From *Bundesrepublik* to *Deutschland*

From *Bundesrepublik* to *Deutschland*

German Politics after Unification

Edited by
Michael G. Huelshoff,
Andrei S. Markovits, and
Simon Reich

Ann Arbor

THE UNIVERSITY OF MICHIGAN PRESS

1996   1995   1994   4   3   2

Library of Congress Cataloging-in-Publication Data

From Bundesrepublik to Deutschland : German politics after unification
  / edited by Michael G. Huelshoff, Andrei S. Markovits, and Simon
  Reich.
       p.   cm. — (Social history, popular culture, and politics in
  Germany)
    Includes bibliographical references and index.
    ISBN 0-472-09527-7 (alk. paper). — ISBN 0-472-06527-0 (pbk. :
  alk. paper)
    1. Germany—Politics and government—1990– 2. Germany—Social
  conditions—1990– 3. Germany—Economic conditions—1990–
  I. Huelshoff, Michael G.   II. Markovits, Andrei S.   III. Reich,
  Simon, 1959–   .   IV. Series.
  JN3972.A58F76   1993
  320.943—dc20   93-16997
                                                                  CIP

A CIP catalogue record for this book is available from the British Library.

The map on page xii is reproduced with the kind permission of the Westermann
Schulbuchverlag GmbH, Brunswick, and the BUSCHE Verlagsgesellschaft mbH,
Dortmund, Germany.

To the many who suffered under the old Germany and Europe,
and in hope for the many who live with the new Germany and Europe.

Acknowledgments

As with all intellectualism, its existence and continuity depends a good deal on institutional involvement and support. First and foremost we would like to mention the valiant—as well as valuable—efforts on the part of the German Academic Exchange Service (DAAD) in making the study of Germany a lively reality in American academic life. Among the DAAD's most notable interventions in this regard is the establishment of a number of visiting professorships at major North American universities. Concretely, the DAAD, in cooperation with these host institutions, makes it possible for highly qualified young German social scientists and contemporary historians to teach German and European politics to American undergraduate and graduate students. This program will expand in the course of the 1990s to include fifteen such positions at as many universities. Additionally, the DAAD funds a variety of programs for North American scholars and students to conduct research and study in Germany. Indeed it is quite probable that virtually every contributor to this volume has at some point in her or his academic career been the beneficiary of one of the DAAD's many programs. The DAAD also runs on an alternating basis summer programs at Cornell and the University of Pennsylvania, as well as an annual summer course at the University of California at Berkeley. These programs are interdisciplinary in character, cater to a wide range of academics, students, and high school teachers, and cover a large spectrum of topics. The DAAD also sponsors over twenty conferences per year. It was such a conference, appropriately titled "Political Science and German Studies" and held before the annual meeting of the American Political Science Association in Atlanta in September 1989, that provided the intellectual and institutional origins for the present book. The Atlanta conference was, in turn, just one in a series of DAAD-sponsored conferences focusing on the interdisciplinary nature of Germany studies.

Additionally, in 1990 three Centers of Excellence in the Study of Germany and Europe were established at Harvard University, Georgetown University, and the University of California at Berkeley, with a DM 45 million grant to be distributed over ten years. A program for German-American Cooperative Research in the Humanities and Social Sciences was scheduled to get underway in 1992, the Bundeskanzler fellowship for advanced students has been running since 1990, and a German-American Academy of Science is expected.

This book is very much a creation of the miraculous events of 1989. As editors, we first published the original papers of the Atlanta conference in a special issue of *German Studies Review*. We subsequently received a contract from the University of Michigan Press to publish a collection of papers based on the ones comprising the special issue of *German Studies Review*. The enormity of the intervening events forced us as authors and editors to shed the usual intellectual complacency associated with the publication of such journal-generated volumes and to concentrate on producing what has essentially become a completely different—and original—collection.

We wish to thank the DAAD for their generous support, without which this project would have been impossible. We particularly would like to thank the former and current Directors of the DAAD's New York office, Manfred Stassen and Wedigo De Vivanco. Wedigo played an especially key role in this project, and we are grateful for his support. Further, we wish to warmly acknowledge the German Studies Association and the editor of the *GSR*, Gerald R. Kleinfeld, for publishing the original papers and for graciously extending copyright permission. It is unlikely that any one individual has done more for interdisciplinary German studies in U.S. academia than Prof. Kleinfeld. We also wish to acknowledge the Busche Verlag, for allowing us to reprint the map from their publication, "Deutschland Tischkalender '92." Finally, we also acknowledge Polity Press/Oxford University Press, for allowing us to reprint Andrei S. Markovits and Philip S. Gorski's contribution from their forthcoming book.

The role of editors cannot be underestimated. We were blessed to have two, Joyce Harrison of the University of Michigan Press, and Geoff Eley, in whose series this book appears. We gratefully acknowledge their guidance, advice, and faith through the birth and maturation of this project.

We also wish to thank those contributors from the first publication, Russ Dalton, Marilyn Rueschemeyer, Brigitta Schultz, and Carl Lankowski, who were unable to continue in the project. Their knowledge and sage commentary informs this product, just as it informed the earlier effort.

Last, and certainly not least, we wish to gratefully acknowledge the secretarial assistance of Ms. Shelley Carlson, without whom this project could never have been completed.

Michael G. Huelshoff, Andrei S. Markovits, and Simon Reich
15 January 1993
Eugene, OR

Contents

Contributors

Christopher S. Allen teaches at the University of Georgia.

Thomas A. Baylis teaches at the University of Texas at San Antonio.

Irwin L. Collier, Jr. teaches at the University of Houston.

John D. Ely teaches at Stanford University.

Arthur M. Hanhardt, Jr. teaches at the University of Oregon.

Jutta A. Helm teaches at Western Illinois University.

Michael G. Huelshoff teaches at the University of New Orleans.

Manfred Kuechler teaches at Hunter College, City University of New York.

Christiane Lemke teaches at the Freie Universität Berlin.

A. James McAdams teaches at the University of Notre Dame.

Andrei S. Markovits teaches at the University of California at Santa Cruz.

Moishe Postone teaches at the University of Chicago.

Simon Reich teaches at the Graduate School of Public and International Affairs, University of Pittsburgh.

Jeremiah M. Riemer teaches at the School for Advanced International Study, Johns Hopkins University.

Hanna Schissler teaches at the University of Minnesota.

James Sperling teaches at the University of Akron.

Introduction

Michael G. Huelshoff and Andrei S. Markovits

There can be little doubt that 1989 has already proven to compare to 1648, 1789, 1918, and 1945 in its epoch-defining significance. Not by chance, this recent date—like its two predecessors in the twentieth century—is inextricably linked to Germany's politics and history. Consequently, it would not be completely erroneous to speak of the twentieth century as a "German century," since Germany was one of the most salient participants in all three critical realignments of global politics during this time. It is surely more than coincidence that a conclusion to the cold war was definitively sealed with the opening of the Berlin Wall on 9 November 1989 and the subsequent unification of the former Federal Republic of Germany (FRG) and the German Democratic Republic (GDR), perhaps the most stark embodiments of the cold war's daily reality.

1989 will also prove to be an epistemological watershed in the social sciences, political science in particular. For just as politics itself after 1945 was decisively shaped by the realities of the post-Yalta world, so, too, was the discipline of political science. Here too, Germany's presence was prototypical. The lens through which political scientists studied Germany was the product of World War II and its immediate legacy, the cold war.

As for World War II, virtually every study of the 1950s and 1960s involving Germany focused on the trauma of national socialism. Ever since the advancing Allied armies uncovered the barbaric deeds of Auschwitz, Buchenwald, and other extermination and concentration camps, social scientists interested in things German tried to answer two simple, but fundamental, questions: How could a culture that epitomized civilization create such barbarism? And, what was needed—institutionally, legally, politically, economically, socially, culturally—to prevent the reemergence of those forces that were largely responsible for the unique atrocities committed in the name of Germany, which the world has come to know under the name Holocaust?

But with a dictatorial Soviet Union confronting the Western Allies in the middle of Germany and Berlin, issues of the cold war also became salient in the study of Germany. Indeed, the cold war divided the study of Germany in the establishment of American and Western political science by analogy to the division of the country proper: those studying West Germany were appropriately integrated into the larger field of comparative politics or international relations, securely anchored in the subdiscipline of West European studies. A much smaller group of scholars who specialized in the study of East Germany remained excluded from this established fraternity, having to form its own associations on the fringes of the much larger subfield of Soviet and East European studies. It is in this context of national socialism and Stalinism that Germany (and things German) assumed a central position in the postwar academic concentration on questions of democracy, political extremism, totalitarianism, and social injustice in the liberal democracies, including the United States and the Federal Republic itself.

Since it was the economic problems of the Weimar Republic that permitted Hitler and his party to attain such prominence, many postwar studies of the Federal Republic concentrated on this new country's economic arrangements. Thus, for example, Western social and political scientists focusing on Germany were preoccupied with—and subsequently rejoiced in—the Federal Republic's "economic miracle." Again responding to the failures of Weimar and the rise of national socialism, Western social scientists were particularly interested in studying the Germans' democratic propensity and its opposite, that is, their authoritarianism. There emerged an array of public opinion surveys and profiles in personal psychology that all tried to measure in one form or another the Germans' reliability as democratic citizens. All of these questions splendidly suited behaviorism and structural functionalism, which—as the hegemonic epistemologies of the time—were in one way or another busily extolling the virtues of the West in a positivist manner. Propelled in good part by the possibility of gathering and analyzing data on a large scale for the first time in the history of the social sciences, behaviorism and structural functionalism were seemingly able to distinguish between good and bad polities by virtue of establishing clear measurements of "modernity." It was only a matter of time and interpretation before the western part of Germany was to become the paragon of a stable and just liberal democracy. This was clearly attained by the late 1950s and early 1960s. Bonn was obviously *not* Weimar, the Germans had definitely become democratic, liberal, and Western. Or had they?

Despite the economic success of the Federal Republic and the apparent stabilization of democratic values among its citizenry, uncertainties remained in some social science circles about the long-run viability of these values and their affinities to the West. Much of this uncertainty was cultivated by a fundamental epistemological challenge to behaviorism and structural functionalism that swept through the academic publics of most advanced industrial societies, notably those of the United States and West Germany. Various forms of modified, though often radical, Marxisms and an array of critical theories, some indeed the direct descendants of the Frankfurt School, provided major intellectual and scholarly alternatives to the dominant modes of academic inquiry. Again, it is significant that this successful epistemological and methodological challenge accorded Germany pride of place through the centrality of such intellectual giants as Max Weber, Karl Marx, Karl Korsch, Theodor Adorno, Max Horkheimer, and Herbert Marcuse. The relevance of their writings to events in, and fundamental changes altering the nature of, advanced capitalism in West Germany and the United States dethroned behaviorism and structural functionalism as the hegemonic discourses in American political science. While the new mode never attained the predominance of the old, it has to this day prevented any single academic epistemology from replicating the exclusive presence enjoyed by behaviorism and structural functionalism until the mid-1960s.

This intellectual—and political—radicalization of the field also renewed the study of the Eastern bloc, including the German Democratic Republic. Ostpolitik also had its ramifications in the epistemologies of political science. A diversity of epistemologies and growing intellectual curiosity concerning the nuances of life in the East replaced cold war–influenced assumptions of uniformity and totalitarian politics. With easing access to the GDR, respectable studies began to emerge depicting various aspects of life under state socialism. A welcome rejection of the previously stifling uniformity of the theories of totalitarianism and a certain fashionable romanticization of socialism characterized the Zeitgeist of the field. With the benefit of hindsight, some of the scholars specializing in the GDR, for example, those who found there an independent political culture, might be criticized for accepting that regime much too uncritically. Even so, their research proved helpful in explaining an otherwise unknown chapter of modern German politics.

While a number of premises linked to the cold war faded in the course of the late 1960s and early 1970s, the essential concern about the viability of German democracy still informed much of the social science study of the Federal Republic. It was, after all, the background of Auschwitz that made political scientists focus on the Federal Republic's repressive measures against political dissidents and others deemed inimical—perhaps even dangerous—to its "liberal democratic basic order." It was also in the context of Germany's troubled history that much attention was devoted to the so-called new social movements and the Greens, who captured the imagination of many and the dread of a significant few. Even the ever-present studies in the neo(or post)-Marxist subfield of political economy that proliferated in the 1970s and the 1980s were ultimately informed by a concern for the daily workings of West German institutions under conditions of "organized capitalism" and "ordered democracy." The verdict was on the whole emphatic: with all its faults, the Federal Republic was a model in the efficiency of its conflict resolution, the management of its economy, and the arrangements of its institutional interactions: Modell Deutschland, the singular success story, constitutional, social, liberal, Western—and normal.

The normalcy of the Bundesrepublik was abruptly transformed into the normalcy of Deutschland during the evening of 9 November 1989 with the fall of the Berlin Wall. Most of the ingredients that had earned the Bundesrepublik the sobriquet of "normal" underwent a qualitative change during that fateful night. Tellingly, 9 November will henceforth always be remembered first and foremost as the day when the Berlin Wall was opened rather than as the ignominious moment when the Nazis unleashed an organized pogrom against the Reich's Jews in 1938. Yet with the cold war definitively over, the period before 1945 has attained greater salience for German politics as well as for political science concerned with Germany.

With unification, key issues that defined the very essence of the Bundesrepublik, such as constitutionalism, federalism, corporatism, gradualism, consociationalism, and efficiency, will recede in significance both in the reality of German politics and in the research agenda for political scientists working on Germany. These issues will not disappear. But in the context of Deutschland they will recede behind hitherto secondary concepts such as nationalism, national identity, and power. The end of the cold war and the precipitous implosion of the Soviet empire has once again placed Deutschland on the center stage of Europe. While these momentous developments have by no means rendered the history of the old Bundesrepublik irrelevant, they have most certainly altered its previous structural, geographic, and political position, which so defined—and stabilized—the post-Yalta world in Europe and beyond. Whereas no serious scholar of contemporary Germany expects a replay of Weimar's weaknesses and the Third Reich's murderous horror, there can be little doubt that these two recent epochs of German history will receive a different interpretation and assume a different political role than they did in the old Bundesrepublik. One of the great successes of the old Bundesrepublik was its making the recurrence of the darker sides of German history virtually unthinkable. Nor will Weimar and the Nazis be replicated in the new Bundesrepublik. But that does not mean *eo ipso* that their political salience and historical Gestalt have remained the same. Today's unified Deutschland renders history much more analytically relevant and politically salient than before 9 November 1989. The changing nature of the object of study will by definition alter the main strains of the research agenda. This, we hope, will pose few problems to political scientists, especially to those well versed in the methodologies of comparative history. It is a telling sign that some of the pioneering work in comparative politics—especially in the European field—has been deeply informed by history.

What makes the study of Germany especially exciting is the immense flux in which most countries in Germany's vicinity find themselves. In the western and southern part of the continent a unique experiment in voluntary supranational state building is transforming the concept of what it means to be European. While the European Community is far from having replaced the nation-state as the primary unit of political identification, it most certainly has created a viable supranational structure whose decrees, policies, and very existence affect virtually every citizen under its reach.

In the Continent's eastern portion a very different change is afoot. The nations of eastern Europe are about to rewrite their histories of the past fifty years. They will have to redefine their memories and create new political models to help forge identities beyond those imposed by Soviet occupation. Whether it wants to or not, Germany will inevitably assume a central role in this complex process. Given Germany's importance to the developments on both sides of the Continent, there can be little question that the new Germany's role in the new Europe must be characterized as hegemonic. This, in turn, should serve as an auspicious framework for political scientists specializing in the area of international relations: Germany as hegemon necessitates a substantial rethinking of conventional theories of international relations, most of which were, of course, products of the bipolarity of the post-Yalta world.

All these developments have rendered the study of Germany exciting. While calculability and a regulated nature bespoke the fundamental success of the Federal Republic's newly attained democratic order, they also lent the country a certain predictable normalcy that—upon occasion—bordered on the drab. They rendered Germany not only stable but a bit boring. (No wonder, then, that it was Greens, neo-Nazis, and urban terrorists who captured students' fantasies about Germany and who, as a consequence, received far too much attention from the press and academia, given their relative insignificance in the Federal Republic's daily political construct.) Indeed, a detailed study by the German Marshall Fund published in 1987 and entitled *Mixed Messages: A Report on the Study of Contemporary Germany in the United States* (by Jackson K. Janes and Helene L. Scher) confirmed the fears of many specialists in the United States that German normalcy was leading to declining interest in Germany and things German among American students. Whereas our evidence to the contrary is merely anecdotal, we are reasonably certain that the amazing events of 1989 have completely reversed this trend. At least as far as the limited experience of the editors of this volume is concerned, it is quite clear that student interest in Germany has never been more pronounced than at the present. We are reasonably certain that this interest will not wane in the future, particularly since Germany's role in Europe and the world will increase substantially.

The book is divided into six sections. Each section comprises papers focusing on the development of the epistemology salient in the issue at hand. Particular attention is given to the fundamental change that German unification wrought in every issue under consideration in this volume.

The themes of continuity versus change and structure versus process can be seen throughout this book, as can the growing understanding of the importance of ideas in comparative politics. In the opening essay, Jutta A. Helm concentrates upon the regularities that social scientists have found in their study of Germany. As we have noted, the stability of German democracy has been and remains a central question in the literature. This concern for structure and stability also informs Manfred Kuechler's analysis of political behavior in Germany, which expands Helm's discussion of German democracy and elite and mass behavior. The search for the bases of stability in the German polity has also influenced the study of the German political economy, despite that approach's seemingly clean break with the mainstream. Much has been made of German neocorporatism, and the German deviations from this model.

Christopher S. Allen's contribution emphasizes the importance of structure in the study of Germany. Allen notes that the relationship between the state and the economy has undergone significant (if slow) change since 1949, reflecting shifts among elites from an organized market to neo-Keynesian, neocorporatist, and finally decentralized management of economic change. Thomas A. Baylis and Irwin L. Collier, Jr., argue the prospects for German-German social rapprochement. The differing expectations of East and West Germans accounts for a significant amount of the dissatisfaction, east and west, with the unification of Germany. These differing expectations, of course, result from the differing historical experiences of the two Germanys—again intertwining structure and process and pointing to the importance of ideology in shaping expectations.

The interaction of structure and political process is particularly evident in the study of women in politics. As Hanna Schissler points out, institutional constraints upon women and the women's movement were quickly reimposed after 1945—despite favorable conditions—with significant consequences for women's economic stability, political influence, and psychological well-being. The implications of this reassertion of male dominance in West Germany clearly still affect women today. Andrei S. Markovits notes that the new women's movement has its roots outside the political mainstream, in the radicalized student movement. When the German abortion debate politicized a broad spectrum of women in the early 1970s, the relatively narrow ideological base of the extant women's movement—brought on by the inhibiting impact of German institutions—could not bring these women within its confines, encouraging a fragmentation of the movement that still troubles women's politics. Christiane Lemke argues that the different experiences and expectations of women east and west further divide the women's movement after unification, and Jeremiah M. Riemer's study of the abortion debate inspired by unification reveals the stifling impacts of process and structure.

The study of German-German relations and the politics of East German collapse and unification are also subject to the effects of structure and process. As A. James McAdams argues, structural arguments alone can not explain developments in German-German relations that patterned the politics of unification. He finds strong evidence of domestic political processes at work in both Germanys before the events of 1989. Arthur M. Hanhardt, Jr., largely concurs: while changes in the international structure provided the necessary conditions leading to the implosion of the SED in the fall of 1989, domestic developments in the former GDR, including the inability of the SED to effectively suppress growing opposition groups, explain why the SED collapsed. With the Berlin Wall breached and the corruption and mismanagement of the SED demonstrated, German unification on West German terms was virtually unstoppable. In the final essay in this section, John D. Ely analyzes one of the more disquieting results of German unification, the rise of right-wing parties in both the eastern and western portions of Germany. He argues that while these groups do not constitute a threat to German democracy, the "new Right" is likely to be a permanent addition to the German polity because of structural shifts in the German economy.

In turning to the future of Germany and Europe, Andrei S. Markovits and Simon Reich point to the importance of ideology and ideas. Building upon Gramsci's model of ideological hegemony, they argue that Germany will become the dominant power in Europe, as the strength of the German economy, its key geographical position, and the weight of its values push Germany into a leadership role. Markovits and Reich note that this hegemonic Germany is decidedly multilateral in its orientation, a point about which Moishe Postone is somewhat more skeptical. He finds developments in recent political debates on both the right and the left that, while not threatening German political stability, require caution when arguing that Germany will remain a good "European citizen." While Michael G. Huelshoff's analysis of German EC policy places the study of Germany into the wider literature on regional integration, his reconstructed model of integration points to the significance of domestic institutions and decision-making processes for German EC policy. German cooperative decision making leads Huelshoff to argue that, in the context of broad German elite and mass endorsement of regional integration, Germany will remain a key force driving toward broader European integration and an effective counterweight to fragmentation in eastern Europe. Institutions and processes interact, according to Huelshoff. James Sperling's analysis of German security policy, however, emphasizes the continued importance of structure in the security field, while noting that political processes are leading the Germans in the long run to build security structures that will transcend NATO.

In the conclusion, Simon Reich shows that structural arguments have come to dominate our analysis of German politics, much to the detriment of our understanding. He advocates a new agenda for study, arguing for a balanced approach that integrates structure, process, and ideology.

One of the main intellectual contributions of this book, then, is to balance structure with process and ideology, moving beyond the strictly structural analyses common in the study of Germany. We do not reject structuralism, but the contributions to the volume seek to improve upon structural analyses by considering structure's interaction with processes and ideas.

PART 1

Germany and Political Science

In the following essay, Jutta A. Helm examines the study of Germany in comparative politics. The central question confronting comparative politics at the end of the Second World War was the prospect for democracy, in Germany and the world. As Helm notes, this question took on a particular importance in the study of German politics, yet the issue also drove much of comparative political study of regions beyond Germany, as the discipline searched for stability in a world divided by the cold war and as it confronted the acceleration of decolonization. This empirical focus coincided with the behavioral revolution, which emphasized the application of scientific method to the study of politics. Although comparativists expressed concern for the stability of German democracy, research findings revealed that the initial hesitancy with which the Germans approached their new democratic institutions was soon replaced by "normal" democratic values, particularly when seen in comparison to other advanced industrial democracies. The discipline turned to the study of elite political behavior and to political economy. As Helm demonstrates, the discipline's initial focus was a natural outgrowth of the behaviorism-driven research paradigm established in the 1950s and 1960s, while the turn to elites and political economy reflected criticisms of this paradigm based in Marxist analysis. Findings in the field of elite behavior reinforced the stability in German politics found in the studies of German democracy, while renewing concern about how democratic its political processes were. In the field of political economy, however, the research findings have indicated the prevalence of change in the German political economy (a theme Christopher S. Allen notes in Part 3 of this book). Finally, German unification encourages us to reexamine the findings of comparative research, particularly in light of the linkages between economic stability and political maturity in Germany.

The Study of Germany in Comparative Politics

Jutta A. Helm

With the publication of a volume entitled *The Struggle for Democracy in Germany* in 1949, Gabriel Almond defined what became the central theme in studies of German politics for the next three decades. The "German Question," in Almond's view, required a twofold answer: demilitarization, largely accomplished at the Potsdam conference in 1945, and democratization, a much more daunting task. Burdened with a legacy of authoritarianism and nationalism, threatened by Communist infiltration and Soviet expansion, most Germans were described as "hold outs," indifferent, caught in a mood of bitterness and futility, unlikely to contribute to the growth of liberal democratic values.[1] Almond and his contributors attempted to spell out a framework for Western policy to reverse this dangerous drift, to give content to the "formal" democracy of West Germany, and thereby to give Western policy strong roots in a most critical area.[2] The essays in Almond's volume assess the strength and the survival of Western values in German history up to the Nazi resistance and various aspects of occupation policy as they bear on democratization and the necessary stabilization of everyday life.

Writing before the formation of the federal government in the spring of 1949, the authors were by no means convinced of the eventual success of this task. "The struggle for democracy in Germany will only begin in earnest when normal conditions of life provide opportunities for a genuine 'grassroots democracy.' . . . Much has been accomplished in many fields, but no real progress has been made in this last connection."[3] The last chapters on political parties and the problem of reorientation highlight the two areas in which scholars during the next decades invested considerable efforts in order to answer the German question: political behavior, notably voting, and political values, beliefs, and attitudes, that is, political culture. Oddly, although Almond tries to answer the German question, he does not define it. But earlier A. J. P. Taylor had already provided what became the standard definition: "How can the peoples of Europe be secured against repeated bouts of German aggression? And how can the German people discover a settled, peaceful form of political existence?"[4] Twenty years later Dahrendorf asked the question even more pointedly: "Why is it that so few in Germany embraced the principle of liberal democracy?"[5] Today, this question has lost some of its urgency. But even now there remains a degree of concern about Germany's democratic credentials, its foreign policy intentions, and its future now that unification has been achieved.

This essay reviews the ongoing debate about German politics of the postwar era. That debate did not occur within a vacuum. Rather, it reflected the priorities and concerns of the field of comparative politics and its synergistic relationship with the behavioral revolution. This was especially true during the fifties and sixties, the period some now refer to as the golden age of comparative politics.[6] Parts one and two of this essay focus on studies of political culture and citizen and elite behavior—the very areas that were then central to the concerns of comparativists. Part three examines a somewhat later development, the turn to matters of political economy. Throughout the focus is on West Germany, as the iron curtain imposed a rather different research agenda for the German Democratic Republic.

Toward a Democratic Political Culture

If Almond and his coauthors worried in 1949 about the chances of democratic values taking root in West Germany, their worries were confirmed by the findings of Almond and Verba's *The Civic Culture,* an empirical investigation of the political culture of democracy in five nations. The concept of political culture was defined as the particular distribution of patterns of orientation (cognitive, affective, evaluative) toward political objects among the citizens of a nation.[7] A democratic, or civic culture, according to Almond and Verba, would be characterized by a mix of traditional and modern orientations. It would be "a pluralistic culture based on communication and persuasion, a culture of consensus and diversity, a culture that permitted change but moderated it."[8] As the authors saw it at the time, the civic culture was most fully realized in Britain and the United States, while Germany did not fit into its parameters.[9] Germans scored high on the cognitive measures of the research instrument: they were aware of and well informed about politics and government, and their voting participation was high. But their affective orientations to the political system were highly pragmatic, suggesting they might not hold up if the system should experience a severe crisis. And their evaluation of the political system, while positive, put a higher premium on its administrative than its political branches. These findings indicated that, in some respects at least, Germans still displayed the orientations of subjects—attentive to political events, but without much confidence in their ability to influence them.

In time, *The Civic Culture* became a classic. The scope of the research, with its focus on five nations, and the urgency of the research question almost guaranteed as much. Like other social scientists, Almond and Verba were looking for the prerequisites of democracy. During the postwar decades this was the single most important research question, and it contributed greatly to the emergence of comparative politics as an organized subfield of political science.[10] While others searched for answers in the social structure of society or in the level of economic development, Almond and his coauthor focused on the cultural underpinnings of a democratic polity. The questions were pressing. The prevention of another breakdown of democracy in Europe and the promotion of democracy in the emerging nations of the Third World were of more than academic interest. And in spite of the criticism that it received, the work set the tone for debates about the future of democracy in the sixties and seventies. It reflected a consensus that West German democracy was tenuous, untested, a "fair-weather democracy." As Dahrendorf put it, "In Germany, if anywhere, protest is the citizen's first obligation. In Germany, . . . however, a great quiet rules among the citizens." The result is "a political system that is authoritarian in effect if not in intention."[11] Would the Federal Republic follow in the footsteps of its only democratic predecessor, the Weimar Republic?

Over time, these fears became increasingly unwarranted. In *The Civic Culture Revisited* a group of scholars took a second look at the original work.[12] They reexamined its theoretical and methodological underpinnings, and the relevance or validity of its findings for the five nations. Writing about Germany, Conradt made a compelling case for a changed citizenry. His findings are particularly convincing in that they are based on a large group of surveys taken at different points in time, avoiding the "snapshot effect" of Almond and Verba's original 1959 survey. And they show that just about every description of values and attitudes in the original work had become dated. New data on system affect and support, civic competence, and political interest all show that West Germany's political orientations were far from static, incapable of evolving into the democratic political culture envisioned by the original authors. There are only two areas of stability over time. The later surveys cited by Conradt continue to show high levels of political cognition and participation (especially voting), both compatible with a democratic political culture.

Like its predecessor, *The Civic Culture Revisited* played a role in reframing the debate about political change in Germany. Its "remade" political culture and the growth of democratic orientations now became key themes in that debate. Other works, notably *Germany Transformed,* amplified the emerging consensus.[13] Based on secondary analysis of ten national surveys between 1953 and 1976, it showed that "the traditional characterization of the average German citizen as [politically] quiescent and uninvolved is no longer appropriate."[14] Instead, citizens demonstrate a good deal of political interest and support of the regime. Their sense of political efficacy is almost as high as that of American citizens. Going beyond the established political-culture framework and building on the work of Inglehart and others, the authors of *Germany Transformed* identified a set of new orientations.[15] A minority of mostly younger, well-educated citizens, socialized in an era of economic growth and political stability, were shifting their priorities from economic and political security to quality of life issues, demanding more democratic participation, freedom of expression, and attention to social issues and the environment.[16] (This kind of generational change was not limited to Germany.) Moreover, the "new politics" had consequences for the political behavior of citizens, a point that will be taken up below.

By the early eighties, political scientists on both sides of the Atlantic had gathered a good amount of evidence indicating that West Germans had erased the democratic deficit in their political culture and now shared values and beliefs very similar to citizens in other democracies. Inglehart's work, drawing on data from a number of multinational opinion surveys commissioned by the European Community since 1973, certainly underlines this conclusion.[17] More recently Scheuch has also emphasized that the notion of a peculiarly German set of political orientations and cultural preferences is erroneous and misdirected. His examination of a vast amount of data from the Eurobarometer surveys reveals that in their basic outlooks and orientations, Germans are a rather stable and, in the European context, "average" population. "The differences that can be found in relation to neighboring countries are rather consistent across various analyses. There are indeed German Germans—but only as a variant of a median European type."[18]

If the questions originally posed by Almond, Almond and Verba, and Dahrendorf have lost their relevance for West Germany, they do enjoy a new timeliness in the East. With the overwhelming majority of the population there lacking any personal experience of democracy, its values, institutions, and practices, it would be miraculous if the authoritarian past had not left its mark on citizens' political outlooks. It has become painfully obvious in recent months, for example, that there is considerably less tolerance of foreigners in the East than in the West.[19] A new research agenda is now probing the extent of value change and its causes in the eastern part of the country. Will generational change be the major independent variable in the remaking of the political culture? How similar should we expect eastern and western political cultures to become? And will the experience of unification modify prevailing outlooks in the West? As social scientists look for answers to these questions, it is helpful to recall Dahrendorf's conclusions. To the extent that Germans have learned that the German Question is not a political question put to others, but a social question Germans put to themselves, there is ground for optimism that a unified Germany will embrace the principle of liberal democracy.[20]

Citizen and Elite Behavior

Mass Political Behavior

No other area of research was so strongly affected by the behavioral revolution as the study of voting behavior. It became a growth industry in American political science, and it left its marks on the study of German politics. While early studies probed the electorate's decisions to support democratic or extremist parties—the spectre of Weimar—later studies focused on approaches originally developed in the study of American voting behavior. Examples are attempts to probe the relevance of party identification and realignment or dealignment in the German context.[21] Overall, voting studies owe a great deal to the growing sophistication of German survey research as well as to the ongoing cooperation between German and American scholars and research institutes.

After 1949 German voters increasingly chose moderate, centrist parties. Even before being outlawed by the Constitutional Court in 1952 and 1956, radical parties on the right and on the left had failed to attract a sizable part of the electorate. A two-and-a-half-party system emerged, with the Free Democratic Party serving as the eternal pivot party, alternating between left-liberal and right-liberal coalitions. Initially, this circumstance was not primarily the result of the electorate's deliberate choice of democratic parties. Rather, in the words of Loewenberg, it was due to "the success of the policies adopted through the new institutions, the absence of alternatives, and the low demands made by these institutions on the political energies of the mass public."[22] Party membership remained low, hovering around 5 percent of the electorate. But the competitive party system won increasing acceptance, as indicated in the impressive rates of voter turnout. Equally important is the fact that "significant portions of the middle class, such as white-collar, upper-level employee strata, including most particularly women and Catholics" now chose the Social Democratic Party (SPD), which became a moderate leftist party with the adoption of the Godesberg Program in 1959.[23] This preference marked a major departure from the traditional voting patterns of the German middle class. But even in 1970 many observers were not completely reassured about voter preferences. In a special issue on the 1969 West German election published by *Comparative Politics,* Herz referred to the "West German experiment in democracy," suggesting that the outcome of that experiment was still unknown. Would it turn out to be another Weimar, a fair-weather democracy, as it were?[24] Of particular concern was the reemergence of the radical Right, along with a radical leftist fringe in the late sixties, each the topic of an article in the special issue. Two elections later, these concerns had faded. Under conditions of economic uncertainty and high unemployment, less than 1 percent of the electorate opted for extremist solutions, leading Cerny to conclude that "West Germans are continuing the process of establishing a functioning democratic political order."[25] And in 1990 Conradt's assessment of the options facing the electorate also stressed the themes of democracy and stability. This time voters faced a rather different political context. Unification had been achieved, and the electorate had grown by the addition of 12 million new voters from the former German Democratic Republic. And although their preferences are volatile, Conradt does not even suggest the possibility of sizable numbers endorsing nondemocratic parties. The election outcome confirmed this assessment. Pocketbook issues seem to have dominated voting decisions in 1990.[26]

Beyond voting, the repertory of political action available to citizens encompasses membership and activism in civic organizations, petitioning, protest behavior, and even violence. As scholars turned to these areas in the 1970s, they uncovered a range of political action that disconfirmed Almond and Verba's earlier evaluation of German citizens as subjects rather than participants in the political process. To some extent, the enlarged repertory of citizen action was influenced by the events of the sixties, resulting in greater citizen assertiveness in most Western democracies. In Germany, citizen initiatives became the preferred organizations, and generational differences in the willingness to play a part in the new groups or to experiment with unconventional forms of political participation were most pronounced. But there was little that was peculiarly German in all this. And virtually all monographs devoted to these issues approach the subject in a comparative framework. Barnes and Kaase focus on direct political action in five democracies.[27] Relying almost exclusively on individual-level variables, the authors show that there is considerable approval of protest behavior everywhere. Predictably, such approval is positively related to education, postmaterialist values, and conventional political activity. The research does not show whether the levels of approval represent an increase over time, or whether they are likely to grow in the future. But the data are consistent with the growing network of citizen initiatives in Germany, many of them focused on environmental issues and nuclear power in particular. This development also is explored by Nelkin and Pollack's study of antinuclear protest in France and West Germany.[28] They show the often elaborate, courageous, and resourceful efforts by (mostly) young ecointellectuals, farmers, and workers challenging the power of bureaucratic elites. Political structures in the two nations account for some differences in the effectiveness of citizen groups. Federalism and the greater importance of courts in Germany rewarded citizen groups' efforts to put nuclear power on the political agenda. The movements themselves seem to illustrate Barnes and Kaase's point about the tendency of citizen action to express itself in limited, issue-based, ad hoc group actions rather than broad socio-political movements for systemic change.[29]

Rochon has explored another example of issue-based group action in his study of peace movements.[30] He argues that the movements in Great Britain, West Germany, the Netherlands, and France are broadly comparable, even though they vary in strategy, tactics, and ideological emphases. For example, in keeping with West Germany's federal structure, the peace movement there operated in a more decentralized manner than in Britain or France. Ideologically, the movement's critique of militarism was broader, linking the reliance on force and hierarchy with patterns of male domination and the domination of nature.[31] But it would be difficult to identify distinctly German traits in the behavior of German peace activists. This conclusion is diametrically opposed to Gress's assessment of Germany's peace movement as rooted in antimodernism, among the most problematic of its cultural traditions.[32] In tone and objective, Rochon and Gress have little in common. Where Rochon attempts to connect peace movements with theories of resource mobilization and new social movements, Gress is committed to the argument that such movements are a threat to Western security. One is left wondering whether a comparative study might have led Gress to different conclusions. Finally, Dalton and Kuechler's volume, *Challenging the Political Order,* should be mentioned. Several chapters examine German movements that challenged the status quo "because these movements marked a dramatic new development for West German society."[33] But the contributors are more interested in testing social-movement theories than writing national case studies. What explains the virtually simultaneous emergence of these movements in most Western democracies? Do they pose a challenge to established parties? How new are the new social movements? Again it would appear that German developments are best understood in a comparative context.

Elite Behavior

The study of political elites was redefined by the behavioral revolution. When an examination of legal documents and biographical data had been de rigueur in the prebehavioral era, researchers now approached elites with structured interviews and standardized questionnaires. This trend also is evident in studies of German elites, most of them concerned with elites in specific institutional contexts. Wildenmann's study is the only cross-sectional analysis, and it focuses on attitudes rather than behavior.[34] Attitudes are also the subject of *The European Administrative Elite* and *Bureaucrats and Politicians in Western Democracies*.[35] These works explore the backgrounds, role definitions, and worldviews of senior-level bureaucrats and elected politicians. But their findings are highly aggregated and do not provide profiles of German politicians or administrators.

The interplay of legislative, executive, and interest-group leaders was explored in three studies.[36] The authors give ample ammunition to those deploring a democratic deficit in decision-making processes in the legislature and executive. With the executive, and especially the chancellor, dominating the legislative process, and the Bundestag, its parties, committees, and extraparliamentary forces merely imposing constraints rather than genuine checks and alternative agendas, Braunthal's description of this process as a "democratic facade" appears to be on target.[37] Deputies from the governing and opposition parties define their role as experts on a narrow range of policy issues. Cooperation and compromise on a legislative agenda couched largely in technical language become the dominant mode of operation. Even parliamentary debates provide little relief from this discourse. Loewenberg calculates that fewer than a fifth of all deputies make over two-thirds of all speeches, all too often addressing the single topic of their expertise.[38] Deputies in all parties have an aversion to unrehearsed debate, an observation that retains its relevance today after numerous procedural reforms designed to enliven parliamentary proceedings. Nor can one quarrel with the author's assertion that the deputies, their representative function not withstanding, in fact keep the public at arm's length.[39] If one were to look for the seeds of the extraparliamentary opposition and its ideology of empowering citizens, one need go no further than the corridors of power in Bonn!

Loewenberg attributed the Bundestag's democratic deficit to the survival of structural and cultural remnants of the Imperial political system, a theme that was echoed by Dyson in his monograph on the peculiar German integration of party, state, and bureaucracy.[40] He was quite successful in identifying the special character taken on by Germany's political parties, which fit themselves into the political space long dominated by state and bureaucracy. In the financing of political parties the implications of this special character are particularly obvious. On the whole, Dyson's argument did not receive much play among American comparativists. It suggested that in some ways, German politics still represented a special case, burdened by the tradition of the Obrigkeitsstaat. At a time when many were including Germany in cross-national studies, in fact downplaying potentially unique aspects of its second democracy, his argument did not fit into the dominant discourse about the German polity.

More than its competitors, the Christian Democratic Union (CDU) and its Bavarian affiliate, the Christian Social Union (CSU), exemplified the peculiarly German role of political parties. A governing force before it became a unified political party, it displayed a strong executive orientation, a feature that turned into a serious handicap once the party found itself on the opposition benches in 1969. Another prominent characteristic was its ideological diffusion, stemming from the rather shallow integration of the various tendencies in the party.[41] As a result, the party's direction was always defined in large measure by its leader or chancellor, suggesting to some that the CDU/CSU was little more than a Kanzlerwahlverein, a machine to secure the election of its candidate for chancellor. The experience of the SPD was rather different. Starting on the opposition benches, with an impressive degree of ideological and organizational cohesion, it lacked a popular candidate for chancellor and an effective electoral strategy. But after its thirteen years as the senior governing party, the tables were turned completely. The SPD still had a popular candidate in Helmut Schmidt, but its organizational and ideological cohesion were badly strained.[42] In opposition after 1982, Social Democrats struggled to integrate the diverse subcultures within their party, very much like the CDU/CSU had done after 1969.[43] Both parties were rocked by what Braunthal subsumed under the heading "external forces": the youth rebellion of the sixties and the ecology and feminist movements of the seventies. Adding changes in the class structure, notably the growing salaried middle class and the declining working class, it is not hard to see that all parties faced considerable challenges. Braunthal traced some of the ensuing internal debates in the SPD, but the full impact of the electoral defection of young, ecology-minded voters was not yet apparent in the time period covered by his analysis.

The Christian Democrats have gone a long way toward embodying the nonideological, catchall party sketched by Kirchheimer's perceptive analysis.[44] Periodic bursts of programmatic debate in the party are routinely snuffed out by the chancellor. The SPD's efforts to become a catchall party have been less successful, even though this was the avowed goal of the conservative party elite. Factions have disputed party goals and strategy, not merely tactical and electoral maneuvers. Internal debate was lively during the seventies and eighties, in marked contrast to the fifties and sixties.[45] And in view of the diverse subcultures within the party, a repetition of the "embracement strategy" of the sixties is not possible now.

Given the importance of Germany's political parties, it is surprising that there are so few book-length studies of the CDU/CSU and the SPD. In contrast, the Green movement and party have attracted a disproportionate amount of attention, much of it focused on the Greens' experiments with grass-roots democracy. On the whole, political scientists were rather unsympathetic to these experiments.[46] A final theme in the literature on elite behavior addresses the federal Constitutional Court. Kommers has produced a very thorough examination of the court's jurisprudence in seven substantive areas, as well as a study of its role in the German political system.[47] His assessment of the court's contribution is very balanced. Few would take issue with the argument that its impact on the formulation of major public policy has been marginal. It has not always steered clear of controversy but succeeded in gaining widespread acceptance for the principle of judicial review in a hostile cultural context.[48] There are many, especially on the left and liberal sides of the political spectrum, who fault the court for tolerating serious erosions of individual liberties. The two areas in which its omissions are thought to be particularly glaring are the response to the terrorist threat, and the rights of civil servants.[49] Was the court's abstinence in these sensitive areas the price paid for mass and elite acceptance of the principle of judicial review?

The Political Economy of Germany

The turn to matters of political economy came from several directions. In American political science, Lindblom's work sensitized scholars to the interconnectedness of politics and economics.[50] In comparative politics, scholars from diverse backgrounds found the established paradigms, namely pluralism and dualism, ineffective in their study of state-society relations.[51] Meanwhile, German analysts had been attentive to the interdependence of politics and economics for some time.[52] Several innovations in German policy-making processes prompted scholars to reexamine the "particular form of institutionalized interaction among organized groups in society."[53] A new conceptual framework for the study of state-society relations emerged: neocorporatism, or societal corporatism. Above all Lehmbruch and Schmitter deserve credit for the rediscovery of corporatism in postwar Europe. Defined as

> a system of interest representation in which the constituent units are organized into a limited number of singular, compulsory, noncompetitive, hierarchically ordered and functionally differentiated categories, recognized or licensed . . . by the state and granted a deliberate representational monopoly within their respective categories in exchange for observing certain controls,

corporatism seemed to provide a useful map for the study of group interaction in a number of societies, including Germany.[54] Here the role of the "peak associations," engaged in continuous, behind-the-scenes bargaining with the executive; the ideology of "social partnership" elevating capital and labor to quasi-official status; the existence of numerous functionally specific parastate agencies with interest-group representation; and a political culture stressing formalism, consensus, and continuous bargaining suggested that corporatist features are well established.[55] Most visible in the efforts to concentrate macroeconomic policy through tripartite, national-level bargaining between government and the peak associations (Concerted Action), corporatist arrangements permeate many other policy areas such as health policy, employment policy, vocational training, and management-labor relations.[56] At subnational levels, networks of meso- and microcorporatism are pervasive.

All of this clearly distinguished the Federal Republic from the neoliberal approaches that became fashionable in Britain and the United States during the 1980s.[57] There have been some superficial similarities. Germany too saw a degree of decentralization of policy-making and even some deregulation. But the much touted Wende, or change of course, never really happened in Germany.[58] More important, and surprising to some, is the accumulating body of evidence showing that corporatist arrangements have contributed to Germany's rather strong economic performance. A number of case studies focused on the big industrial sectors show how dense networks of public and private actors—their well-articulated differences notwithstanding—cooperate to achieve desired results.[59] In an ideal-typical scenario, this cooperation takes the following forms: the Ministry of Research and Technology funds research and development projects, typically initiated by industries in conjunction with a research institute; state governments disseminate new technologies to potential users, often including small firms; large firms and smaller suppliers cooperate to fine-tune new technologies to their specific needs; labor unions are involved through vocational training programs and negotiate with employers regarding the organization of the work place; governments support trade and export promotion. Cooperative networks of this density are by no means uniformly spread over all sectors and regions of the German economy. Usually the automobile industry and the mechanical engineering sector, especially in Baden-Württemberg, are cited as the best examples of public-private sector incorporation.

Corporatism has also been a pattern in the resolution of major economic crises. The consolidation of the coal industry in 1968, achieved through the quasi-nationalization of productive mines, drastic reductions in output, generous terms for the steel industry, and exemplary income support for redundant miners, is the best example. To accomplish this, the Ministry of Economics convened a series of "coal rounds," with mining and steel companies, labor unions, and government hammering out a solution. German politicians and union leaders proudly cite this case as a positive response to corporate failure.[60] Critics, however, argue that such "crisis cartels" have retarded innovation in troubled sectors or regions, in fact stabilizing decaying structures.[61]

Besides shedding a good deal of light on decision making in corporatist structures, the political economy approach has also sharpened our understanding of the institutions involved in the policy process. There is now a consensus that the Federal Republic is not a strong state. In view of traditional interpretations linking German authoritarianism to an all-powerful state structure, this represents a major change.[62] Whether it is an entirely welcome change is another matter. As the contours of public and private institutions become increasingly blurred, the "formative functions of the state are relativized. The respective situation determines state activities. The state lacks a grand strategy or agenda and adopts a pragmatic or opportunistic attitude towards outcomes."[63] Interelite bargaining, described earlier by Dahrendorf as a "cartel of anxiety," is essential to the maintenance of pragmatic outlooks. And the bargaining networks usually survive electoral challenges. For example, after 1976 the CDU/CSU's majority in the Federal Council guaranteed it a de facto veto over all policies requiring council approval. Currently the SPD enjoys the same opportunity to cogovern.

Corporatism does create the risk for political parties of turning into bland extensions of the state machinery, a risk that appears more real in view of their convergence on centrist positions. Braunthal has shown that ideological debate was lively in the SPD during the seventies and eighties. But the party paid a high price for this when in 1987 internal divisions undermined the chances of its popular candidate for chancellor, Johannes Rau. Three new parties, the Greens, the Republicans, and the Party of Democratic Socialism (successor of the Socialist Unity Party) provide the major parties with some incentives to avoid overly homogenized campaigns. In the past, voters have rewarded small parties that articulated well-defined issue positions, diverging from the catchall strategy of its major rivals. At this time, within the rather fluid electoral context, there are opportunities for small parties. And predictions for what might be the first "normal election" in unified Germany in 1994 are impossible.

Finally, neocorporatism and the political economy approach have highlighted the pivotal role of the centralized peak associations of business and labor. Of the two, business associations, dominated by the all-powerful Federation of German Industry (BDI), have operated in a rather centralized fashion. Not shying away from confrontations such as its decision in 1977 to challenge the constitutionality of the 1976 Codetermination Act, business has gained much from its continuing involvement in corporatist structures. Not the least of its gains is the willingness of elite and mass publics to attend to the problems of German business in a global economy. This willingness was quite obvious during the Social-Liberal coalition government, which had come to power in 1969 with promises of substantial redistribution and reform.[64]

Organized labor could not count on the same degree of responsiveness to its needs. Divided into sixteen industrial unions, its national federation, the German Trade Union Federation (DGB), does not wield centralized power to the same degree as the BDI. The industrial unions guard their autonomy rather jealously, complicating labor's pursuit of a united front on important issues. One example was the DGB's position on the issue of work-time reduction, conceived in part as a response to stubbornly high unemployment in the late seventies and eighties. While the concept of work-time reduction enjoyed near-unanimous support in all unions, there have been differences between the national federation and the Metal Worker Union on the one hand, favoring a reduced work week, and the Chemical Workers Union, preferring earlier retirement instead.

Their deep involvement in corporatist structures at all levels has not prevented unions or business from resorting to open conflict or confrontation when important issues are at stake. In 1984, strikes and subsequent lockouts in the metal and printing industries left the system of corporatist intermediation deeply strained. Government-union relations were at an all-time low, and legislation raising the costs of a strike for unions was introduced and passed. Employers used every opportunity to weaken solidaristic union strategies. In lieu of contractual agreements on wage and work-time issues, they offered firm-specific incentives, negotiated with their often more compliant works councils. Even so, the business community sees organized labor as "a stable, predictable and indispensable participant in the Federal Republic's industrial, economic and political life."[65]

Conclusion

Comparativists who turned their attention to Germany in the forties and fifties were, above all, concerned with the prospects for democracy. This was a reflection of the fact that democratization was the single most important research question for comparativists at the time. Answers to this question were sought primarily in the study of Germany's political culture. Initially there was less interest in political institutions, as these had been designed under the watchful eye of the Allied powers, notably the United States. But when institutions and elite behavior were examined, a number of authors identified legacies of the past here as well. Some institutional practices betrayed a whiff of the Obrigkeitsstaat. Mention could be made here of the chancellor's often contemptuous treatment of the opposition, or the dry, expert-dominated nature of parliamentary proceedings. The political economy approach was not well established in comparative politics until the mid- to late seventies.

In their critical studies of German politics, the concerns of American scholars were often confirmed by the insights of German scholars. Dahrendorf's work certainly was widely read, and although different in perspective and approach, it highlighted many of Almond and Verba's conclusions. Émigré scholars, like Kirchheimer, also added important arguments. All shared a preoccupation with the distinctiveness of German politics. This focus faded slowly. In 1971, Grosser described Germany as a normal state and society and went on to explain that if "we have drawn comparisons with France and Britain more frequently than with the G.D.R., it is . . . above all because the analogies in Western Europe are so much closer and more numerous than those between the two Germanies."[66] Twelve years later, Katzenstein expressed the widely held view that fears of a revival of German militarism and authoritarianism were receding. And in 1989 he emphasized the comparability rather than the exceptionalism of West Germany.[67] Over the forty-year history of Germany's second experiment with democracy, comparative research has amassed much evidence that the gulf between Germany and the West has been bridged.

In time, comparativists moved from a preoccupation with the single theme of democratization to a more varied and specialized agenda. The search for a grand theory of politics was abandoned in the late sixties and seventies in favor of midlevel approaches and an interest in specific subunits of the political process.[68] This coincided with the growth of comparative approaches as opposed to single-country studies. Increasingly, Germany appeared as one of several cases in comparative analyses. This was aided by the growing availability of comparative data sets like the Eurobarometer and European Consortium for Political Research. But it was also a consequence of the perception of "normalcy" that had settled over the West German landscape. The fact that the Federal Republic did not experience dramatic changes or upheavals also undermined the single-case-study approach. Some argue whether this growing perception of normalcy reflected a decline of interest in things German. But few would challenge the argument that the quick and unexpected unification of East and West Germany opens up a new agenda for scholars of German politics and society. Convention papers already reveal the contours of that agenda. Studies of the political culture of eastern citizens were available very quickly. Their political behavior—conventional and unconventional—will take more time to gain some recognizable shape. Studies of the new institutions will focus on elite recruitment and socialization. The party system, namely the extension of the western parties to the East, is of obvious interest. These are important areas for political scientists to address. But there are questions of greater urgency. Two will be raised here.

Of most obvious concern is the likelihood of the successful extension of the Federal Republic's economy and economic-policy framework to the East. With implications that reach well beyond the German case, German experts have noted the political significance of the economic miracle for the Federal Republic. Can west German experts now engineer another economic miracle in the East? The global economic context would seem to be much less favorable this time around. On the other hand, Easterners are guaranteed a steady inflow of expertise and capital from the West. Even so, there will be difficult times ahead. Apart from the likely political ramifications of economic stagnation in the East, the social and cultural implications are equally alarming. Will the five new eastern states develop into Germany's Mezzogiorno, resentful and resented, economically dependent on cash flows from the West and/or the European Community? As these and related issues are already receiving considerable attention, it is unlikely that scholars will ignore the development of the new political economy in east Germany. This cannot, however, be assumed to apply to the second question as well.

Are the west German institutions—political, economic, and social— able to absorb the shock waves that will no doubt continue to roll from the East toward the West? The Federal Republic had developed into a polity characterized by stable institutions constantly adjusting to new circum- stances.[69] West Germany managed change *within* stable institutions. This leaves the question whether this pattern of change can be maintained in the future. At this early juncture, the answer would appear to be positive. The widely supported decision to unite East and West Germany according to Article 23 of the Basic Law, allowing new states to join the federation, is a good example. Other nations might have opted for the opportunity to achieve unification with the adoption of a new constitution, as outlined in Article 146. But this example of managing change, major though it was, provides no guarantees for the future. A related issue deals with the likelihood that change will not always be a one-way street, going from the West to the East, as the actors of the Federal Republic extend its framework into the East. It is extremely likely that western institutions and practices will themselves be changed in this process. Unsettling though this may be, comparativists must be open to this possibility.

The experience of unification should reenergize and revitalize the study of German politics. After the experiment with democracy, the country is now undergoing the experiment of unification.

NOTES

1. Gabriel A. Almond, ed., *The Struggle for Democracy in Germany* (New York: Russel & Russel, 1965), vi.

2. Ibid., vii.

3. Clara Menck, "The Problem of Reorientation," in Almond, *Struggle for Democracy,* 306.

4. A. J. P. Taylor, *The Course of German History* (London: Hamish Hamilton, 1945). Cited in Ralf Dahrendorf, *Society and Democracy in Germany* (Garden City, N.Y.: Anchor Books, 1969), 8.

5. Dahrendorf, *Society and Democracy,* 14. This book was first published in Germany in 1965.

6. Russell J. Dalton, "Comparative Politics of the Industrial Democracies: From the Golden Age to Island Hopping," *Political Science: Looking to the Future,* ed. William Crotty, vol. 2, *Comparative Politics, Policy, and International Relations* (Evanston, Ill.: Northwestern University Press, 1991), 17.

7. Gabriel Almond and Sidney Verba, *The Civic Culture: Political Attitudes and Democracy in Five Nations* (Princeton: Princeton University Press, 1963), 13.

8. Ibid., 6.

9. Ibid., 312–13.

10. Dalton, "Comparative Politics," 16.

11. Dahrendorf, *Society and Democracy,* 325, 424.

12. Gabriel Almond and Sidney Verba, eds., *The Civic Culture Revisited* (Boston: Little Brown, 1980).

13. Kendall Baker, Russell J. Dalton, and Kai Hildebrandt, *Germany Transformed* (Cambridge: Harvard University Press, 1981).

14. Ibid., 69.

15. Ronald Inglehart, *The Silent Revolution: Changing Values and Political Styles among Western Publics* (Princeton: Princeton University Press, 1977).

16. Baker, Dalton, and Hildebrandt, *Germany Transformed,* part 2.

17. Inglehart, *Silent Revolution.*

18. Erwin K. Scheuch, "Die Suche nach der Besonderheit der heutigen Deutschen," *Kölner Zeitschrift für Soziologie und Sozialpsychologie* 42 (1990): 750. The quote was translated by the author.

19. Deutsches Jugendinstitut, *Deutsche Schüler im Sommer 1990: Skeptische Demokraten auf dem Weg in ein vereintes Deutschland,* Arbeitspapier 3–019 (Munich: Deutsches Jugendinstitut, 1990), 18.

20. Dahrendorf, *Society and Democracy,* 426.

21. Russell J. Dalton, Scott Flanagan, and Paul Allen Beck, eds., *Electoral Change in Advanced Industrial Democracies* (Princeton: Princeton University Press, 1984).

22. Gerhard Loewenberg, "The Development of the German Party System," in *Germany at the Polls,* ed. Karl H. Cerny (Washington, D.C.: American Enterprise Institute, 1978), 24.

23. John H. Herz, "A Statement by the Issue Editor," *Comparative Politics* 2 (1970): 520.

24. Ibid., 520–21.

25. Cerny, *Germany at the Polls,* preface, n.p.

26. Compare, respectively, David P. Conradt, *Unified Germany at the Polls,* German Issues 9 (Washington, D.C.: American Institute for Contemporary German Studies, 1990), and Manfred Kuechler, "Anschluss über alles?—What Did the Voter Decide in the 1990 German Elections?" (Paper delivered at the Annual Meeting of the Midwest Political Science Association, 1991).

27. Samuel Barnes and Max Kaase, *Political Action: Mass Participation in Five Western Democracies* (Beverly Hills, Calif.: Sage, 1979).

28. Dorothy Nelkin and Michael Pollak, *The Atom Besieged* (Cambridge: MIT Press, 1981).

29. Barnes and Kaase, *Political Action,* 49.

30. Thomas T. Rochon, *Mobilizing for Peace* (Princeton: Princeton University Press, 1988).

31. Ibid., 213.

32. David Gress, *Peace and Survival* (Stanford, Calif.: Hoover Institution Press, 1985).

33. Russell J. Dalton and Manfred Kuechler, eds., *Challenging the Political Order: New Social and Political Movements in Western Democracies* (Cambridge and New York: Oxford University Press, 1990), 4.

34. Rudolf Wildenmann et al., *Führungsschicht in der Bundesrepublik Deutschland* (Mannheim: Lehrstuhl für politische Wissenschaft, 1981).

35. John A. Armstrong, *The European Administrative Elite* (Princeton: Princeton University Press, 1973); Joel Aberbach, Robert Putnam, and Bert Rockman, *Bureaucrats and Politicians in Western Democracies* (Cambridge: Harvard University Press, 1981).

36. See, respectively, Gerhard Loewenberg, *Parliament in the German Political System* (Ithaca: Cornell University Press, 1967); Gerard Braunthal, *The West German Legislative Process* (Ithaca: Cornell University Press, 1972); and William Safran, *Veto-Group Politics* (San Francisco: Chandler, 1967).

37. Braunthal, *Legislative Process,* 244.

38. Ibid., 387.

39. Ibid., 435.

40. Loewenberg, *Parliament,* 434; Kenneth H. F. Dyson, *Party, State, and Bureaucracy in Western Germany* (Beverly Hills, Calif.: Sage, 1977).

41. Geoffrey Pridham, *Christian Democracy in Western Germany* (New York: St. Martin's, 1977), 349, 33, 223.

42. Gerard Braunthal, *The West German Social Democrats, 1969–1983* (Boulder, Colo.: Westview), chs. 3, 8.

43. Ibid., 229–300.

44. Otto Kirchheimer, "The Waning of Opposition in Parliamentary Regimes," *Social Research* 24 (1957): 127–56.

45. Otto Kirchheimer, "Germany: The Vanishing Opposition," in *Political Opposi-tions in Western Democracies,* ed. Robert Dahl (New Haven: Yale University Press, 1966), 250.

46. Gerd Langguth, *The Green Factor in German Politics: From Protest Move-ment to Political Party* (Boulder, Colo.: Westview, 1986).

47. Donald P. Kommers, *The Constitutional Jurisprudence of the Federal Republic of Germany* (Durham, N.C.: Duke University Press, 1989), and *Judicial Politics in West Germany* (Beverly Hills, Calif.: Sage, 1976).

48. Ibid., 302, 214.

49. Gregg O. Kvistad, "Civil Liberties and German State Employees," *German Politics and Society* 19 (1990): 14–26.

50. Charles Lindblom, *Politics and Markets* (New York: Basic Books, 1977).

51. Suzanne D. Berger, ed., *Organizing Interests in Western Europe* (New York: Cambridge University Press, 1981), 1.

52. Karl Hardach, *The Political Economy of Germany in the Twentieth Century* (Berkeley and Los Angeles: University of California Press, 1980), 6.

53. Andrei S. Markovits, "Introduction: Model Germany—A Cursory Overview of a Complex Construct," in *The Political Economy of West Germany: Modell Deutschland,* ed. Andrei S. Markovits (New York: Praeger, 1982), 9.

54. Philippe C. Schmitter and Gerhard Lehmbruch, eds., *Trends toward Corpora-tist Intermediation* (Beverly Hills, Calif.: Sage, 1979), 13; see also Gerhard Lehmbruch and Philippe C. Schmitter, eds., *Patterns of Corporatist Policy Making* (Beverly Hills, Calif.: Sage, 1982).

55. Schmitter and Lehmbruch, *Trends,* 19.

56. Gerhard Lehmbruch, "Introduction: Neo-Corporatism in Comparative Perspec-tive," in Lehmbruch and Schmitter, *Patterns,* 20.

57. Gerhard Fuchs and Andrew Koch, "Corporatism and 'Political Context' in the Federal Republic of Germany" (Paper delivered at the Annual Meeting of the Midwest Political Science Association, 1990), 14.

58. Peter J. Katzenstein, *Industry and Politics in West Germany* (Ithaca: Cornell University Press, 1989), 332, 346; Simon Bulmer and Peter Humphreys, "Kohl, Corporatism, and Congruence: The West German Model under Challenge," in *The Changing Agenda of West German Public Policy,* ed. Simon Bulmer (Brookfield: Gower, 1989), 177.

59. Katzenstein, *Industry and Poitics,* part 3.

60. Jutta A. Helm, "Structural Change in the Ruhr Valley: What Price Social Peace?" in *The Federal Republic of Germany at Forty,* ed. Peter H. Merkl (New York: New York University Press, 1989), 202.

61. Joachim Jens Hesse, ed., *Die Erneuerung alter Industrieregionen* (Baden-Baden: Nomos, 1988), 564.

62. Charles S. Maier, "Bonn ist doch Weimar: Informal Reflections on the Histori-cal Legacy of the Federal Republic," in Markovits, *Political Economy,* 188; Peter J. Katzenstein, "Problem or Model? West Germany in the 1980's," *World Politics* 32 (1982): 577–98; Peter J. Katzenstein, *Policy and Politics in West Germany: The Growth of a Semi-Sovereign State* (Philadelphia: Temple University Press, 1987).

63. Fuchs and Koch, "Corporatism," 15.

64. Douglas Webber, "A Relationship of 'Critical Partnership'? Capital and the Social-Liberal Coalition in West Germany," in *Capital and Politics in Western Europe,* ed. David Marsh (London: Frank Cass, 1983), 79–80.

65. Andrei S. Markovits, *The Politics of the West German Trade Unions* (New York: Cambridge University Press, 1986), 441, 415.

66. Alfred Grosser, *Germany in Our Time* (New York: Praeger, 1971), 330.

67. Katzenstein, "Problem or Model?" 577; Katzenstein, *Industry and Politics,* 5.

68. Dalton, "Comparative Politics," 27.

69. Katzenstein, *Industry and Politics,* 6, 329.

PART 2

Political Behavior

As Jutta A. Helm noted in the last essay, a key question about Germany after World War II was the stability of its democracy. While the initial surveys conducted after the war suggested that democratic values were not widely held in West Germany, the economic and political successes of the West Germans strengthened public belief in democracy in the ensuing decades. Yet right-wing challenges to the democratic norms of the Federal Republic persisted after 1949 and may reflect underlying authoritarian value patterns in the German public. In this essay, Manfred Kuechler explores the changing nature of German democracy. He notes the forces that stabilized German democracy after the war, analyzes the challenges to the democratic value system that developed, and examines the impacts of German unification on system support in both east and west Germany. His conclusions are positive: despite challenges posed by the integration of 16 million East German citizens into the western political order and value system, German democracy seems strongly rooted in unified Germany.

Political Attitudes and Behavior in Germany: The Making of a Democratic Society

Manfred Kuechler

The political preferences of the German public have been under intense scrutiny ever since the end of World War II. While study and analysis of public opinion and mass political behavior are important for a comprehensive assessment of any nation's political state, Germany is a special case. The first attempt to establish a Western-style democracy after World War I failed quickly. The Weimar Republic collapsed after little more than a decade, when the German electorate voted Hitler into power. No coup was needed. German democracy went into self-destruction. After the end of World War II Germany was divided, and the two parts went different routes. Under the auspices of the United States, Great Britain, and France one part adopted a Western-style democratic system formally known as the Federal Republic of Germany (FRG). The other part became a satellite of the Soviet Union under Communist rule formally known as the German Democratic Republic (GDR).[1] Given the constraints set by a Communist regime, research on public opinion and mass political behavior in East Germany was very limited. Attention was focused on West Germany. Would the (West) German public truly adopt democratic norms and values? Would a commitment to the democratic system endure times of economic hardship or internal strife? In short, would the Germans develop and maintain a civic culture? As discussed in more detail below, by the 1980s most scholars agreed that West Germany had been transformed into a stable democracy, that its citizenry was beyond reproach with respect to its commitment to democratic principles and procedures.

The surprising demise of the Communist regime in East Germany and the subsequent push for unification revitalized a seemingly moot agenda. Would the East Germans fully embrace Western democratic norms and values, even if economic rewards were slow in coming? Would the West Germans be willing to share, would they be willing to bear with a difficult transition period? Would the newly united Germany continue to be the "model democracy" the western part has been noted for? Or, would democracy in Germany crumble once more under the burden of a drastic change in the economic structure and in the social fabric? Mass sentiment in Germany, then, seems crucial for the stability of the domestic political system and for the international order in Europe.

Some problems notwithstanding, survey research provides the tools to monitor the sentiment of the masses in a controlled, systematic, and quantitative way.[2] Information gained from survey research played an important role in shaping the image of postwar Germany, for example as presented in introductory American texts on the subject.[3] Survey research as a scholarly method is relatively new, not fully recognized before the landmark study on the American soldier.[4] The new method was quickly put to use in Germany after the end of World War II. With the possible exception of the United States, the amount of political survey data on the German public is unsurpassed in any other nation. Political surveys of the German citizenry started with the creation of a survey unit within the Information Control Division of the Office of Military Government, United States (OMGUS). This unit conducted seventy-two surveys of varying size and scope in the period from October 1945 to September 1949.[5] After the promulgation of the Federal Republic, these surveys were followed by a similar series, now conducted by the Reactions Analysis Staff, Office of Public Affairs, Office of the U.S. High Commissioner for Germany (HICOG) till 1955,[6] and subsequently by surveys commissioned by the United States Information Agency (USIA).[7] In addition, commercial German survey research firms were established as early as the late 1940s, most notably the Institut für Demoskopie in Allensbach. Its cofounder, Elisabeth Noelle-Neumann, later also held a chair in journalism and communications at the University of Mainz. She came to often controversial prominence both as a scholar and as a pollster and political advisor to conservative German governments.

Only a fraction of this abundance of survey data on political attitudes and behavior of the German public, though, resulted from systematically designed scholarly studies spanning extended periods of time. Also, many of these data are not (easily) accessible. Often, selected tables are available but not the full data set necessary to conduct secondary statistical analysis. The prime freely accessible source for political survey data over time is the series of election studies initiated by Rudolf Wildenmann and Erwin K. Scheuch in Cologne with the 1961 election. The series was continued first at the University of Mannheim by Rudolf Wildenmann, then since 1974 by a nonprofit organization known as the Forschungsgruppe Wahlen through all subsequent elections. These studies have involved leading German scholars in the field—such as Max Kaase, Hans-Dieter Klingemann, and Franz-Urban Pappi—as collaborators and advisors.[8] Apart from practicality, a focus on elections is warranted on theoretical grounds. After all, political attitudes and beliefs come to bear most directly at the polls.

In this chapter, I will summarize important findings as they relate to the future of the political system in Germany and to the stability of the democratic order, as well as to changes in the process of interest intermediation, to the role of parties, and to the composition of the party system.[9] More detailed overviews can be found in other studies.[10] A series of volumes edited by Kaase and von Beyme, Kaase and Klingemann, Klingemann and Kaase, and Oberndörfer, Rattinger, and Schmitt provide comprehensive coverage of voting behavior in Germany.[11] In addition, a recent English-language volume offers a descriptive account of German politics and elections in the 1980s.[12]

In the first part of this chapter I will deal with the rebirth of democracy in West Germany after World War II. Then I will discuss the process of German unification from the emergence of major dissatisfaction in East Germany in the mid-1980s, to formal unification in 1990, to the yet-to-be-completed actual merging of two vastly different social and political systems. I will use data on mass sentiment in both east and west Germany up to the fall of 1991.[13] In an appendix, I will provide a brief discussion of sources of data and their availability.

The Rebirth of Democracy in West Germany

Social Cleavages and Political Parties

Typically, turmoil, radical changes, and revolutions attract much more attention than stability and evolutionary development. Yet, the most striking characteristic of postwar Germany is the relative ease with which a new political order was established and a high degree of political stability achieved. In a span of just eight years the number of parties in the Bundestag was reduced from over ten to just three (Christian Democratic Union/Christian Social Union [CDU/CSU], Social Democratic Party [SPD], Free Democratic Party [FDP]), which held their monopoly till the entry of the Greens in 1983.[14] Several changes in the electoral laws, most notably the 5-percent threshold, helped to accelerate this concentration process and later prevented the rise of new parties trying to capitalize on temporary dissatisfaction. However, the main reason for the stability of the German party system and, in turn, the stability of German governments was the formation of strong ties between the major parties and sizable segments of the electorate.

Turnout for the first general elections in 1949 was close to 80 percent and then oscillated between about 85 and 90 percent in the next four decades before it reached a low of 77.8 percent in the first pan-German elections in December 1990.[15] High turnout across various social groups and few votes for parties that did not fully endorse democratic principles, then, provided solid mass support for the emerging new order. The choice between (democratic) parties in Germany, though, has been strongly predetermined by sociodemographic characteristics of the voter, such as religious affiliation, frequency of church attendance, union membership, and subjective class identification. The Social Democrats regained their traditional clientele of union-oriented workers from the pre-Nazi era. The newly formed Christian Democrats aimed to represent Christian, not just Catholic, values and quickly foiled the attempt to reestablish the strictly Catholic Zentrum party of the Weimar Republic. Perhaps more importantly, the CDU represented a non-socialist, "humane capitalist" approach to building the German economy (Sozialemarktwirtschaft) that was in stark contrast to the course taken in East Germany and thus immediately appealed to a large segment of the population. In the process, the tangible results from its economic policies widened the CDU's structural advantage, a significantly larger pool of potential voters than its main competitor commanded.[16] In this constellation the Liberals gained a pivotal role, largely deciding which of the two major parties would lead the government—the first SPD-led government, however, not being formed before 1969. It may appear that a small party (rarely exceeding 10 percent of the popular vote) is exercising an undue influence on the allocation of political power. However, surveys consistently show that a solid majority of the electorate prefers to have the FDP represented in parliament. The FDP's occasional failure to clear the 5-percent threshold in state and other elections must be seen as the result of normal ebbs and flows in the standing of a party with an average vote share close to the threshold. In the past, these failures have often been mistaken as an indication of the FDP's final decline. The elections to the European Parliament are just one example. Here, after the party missed by a fraction in the elections of 1984, the FDP easily surpassed 5 percent in 1989. The German electorate perceives the FDP as a liberal corrective to the CDU in matters of civil liberties and foreign policy and as a corrective to the SPD with respect to economic policy. The FDP, then, is an acceptable choice to a much larger segment of voters than its average share of the vote seems to suggest. Yet, its core clientele has always been small and most likely will remain small. Its composition may change again, however, as it did in the late 1960s, when Left libertarianism replaced economic liberalism as the party's prime focus. Apart from its core clientele, the FDP needs the support of voters who temporarily abandon the major party of their choice to support the liberal cause. What appears at first sight as immobility of the German party system is the net result of a more intricate balancing process resulting in long-term stability. And the German voters have shown considerable sophistication in making their choice.

A New Era of Volatility?

After the formation of the Social-Liberal coalition in 1969, its slim parliamentary majority quickly faded. A number of right-wing Liberals left the party and fueled an unsuccessful attempt to replace Willy Brandt as chancellor by a vote of nonconfidence. The SPD emerged from the out-of-cycle elections in 1972 as the strongest party (a feat never accomplished again), producing a comfortable margin for a new SPD/FDP coalition. But the traditional determinants of voting behavior were insufficient to explain the outcome of the 1972 election. Social change has led to a constant decline in the number of blue-collar workers—the traditional clientele of the SPD—and to a simultaneous rise of what was labeled as the "urban middle class."[17] Precipitated by changes in mass communication (the omnipresence of television) and drastically increased educational opportunities, a process sometimes labeled as *individualization* had set in. In this process, ties to family, church, and community, as well as identification with social groups—for example, the trade unions—become less important. The impact of the individuals' social backgrounds on their life choices is receding, and a multitude of options becomes available. It is plausible to assume that political choices would be affected as well, that volatility would replace social-cleavage voting as the norm. Unresolved in the 1970s, the debate on the extent of voter volatility (and all its implications for the stability of the established political order) continues and is not likely to be settled soon.[18] On the one hand, it is well established that the traditional core clienteles of the major parties are declining in size. On the other hand, the association between sociodemographic background and vote choice has not changed much over the last ten or fifteen years.[19] According to recall of past voting behavior in surveys, the major parties retain approximately 75 to 80 percent of their voters from one election to the next. Given tactical voting (e.g., voting for the FDP, as discussed above) and random abstention, the segment of truly volatile voters does not appear to be very large. In spite of all social change, the traditional ties between voters and parties seem largely unaltered. In my opinion, there is no strong evidence for a process of dealignment and realignment in Germany.[20] Unfortunately, it is extremely difficult to separate long-term ties to a particular party from more transient preferences. In the German context, no reliable measure exists to gauge the extent and intensity of what is called *party identification*. This concept was developed by the dominant Michigan School of voting behavior. It refers to a long-term inclination towards a particular party, developed as early as childhood and adolescence under parental influence. In the United States, institutional arrangements accentuate a difference between party identification and current voting preference. In many states voters need to register as Democrats or Republicans to exercise their voting rights. In most cases they will register in line with their general preference. American parties, however, exercise little control over a candidate's specific agenda. Consequently, it is quite common that in a given election, the candidate of the other party appears more attractive. In contrast, voting registration in Germany is automatic and nonpartisan. No more than 4 to 5 percent of the electorate are formal, dues-paying members of a political party. Thus, the analytic concept of party identification does not have manifest behavioral correlates in the everyday life of the average German citizen.[21] However, the question of how well party identification has been or can be measured in the German context is controversial. In particular, Falter and Rattinger have presented elaborate attempts at a "normal vote analysis."[22]

New Politics and the Rise of the Greens

An integral part of the dealignment thesis is the assertion that as part of a more fundamental change,[23] new issues and interests have replaced traditional concerns.[24] Consequently, the old alliances between parties and specific segments of the electorate are gradually superseded by new alliances. In particular, the rise of "new social movements" and their party correlate, the Greens, may be seen as a manifestation of this ongoing change. Before their entry into the Bundestag in 1983, the Greens gained representation on the municipal level as well as in several state (Länder) legislatures. By now, the Greens must be considered as a permanent addition to the German party system.[25] Yet, it needs to be determined (*a*) whether new interests and issues replace or, more likely, just supplement traditional economic interests and (*b*) whether the established parties will be flexible enough to successfully respond to these challenges to the existing political order.[26]

As to the first point: survey data show without doubt that the issues of environmental protection, nuclear energy, and disarmament have become highly salient topics on the political agenda for the elections of 1987 and beyond. Apparently, the nuclear disaster at Chernobyl was essential in reshaping the thinking of large parts of the electorate across traditional ideological lines. Also, the impact of perceived party competence in dealing with these problems on the vote choice has increased. Yet, traditional economic concerns have held their ground.[27] As to the second point: there is strong evidence from the election studies and from other political surveys that the Greens and the SPD compete for the same segment of the electorate. Among adherents of the Greens, the SPD—almost uniformly—is the party liked

second best. It is the only other party rated favorably on a scale from −5 to
+5. In functional terms, then, the Greens are a split-off from the SPD
appealing to the educated young of libertarian conviction. Consequently, the
parliamentary entry of the Greens does not signify a major change in the
composition of the German party system and in the alignment between voters
and parties.[28] Overall, then, the most significant impact of new social movements may be indirect, by inducing change in the established parties resulting
in long-term stability.[29]

System Support and Stability of Democratic Convictions

Another important aspect of mass political attitudes is the support for the
democratic system in general, or *diffuse support*—to employ the vague but
widely used term Easton has coined.[30] On the one hand, survey data seemed
to indicate a rather rapid adoption of the democratic system in West Germany
during the 1950s.[31] On the other hand, serious doubt prevailed about how far
the support for the democratic system would go. This doubt was most prominently expressed by Almond and Verba in *Civic Culture,* a study of political
attitudes and democracy in five nations (United States, United Kingdom,
Germany, Italy, and Mexico). They claimed that, in Germany, "though there
is relatively widespread satisfaction with political output, this is not matched
by more general system affect."[32] Germans tended "to lack a more general
attachment to the system on the symbolic level" and displayed a "detached,
practical, and almost cynical attitude towards politics." Almond and Verba
saw serious limitations in the Germans' ability to cooperate politically. As a
consequence, support for democracy was likely to continue as long as the
system provided for economic well-being. However, in times of deficiencies—most notably economic hardship—the West Germans might quickly
withdraw their support.

The *Civic Culture* study has been sharply criticized on both methodological and conceptual grounds. First, key parts of the questionnaire administered by Almond and Verba may not produce valid data in the German
context.[33] Second, as a one-time survey, the study could not address change
over time. Later analyses focused on the ongoing process of democratization,
using a multitude of available survey data, and thoroughly refuted the original assessment by Almond and Verba.[34] In Conradt's analysis, "The Bonn
Republic, unlike its predecessor [the Weimar Republic], has built up a reserve of cultural support which should enable it to deal with these future
issues of the quality and extent of democracy at least as effectively as other
'late capitalist' Western democracies."[35] Particularly notable is the change
in political interest and participation apart from continuing high turnout in
elections. For example, in 1953 more than 60 percent of the respondents said

they never discussed politics; by 1972, this figure was down to 15 percent.[36] Similarly, the percentage of Germans interested in politics rose from 27 percent in 1952 to 50 percent in 1977.[37] However, some caution seems to be in order. Most of this increase may be due to the omnipresence of television and an almost unavoidable exposure to political news. While superficial interest in politics has certainly increased, genuine involvement in politics may not have increased as much. Also, in contrast to political interest, political knowledge is still at a fairly low level.[38] Yet, the support for key elements of a democratic system increased. In 1953, only half of the Germans believed that it was best to have several parties; by 1979 support for a multiparty system had increased to 86 percent.[39] Similarly, in 1953 political efficacy was low. Only one-third of the Germans felt that they could do something if they were dissatisfied with the government. By 1979, this figure had risen to 59 percent.[40] These and other data constitute an impressive array of empirical evidence assuaging major concerns expressed by Almond and Verba. Conradt even rated West Germany as a "model stable democracy."[41]

In addition, the cross-national "Political Action" study and other studies on political participation[42] do not provide any evidence that patterns of political participation in Germany are markedly different from those in other Western democracies. There is good reason to believe, then, that the Germans have fully embraced democracy, that the process of democratization is irreversible and immune to any challenge. Still, some doubts remain.

Times of Challenge

Germany has gone through a long period of economic growth and ever-rising affluence for the overwhelming majority of the population. The political system has continually provided economic benefits at levels never attained before. The Germans, then, experienced democracy and affluence as part of one package. Acceptance of democratic norms and values is high, but at the same time affluence is taken for granted. A true test of an unwavering commitment to democracy in times of hardship has yet to come. So far, when compared to other Western nations, Germany has experienced rather mild economic setbacks only. But at these times of modest challenge, there were some indications that the Germans' belief in the democratic system can be shaken.

Germany has gone through several cycles of emerging right-wing extremism and surprising electoral success of right-wing or downright neo-Nazi parties. So far, these cycles were short-lived, and antidemocratic forces never gained enough momentum to put the established political order in jeopardy. In addition, none of the right-wing parties and organizations has been able to provide continuity through the ebbs and flows of extremist mass appeal.

Over the years, right-wing extremism has changed its face, and generational replacement has altered the composition of its clientele. Today, nazism and anti-Semitism no longer epitomize the ideology of the Right—though anti-Semitism is not extinct in Germany. The changing face of right-wing forces may invite scholars to deal with each occurrence separately. If spells of extremism are analyzed this way, doubts about the stability of the democratic order in Germany can be dismissed rather easily—as normal deviations from the democratic mainstream caused by singular issues and temporary disenchantment. While this mode of analysis may be appropriate for similar spells of extremism in old, established democracies like Great Britain or France (e.g., most recently Le Pen's Front National), more caution should be used in the German case. It seems wiser to look for a latent movement, an undercurrent that, contingent upon precipitating events and favorable conditions, will manifest itself in varying shapes and forms. What, then, may be at the core of these spells of right-wing extremism? I see a continued—though mostly latent—prevalence of authoritarian belief systems in significant parts of the German public. These beliefs emerge and become relevant for political behavior whenever threats to economic affluence, coupled with a threat to the established order and a lack of strong political leadership, are perceived. This particular combination of factors, an authoritarian syndrome, seems to be present in all of the more serious spells of right-wing activity or declining support for the democratic system.

The first economic recession in the late 1960s led to the fall of the Christian Democratic government and the resignation of Chancellor Erhardt, once widely acclaimed as the father of the German Wirtschaftswunder, the economic miracle. Subsequently, a neo-Nazi party (the NPD) gained 4.3 percent of the vote in the 1969 elections. However, it was barred from parliamentary representation by the 5-percent rule and quickly lost momentum.[43]

The more serious economic crisis in the early 1980s, with a simultaneous increase of both inflation and unemployment, was accompanied by a drastic fall in the level of satisfaction with democracy.[44] At the same time, Germany had been shaken by a wave of terrorist attacks (e.g., the Baader-Meinhof Gang or "Red Army Fraction," in their self-description) and the assassination of several prominent figures in business and government, including the federal chief prosecutor and the chief executive officer of the Mercedes motor company. But satisfaction with democracy rose to its previous level once inflation was curbed, the economic situation was perceived more favorably, and terrorist activity subsided.[45]

In January 1989, another right-wing party, the Republicans, had spectacular electoral success in the Berlin (state) elections. Subsequently, they surged in public opinion polls and recorded significant gains in the municipal elections in Hesse, as well as in the nationwide European Parliament elections of June 1989.[46] In early 1989, however, Germany did not experience an economic crisis, though high levels of unemployment continued. Rather, the public's perception seemed to be unduly influenced by relatively minor issues like the introduction of effective ways to tax interest income (the later hastily rescinded Quellensteuer), or apparently unjustified privileges for Aussiedler—immigrants of German descent from eastern European countries. While dissatisfaction with the government on these issues was widespread, support for the Republicans was largely restricted to voters of right-wing ideological orientation. For many years, this segment of the electorate had been effectively integrated into the CDU, and most importantly into the Bavarian CSU, due to the appeal of strong leaders like Konrad Adenauer and Franz-Josef Strauss. The lack of inspiring political leadership had made the right-wing clientele of the CDU and CSU susceptible to alternatives that the Republicans seemed to provide.[47]

The dramatic events leading to German unification left the Republicans on the sidelines. In the December 1990 elections they captured 2.1 percent of the total vote and just 1.3 percent in the east. And they were not able to capitalize on the disenchantment and dissatisfaction with the consequences of unification in the following year. In four state elections in 1991, they did not capture more than 2 percent of the vote anywhere. Their results in national polls were at the same level. In April 1992, however, they registered a stunning success in the state elections in Baden-Württemberg and seized 10.9 percent of the vote—mostly at the expense of the Christian Democrats. Subsequently, through the summer into fall of 1992, national polls showed the Republicans as the vote choice of seven to eight percent of the respondents. Given a host of internal organizational problems and leadership disputes, the Republicans may not become a serious contender in the next elections. Still, it is worthwhile to note differences and similarities between the Republicans and the neo-Nazi NPD. The Republicans are not a neo-Nazi party in the immediate sense, irrespective of the sometimes overemphasized military record of their leader, Franz Schönhuber. Hitler's Kampf is not theirs; anti-Semitism is not one of their key programmatic concerns. At the same time, the Republicans appeal to petit bourgeois fears of losing ground both economically and culturally to whatever appears as foreign. They appeal to visions of national grandeur and supremacy, to be upheld in a hostile world. They walk a thin line between legitimate conservatism of the patriotic kind and outright national and racial chauvinism. In contrast to the NPD, the Republicans are shrewd enough to stay in the twilight zone. They carefully avoid blatant Nazi symbolism and rhetoric of the past. The distance between Republicans and the NPD is also reflected in the party preferences of their clienteles. Survey data from spring 1989 showed that adherents of the NPD also felt close to the Republicans, but that the reverse was not true. Overwhelmingly, the party of second choice among adherents of the Republicans is the CDU/CSU, not the NPD.

The success of the Republicans may be temporary. However, another extremist party may emerge as long as a significant part of the German public is susceptible to the authoritarian syndrome described above. In the fall of 1991, the now united Germany experienced a new wave of xenophobia and right-wing extremism. Over the course of just four weeks, an estimated 500 attacks took place by right-wing youth against foreigners.[48] A right-wing party, the German People's Union (DVU), gained more than 6 percent of the vote in the Bremen state elections, in addition to 1.5 percent for the Republicans. Both parties exploited the fear of many Germans that they will become overburdened by immigrants, and both parties have their strongest support among young male workers. At the same time, the share for the Social Democrats dropped by more than 10 percent to just under 40 percent, while the conservative Christian Democrats also made gains—recovering from a devastating loss four years earlier. Bremen is the least populated state in Germany (just a little over half a million eligible voters), and the DVU may not be able to spread to other states. However, the issue of benefits for Aussiedler, foreigners, and asylum seekers has regained a top spot on the issue agenda. The established parties are hard-pressed to come up with solutions satisfying the public, but still in consonance with previously proclaimed goals and policies. Maybe the process of actual unification in a reshaping Europe will turn out to be the true test of the stability of the Germans' democratic convictions. Hopefully, this test will dispel all remaining doubts about the civility of the Germans—east and west.

The Process of Unification

Political Attitudes in Communist East Germany

There is no comparable host of data on political attitudes and behavior in the GDR. In particular, there are practically no data at all for the 1950s and the early 1960s. The situation changed in 1966, when the Central Institute for Youth Research (ZIJ) was founded in Leipzig. It was charged with conducting studies on the "socialist personality" and on character development among adolescents and young adults to aid the Communist party in pursuing its goals. Despite frequent conflicts with Communist party headquarters, the ZIJ under the direction of Walter Friedrich—himself an avowed Communist, but a dedicated scholar as well—managed to survive. In the 1970s and 1980s the ZIJ conducted ten to fifteen studies per year, including several major longitudinal studies covering spans of five to twelve years.[49] The choice of topics had to be cleared with party officials. Often some ingenuity was needed to continue a line of research inconsistent with official party doctrine. For example, in 1974 the Communist party officially declared that equal rights for men and women had been fully realized in East Germany. Consequently, no further research on the situation of women was needed—and none was permitted. However, omnibus-type surveys provided opportunities to include at least a limited number of questions related to topics deemed unnecessary or counterrevolutionary by party officials.

Given its initial charge to study youth, samples of ZIJ studies were selected from young workers, apprentices (young people in training for a skilled trade), and high school and university students. Typically, researchers at ZIJ administered questionnaires to groups in their natural setting, for example, to classes in high schools and universities and to work collectives in plants and factories, for immediate completion and subsequent recollection in the group setting. This system provided reasonable assurance that responses would indeed not be attributed to specific individuals and that the data would be used for statistical analysis only. The political context of a totalitarian regime did not allow for random sampling (of the population at large) or for individual personal interviews. But apart from these methodological differences to research in the West, the ZIJ studies were quite sophisticated with respect to research design and questionnaire construction. In my opinion, these data constitute an invaluable source of information on political and social attitudes in Communist East Germany.[50] Most of the research was not published at the time. Reports on findings were produced in a few copies only, and their circulation was severely restricted. It will take some time to fully analyze the data collected under the old regime. For the time being, Friedrich and Griese provide a very useful summary of the research conducted at ZIJ.[51]

With respect to political ideology, the ZIJ data depict some remarkable trends over time. From 1970 to about 1987, solid majorities of young people identified with the Communist regime.[52] Then, unequivocal support among young workers and apprentices dropped to about 30 percent in May 1988 and to below 20 percent in October 1989. University students lagged behind, but showed a similar downward trend, reaching some 35 percent in February 1989.[53] This may seem surprising given the leading role of university students in challenging established authority in the West, for example in the 1960s. However, the Communist party exercised strict control over access to universities, and admission was based on "political reliability" as well as on academic qualification. By selection, then, university students were the segment of the youth most supportive, not most critical, of the Communist regime. In contrast, students in ninth and tenth grade showed the least identification with the GDR.

A similar trend shows in the opinion about the prospects of socialism.[54] In 1970 and beyond, less than about 20 percent of young workers and apprentices and less than 10 percent of university students doubted that socialism would prevail. Then, this percentages rose to well over 50 percent for young workers in 1988 and to close to 50 percent for students in 1989.[55] These and other indicators show quite clearly that a solid majority of young people were supportive of socialist ideology and of the GDR regime till the mid-1980s. Support then eroded quite quickly as the failures of the Communist regime became more visible. As the spirit of glasnost captured neighboring Communist countries, the Honecker regime responded with stubborn dogmatism, further alienating its people and continuously losing credibility. Classified ZIJ research reports had provided early warnings, but the party leadership chose to ignore the message.

East Germany in Transition

The events leading to the collapse of East Germany are explored by Arthur M. Hanhardt, Jr., in this volume. Once the former Communist regime collapsed, western-style public opinion research quickly spread to East Germany. Combining forces with a marketing research institute that had been using sampling procedures similar to those in the West, the ZIJ started a series of general population surveys focusing on issues related to the current political development.[56] In East Berlin, a group of researchers at the Academy of Science designed a study to explore all aspects of life in an era of rapid transition. A first round of data collection was completed in January 1990, with a replication in March 1991.[57] At the same time, public opinion research companies from West Germany moved to cover the new territory by setting up their own operations and/or establishing ties with East German groups emerging from social-research units at universities and academies in East Berlin and elsewhere. However, data from this transition period needs to be viewed with some caution. For one, the East German population was not used to freely express political opinions to a stranger (the interviewer). Secondly, political attitudes and opinions seemed to be very much in flux, subject to many short-term effects. And, last but not least, it took time to build reliable field organizations, that is, to establish sound sampling procedures as well as to train professionally minded interviewer staffs. Probably up to about fall of 1990, on average, East German data are less reliable and more prone to bias than comparable data for the West. Still, they provide valuable insights.

Much to the disappointment of the civil-rights activists, the East Germans quickly embraced the concept of quick unification, an accession to the West rather than a merger on equal terms. In the first free election on 18

March 1990 they presented Chancellor Kohl's conservative Christian Democratic party and its allies with an overwhelming victory of nearly 50 percent of the popular vote, leaving the Social Democrats trailing far behind with a little over 22 percent.[58] Groups and parties that emerged from the civil-rights movements received less than 5 percent of the popular vote. The promise of affluence had proven much more enticing than the prospect of reform from within. In April 1990, over 90 percent of the East Germans (compared to some 75 percent of the West Germans) were "pleased" or "very pleased" that—leaving aside detailed plans and procedures—German unification was more or less agreed upon.[59] Both East and West Germans anticipated economic gains by unification, though expectations ran considerably higher in the East. Like the East Germans, the West Germans were largely supportive of the unification course, though in the first half of 1990 roughly two-thirds of the West Germans would have preferred a slower, more deliberate pace. The West Germans were wary of unintended consequences, of difficulties in reconciling the two different social systems. Above all, only a quarter of the West Germans were fully prepared to make sacrifices. Consequently, the Kohl government promised that unification would be self-financing, that it would not require major sacrifices on part of the West Germans—a vision far removed from reality. This, however, became fully apparent to the public only after the December 1990 elections.

The unification of two Germanys, then, can be seen as a marriage of convenience rather than the consummation of long-harbored deep affection. Not unlike the West Germans in the 1950s, the East Germans were ready to embrace Western democracy as part and parcel of a promised steep increase in material wealth. Unlike the West Germans in the 1950s, however, the East Germans expected quick delivery, encouraged by irresponsible campaign rhetoric and blatant pork barrel politics early on. For example, in a deliberate—and successful—attempt to swing the vote in the March 1990 elections, Chancellor Kohl announced a very generous, but economically unwise, scheme to exchange worthless East German currency for West German money against strong warnings by the Federal Reserve Board (Bundesbank). Sooner or later, the East German expectations had to be disappointed.

After Formal Unification

Sure enough, a surge of massive discontent on part of the east Germans surfaced in early 1991 and proved to be persistent. Starting in November 1990, after formal unification, the monthly Politbarometer surveys include a separate sample of east Germans. This allowed tracking of mass sentiment in east Germany as precisely as in west Germany from then on.

These surveys show that, continuously, between 70 and 80 percent of east respondents are "more dissatisfied than satisfied" with regard to reaching the western standard of living; over 75 percent feel that the Bonn government is not doing enough for them; over 50 percent say that their expectations of unification with respect to their personal situation were "mostly unmet," over 40 percent find the course of unification overall as "worse than expected." The percentage of employed respondents who feel that their job is not secure declined slightly from 60 percent in January 1991 to over 50 percent in September 1991, to still some 45 percent in September 1992. The work by the agency in charge of privatization of state-owned plants and factories (Treuhandanstalt) is rated as "on the poor side (eher nicht gut)" by between 80 and 90 percent of all respondents.[60] West Germans view the same issues markedly differently: in the fall of 1991, only about 40 percent are critical of the Treuhand, just about a quarter think that the Bonn government does not do enough, and two-thirds of the west Germans continue to feel that the dissatisfaction of the east Germans is "not justified." The measures taken by the government in March to markedly increase assistance to the east German states—at the price of a new record in public indebtedness—seems to have placated critics in the West, but the mood of the masses in the East hardly changed.

West and east Germans still seem to be far apart—and they experience major communication problems. This clearly shows in the responses to a series of questions related to general characteristics (or stereotypes) of Germans east and west.[61] Respondents were asked to evaluate a series of seven properties (being orderly, overbearing, diligent, courageous, patriotic, greedy, and friendly) as they pertain to their own group (self-image), to the other Germans, and to the perception of their own group by the other Germans. By and large, self-image and the image held by the other group correspond. For example, 60 percent of the west Germans admit that they—west Germans—are overbearing, and about the same percentage of east Germans see the west Germans as overbearing. One notable difference is diligence. Over 90 percent of the east Germans feel that they themselves are diligent compared to only some 50 percent of west Germans who see the east Germans this way. However, only 25 percent of the east Germans think that the west Germans consider them as diligent. Similarly, only 35 percent of the west Germans think that the east Germans are greedy; but over 70 percent of the east Germans feel that the west Germans perceive them as greedy. These are just two examples of "negative anticipation." Given the objective difficulties that unification poses, the problems in communication between east and west Germans add an additional hurdle.

For the time being, however, lack of understanding rather than downright hostility governs the relationship between east and west Germans. It seems that a common enemy serves to divert any latent intra-German conflicts. The issue of foreigners, asylum seekers, and so-called Aussiedler,[62] which had achieved a top spot on the list of most important problems facing the nation in 1989 before the fall of the Wall, reemerged in the summer of 1991. About 45 percent of the west Germans named this problem as one of two most important ones. For east Germany the comparable figure is much lower, since east Germans are still preoccupied with their economic plight. Unemployment and issues related to standard of living capture the spots on the very top of their problem list. However, the east Germans are no less xenophobic. In the fall of 1991, well over 50 percent do not think it is right that Germany hosts many foreigners, and some 20 percent do not agree with the constitutional right to political asylum (Article 16 of the Basic Law), surpassing comparable figures for west Germany. In September 1992, 90 percent of the east Germans and 75 percent of the west Germans think that Germany cannot cope with the large number of asylum seekers. Also, 87 percent in the east and 72 percent in the west feel that most asylum seekers abuse the provision in the constitution; almost as many Germans are in favor of changing the Basic Law to curb the stream of asylum seekers. What was apparent to some early on has become an undisputed fact by the fall of 1992: the process of actual unification will be difficult and tedious; an extended period of internal strife lies ahead. In this situation, the people's commitment to democratic norms and values will be crucial. Given their long history of authoritarian rule and their disprivileged economic position, the east Germans may be particularly susceptible to sway from the path of democracy.

However, data from early 1990 seem to indicate the opposite. The Wildenmann study of April 1990 included an established set of nine items measuring agreement with key democratic values.[63] Only three items showed a difference between east Germans and west Germans in the mean response on a six-point agree-disagree scale.[64] East Germans were significantly more likely to disagree that "conflicts between different interest groups and their demands on the government are adverse to the welfare of all," that "a citizen forfeits the right to strike and to demonstrate if he threatens public order," and that "it is not the job of the opposition to critique the government, rather it should support the government's work." In all three cases, of course, disagreement is the "right" response in view of democratic norms. Had the east Germans turned into model democrats less than half a year after the fall of the Communist regime? Or were they "closet democrats" all along? Several explanations for these somewhat surprising results are plausible.[65] For one, east Germans may have answered the question with the old government and the powerful "Monday demonstrations" still in mind. Their responses, then, may signify their support for the civil-rights movement of fall 1989 rather than generalized support for the rights of dissenters in a democracy.

Secondly, as a matter of survival during the Communist regime, east Germans have learned to express the "right" opinion in public. Their responses may also indicate that they quickly adjusted to a set of new norms and values. At any rate, serious doubt remains as to how deeply rooted these beliefs are.

The east German longitudinal study "Leben '91" provides some indication of how quickly beliefs may change.[66] In January 1990, close to 60 percent of the respondents felt it "very important" and additional 30 percent "important" to live in a pluralistic society with competing parties. By March 1991, only 15 percent still found this "very important," and 35 percent found it "important."[67] In 1990, 40 percent of the respondents strove to be politically active "to a high degree"; by 1991, only 7 percent expressed such aspirations.[68] In 1990, over 60 percent expected an improvement in the conditions for democratic development; by 1991, just 40 percent expected improvements, but almost 20 percent anticipated some deterioration.[69] Finally, throughout 1991 less than half of the east Germans were "more satisfied" than "more dissatisfied" with democracy and the political system in Germany, according to the monthly Politbarometer surveys—after a high of 54 percent in December 1990. By fall 1992, satisfaction with democracy had dropped to just 34 percent.

Conclusion

At this point, in the fall of 1992, it is too early to tell how well the newly united Germany will weather its current problems. Political attitudes and behavior of the east Germans are volatile. Early enthusiasm for a merger with the West has given place to massive dissatisfaction. Disappointment over slow economic progress has markedly changed party preference.[70] More important, confidence in the established parties has decreased overall. By now, even the Kohl government no longer proclaims that a significant upswing is imminent. A long and thorny way lies ahead, and dissatisfaction in east Germany is not likely to dissipate soon. Rather, volatile beliefs in democratic norms and values may erode further. A series of brutal, violent attacks on foreigners—most notably the prolonged riots in Rostock in August 1992 where sympathetic crowds of locals sided with "skinheads" and other extremists—has invoked memories of Germany's darkest past. Only small numbers of people may actively engage in violence against foreigners. Yet, almost two-thirds of east Germans (in contrast to only one-third of the west Germans) find fault with the fact that Germany houses many foreigners.

In west Germany, optimism prevailed till about mid-1991. Despite some grumbling over a substantial tax hike to finance the cost of unity, west Germans continued to have a positive outlook on their own economy and on their political system. As a matter of fact, the west German economy had fared extremely well. However, drastically increased public indebtedness may cause serious problems in the long run. Starting in the second half of 1991, the public's mood began to change. The outlook on the economy became more skeptical. Immediate concern, however, focused on the influx of large numbers of people seeking refuge in Germany. Fear, anxiety, and downright xenophobia are spreading widely in both west and east Germany. Like in east Germany, only a small minority engages in acts of open physical aggression against foreigners, but Politbarometer data for September 1992 show that one in seven west Germans condones such acts. At the same time, politicians of all democratic parties have gone on record to denounce the violence and a series of demonstrations against xenophobia and right-wing extremism have been staged.

There is reason for concern. Yet, there is reason for hope as well. Over forty years of socialization into democratic norms and values may have built up enough resistance to authoritarian ideologies in the postwar generations of west Germans to resist the drift to the right. The right-wing virus may spread further, but democratic antibodies should keep it in check. In addition, the Germans have learned to be pragmatic. Kohl's vision of "winners only" was at best naive. Now there is a distinct possibility that all will lose. The west Germans need to accept the fact that unification has its price and that sacrifices are necessary; the east Germans need to grow more patient and find solace in the actual, but gradual gains already made. Wary of ideologies, the Germans—east and west—will probably choose to be pragmatic. Unfortunately, Germany lacks political leadership in these difficult times. Both government and opposition are held in low esteem by the public; Chancellor Kohl's popularity has sagged even further, and most popular among the current politicians is semiretired Hans-Dietrich Genscher, the former foreign minister. Without strong democratic leadership, the new Germany faces a crucial test of its civility and its democratic order.

Appendix: Data sources

Currently, the main generally accessible data source on political attitudes and behavior in Germany are the German Election Studies. Since 1974 an independent nonprofit organization, the Forschungsgruppe Wahlen e.V. headed by Manfred Berger, Wolfgang Gibowski (replaced by Matthias Jung in 1991), and Dieter Roth, has conducted these studies under a long-term funding agreement with one of the two major television channels (ZDF). For some elections supplementary funding (e.g., for postelection studies) was obtained from the Deutsche Forschungsgemeinschaft—the German equivalent to the National Science Foundation. All these election studies, more recently accompanied by monthly Politbarometer surveys, are freely available through the Central Archives for Empirical Research (ZA) at the University of Cologne, Germany, and—with additional time delay—through ICPSR at the University of Michigan.[71]

Another series of scholarly election studies has been conducted at the social science research institute Sozialwissenschaftliches Forschungsinstitut of the CDU-affiliated Konrad-Adenauer Foundation. Unfortunately, the institute has been reluctant to make these studies generally available through the Central Archives. Selective access only is granted by Noelle-Neumann's Allensbach Institute as well.[72] Allensbach's holdings are particularly valuable, since its work dates back to the very beginning of the Federal Republic. Other commercial institutes, most notably the German Gallup affiliate (EMNID in Bielefeld), are more cooperative in supplying data to the Central Archives. However, data set deposits are irregular and—requiring permission from the sponsor—often exclude studies most pertinent to the topics discussed in this chapter.

Another easily accessible source is the semiannual Eurobarometer surveys, conducted in the (currently twelve-) member countries of the European Community and directed by first Jean-René Rabier and later Karlheinz Reif at the European Commission in Brussels, Belgium. However, the set of regularly repeated questions ("trend questions") is rather small, and the quality of data collection is uneven. Selected results (marginal distribution for each country) are published in a special series soon after completion of the survey.[73] Data sets are available through ICPSR with a time delay of about three years.[74]

A multitude of political surveys commissioned by political parties or affiliated organizations, the media, and various government agencies are virtually inaccessible beyond what is selectively published. In contrast to the United States, Germany does not have a Freedom of Information Act or a functional equivalent that would require public access to surveys commissioned by government agencies, such as the Ministry of the Interior or the Information Agency (Bundespresseamt). There is little hope that this situation will change in the near future.

However, another important series of surveys is in the public domain, although access to these data is very cumbersome in practical terms. These are the surveys (including blocks of questions in omnibus surveys) commissioned by the USIA.[75] Selective studies from the 1950s are available from the Cologne archive, and studies from the 1960s up to 1974 are distributed by the Roper center.[76] In principle, all surveys from 1974 on are deposited with the U.S. National Archives in Washington, D.C., with a time delay not exceeding three years. Each year, the USIA commissions an average of three to four major surveys on Germany. A set of standard questions repeated since the 1970s makes these holdings a most important source of information on political attitudes and behavior in Germany. Copies of data sets can be obtained at a nominal fee. Unfortunately, the studies are poorly documented, and many of the data sets are in bad technical shape (undocumented code changes, loss of information due to improper handling of the column binary format, etc). Without direct access to the USIA and their own archive, a full reconstruction of these surveys is not possible.

Finally, the East German ZIJ studies and research reports will become generally available. While some documentation has been lost, practically all data sets from the mid-1970s onward have been secured. However, reformatting to common software standards in the West and proper documentation will require a major effort. By summer 1993, however, most of these studies should be available from the Cologne archives. Printed research reports will be archived by the Information Center for Social Sciences (IZ Sozialwissenschaften) in Bonn and will be available from there.

NOTES

1. Obviously, in the Communist world, the words *democratic* and *republic* have a meaning quite different from that in the West. To simplify the language, I use these terms in the Western meaning unless otherwise noted.

2. It is important to recognize the inherent limitations of even the most carefully collected survey data. To promote the cause of systematic empirical analysis of political attitudes and behaviors, we need to be aware of the pitfalls without conceding the terrain to those who dismiss this approach as dealing with superficial, irrelevant data that can be manipulated at will. A discussion of the methodological problems involved—as they relate to this specific topic—can be found in Manfred Kuechler, "Political Attitudes and Behavior in West Germany: Feats and Failures, Pitfalls and Promises of Survey Research," *German Studies Review,* DAAD special issue (1990): 153–71.

3. See David P. Conradt, *The German Polity,* 3d. ed. (New York: Longman, 1986); Russell J. Dalton, *Politics in West Germany* (Glenview, Ill.: Scott, Foresman, 1989); and to a lesser degree M. Donald Hancock, *West Germany—The Politics of Democratic Corporatism* (Chatham, N.J.: Chatham House, 1989).

4. Samuel A. Stouffer et al., *Studies in Social Psychology in World War II,* 4 vols., (Princeton: Princeton University Press, 1947–50).

5. See Anna J. Merritt and Richard L. Merritt, eds., *Public Opinion in Semisovereign Germany: The HICOG Surveys, 1949–1955* (Urbana: University of Illinois Press, 1980).

6. Ibid.

7. These activities of the USIA continue till today in Germany and other countries in Europe and around the world. See the Appendix on data sources for more details.

8. A first academic election study was conducted in 1953. Differences in content and wording of questions severely limit comparisons with the later studies, however.

9. A discussion of this broader range of topics can be found in the deliberations of a study group convened by Rudolf Wildenmann. See Rudolf Wildenmann et al., *Volksparteien—Ratlose Riesen?* (Baden-Baden: Nomos, 1989).

10. Manfred Kuechler, "What Has Electoral Sociology in West Germany Achieved? A Critical Review," in *Elections and Parties,* ed. Max Kaase and Klaus von Beyme (London: Sage, 1978); Manfred Kuechler, "Interessenwahrnehmung und Wahlverhalten—Perspektiven und Ergebnisse der neueren Wahlforschung," *Zeitschrift für Politik* 27 (1980): 277–90; and Manfred Kuechler, "Wahl- und Surveyforschung," *Politische Vierteljahresschrift* 27, special issue 17 (1986): 194–208.

11. Kaase and von Beyme, *Elections and Parties;* Max Kaase and Hans-Dieter Klingemann, eds., *Wahlen und politisches System* (Opladen: Westdeutscher, 1983); Max Kaase and Hans-Dieter Klingemann, eds., *Wahlen und Wähler: Analysen aus Anlass der Bundestagswahl 1987* (Opladen: Westdeutscher, 1990); Hans-Dieter Klingemann and Max Kaase, eds., *Wahlen und politischer Prozess* (Opladen: Westdeutscher, 1986); Dieter Oberndörfer, Hans Rattinger, and Karl Schmitt, eds., *Wirtschaftlicher Wandel, Religiöser Wandel, und Wertewandel* (Berlin: Duncker and Humblot, 1985).

12. Karl H. Cerny, ed., *Germany at the Polls: The Bundestag Elections of the 1980s* (Durham, N.C.: Duke University Press, 1990).

13. I will use the terms East and West Germany to denote the separate political entities before formal unification on 3 October 1990. The two regions in the unified Germany (formally known as neue Bundesländer and alte Bundesländer) will be termed east and west Germany. Also, when apparent from context, I will omit the qualifier *west*.

14. In 1957, a fourth party (Deutsche Partei—DP) failed the 5-percent threshold but was awarded seventeen parliamentary seats by virtue of winning the direct seat in three constituencies (Wahlkreis) due to an alliance with the CDU. In practical terms, the DP merged with the CDU and was formally dissolved some time later. The Bavarian sister party of the CDU, the CSU, is not considered as a separate party here, since the CDU and the CSU do not compete directly at the polls due to their regional limitations.

15. High turnout, however, does not necessarily indicate that democracy is working well and vice versa. For example, in the 1932 elections—when the Nazis emerged as the strongest party—turnout was 84.1 percent. In contrast, several stable democracies, including the United States, have a long tradition of low voter turnout.

16. In an effort to overcome this structural deficit the SPD adopted the Godesberg Program in 1959, denouncing its socialist roots and trying to present itself as a party open to all segments of the electorate—as a Volkspartei.

17. Werner Kaltefleiter, *Zwischen Konsens und Krise: Eine Analyse der Bundestagswahl 1972* (Cologne: Heymanns, 1973).

18. Hans-Dieter Klingemann, "The Fragile Stability: Electoral Volatility in West Germany 1949–1983," in *Electoral Change in Western Democracies: Patterns and Sources of Electoral Volatility,* ed. Ivor Crewe and David Denver (New York: St. Martin's, 1985).

19. For more detailed discussion on the persistence of traditional social cleavages

in German voting behavior, see Hans-Dieter Klingemann, "Soziale Lagerung, Schichtbewusstsein, und politisches Verhalten: Die Arbeiterschaft der Bundesrepublik Deutschland im historischen und internationalen Vergleich," in *Das Ende der Arbeiterbewegung in Deutschland?* ed. Rolf Ebbighausen and Fritz Tiemann (Opladen: Westdeutscher, 1984); Franz-Urban Pappi, "Das Wahlverhalten sozialer Gruppen bei der Bundestagswahl im Zeitvergleich," in Klingemann and Kaase, *Wahlen und politischer Prozess;* Karl Schmitt, *Konfession und politisches Verhalten in der Bundesrepublik Deutschland* (Berlin: Duncker & Humblot, 1989).

20. For opposite views, see Kendall Baker, Russell J. Dalton, and Kai Hildebrandt, *Germany Transformed* (Cambridge: Harvard University Press, 1981); and Russell J. Dalton, "The West German Party System between Two Ages," in *Electoral Change in Advanced Industrial Democracies: Realignment or Dealignment?* ed. Russell J. Dalton, Scott C. Flanagan, and Paul Allen Beck (Princeton: Princeton University Press, 1984).

21. Still, survey respondents obligingly answer questions supposedly measuring party identification. For example, starting with April 1991 the monthly Politbarometer survey includes such a question—long used in the West—in its east German version as well. Based on these surveys, more than 60 percent of the east Germans (slightly less than the approximately 70 percent in west Germany) supposedly identify with a specific party. Yet, history has not given them much time to establish a long-term preference.

22. In the conceptual framework of the Michigan School, a normal vote analysis tries to determine the relative impact of long-term (party identification) versus short-term (candidates, issues) factors. It also aims to identify "critical elections," which mark the beginning of permanent changes in long-term alliances (dealignment, realignment). See Jürgen Falter and Hans Rattinger, "Parteien, Kandidaten, und politische Streitfragen bei der Bundestagswahl 1980: Möglichkeiten und Grenzen der Normal-Vote-Analyse," in Kaase and Klingemann, *Wahlen und politisches System*; and Jürgen Falter and Hans Rattinger, "Die Bundestagswahl 1983: Eine Normalwahlanalyse," in Klingemann and Kaase, *Wahlen und politischer Prozess*.

23. Ronald Inglehart, *The Silent Revolution: Changing Values and Political Styles among Western Publics* (Princeton: Princeton University Press, 1977); and Ronald Inglehart, *Culture Shift in Advanced Industrial Society* (Princeton: Princeton University Press, 1989).

24. Dalton, "West German Party System"; Russell J. Dalton, "Wertwandel oder Wertwende: Die neue Politik und Parteienpolarisierung," in Klingemann and Kaase, eds. *Wahlen und politischer Prozess*.

25. Their failure to pass the 5-percent threshold in December 1990 elections appears to be a temporary setback only. Throughout 1991, their standings in the polls is quite solid and well above 5 percent. Had the west German Greens pursued a formal alliance with the east German Greens for the December 1990 elections, such an alliance would have gained thirty-five seats—in contrast to the eight seats now held by the east German alliance of Greens and Bündnis 90.

26. Russell J. Dalton and Manfred Kuechler, eds., *Challenging the Political Or-*

der: New Social and Political Movements in Western Democracies (Cambridge: Polity and New York: Oxford University Press, 1990).

27. Manfred Kuechler, "Ökologie statt Ökonomie—Wandelnde Wählerpräferenzen?" in Kaase and Klingemann, *Wahlen und Wähler*.

28. However, there are several significant consequences. Particularly on the state level, the emergence of the Greens does make a difference in terms of coalition options. Also, the functional split between Social Democrats and Greens may increase the chances of a full mobilization of voters on the left of the political spectrum at election time.

29. Manfred Kuechler and Russell J. Dalton, "New Social Movements and the Political Order: Inducing Change for Long-Term Stability?" in Dalton and Kuechler, *Challenging the Political Order*.

30. David Easton, *A Systems Analysis of Political Life* (Chicago: University of Chicago Press, 1965).

31. G. R. Boynton and Gerhard Loewenberg, "The Development of Public Support for Parliament in Germany, 1951–59," *British Journal of Political Science* 3 (1973): 169–89.

32. Gabriel A. Almond and Sidney Verba, *The Civic Culture: Political Attitudes and Democracy in Five Nations* (Princeton: Princeton University Press, 1963), 429.

33. Erwin K. Scheuch, "The Cross-Cultural Use of Sample Surveys: Problems of Comparability," in *Comparative Research Across Cultures and Nations,* ed. Stein Rokkan (Paris: Mouton, 1968).

34. Baker, Dalton, and Hildebrandt, *Germany Transformed;* and David P. Conradt, "Changing German Political Culture," in *The Civic Culture Revisited,* ed. Gabriel Almond and Sidney Verba (Boston: Little, Brown 1980).

35. Conrad, "Changing Culture," 265.

36. Baker, Dalton, and Hildebrandt, *Germany Transformed,* 40.

37. Conradt, "Changing Culture," 1980, 239.

38. Suzanne Schüttemeyer, *Bundestag und Bürger im Spiegel der Demoskopie* (Opladen: Westdeutscher, 1986).

39. Institut für Demoskopie Allensbach, *Eine Generation später: Bundesrepublik Deutschland 1953–1979* (Allensbach: [Institut für Demoskopie] IfD, 1981), table 80.

40. Institut für Demoskopie Allenbach, *Eine Generation später,* table 85.

41. Conradt, "Changing Culture," 265.

42. See Samuel H. Barnes et al., *Political Action: Mass Participation in Five Western Democracies* (Beverly Hills, Calif.: Sage, 1979); M. Kent Jennings and Jan van Deth, eds., *Continuities in Political Action: A Longitudinal Study of Political Orientations in Three Western Democracies* (Berlin: de Gruyter, 1989); and Edward N. Muller, *Aggressive Political Participation* (Princeton: Princeton University Press, 1979).

43. Though still in existence today, the NPD is a truly insignificant splinter party.

44. Levels of satisfaction with democracy in Germany have been high—both in absolute terms as well as in relation to its European neighbors. See Manfred Kuechler, "Dynamics of Mass Political Support in Western Europe: Methodological Problems and Preliminary Findings," in *Eurobarometer—The Dynamics of European Opinion,*

ed. Karlheinz Reif and Ronald Inglehart (London: Macmillan, 1991). Even at its lowest point, about half of the electorate expressed more satisfaction than dissatisfaction. Given measurement problems, though, relative change in satisfaction is a more valid indicator than absolute level of satisfaction.

45. For a detailed analysis, see Manfred Kuechler, "A Trend Analysis of System Support in West Germany, 1976–1986." (Paper delivered at the Annual Meeting of the Southern Political Science Association, Atlanta, 1986).

46. Due to organizational problems, the Republicans did not contest many of the local elections in Hesse. Taking their place, the openly neo-Nazi NPD gained almost 7 percent of the popular vote in the city of Frankfurt. Overall, the Republicans gained 7.1 percent of the vote nationwide for six of the eighty-one German seats in the European Parliament in Strasbourg. In the state of Bavaria, they captured a stunning 14.6 percent of the vote. This electoral success was in contrast to the results of major preelection surveys (e.g., the Politbarometer of May 1989 and Eurobarometer 31 of April 1989), which seemed to indicate a decline in public support for the Republicans after the surge earlier that year. According to these surveys, a result very close to the 5 percent threshold was to be expected.

47. Chancellor Kohl established himself as a dynamic and forceful leader—apart from being a shrewd master of the Christian Democrat party "machine"—only after the collapse of the Communist regime in East Germany by vigorously and successfully pursuing a course of quick unification.

48. As reported in *The Week in Germany,* a publication by the government-funded German Information Center in New York, 11 October 1991, 1.

49. Walter Friedrich and Hartmut Griese, eds., *Jugend und Jugendforschung in der DDR* (Opladen: Leske and Budrich, 1991), 14.

50. My judgment is based on a review of original questionnaires and research reports as well as talks with several senior researchers at ZIJ in the summer of 1991.

51. Friedrich and Griese, *Jugend und Jugendforschung.*

52. Till 1979, respondents were asked whether they were proud to be a citizen of their socialist country. Subsequently, the statement read: "I feel very close to the German Democratic Republic."

53. Friedrich and Griese, *Jugend und Jugendforschung,* 139.

54. Respondents were asked to evaluate the following statement: "Socialism will win all over the world."

55. Friedrich and Griese, *Jugend und Jugendforschung,* 145.

56. "Studie zur aktuellen sozialen Lage Jugendlicher nach der Vereinigung" (Zentralinstitut für Jugendforschung Leipzig, Leipzig, 1990, mimeographed). Between November 1989 and December 1990 nine surveys were conducted, two of which were sponsored by the west German weekly *Der Spiegel*—a publication roughly equivalent to *Newsweek* or *Time* in the United States. Not protected by the unification treaty, the ZIJ was virtually shut down on 31 December 1990. However, it was allowed to keep a small portion of its previous staff and to keep operating as a subsidiary of the government-funded German Youth Institute (DJI) in Munich. As such, it may be able to regain a leading role in east German social research.

57. Michael Häder, ed., *Denken und Handeln in der Krise* (Berlin: Akademie,

1991); and Brigitte Hausstein, "Leben '91—Daten und Feldbericht" (Institut für Soziologie und Sozialpolitik, Berlin, 1991, mimeographed). Both times a multistage random sample of persons eighteen years and above was used. "Interviewers" delivered questionnaires for self-completion to the respondent's home.

58. This figure does not include another 5 percent for the Liberals, the coalition partner of the CDU in West Germany. Public opinion polls up to early March 1990 had given a clear edge to the Social Democrats. For example, the ZIJ surveys had the SPD leading 53 to 13 percent in February and 34 to 22 percent in March. See "Studie," 35.

59. Unless otherwise noted these and the following data are taken from Manfred Kuechler, "The Road to German Unity: Mass Sentiment in East and West Germany," *Public Opinion Quarterly* 56 (1992): 53–76, where data from various sources are used to trace mass sentiment on the unification issue. A prime source was a study conducted by Rudolf Wildenmann at the University of Mannheim, West Germany, in April 1990, in both East and West Germany—also referred to as the Wildenmann surveys.

60. These and the following figures are excerpted from mimeographed reports on the monthly Politbarometer published by the Forschungsgruppe Wahlen (FGW) in Mannheim.

61. These questions were included in the August 1991 Politbarometer survey; figures are excerpted from the mimeographed report issued by the FGW Mannheim.

62. Aussiedler are people of German descent living in eastern European countries like Romania or Poland or in the former Soviet Union. They are considered German citizens and are allowed to move to Germany without restrictions. Many of those who have moved to Germany recently do not speak German and are unfamiliar with German customs and culture. In addition, given the lack of hard evidence, German authorities find it often difficult to assess the validity of a claim to German ancestry.

63. These items were developed by Max Kaase, "Demokratische Einstellung in der Bundesrepublik Deutschland," in *Sozialwissenschaftliches Jahrbuch für Politik,* ed. Rudolf Wildenmann, vol. 2 (Munich: Olzog, 1971).

64. Manfred Kuechler, "Pocketbook Patriotism" (Paper delivered at the Annual Meeting of the American Political Science Association, San Francisco, 1990).

65. See also Russell J. Dalton, "Communists and Democrats: Attitudes towards Democracy in the Two Germanies" (Paper delivered at the Annual Meetings of the American Political Science Association, Washington, D.C., 1991).

66. As mentioned before, data from the very early period may be less reliable. The changes reported here may be exaggerated due to methodological problems.

67. Hausstein, "Leben '91," 21.

68. Hausstein, "Leben '91," 147.

69. Hausstein, "Leben '91," 160.

70. In the monthly Politbarometer surveys, the percentage of respondents who ranked the CDU/CSU as the "party liked best" went down from 44 to 25 between December 1990 and September 1991, whereas the percentage for the SPD went up from 26 to 45 points. Similarly, the FDP decreased from 16 to 10 percentage points, while Greens and Bündnis 90 increased from 6 to 11 percent.

71. The Inter-University Consortium for Political and Social Research (ICPSR), founded in 1962, is a partnership between the Institute for Social Research at the University of Michigan and practically all major universities in the United States and Canada. Similar archives in Australia, Germany (the Central Archive at the University of Cologne), Great Britain, the Netherlands, Norway, and Sweden are also included.

72. In the past, American scholars seemed to have obtained access more easily than German researchers. However, access is generally restricted to printed documentation of marginals and cross-tabulations—in contrast to access to the original data sets.

73. The publication "Eurobarometer" can be obtained free of charge from the Directorate-General for Information, Communication, and Culture in Brussels in both French and English.

74. In general, the holdings of ICPSR can be searched by accessing a database with the SPIRES (Stanford Public Information Retrieval System) software either directly in Michigan via an electronic network (which requires a computer account with the University of Michigan) or locally if a member institution chooses to implement and update this source.

75. The following information is based on personal communication from Hans Rattinger, whose advice I very much appreciate. In the late 1980s, Rattinger explored USIA data holdings in preparation for a temporal analysis of German public opinion on matters of national security.

76. The Roper Center for Public Opinion Research is a nonprofit research library with offices on the campus of the University of Connecticut in Storrs, Conn.

PART 3

Political Economy

The Germany polity faces two key economic challenges in this decade: the unification of the east and west German economies, and the completion of the internal market in the European Community. In the first contribution, Christopher S. Allen analyzes the development of economic policy-making in the Federal Republic since 1949. He notes that macrolevel coordination and neocorporatism gave way to regional or mesocorporatism in the early 1980s, although our understanding of policy-making at the meso level is weak. The importance of this analysis is clear: German unification has come on west German terms, and the ways reconstruction and revision of the east German economy is accomplished will be largely influenced by west German experience. Further, unified Germany will play an even greater role in the EC than the old Federal Republic. Allen lays out a challenging research agenda for scholars interested in understanding the political economy of German unification and German participation in Europe.

The controversy over the economic dimension of unification is taken up by the following two contributions. Thomas A. Baylis argues that the speed at which German unification was achieved, in the context of west Germany's links to the liberal international economic order, has placed the east German economy in a position even worse than that facing the other reforming economies of eastern Europe. While the east Germans benefit greatly from west German social policies, which in contrast to east European states have kept standards of living from declining, the cost of these outlays have generated animosity in the West that is directed to the East. Large-scale industrial restructuring in the East has contributed to east German anxiety, and coupled with perceived arrogance on the part of the Wessis, has increased east German animosities as well. Baylis concludes that the prospects for social unification have been weakened by west German economic policy.

Irwin L. Collier, Jr., in contrast, paints a rosier picture of the long-term prospects for the east German economy. While noting the subjective sources of uncertainty—fully 50 percent of the east German work force has experienced a major change in employment since 1989—and the consequences of differing distributional ethics between east and west Germans, Collier argues that, given extant political constraints, the economic transformation in the East has been managed reasonably well. He concludes that in the long run the prospects for economic growth and stability in the East are as close to a sure bet as to be found in economics. He also notes the indicators to follow to determine if his optimism is justified.

From Social Market to Mesocorporatism to European Integration: The Politics of German Economic Policy

Christopher S. Allen

This chapter reviews the major approaches used to analyze the political economy of the Federal Republic during its first forty years, which culminated with German unification. The chapter is organized in five sections. The first looks at the Wirtschaftswunder and Sozialemarktwirtschaft phase of the 1950s and early 1960s. It argues that economic policy established not so much a free market as framework regulations that provided order to market activity. While this policy clearly represented a step away the state-centered economy of the Nazi period, it did build on a late-nineteenth-century legacy of coordination between the private and public sectors. Thus, it represented something more than a Christian Democratic welfare state overlaid on a free-market economy. The second portion of the article explains the all-too-brief German experience with Keynesianism during the late 1960s and very early 1970s. Keynesianism in West Germany was short-lived because dominant policymakers felt it irrelevant for the Federal Republic, not because of any deep-seated hostility to Keynesianism as a school of thought. The third portion looks at the Modell Deutschland era of (macro)corporatism, often seen as coterminus with the Helmut Schmidt era (1974–82). The article will argue, however, that this period was also short-lived and that, if macrocorporatism was the glue that held the model together, it did not last even as long as Schmidt's last government. The fourth portion looks at the politics of industrial adjustment during the governments of Helmut Kohl during the 1980s. It argues that corporatism was a useful analytical tool during this period, but that one had to use a *meso*corporatism comprehending the dynamics of both sectoral and regional economic adaptation. Subnational patterns of adjustment were particularly important because the Kohl center-right governments—as national actors—were less influential in corporatist behavior than were the Länder governments and peak industry organizations—as regional and sectoral actors. The fifth portion analyzes German economic policy through the twin prisms of German unification and European integration in the early 1990s. It argues that German economic policy faces the significant task of integrating the German *meso-* (sectoral and regional policies) with *meta-* (Europe-wide) policies in the period after German unification and European integration. Moreover, this task is exacerbated by by the potentially contradictory pressures of generating sufficient growth to manage unification well, without this suggesting to its neighbors that this strength is a vehicle for economic domination of Europe.

Wirtschaftswunder and Sozialemarktwirtschaft

The first two decades after the war in the Federal Republic did not provide a supportive environment for the development of a consumer-led economic recovery. Primacy was placed on the rebuilding of economic infrastructure and an investment climate that would enable the Federal Republic to recreate internationally competitive industries.[1] This section will show how a series of institutions, policies, and ideologies favored an "organized" supply-side policy, biased in favor of industry, that produced annual economic growth averaging more than 7 percent per year from 1950 to 1963 (i.e., the Wirtschaftswunder).[2] In return for this tilt in favor of capital investment, the Adenauer regime created a welfare state (Sozialemarktwirtschaft) that provided a partial cushion for those not favored by the dominant economic policy.[3]

These policies were mutually reinforcing; they created an economic structure and culture that delayed the arrival of demand-side Keynesianism until at least the mid-1960s.[4] They even limited the impact of policies oriented toward consumer demand when they arrived in the 1960s. The remainder of this section will briefly trace the course of West German economic policy with a view to understanding more precisely how it delayed more Keynesian policies until in the mid-1960s and circumscribed them even then.

Despite the gamble, the economic results that followed currency reform, price control, and similar social market policies were highly encouraging. Inflation did rise for the first few months, but the relatively quick transition to the new currency and the arrival of aid from the Marshall Plan in early 1949 brought inflation under 2 percent by 1952, a figure it did not exceed for the rest of the decade. Unemployment shot up because, under the system of decontrolling prices, it was no longer necessary to have a public sector "job" to get ration coupons and because a wave of Eastern European immigrants swelled the ranks of the German labor force as the cold war intensified. Hence, unemployment averaged 9.4 percent from 1950 to 1954, but its effects were offset by a level of economic growth that averaged 8 percent during the 1950s, the low cost of such basic necessities as food, utilities, and rent, and the introduction of a basic system of social security, which formed the "social" part of the Sozialemarktwirtschaft. It provided a floor under which working class West Germans would not fall.

These policies were politically as well as economically successful.[5] Currency reform and decontrol of prices were in effect ratified by the election of the first West German government at the founding of the Federal Republic in 1949, and the continuing success of the policies generated support for the center-right governments of Konrad Adenauer and Ludwig Erhard for over fifteen years. Germany was initially governed by a center-right coalition of Christian Democrats (CDU/CSU) and Free Democrats (FDP). This coalition won again in 1953; the Christian Democrats won an outright majority in 1957, and the FDP rejoined the CDU/CSU in coalition in 1961. In all of these governments Konrad Adenauer was the chancellor and Ludwig Erhard remained as economics minister, providing highly consistent economic policy and a stable political setting for private-sector development. The government and Germany's leading economists shared a comparable vision of the economy. They agreed that government policy should steer a middle course between the unpredictability of complete laissez faire and the distortions that central planning might introduce into market mechanisms for the allocation of goods.[6]

In short, during the 1950s and early 1960s, German policymakers followed a strategy that relied on exports of capital goods to rejuvenate the economy. In retrospect, it turned out to be an extraordinarily fortuitous choice. The investment-goods sectors were well positioned to serve the growing needs of the industrialized world during the 1950s,[7] and their strong export performance provided key contributions to the economic infrastructure of other Western European countries. These sectors also took advantage of the demand for their goods that resulted from the boom accompanying the Korean War. In fact, even the tight money policy established in the late 1940s began to seem desirable, as low rates of domestic inflation enhanced the competitiveness of West German exports and generated high profits out of which further growth could be fueled. In all these respects, the policy formed a coherent package whose success reinforced support for each of its elements.

The Brief Keynesian Interlude

Between the late 1950s and early 1960s, however, several changes took place that seemed to open the door toward a more stimulative, demand-oriented,

Keynesian set of policies in the Federal Republic. This door was finally opened by the mid-1960s. The initial impetus lay in two exogenous events: the opening of the West German economy to the rest of Europe; and a sharp drop in the available supply of labor with the building of the Berlin Wall in 1961. Three other factors in the shift toward Keynesianism during the mid-1960s were endogenous. They included attempts by the Social Democratic Party (Sozialdemokratische Partei Deutschlands—SPD) and the German Trade Union Confederation (Deutsche Gewerkschaftsbund—DGB) to incorporate policies of stimulating demand into their economic programs; efforts by the CDU/CSU-FDP coalition to emphasize more explicitly the social part of the social market economy; and the creation of an independent council of experts to offer outside analysis on economic matters. Together, these developments contributed to a growing feeling that the conditions that had generated German growth in the 1950s had changed and new policies might be required to deal with the evolving situation. This belief reached a dramatic height in 1965 and 1966, when the economy experienced its first postwar recession, but it had been gaining force for some time before then.

While all five of these factors are important, limitations of space require that this chapter concentrate on the last endogenous factor, the Council of Economic Experts.[8] A more deliberate step toward Keynesianism was taken with the creation of a Council of Experts (Sachverständigenrat), known colloquially as the Five Wise Men, in 1963. The council was to provide an institutional means for canvasing the opinions of the country's leading economists, both on recent economic changes and on the Left's new interest in Keynesianism.[9] That pressure intensified in the 1960s as the annual growth rate slowed down to 4.1 percent and 3.5 percent during 1962 and 1963. It only rebounded to 6.6 percent and 5.6 percent during 1964 and 1965 before falling off again to 2.9 percent in 1966 and −0.2 percent in 1967.[10] Adenauer and Erhard turned to the academic economists—in Germany, a profession of considerable esteem—to bolster the government and undercut the Left. The center-right government assumed that most private economists would support the policies of the social market economy. But, the council soon became a forum for the articulation of some Keynesian ideas and gave them institutional legitimacy. Karl Schiller himself was not on the council, but his role within the SPD heightened critical views of the social market economy, and he pressed members of the council on Keynesian policies.[11] Schiller had been advising the SPD and the unions to add reflation to their traditional platform since the mid-1950s. By the mid-1960s, both he and they—the SPD and DGB—were well placed to push Keynesianism on the Federal Republic.[12]

The SPD's entry into government with the Grand Coalition in 1966 finally allowed Keynesians access to the policy arena, and, as economics minister, Schiller helped pass a Stability and Growth Law in 1967. The law officially recognized the government's responsibility for employment and mandated macroeconomic measures to secure the goals of the "magic polygon," consisting of price stability, economic growth, full employment, and balanced trade.[13] However, the first and fourth goals outlined in this polygon received much more stress than did the second and third. Debate about this legislation began in 1965, and the lines of battle were quickly drawn. The Social Democrats and the trade unions sought additional macroeconomic measures to safeguard employment and growth. The business community, banks, and center-right parties felt that major new measures were superfluous, as the social market economy needed only fine tuning. This alignment suggests that the Keynesian forces faced an uphill battle. Nevertheless, the law was passed.

However, legislation is usually only the beginning of policy, as several factors continued to constrain the full implementation of Keynesianism in Germany. Two important constraints on the Schiller-influenced Social Democratic party were, first, its coalition partners (the CDU/CSU during the Grand Coalition and the FDP from 1969 to 1982), since the Social Democrats *never* governed with an absolute majority; and, second, the fiercely independent Bundesbank, which exercised great influence over monetary policy. Thus the most that the Federal Republic was able to achieve on this front is what Riemer has called a "qualified Keynesian design." Not surprisingly, even this qualified design proved short-lived. Its high point was the 1969–72 period, when Social Democrats controlled both the economics and finance ministries (Schiller was forced to give the Economics Ministry to the FDP as part of a political compromise in 1971). This was a period when

> Schiller succeeded in installing global guidance—which was under suspicion of being a planned economy—simply by maintaining that state guidance was intended to affect only macro relations, while the freedom and autonomy of those responsible for the allocation process would not be disturbed thereby.[14]

The government successfully survived wildcat strikes for higher wages in 1969 and expanded the welfare state in the reform euphoria of the Willy Brandt–led government. It even smoothly handled the upward revaluation of the DM during the early 1970s in the face of a weakening dollar, as the Bretton Woods system broke down. Yet, because Keynesianism was subject to the tight-money policies of an independent Bundesbank, even in the mid-1960s there was an upper limit to these experiments. And after Schmidt replaced Schiller as the de facto—if not de jure—economic leader in the Brandt government, the SPD itself showed increased concern about inflation.

When reflationary policies began to produce an average inflation rate of 5.5 percent in the early 1970s,[15] the Bundesbank reined in the Keynesian experiment in order to keep wages in check, a common response in such situations. Yet Keynesianism's true demise was caused by the recession of 1974–75, induced by the oil crisis, and the replacement of Brandt by Helmut Schmidt as chancellor in 1974. The oil crisis brought stagflation, which undermined contemporary Keynesian thinking. Schmidt's rise in the SPD was important because he generally favored fiscally conservative policies. Under his aegis, the Keynesian experiment of the late 1960s gradually gave way, and—although the Schmidt government did not use the term—the social market economic paradigm was applied once again.[16]

Modell Deutschland and Macrocorporatism: Oversold and Underrealized

By the time of the first oil crisis in 1973, Keynesianism had gone as far as it would in the Federal Republic. Yet it did not cause alarm at the time among those arguing for a progressive set of economic policies. For Keynesianism had already been overtaken by another set of policies, macrocorporatism, that supposedly provided a more direct way to combine economic coordination with generous wages and social benefits, which became greater demands of both the unions and the SPD from the late 1960s until the late 1970s. This German model of tripartite coordination among the state and the peak associations of business and organized labor was offered by some observers, many of them in the United States, as a step beyond Keynesianism that combined economic efficiency with social justice. But macrocorporatism on the German model proved far less effective than its adherents claimed. In fact, the Concerted Action meetings among business, labor, and the state that began in the mid-1960s proved remarkably ineffective as a tool of policy for either the Grand Coalition (1966–69) or the center-left SPD-FDP coalition from 1969–82. In fact, the DGB explicitly left the "Concerted Action" discussions in 1976 after organized business objected to a broadening of the Mitbestimmung laws.

Corporatism has been the dominant theoretical approach in analyzing the role of the major actors (business, labor, and government policymakers) in this process of economic adjustment and renewal. Corporatist theory had its roots in the early twentieth century, but was revived in the 1970s when the peak (or national) associations of organized business and organized labor came together in an institutional forum facilitated by (generally Social Democratic) governments to address problems common to all three actors, such as collective bargaining, industrial policy, and international competitiveness.[17] Yet the region- and sector-specific nature of economic problems in most advanced industrialized nations during the 1980s, the Federal Republic included, has undercut the effectiveness of *national* corporatist institutions established to deal with economic adjustment.

In the Federal Republic, the specialty automobile, machine-tool, and industrial electronics industries of the South have performed better than the declining steel and shipbuilding sectors of the North. Despite the development of these regional and sectoral disparities in the past decade, political scientists have been slow to develop a theoretical paradigm for analyzing how governments can address them. Macrocorporatism,[18] which has traditionally emphasized coordinated action among organized business, organized labor, and government at the national level, has not effectively addressed these sectoral and regional discrepancies. The centrifugal tendencies engendered by these changes in the political economy eroded the solidarity among the various national parties that participated in macrocorporatist institutions. The corporatist paradigm proved too focused on macrolevel analysis to address the specifics of regional and sectoral adjustment. In short, the German model developed serious strains, most notably among the older industries of the northern part of the Federal Republic.

Many proponents of corporatism began to recast the theory to examine peak associations of business, but within specific industries. For example, rather than analyzing the Federation of German Industry (BDI) or the Federation of German Employers (BDA), attention shifted to the Chemical Industry Association (VCI) and the Chemical Industry Employers Association (BVAC).[19] Building on a variation of institutional economics first offered by Hans-Rudolf Peters,[20] corporatism was modified from its national focus to an industry-specific (meso) focus. This new approach was empirically tested in numerous cross-national studies of business associations in specific sectors of the economy.[21] The strength of these studies was their ability to disaggregate the interests of organized business and demonstrate the different strategies used by employers in different sectors. Among the specific advantages of these cross-national approaches was the ability to distinguish practices that fostered cohesiveness from those that fostered divisiveness among employer and industry associations. They were also able to analyze the different strategies pursued by businesses within the same industry but in different countries.

As important as the step from macro- to mesocorporatism has been in analyzing the sectoral distinctiveness of organized business, two other components of the corporatist triad (labor and government) have been much underrepresented in this literature, with government being almost invisible. While sector-specific labor unions have at least had a shadowy reference in these studies, regional governments have not been addressed at all. Important sectors of industry in advanced capitalist countries tend to concentrate in particular regions. Moreover, the ideological predisposition in the 1980s against the national government's managing industrial policy—the Thatcher and Reagan governments being the most notable examples—has thrust many problems of industrial adjustment onto subnational governments. Given that regional governments, out of necessity, have taken a much more active role in formulating and executing strategies of industrial adjustment, the omission of regional politics from the mesocorporatist literature seems particularly unfortunate.

What are the implications of these regional developments on theories of contemporary political economy? Can the mesocorporatist approach, which emphasizes industry-specific business associations, make a useful contribution? The change in focus from the national level to the industry level is important, but the mesocorporatist literature still lacks an explicit treatment of the *politics* of industrial adjustment. Region- and sector-specific tensions demand an approach that can help us understand why some regional governments respond aggressively to these challenges, while others seem unable to respond. The mesopolitics of regional activity is particularly important in that much of the macrocorporatist literature identified country-specific patterns of business, labor, and government interaction. The political economies of entire countries were thus described as either corporatist or pluralist. In this literature, pluralism has been described as the absence of corporatism.[22] Yet if the national laws of particular countries allow or prohibit specific national patterns of corporatist interaction, why have there been such different patterns of industrial adjustment *within* nation-states? These varieties of response in different regions suggest that the legal foundations upon which macrocorporatism has relied to explain patterns in specific countries cannot comprehend the particular politics of industrial adjustment in different regions of the same nation. If mesocorporatism could combine an analysis of private-sector regional and sectoral actors with one encompassing regional public-sector actors, a useful theoretical model might be developed for understanding the dominant contemporary patterns of industrial change in the political economies of advanced capitalist countries.

Toward a Politics of Mesocorporatism

To prove useful, mesocorporatism must go beyond analysis of contemporary sector- and region-specific industrial dislocation to distinguish regional governments that have only recently acquired their own industrial policy mechanisms from those in which mechanisms of response have become institutionalized over time. For mesocorporatist theory, countries with deeply institutionalized patterns of response may be more adept than regional governments that have only recently developed such skills.

In the Federal Republic, the active involvement of regional governments in economic policy-making is not new. Precisely because the Federal Republic's Länder were constituent states, they were able to develop their own regional versions of Ordnungspolitik and mesocorporatism in ways that the federal government could not. The Land governments undertook mesopolitical intervention in the economy in the name of regional autonomy, not in the name of centralized economic planning. Because different regions had different economic needs and industrial foundations, these powers of intervention were all the more legitimate.[23] The Länder governments encouraged banks to direct investment and loans to stimulate regional industrial development. They encouraged cooperation among regional firms—many in the same industry—to spur international competition.[24] In so doing, they avoided violation of the Cartel Law of 1957, because this coordination did not impede domestic competition. They also invested heavily in vocational education to provide the skills so necessary for high-quality manufacturing goods, the core of the West German economy. Organized business and organized labor also had a direct role in shaping curricula in the vocational education system to improve worker skills.[25]

Regional governments worked closely with the actors in different industries in ways that the national government was unwilling and perhaps unable to undertake.[26] These Land policies made important contributions to the Federal Republic's rapid postwar economic growth. The flexibility to produce specialized, high-quality, internationally competitive products, so characteristic of the leading West German sectors (automobiles, chemicals, machine tools, and industrial electronics), has been specifically enhanced by regional government policies.[27] Yet these policies were often opaque to those unaware of the importance of the deeply institutionalized pattern of regional-government intervention in the economy, as well as to those who had an image of a West German economy based on American-style, free-market principles.

Regional government powers became even more important in the 1980s, for two reasons in particular. The economic problems that developed after 1973 were much more sector- and region-specific than they had been during the postwar reconstruction period.[28] And the center-right Kohl government after 1982 intervened in economic affairs less than did the SPD-led governments of Willy Brandt and Helmut Schmidt from 1969 to 1982. Therefore, regional governments in the 1980s more often took active steps on their own. (They also pressed the federal government, with only partial success, for increased aid and coordination and implored the federal government to prevent the reductions of certain subsidies for hard-hit industries.)[29]

Taken together, these policies quietly laid to rest the "Eurosclerosis" arguments of the early 1980s.[30] The German economy retained the third highest GNP of capitalist countries, behind the United States and Japan (with one-fourth the population of the former and one-half the population of the latter). These policies enabled the German economy to combine order and adaptation—a kind of "shared capitalism"—in ways that both free-market and statist analyses would not recognize.[31] The hitherto sole focus of meso-corporatist analysis on business interest associations would be theoretically enhanced by much closer attention to the politics of these regional governments.

The introduction of the concept of mesocorporatism to address the regional and sectoral dislocation of advanced capitalist countries has been a welcome innovation from the macrocorporatist models of the 1970s. The examination of sector-specific producer groups was important in disaggregating the actions of employers (and, indirectly, unions) under different structural circumstances. However, because this literature has neglected the politics of industrial adjustment in subnational governments, the mesocorporatist approach remains incomplete. If corporatist theory is to retain validity or explanatory power, it needs to be tested more thoroughly by looking at the specifics of economic policy within regional governments in industrialized nations.

What this section has tried to suggest is that the regional politics of industrial adjustment in the 1980s were particularly important. Clearly, the three federal German Länder have differed in the structure of their economies, leading some scholars to argue that the outcomes of industrial policy are constrained, if not determined, by the type and economic condition of the industries that dominate a region. Yet, as important as the economic conditions are, other political outcomes were possible in the Länder. Regions in other countries facing similar types of structural dislocation have not had the same success in promoting industrial modernization or managing decline as these three German Länder.

As impressive as these regional successes have been for the Federal Republic, within them lie the seeds for important questions that temper these stories of political development and adjustment. The two most successful Länder have been Baden-Württemberg and Bavaria. Both have been ruled by Christian Democratic governments for the entire postwar period. Does this mean that the most successful regional industrial adjustment strategies are only possible under center-right governments? What options are available to northern Länder that contain older and less flexible economic bases and that are governed by Social Democrats? Is it possible to establish framework policies among business, labor, and government under Social Democratic auspices, or will business resist? These questions suggest a more fundamental issue, namely, to what extent can we speak of success for a country if all regions do not share in it? In other words, will regional industrial policy ever serve as a model for national economic success? Or will the increasing disparity among regions lead to a fragmentation that increases political and economic uncertainty, which might even threaten those regions that have experienced the greatest successes? In conclusion, the more fundamental task is to find models that will enable all regions to enjoy prosperity and thereby make macroeconomic success greater than the sum of its mesoeconomic parts.

German Unification and European Integration

The issue of regional disparities, intra-German as well as intra-European, is at the heart of the challenges facing German economic policy in the 1990s. The five new states of the former East Germany clearly have more serious challenges facing them than do the northern states of the former West Germany. But the concept of regional disparities are also manifest at a European level, in the contrasts between strong countries, like Germany, and weak countries, like some in southern Europe. The task for German economic policy, in the midst of these phenomena, is to develop a strategy that can enhance economic growth for its five new states, and for the rest of Europe, without incurring the suspicion of other nation-states that Germany is dominating Europe.[32]

The domestic disparity can be seen in the quite different projections for growth in the two portions of the united Germany immediately after unification. The former West Germany could foresee approximately 3 percent growth during the early 1990s, while the former East Germany anticipated struggling through a decline in economic growth of up to 10 percent for the first few years of the 1990s.

There were several obstacles to insuring more robust economic growth in eastern Germany. One was the unresolved issue of property ownership. The treaty governing German unification stipulated that any property confiscated had to be paid at "current market value." The difficulty here was that capitalist market relations were only just beginning, resulting in an uneven transition to market prices for specific properties, depending on their location. But if compensation proved to be difficult, then that alternative option, restitution, was even worse. The return of confiscated property that dated from the Nazi period and stretched though the GDR period proved to be an administrative nightmare. Some 1.2 million claims were filed by early 1991, a condition that made the ultimate disposition of these properties and a transition to other uses all the more difficult.

Resolution of some of the commercial property issues moved more quickly. Under the auspices of the Treuhandanstalt (Trusteeship Agency), commonly called the Treuhand, the disposition of the former state holdings of the GDR was pressed in rapid fashion. The agency, under the leadership of Birgit Breuel who replaced the assassinated Detlev Röhwetter, saw its mission as a crash program to get the former GDR economy functioning as soon as possible. The most profitable firms were sold off quickly to mostly western German buyers for relatively high value, while others remained under the Treuhand's management in the hope that the agency's "turnaround" specialists would help salvage those firms that were salvageable. A third group of firms, the least competitive, were liquidated under the assumption that they could neither be sold nor made profitable, even under the Treuhand's guidance. Some harshly criticized the Treuhand's actions as "cream skimming," selling off what was easy to sell and quickly closing potentially profitable firms without seeing if they could be salvaged. Some critics, mostly from the SPD, Green opposition, and the unions, made the more general argument that the Treuhand's policies paid little heed to the networks of enterprises within specific sectors and offering each other necessary skills, which would have to be nurtured if the region as a whole were to be resuscitated.

In addition to this privatization strategy, pursued by the Treuhand under the auspices of the CDU-CSU/FDP government, there was also a more recognizable "organized capitalist" pattern being pursued by some of the largest western German firms and industries. The major private-sector actors and most of their public-sector counterparts have a distinct vision and set of preferences for rebuilding this region. As one example, these firms, the banking system, and public sector agencies other than the Treuhand preferred to rebuild the infrastructure and preferred investment goods over consumption goods. Many of the western German firms and banks argued that a secure foundation must be built before one could speak of a sustainable pattern of economic growth. A glance at the history of German industrialization in the late nineteenth century as well as at the history of the reindustrialization of the economic miracle years produces some important parallels to the present economic policy in the five new Bundesländer. This historical parallel was understood by the major western German banks, which hired former executives to consult regarding their experiences during the late 1940s and early 1950s. Contemporary officials realized that the tasks of adopting a new currency, allocating large amounts of investment, and developing the infrastructural services to support the five new Bundesländer were not new needs. Rather, they had distinct antecedents during two earlier periods of German history, and contemporary German officials were motivated to try to jog these institutional memories for industrial regeneration. Although the integration of eastern German states into a functioning Federal Republic's economy was not to be an instant task, there remained powerful reservoirs from which to draw. Yet, as the political turmoil around property compensation as well as the rise in antiforeigner action on the part of neo-Nazi groups has shown, German unification may have considerable domestic costs before bearing fruit.

As for the single European market and German economic policy, many Europeans became apprehensive when they realized that the Federal Republic, the leading economic power in Europe prior to German unification, was to increase its geographical size, its population, and its potential political power. Yet despite Germany's hegemonic economic and political position during the first half of the twentieth century, several factors militated against Germany's European economic policy replicating this earlier history. First, most German economic actors realized that the country's success could not be insured by unilaterally dominating other countries as an enlarged sovereign state, or by infiltrating the institutions of the EC to control Europe more surreptitiously. Rather, Germany's primary task was to use its own economic strength as a foundation that would enhance the larger economic efficacy of the single european market. Second, the deep embedding of parliamentary democratic regimes in Europe stood in sharp contrast to the political instability of the interwar period. And despite the political instability in eastern Europe in the early 1990s, and the increased antipathy toward foreigners within western Europe, functioning parliamentary institutions served as a stabilizing buffer against this turmoil.

With respect to specific economic policies toward Europe by German policymakers, the Federal Republic's long experience with federalism has had salutary effects on shaping economic policy for Germany's interaction with the EC and the single European market. In its evolution in the 1990s, the single European market bears strong resemblance to a national federal system, writ large. In fact, the primary criticism of the institutional integration of Europe comes from Britain and takes the form of warnings against the increased centralized power of a federal Europe. For German economic policy, the task is one of extending frameworks that have proven economically effective and politically accountable in dealing with *meso* problems at the domestic level, to the *meta* level of the European Community. Germany's goals for a united European market are for 1) European Union citizenship, allowing broader voting rights for all EC citizens; 2) a stronger European Parliament, to democratize many of the decisions now taken by the appointed EC Commission; 3) Majority rule, rather than the unanimity of the twelve states now required on most issues (a theme Britain has long resisted); 4) expansion of the EC's powers in several areas, including development policy, environment, social issues, and increased social cohesion (these policies would be based on market and subsidiarity principles); and 5) a federative structure, one that would not impose a central authority on European citizens.[33] Germany hopes that British (and other nations') concerns over a stronger Europe can be overcome by the market orientation of its goals and the strong adherence to the subsidiary principle, namely that only those actions that cannot be performed at lower levels should be taken to higher (i.e., European) levels. German policymakers argue that these are the essence of the policies pursued for the forty years of the Federal Republic that have produced both a strong economy and a responsible polity.

NOTES

An early version of this article was first published as "From Social Market to Meso-Corporatism: The Politics of West German Economic Policy." *German Studies Review,* DAAD special issue (Fall 1990), 13–25. In paper form, it was first presented at the DAAD conference on Political Science and German Studies, Atlanta, Ga., August 29–30, 1989. I am grateful to the DAAD for its support. Portions of this article were drawn from the author's "The Underdevelopment of Keynesianism in the Federal Republic of Germany," in *The Political Power of Economic Ideas: Keynesianism Across Nations,* ed. Peter A. Hall (Princeton: Princeton University Press, 1989), 263–89; Christopher S. Allen and Jeremiah Riemer, "The Industrial Policy Controversy in West Germany: Organized Adjustment and the Emergence of Meso-Corporatism," in *The Politics of Economic Adjustment: A Comparative Study of Corporatism, Privatization, and Pluralism,* ed. Richard Fogelsong and Joel Wolfe (Chicago: Greenwood Press, 1989), 45–64; and Christopher S. Allen, "Regional Governments and Economic Policies in West Germany: The 'Meso' Politics of Industrial Adjustment," *Publius* 19 (1989): 147–64. For extended treatment of these issues, please consult the relevant articles. I would also like to thank Angela Denton for her excellent research assistance.

1. Karl Hardach, *The Political Economy of Germany in the Twentieth Century* (Berkeley and Los Angeles: University of California Press, 1980), 94–95.

2. Henry C. Wallich, *Mainsprings of the German Revival* (New Haven: Yale University Press, 1955), 113–52.

3. Ludwig Erhard, *Deutsche Wirtschaftspolitik: Der Weg der sozialen Marktwirtschaft* (Düsseldorf: Econ, 1962).

4. Dudley Dillard, "The Influence of Keynesian Thought on German Economic Policy," in *The Policy Consequences of John Maynard Keynes,* ed. Harold L. Wattel (Armonck, N.Y.: M. E. Sharpe, 1985).

5. For a critical view of postwar West German economic policy, one that thought that high unemployment and the lack of egalitarianism were a sign of failure, see Heinz Abosch, *The Menace of the Miracle* (New York: Monthly Review Press, 1963).

6. Werner Kaltefleiter, *Wirtschaft und Politik in Deutschland,* 2d ed. (Cologne: Westdeutscher, 1968), 96–176.

7. Michael Kreile, "West Germany: The Dynamics of Expansion," in *Between Power and Plenty,* ed. Peter J. Katzenstein (Madison: University of Wisconsin Press, 1978), 191–224.

8. See the author's note above for my treatment of these other factors in other published sources.

9. See Henry C. Wallich, "The American Council of Economic Advisors and the German *Sachverständigenrat:* A Study in the Economics of Advice," *Quarterly Journal of Economics* 82 (1968): 349–79.

10. Hardach, *Political Economy of Germany,* 162.

11. Schiller was able to mobilize some support during the mid-1960s among the more pragmatic non-Keynesians who dominated the council, but Keynesianism was very limited within the council previously and subsequently.

12. Karl Schiller, "Gesprach," in *Wohin steuert die deutsche Wirtschaft?* ed. Leo Brawand (Munich: Kurt Desch, 1971), 25–48.

13. Much of the following account is drawn from Jeremiah M. Riemer, "Crisis and Intervention in the West German Economy: A Political Analysis of Changes in the Policy Machinery during the 1960s and 1970s" (Ph.D. diss., Cornell University, 1983); "Alterations in the Design of Model Germany: Critical Innovations in the Policy Machinery for Economic Steering," in *The Political Economy of West Germany: Modell Deutschland,* ed. Andrei S. Markovits (New York: Praeger, 1982), 53–89; and "West German Crisis Management: Stability and Change in the Post-Keynesian Age," in *The Political Economy of Advanced Industrial Societies,* ed. Norman Vig and Stephen Schier (New York: Holmes and Maier, 1985).

14. Hans-Peter Spahn, *Die Stabilitätspolitik des Sachverständigenrats* (Frankfurt am Main: Campus, 1979), 53, quoted in Riemer, "Crisis and Intervention," 113; translation Riemer's.

15. Norbert Kloten, Karl-Heinz Ketterer, and Rainer Vollmer, "West Germany's Stabilization Performance," in *The Politics of Inflation and Economic Stagnation,* ed. Leon Lindberg and Charles S. Maier (Washington: Brookings Institution, 1985), 360.

16. For the difficulties in pushing for full-employment Keynesianism in West Germany, see Fritz W. Scharpf, "Economic and Institutional Constraints of Full Employment Strategies: Sweden, Austria, and Western Germany, 1973–82," in *Order and Conflict in Contemporary Capitalism,* ed. John H. Goldthorpe (New York: Oxford University Press, 1984), 257–90.

17. See Philippe C. Schmitter and Gerhard Lehmbruch, eds., *Trends toward Corporatist Intermediation* (Beverly Hills, Calif.: Sage, 1979).

18. Schmitter and Lembruch, *Trends.* For treatment of this approach as it has applied to the Federal Republic of Germany, see Markovits, *Political Economy.*

19. Christopher S. Allen, "The Political Consequences of Change in the West German Chemical Industry," in *Industry, Politics and Change in West Germany: Toward the Third West German Republic,* ed. Peter J. Katzenstein (Ithaca: Cornell University Press, 1989), 157–84.

20. Hans-Rudolf Peters, *Grundlagen der Mesoökonomie und Strukturpolitik* (Bern: P. Haupt, 1981); and *Sektorale Structurpolitik* (Munich: Oldenbourg, 1988). See also: Lee Preston, "A Perspective on Meso-economics." Discussion Article, International Institute of Management, Wissenschaftszentrum Berlin, October 1984.

21. Wolfgang Streeck and Philippe Schmitter, *Private Interest Government* (Beverly Hills, Calif.: Sage, 1985); Alan Cawson, *Organized Interests and the State*

(Beverly Hills, Calif.: Sage, 1985); and Wyn Grant, ed., *Business Interests, Organizational Development and Private Interest Government* (Berlin and New York: Walter de Gruyter, 1987).

22. Manfred Schmidt, "Arbeitslosigkeit und Vollbeschäftigungspolitik," *Leviathan* 11 (1983): 451–71.

23. George W. Hoffman, ed., *Federalism and Regional Development: Case Studies on the Experiences in the United States and the Federal Republic of Germany* (Austin: University of Texas Press, 1981).

24. Nevil Johnson and Allan Cochrane, *Economic Policy-making by Local Authorities in Britain and Western Germany* (London: Allen and Unwin, 1981).

25. Akademie für Raumforschung und Landesplanung, *Qualität von Arbeitsmärkten und regionale Entwicklung* (Hannover: Curt R. Vincent 1982); and Theo Bühler and Wolfgang Steinle, "Regionale Beschäftigungsförderung—Erfahrungen aus Modellversuchen zur Förderung des endogenen Entwicklungspotentials" (1985, Typescript).

26. Ibid.

27. Charles Sabel, *Work and Politics* (Cambridge: Cambridge University Press, 1982).

28. Thomas O. Hueglin, "Regionalism in Western Europe: Conceptual Problems of a New Political Perspective," *Comparative Politics* 18 (1986): 439–58.

29. Klaus von Dohnanyi and Bernhard Gahlen, "Regionale und sektorale Strukturpolitik für die 80er Jahre" (Paper delivered at the conference on Politik und Wissenschaft at the Research Institute of the Friedrich Ebert Stiftung, Bonn, 8 February 1984); M. Konukuiewitz, "Urban Economic Development and Intergovernmental Policymaking in West Germany," *Environment and Planning C: Government and Policy* 4 (1986): 471–79; and Wolfgang Fach, "Industrial Modernization and the Federal System: A Comparative Study on Decentralization of Innovation Policies," *Regional Innovation and Decentralization,* ed. Ulrich Hilpert (London: Routledge, 1989).

30. Bruce Nussbaum, *The World after Oil* (New York: Simon and Schuster, 1983).

31. Herbert E. Striner, *Regaining the Lead: Policies for Economic Growth* (New York: Praeger, 1984).

32. Portions of the following are based on my section "Germany" in Mark Kesselman et al., *European Politics in Transition,* 2d ed. (Lexington, Mass.: D. C. Heath, 1992).

33. German Information Center, ed. *The Week in Germany,* 6 December 1991, 1.

Transforming the East German Economy: Shock without Therapy

Thomas A. Baylis

The new Länder of eastern Germany and the other post-Communist states of eastern Europe are undertaking an experiment no less breathtaking for the fact that it has now become familiar: the transformation of state-owned, centrally planned and managed economic systems into functioning capitalist market economies. Although there are no real precedents for such a metamorphosis and as yet no clear signs of success in any of the countries now undergoing it, neither German nor east European leaders have wanted for advice concerning the goals, methods, and pace of the transformation. Western economists (joined by many eastern ones), funding agency officials, bankers, businessmen, and politicians have joined in a chorus marred by only a few discordant voices: the shift to the market must be rapid, comprehensive, and uncompromising.

The formula that the West has commended to the embattled leaders of the fledgling east European democracies is popularly called "shock therapy," or, sometimes, the "big bang." It requires the prompt introduction of the institutions and rules of market economies, the speedy transfer of both small and large enterprises from state to private ownership and control, the sharp curtailment of state regulation and subsidy, and the rapid opening of each economy to foreign investment and competition, supported by decisive steps toward full convertibility of the local currency. It is widely conceded that such changes will be painful for many social groups, and that some sort of "safety net" must therefore be furnished for the most endangered of the victims. But advocates agree that the pain will be unavoidable in any circumstances, and it is best to get it over with as swiftly as possible. The very "shock" of sudden and drastic change that eliminates most of the protective niches the old economic system provided for state bureaucrats, managers, workers, and other citizens, they contend, is the best way to get the economy moving out of its post-Communist doldrums toward Western-style prosperity.[1]

Articulate dissent from this formula has been exceptional. Resistance to its implementation, however, has not. Workers have struck or staged demonstrations when their jobs have been threatened or the value of their paychecks slashed; their unions have demanded, and often received, wage and benefit improvements that dismayed economists immediately observe are unjustified by productivity gains and subversive of genuine recovery. Eastern Europe's inexperienced politicians, responding to the disaffection of their constituents with at least as much alacrity as their western counterparts, have sought compromises and delays. They are aware that popular vengeance for economic privation is likely to be wreaked upon *them*—the emphatic repudiation of the Balcerowicz reforms by the Polish electorate in October 1991 is only the most dramatic example of several. "We listened to the West, and we made too big a leap," remarked Lech Walesa just before the election.[2] Governments in Bulgaria and Romania have also been driven from power in the wake of surging economic discontent, and Hungary's has lost much of its popular support; the breakup of Czechoslovakia can also be attributed in part to Slovak resistance to economic reform. Such resistance—along with the sheer organizational and psychological obstacles to entirely remaking fundamental economic institutions and rules—has greatly slowed the actual pace of change even in those countries most strongly committed to shock therapy. Economists given the task of applying the therapy sometimes have difficulty concealing their impatience. Mihaly Kupa, the finance minister of Hungary, has voiced a complaint that many of his counterparts elsewhere would be quick to endorse: "There are too many compromises and too few decisions. I am an economist, not a politician."[3]

In the former German Democratic Republic, however, the pace of economic transformation has been unrelenting. The process of unification brought to the east German states a form of shock therapy that not even the most devoted Friedmanite elsewhere in the former Soviet bloc would have dared to advocate. Ironically, this radical economic course was dictated more by the calculations of politicians than the designs of economists—indeed, many economists warned against it. Their misgivings seem amply to have been confirmed by subsequent events. The shock has been drastic; the amount of therapy it has provided, to date, small. There are even those who suggest that the patient might have been better off had he not submitted to treatment in the first place.[4]

In this chapter I will review the measures of economic transformation undertaken in the former GDR, assess the results to date, and consider the region's prospects for the near future. The consequences of economic policy, it should be emphasized, are never purely economic. Accordingly, I will consider not only the economic impact of German shock therapy, but also its political, social, and psychological effects. Indices of GNP growth or the improvement of purchasing power are not by themselves adequate measures of the success of any economic reform program, east or west.

Starting Points

After the revolutions of 1989 swept Communist parties from power in eastern Europe and it had become apparent that the GDR was on an irreversible course toward unity with the Federal Republic, commentators were quick to point to the special advantages eastern Germany would enjoy in comparison with its former Council for Mutual Economic Assistance (CMEA) partners as it sought to adjust to the discipline of the capitalist market. The GDR, after all, had the reputation of being the most economically advanced of all the Communist states. Its standard of living, measured by Western estimates of GNP per capita and such other indices as the ratio of automobiles, refrigerators, and washing machines to households, and the comparatively favorable level of housing and medical care, seemed significantly to exceed that of its eastern neighbors. Its technology seemed more advanced—in 1988, for example, the GDR proudly announced that its electronics industry had produced a one-megabit computer chip—and the regime had incessantly cited what seemed to be impressive statistics on the introduction of computer-based manufacturing techniques and industrial robots in its enterprises.[5] The high rate of labor utilization and the repeated complaints of a labor shortage in the GDR made it easy to believe that the country did not suffer from the hidden unemployment that observers knew lay just beneath the surface of the economies of the other East European countries. The GDR had also been in absolute terms the most successful of the East European states in exporting goods to Western markets. Thus, it was thought, the country would have a substantially easier time adjusting to market conditions than its neighbors.

Moreoever, the GDR, unlike these neighbors, would have almost limitless access to the impressive resources of the Federal Republic for capital investment, technological modernization, the war on pollution, and the support of the safety net. The government of a newly united Germany, commentators believed, could not allow its efforts to rebuild the east German economy and to integrate it into the German economy as a whole to fail. In addition, the former GDR would benefit from its immediate membership (cushioned by transitional provisions) in the European Community, which other east European states would not be permitted to join for many years.

This optimistic prognosis has proven incorrect, not because the other east European states have fared better than expected, but because the former GDR has fared much worse. We now know that official GDR statistics had concealed economic problems far more severe and a technological lag far greater than anyone had imagined. In the last decade of Communist rule, the

GDR's inability to find the resources needed to renew its aging industrial plant had proven especially damaging.[6] But not everything can be blamed on the multiple sins of kommunistische Misswirtschaft, in spite of its usefulness as a scapegoat. To understand fully the sources of the east German Misere, we need to examine the basic policies followed by the German government(s) once the drive toward unification was underway, and then examine some of the consequences of those policies.

Monetary Union and Its Consequences

What is most striking to the external observer is the remarkable haste with which pivotal economic measures were adopted and implemented, in contrast to the usually deliberate pace and incremental character of economic policy change in democratic countries. The haste, we know, was driven by electoral politics in both parts of Germany, and by growing alarm over the continuing migration of East Germans to the West in the months following the fall of the Berlin Wall, an exodus that had reached some 2,000 a day by early 1990. The belief was also widespread that a window of opportunity for achieving German unity had opened that might soon again be closed. Chancellor Helmut Kohl seized the initiative in the drive toward unification and thereby succeeded in reversing the dwindling fortunes of his Christian Democratic Union.[7] His cabinet's endorsement of quick monetary union, while initially opposed by Bundesbank chairman Karl-Otto Pöhl and other economists, was instrumental in the landslide victory of the East German CDU and its allies in the GDR's elections of 18 March. The alliance's promise that most, if not all, East German savings would be converted to West marks at the rate of 1:1, and the Kohl government's parallel assurances to West Germans that the costs of unification could be met without an increase in taxes lent a momentum to the process that proved impossible to contain. By 18 May the two Germanies had completed and signed a treaty on monetary, economic, and social union. Under its terms the GDR ceded its financial sovereignty to the Federal Republic and committed itself to building a "social market economy," and to bringing its tax, welfare, and labor laws into line with the West's. On 1 July the treaty went into effect; de jure political unification three months later was no more than a formality.

The effect of these measures was to catapult the GDR's firms and their workers, virtually unprotected, into competition with one of the most efficient and technologically advanced western economies—as well as with the economies of the Federal Republic's partners in the European Community, Japan, and other wealthy capitalist states. Elsewhere in eastern Europe the opening to the West could be cushioned through the use of tariffs, exchange controls, and other protective mechanisms. Above all, countries like

Hungary, Poland, and Czechoslovakia could (and did) fix the exchange rate of their currencies so as to make western imports expensive for their citizens and the western selling prices of their own products low. Adjustment of the exchange rate also kept down potential wage costs for prospective western investors. For the GDR, the terms of economic union foreclosed such possibilities.

The 1 July date meant that there was virtually no time to carry out reforms and other preparations that might have permitted at least some east German enterprises to be competitive in the DM market. It is well to recall that the East German economic system, even had it been far less flawed than it was, had never been designed to compete in an international capitalist marketplace. It had been constructed to produce goods for captive markets at home and in the Soviet Union and other CMEA countries, while avoiding excessive dependence on capitalist suppliers. The GDR had concentrated investment in areas such as microelectronics, in which it was a critical supplier to the entire Soviet bloc but could not hope to be competitive with leading Western producers. It also invested heavily in efforts to reclaim more of its dwindling reserves of brown coal, so as to reduce its energy import requirements. Even products offered for sale to the West did not have to be profitable in conventional market terms as long as they could bring in badly needed hard currency—or be bartered under the rules of inter-German trade for needed West German products.[8] Full employment was a higher priority than cost efficiency, and the fulfillment of quantitative planning targets was more important than quality of product and technological innovation, however much rhetoric might be devoted to the latter. Under these circumstances, the inability of east German managers and workers to adapt to a radically changed economic environment is unsurprising.

Both before and after economic union, a great deal of controversy surrounded the rate at which East marks were to be exchanged for West marks. For the first 4,000 marks of savings (2,000 for children under fifteen, 6,000 for those sixty and over) and wages and salaries, a 1:1 rate was applied; for everything else, including the reserves of economic enterprises, the rate was one deutsche mark for two East marks. Critics charged that these rates were far too generous, given the differences in productivity of the two Germanys; only a much lower rate would allow GDR firms to be competitive. Since average East German wages even at a 1:1 rate were less than half those of West Germany, however, a lower rate was politically and socially unthinkable: it would doubtless have pushed the migration rate still higher, lowered the level of East German morale even more, and denied Chancellor Kohl and his party the political dividends of unity.

The east German trusteeship agency, the Treuhandanstalt, set up originally under the Modrow government to administer state property during the transition to a market economy, became a critical institution in the process of economic transformation. The Treuhand's thankless task was to privatize, modernize, or where necessary liquidate some 10,000 East German state-owned firms. From the outset, the balance of priorities among these goals has been the object of intense controversy, but the greatest emphasis to date has been on privatization.[9] By September 1991 some 3,800 firms had been sold, most of them small, with industrial enterprises significantly underrepresented.[10] All but a handful went to west German companies, usually on generous terms. Those purchasers promising to maintain a certain (although usually sharply reduced) level of employment and to make substantial new investments were favored. East German critics charged that some firms, including such well-known ones as the state airline Interflug, were being closed too quickly and with too little regard for the employeees thrown out of work; some western economists, by contrast, contended that too many firms were being kept alive, and jobs accordingly maintained, when there was no possibility of their becoming profitable.[11] A Treuhand vice-president enunciated the organization's ostensible policy: "A company is not worth reconstructing if it seems that even in two or three years' time it will not be in the black." He admitted, however, that exceptions would be made, notably in the chemical industry;[12] others predicted that the state, having sold the most attractive properties and faced with already high unemployment figures, would be forced to limit further closures and expand its own modernizing role.[13]

One factor that slowed western investment and introduced added elements of uncertainty into the lives of many east Germans was the agreement of the two states to return to their previous owners or their heirs certain properties seized during the forty years of Communist rule, or to provide compensation for them. The principle giving priority to "restitution over compensation," although qualified in a number of ways, proved especially troublesome to implement equitably. The number of legal claims filed now exceeds 1 million; not only the title to much of the land needed for business enterprises is in dispute, but also the right of many east Germans to homes they have lived in for years.[14]

A measure more welcome to east Germans has been the extension of the generous, and expensive, West German social safety net to the former GDR. The system of unemployment benefits and welfare payments for those who have exhausted such benefits has been of particular importance in easing the material strains of unity. East German pensions, while still just 65 percent of those in the West, have been improved over Communist-era levels. East Germans have seen other social benefits curtailed or eliminated, however, such as the GDR's generous maternity-leave provisions (the Baby-Jahr), its system of virtually universal preschool care, and many of the young people's clubs formerly operated by the Free German Youth.[15] As this list suggests, women, who have also lost their jobs in disproportionate numbers, have been particularly hard hit by the changes in social benefits.

The Economic Collapse

By 1991 industrial production in the former GDR had dropped to one-third the level of 1989.[16] Both foreign and domestic markets had all but collapsed. Although in the late 1980s nearly half of the GDR's trade had been with the West,[17] many of the goods exported had been sold at artificially low prices—the reliable but technologically outmoded Praktika camera is an example—which could not cover the actual costs of production under market conditions after the changeover in currency. The GDR's trade with the Soviet Union and other countries in eastern Europe came to an abrupt halt once east German enterprises were forced to demand payment in hard currencies. (For their part, GDR firms canceled contracts for the purchase of goods from its east European neighbors, thus intensifying their own economic crises.) Only government guaranteed Hermes credits permitted the revival of some of eastern Germany's Soviet and east European trade.

The collapse of the domestic market, however, proved the most damaging, psychologically as well as economically. In the days preceding 1 July, most East German stores closed, stripped their shelves of goods produced domestically, and replaced them with Western products. Their managers had not underestimated the enormous hunger of GDR citizens for Western consumer goods. Overnight the decade-long waiting period for Trabant automobiles disappeared. In spite of some expressions of nostalgia for the faithful "Trabi," East Germans rushed to buy Volkswagens and Opels with their newly acquired DM. The East German shoe industry, which in 1989 had employed 40,000 workers, suddenly found its products unwanted.[18] East German farmers found themselves unable to sell their produce either to state stores or the rapidly proliferating branches of western chains; consumers even gave western eggs preference over those laid by state socialist chickens. Only gradually did awareness of the self-destructive character of this behavior grow sufficiently to allow a modest revival of the sales of domestic agricultural products.

By July 1991, unemployment in the former GDR exceeded 1 million, more than 12 percent of the workforce, but this figure vastly understated the extent of the problem. Another 1.45 million were on "short-time" work, which in many cases meant no work at all, but still for the moment receiving pay. Many over 55 were pushed into early retirement; others were kept off the unemployment rolls only through retraining or work creation ("ABM") programs. Some 300,000 took jobs in the West but continued to live in the

East, and the rate of migration to the West continued at a level estimated at 15,000 each month.[19] Taken together, the number of those without regular work in the old GDR was approaching 40 percent of the work force and was expected to go higher.[20]

Was there ever a realistic political alternative to the course that led to these unhappy results?[21] There is no gainsaying the enormous pressures for economic and political union that the collapse of the Communist regime, the renewed migration, and the mounting economic disarray of the GDR produced. But it is worth noting that as late as the beginning of March 1990 44 percent of East Germans and 46 percent of West Germans surveyed by Infratest still favored a gradual approach to unification, beginning with a confederation and moving toward full unity only after some years.[22] Influential figures in the Federal Republic, including not only Pöhl but also Federal President von Weizsäcker and the SPD chancellor candidate Oskar Lafontaine, warned of the dangers of excessive haste. The then-economics minister Helmut Haussmann proposed a gradual program for the marketization of the East German economy at the same February cabinet meeting that decided instead to propose a rapid currency union.[23] It is arguable that had the chancellor taken a strong position in support of a gradualist course, promising the necessary support for market reforms, including steps toward internal convertibility of the East mark, and candidly underlining the dangers already spelled out by Pöhl and the potential costs to the West German taxpayer, it could have carried the day. But such a course would probably have required a different chancellor. Moreoever, it is by no means certain that a gradualist course would have reduced the economic gap and made full unity more palatable later on.

West German Assistance and Its Effects

The government's decision to press for rapid unity and its accompanying promise to bring the former GDR up to the economic level of the old Länder as quickly as possible implied a commitment to supply substantial financial assistance, but few anticipated just how massive the infusion of funds would have to be. By late 1991 the estimated total for that year had reached $95 billion,[24] with a similar amount projected for 1992. Another $4 billion came from the European Community. No other east European country could expect even a fraction of that amount in Western aid; according to one source, total foreign assistance to Poland, Hungary, and Czechoslovakia together was less than one-tenth that extended to east Germany.[25] Yet even that sum did not ensure a quick and successful economic transformation.

The Kohl government's initial promise to finance east German recovery entirely through borrowing, unrealistic if not dishonest from the outset, had to be abandoned just after the all-German elections of December 1990. The substantial increases in the sales and income taxes that were required gave the costs of union still greater immediacy to a west German public already grudging in its generosity toward the East. German government deficits continued to mount, however, earning the country the sort of rebuke from the International Monetary Fund that Germans had once thought was reserved for less disciplined nations, such as the United States or France.[26]

About two-thirds of west German assistance, most of it from the federal government but some from the old Länder, went to support consumption. That was true of the large sums necessary for various transfer payments—for unemployment compensation, pensions, and other social measures. Support for ABM, job retraining, and other labor-market measures was also costly, although they helped keep unemployment payments down.

The governments of the new eastern German Länder and communes had to meet desperate needs with rapidly declining revenues. According to estimates of the German Institute for Economic Research (DIW), eastern German states would take in one-third the revenues per capita of their western counterparts in 1991, and east German communes just 10 percent. Some (but not all) of this gap was to be met by payments from the German Unity fund—which, however, were scheduled to drop rapidly in 1992 and subsequent years.[27]

Additional western funds were required to cover the deficits of the Treuhand (an estimated DM 21 billion in 1991) and to subsidize private investment.[28] Support for the latter included a 12 percent investment subsidy for 1991 (8 percent in 1992) and generous depreciation allowances. The government poured substantial sums into rebuilding the east German infrastructure, most notably telecommunications, roads, and the rail system. Additional sums were required for dealing with eastern Germany's massive environmental problems.[29] Much of the money for public investment and labor market programs was to come from the Gemeinschaftswerk Aufschwung Ost (Joint Project Upward Bound East), approved in early 1991 and amounting to DM 24 billion over two years.

A large proportion of this assistance, it should be noted, quickly flowed back to the West, and helps account for the economic boom that sent west German profits to their highest level since the end of the 1960s at a time when other western economies were slipping into recession.[30] As Peter Christ has rather acerbically put it, moneys intended to generate an Aufschwung Ost created instead an Aufschwung West; east Germans bought western products, western construction companies were hired to carry out projects in the East, and western investors profited from the higher interest rates produced by heavy government borrowing. The restitution of east German property to owners living in the West promised to add to the latter's prosperity. Overall,

Christ points out, unification appears to have made the distribution of wealth between east and west even more unequal than it previously had been.[31]

A related consequence of economic unity and the policies of the Treuhand has been to place the ownership of east German businesses largely in west German hands. Because of the shortage of east German capital and the reluctance of foreign investors, all but a handful of Treuhand's sales of firms have been to west German companies. The proportion of foreign ownership is far lower than in western Germany itself, or any other advanced western nation. Overall, eastern Germany is quite literally becoming an economic colony of west German capital, and it is hard to see that fact changing for decades to come. The Treuhand has not pursued plans like those undertaken in Poland and Czechoslovakia to create domestic capital holdings by issuing free or low-cost vouchers for stock purchases either to a privatized enterprise's employees or citizens at large;[32] it has, however, arranged some 500 "management buy-outs."[33] The only real exception to the dominance of west German capital may be in the small business sector; 420,000 such firms have reportedly opened since unification, but failures are frequent.[34] "All in all, exaggerated expectations that a capable middle class will quickly arise in the new states must be scaled back [zurückgeschraubt] to realistic levels," remarks a joint report of the DIW and the Kiel Institute for the World Economy.[35]

In one important respect, however, east Germans have fared much better than their east European counterparts: their average standard of living, rather than falling sharply, seems to have improved. Pensioners, whose real income has reportedly grown by 50 percent since 1989, have especially benefited.[36] The reason lies partly in the generous transfer payments mentioned above and partly in the successful efforts of west German unions to raise east German wages, now said to be about 60 percent of the west German level.[37] These appear to have offset the reduction or elimination of subsidies for food staples, public transportation, the arts and culture, and, above all, housing that were so much a hallmark of the old GDR's economic order. Thus east Germans, unlike other east Europeans who cannot afford to buy the attractive goods now on their store shelves, have been able to taste some of the pleasures of Western consumption denied to them for so long. How much this offsets the unprecedented unemployment and the deep uncertainty over the economic future that pervades the GDR is another question.

Social and Psychological Consequences

That the estrangement between Ossis and Wessis has deepened since unification can hardly be doubted. Opinion surveys confirm countless more anecdotal accounts of the stereotypes held by each side.[38] East Germans view west Germans as arrogant, as Besserwessis all too eager to instruct their poorer cousins in the superior ways of market economics and pluralistic politics. West Germans view east Germans as lazy and improvident, whining for handouts at the expense of the west German taxpayer; years of Communist rule have, it is thought, drained them of any trace of ambition, energy, or imagination. Given these attitudes, it is not surprising that 84 percent of the east Germans surveyed in mid-1991 viewed themselves as "second class Germans."[39]

While talk of a "collective psychological breakdown" in the old GDR may be exaggerated,[40] there can be no doubt that the degree of demoralization and alienation and the feeling of collective inferiority is intense. "Everyone is suspicious, and everyone suspects," writes a German psychiatrist. "Values that were binding and predictable in the past are gone without the establishment of new equivalents."[41] In such circumstances, scapegoating flourishes, and the popularity of the Bonzentelefon for denouncing ex-Communist officials[42] as well as the outbursts of right-wing extremism and the attacks on immigrants become somewhat easier to comprehend.

The largely accurate feeling of east Germans that the future of the new Länder is being determined primarily by west German elites contributes significantly to the estrangement. The pool of able, well-educated, and experienced east Germans not tainted by their association with the old regime and thus available for leadership positions after the Wende was undoubtedly even smaller than it was in Hungary or Poland, where political criteria for recruitment were more loosely applied, or in Czechoslovakia, where a number of figures associated with the 1968 reforms remained, albeit in menial jobs. The pervasiveness of the Stasi in East German life probably made it inevitable that even important opposition figures would be found to have been compromised. Thus, west Germans have moved into key positions in government, administration, and the economy, although eastern Germans typically remain at the middle levels as their subordinates, a relationship that the latter can hardly help but see as colonial.[43] Three of the new Länder (along with reunited Berlin) now have west German minister-presidents, and three have west German finance ministers. Perhaps still more disquieting is the thin representation of east Germans on the national level, a reality exemplified by the departure of the former GDR Prime Minister de Maiziere from his government and party posts and by the fact that only two of the thirteen members of the SPD's Presidium are from the new states.[44] What this means is that east Germans have been left with remarkably little say in working out their problems and rebuilding their society and economy.

Prospects

The legacy of German shock therapy thus promises to be painful and enduring. The high level of government investment and the more cautious but still
substantial contributions of the private sector probably insure that some sort
of economic upturn will come in the old GDR, barring a severe all-German
economic slump unleashed by high public debt, rising inflation, and high
interest rates. The construction and service industries have already shown
some signs of improvement, and the decision to transfer the seat of government should give a substantial economic boost to the area around Berlin. The
disparity in average incomes and the standard of living between the two parts
of Germany is likely gradually to diminish, thanks in part to the efforts of the
unions. But the economic gap will persist, probably for decades. Capital and
wealth will remain largely in the West; eastern firms will remain branches
or subsidiaries of western companies; the East will serve at best as the
"extended workbench" (verlängerte Werkbank) of the West. Joblessness will
remain high for some time,[45] and more east Germans will emigrate to the
West in pursuit of employment. The psychological and cultural gap is also
likely to persist: the example of southern Italy comes irresistibly to mind.
The new Germany, in the words of the SPD leader Karlheinz Blessing, may
be characterized by "a loss of social homogeneity [and] the solidifying
[Versäulung] of different cultures, which stand beside one another speechless
and without relations."[46]

NOTES

1. For an uncompromising statement of this position, see Jan S. Prybla, "The
Road From Socialism," *Problems of Communism* 40 (January–April 1991): 1–17.
2. *New York Times*, 25 October 1991, sec. C. All references to the *Times* are to
the national edition.
3. *Magyar Hirlap*, 13 May 1991, translated in Foreign Broadcast Information
Service—Eastern Europe, *Daily Report*, 15 May 1991, 19.
4. According to a mid-1991 Emnid survey for *Der Spiegel*, 49 percent of east
Germans questioned felt that most or a "large number" of their countrymen viewed
reunification as a mistake. *Der Spiegel*, 22 July 1991, 26.
5. The statistics were based, however, on extraordinarily creative definitions of
CAD/CAM systems and robots. See Fred Klinger, "Organisation und Innovation—die
Grenzen der Fabrikautomatisierung," in *Die DDR in der Ära Honecker*, ed. Gert-
Joachim Glaessner (Opladen: Westdeutscher, 1988), esp. 397–98; also Mike Dennis,
"Scientific-Technical Progress, Ideological Legitimation, and Political Change in the
German Democratic Republic," in *Studies in GDR Culture and Society 10*, ed. Margy
Gerber et al. (Lanham, Md.: University Press of America, 1991), 1–29; Gary Geipel,

"Politics and Computers in the German Democratic Republic: The Robotron Combine," in *Studies in GDR Culture and Society 8,* ed. Margy Gerber et al. (Lanham, Md.: University Press of America, 1988), 83–98.

6. See Carl-Heinz Janson, *Totengräber der DDR* (Düsseldorf: Econ, 1991), 68–81. The sharp decline in investment in most sectors of the GDR economy was due in part to the high cost of servicing the hard-currency debt accumulated in the 1970s, in part to the priority given to microelectronics and the expansion of brown coal production, and in part to the unwillingness of the SED leadership to risk cutting back on costly social programs.

7. See Clay Clemens, "Helmut Kohl's CDU and German Unification: The Price of Success," *German Politics and Society,* no. 22 (1991): 33–44.

8. "Everything was sold that could be sold [to the west], even if only ten pfennigs came back for every Mark spent." Janson, *Totengräber der DDR,* 66.

9. "The emphasis that has been placed on privatization has, together with the administrative emergency, favored a type of entrepreneur who views the word 'social' only as a trade union slogan and, together with self-seeking functionaries of the old GDR, puts into practice Marxist-Leninist teachings about the dog-eat-dog morality [Wolfsmoral] of capitalism." Ilse Spittmann, "Korrektur der Prioritäten," *Deutschland Archiv* 24 (1991): 450.

10. "Gesamtwirtschaftliche und unternehmerische Anpassungsprozesse in Ostdeutschland," *DIW Wochenbericht,* 13 June 1991, 332; *Treuhandanstalt Informationen,* November 1991, 1, 12. Of the 1,250 firms sold by the *Treuhand*'s central administration, 176 were sold to foreign buyers. The other 2,550 were smaller firms sold by *Treuhand*'s regional branches, nearly all, presumably, to German purchasers.

11. See, e.g., *New York Times,* 22 October 1991, sec. C.

12. *Frankfurter Rundschau,* 9 September 1991, translated in *German Tribune,* 22 September 1991, 6.

13. Roger de Weck, "Mühsame Geduldsprobe," *Die Zeit,* 11 October 1991, 9. All references to *Die Zeit* are to the North American edition.

14. Dieter Fedderson, "GDR Emigres and Property Rights," *German Politics and Society,* no. 22 (1991): 47–61. See also Katie Hafner, "The House We Lived In," *New York Times Magazine,* 10 November 1991, 32ff.

15. See *Tagesspiegel* (Berlin), 11 August 1991.

16. "Tendenz der Wirtschaftsentwicklung 1991/92," *DIW Wochenbericht,* 27 June 1991, 365.

17. Official East German statistics had previously attributed just 30 percent of the GDR's trade to the industrialized West, but a recalculation using realistic values for the ruble and Western currencies showed the Western share to have been much higher. See Statistisches Amt der DDR, *Statistisches Jahrbuch der Deutschen Demokratischen Republik '90* (Berlin: Rudolf Haufe, 1990), 277.

18. *Financial Times,* July 14–15, 1990.

19. Employment in west Germany rose by 680,000 between April 1990 and April 1991. Marvin Jackson, "One Year after German Economic Union," *Report on Eastern Europe,* 28 June 1991, 45.

20. See the figures in Peter Christ, "Das Land der zwei Geschwindigkeiten," *Die*

Zeit, 11 October 1991, 11; Christ, "Der Fortschritt ist eine Schnecke," *Die Zeit,* 5 July 1991, 9.

21. For a forceful if not entirely persuasive argument that there was not, see Klaus von Beyme, "The Legitimation of German Unification between National and Democratic Principles," *German Politics and Society,* no. 22 (1991): 1–17.

22. See "Grosse Mehrheit für Einheit," *Informationen,* 30 March 1990, 2.

23. Christ, "Fortschritt," 9.

24. *New York Times,* 22 Oct. 1991, sec. C.

25. Jochen Steinmayr, "Die Sonntagskinder des Umbruchs," *Die Zeit,* 25 October 1991, 4.

26. Roger de Weck, "Tadel für die Musterschüler," *Die Zeit,* 25 October 1991, 1.

27. See "Gesamtwirtschaftliche," 343.

28. *Berliner Zeitung,* 15 August 1991.

29. For details, see "Gesamtwirtschaftliche," 344–46.

30. "Tendenz," 368.

31. Christ, "Das Land," 11.

32. See *New York Times,* 10 October 1991, sec. C; 10 November 1991, sec. A. The ambitious Polish plan has, however, run into serious difficulties. See Ben Slay, "The 'Mass Privatization' Plan Unravels," *Report on Eastern Europe,* 1 November 1991, 13–18.

33. *Financial Times,* 30 July 1991.

34. *Washington Post,* 29 September 1991, sec. A.

35. "Gesamtwirtschaftliche," 342.

36. *Tagesspiegel* (Berlin), 10 August 1991. The reported increase, which was 20 percent for a family of four with one member employed and one unemployed, did not take into account the slashing of subsidies for rent and other items that took place on 1 October.

37. *Washington Post,* 29 September 1991, sec. A. The unions are reportedly seeking to equalize wages in the two parts of Germany within two to three years. Michael Fichter, "From Transmission Belt to Social Partnership," *German Politics and Society,* no. 22 (1991): 35.

38. See *Der Spiegel,* 22 July 1991, 24–29; 29 July 1991, 41–49; Anne Köhler and Richard Hilmer, "Ein Jahr Wirtschafts-, Währungs- und Sozialunion," *Deutschland Archiv* 24 (1991): 931–35.

39. *Der Spiegel,* 22 July 1991, 28.

40. David Gow, "Kohl Blamed for Perceived Failure of Reunification," *Manchester Guardian Weekly,* 7 April 1991, 9.

41. Jochen Neumann, "Psychiatry in Eastern Europe Today," *American Journal of Psychiatry,* 148 (1991): 1386–89.

42. *Tagesspiegel* (Berlin), 9 August 1991; *Austin American-Statesman,* 20 October 1991, sec. A. The *Bonzentelefon* is sponsored by the leader of the Berlin CDU's parliamentary caucus and promoted by Rupert Murdoch's east German daily *Super!,* a publication whose popularity has been attributed to its efforts to cater to the resentments of east Germans against both *Wessis* and former Communists.

43. For example, over half of the higher civil servants but just one-quarter of all

the bureaucrats in government ministries in the state of Brandenburg are reported to be from the west. *Tagesspiegel* (Berlin), 9 August 1991.

44. *Tagesspiegel* (Berlin), 7 September 1991; *Mannheimer Morgen,* 16 September 1991. Both translated in *German Tribune,* 22 September 1991, 3. See also Nina Grunenberg, "Salut für einen politischen Selbstmörder," *Die Zeit,* 20 September 1991, 3.

45. "It is well documented that German industry has not created jobs in the last twenty years but has become increasingly efficient while hiring fewer workers. Even if German industry invests heavily in the east German economy, it is unlikely to offset high unemployment in the short term." Thomas Koelble, "After the Deluge: Unification and the Political Parties in Germany," *German Politics and Society,* no. 22 (1991): 54.

46. Cited in Christ, "Das Land," 11.

German Economic Integration: The Case for Optimism

Irwin L. Collier, Jr.

> Eine Republik zu bauen aus den Materialien einer niedergerissenen Monarchie ist freilich ein schweres Problem. Es geht nicht, ohne bis erst jeder Stein anders gehauen ist, und dazu gehört Zeit.

> To build a republic from the material of a demolished monarchy is a difficult task to be sure. It won't happen until each stone has been recut, and that takes time.
>
> —Georg Christoph Lichtenberg, *Aphorismen 1793–96*

Introduction

Ever since Thomas Carlyle succeeded in tagging economics as the dismal science, economists have found themselves typecast in the role of Dr. Gloom, a character that gives far more pleasure to play than one should ever admit in public. The economic reconstruction of the new states of the post-Wall Federal Republic of Germany provides economists with an opportunity to argue a cheerful brief instead. This might seem strange to anyone who has traveled through the new states of the FRG, where one observes (as described by Thomas A. Baylis in his chapter) far less cheer than widespread pessimism compounded by a bitterness resulting from perceived injustice. Uncertain or lost jobs, quadrupled rents, and the pay gap between Wessi and Ossi loom far larger in the average easterner's consciousness than the new family car, VCR, and holidays in western Europe. The purpose of this chapter is to count the blessings that together provide a solid basis for optimism concerning the present and future course of German economic integration.

The first argument in the case for optimism is also its strongest: namely, the long-run economic prospects for the new states of the FRG are as close to a sure bet as economics can ever offer. In the first section of this chapter the sources of the anticipated "integration dividend" are described. Due to human impatience, the next set of important questions includes the size of the up-front costs of adjustment to the new order (and who pays) and whether economic policy has hastened or delayed the payment of the integration dividend. The second section examines a few of the adjustments forced by economic integration and assesses the strength of the social safety net for the new states that is anchored in the west German economy. Given that an economic revolution with political and social complications both of domestic and international origin has taken place, it is argued in the third section that the actual implementation of policies bearing on integration has been remarkably successful, with significant learning on the job. Because economic integration is taking place within a context of democratic politics, the widespread anxiety and sense of being unfairly treated shared by many east Germans warrents serious attention, even accepting the validity of the optimistic case. In the fourth section the impact of personal uncertainty and the fundamental difference in distributive ethics held in East and West are identified as the sources of the prevailing gloom in the new states of the FRG. The process of the integration of the post-Wall German economies is still in an early stage. Because long-run arguments are always premised on certain assumptions as to likely future developments and policies, the concluding section of the chapter reviews the expected sequence of events implicit in the optimistic case.

The Light at the End of the Tunnel:
The "Integration Dividend"

One of the hallmarks of human rationality is that future costs and benefits matter in deciding our actions today. The belief shared by the vast majority of the east German population and expressed in the outcome of the first free elections in the German Democratic Republic (GDR) in March 1990, that is, that the old order of the GDR should be replaced with the political, economic, and social order of West Germany in toto, reflected a widely shared consensus in east Germany that the costs of adjustment would be more than compensated by the ultimate benefits of economic and political integration.[1] The failure of imagination in East and West alike to anticipate the actual course taken by the eastern economy is at least partially due to the relative salience of economic life in the west compared to the (then) indistinct future costs of adjustment required to achieve that long-run of prosperity. This is not the first time in human affairs that impatience and imperfect foresight have traveled together.[2]

The economic integration dividend for the east German economy can be loosely defined as the difference between projected living standards at the end of the process of economic integration and the living standards that would have resulted from a hypothetical continuation of the Honecker-era economy. Clearly two aspects are involved: an assessment of where the GDR economy was heading as well as the direction taken by the new states. That difference must be compared to the costs of dislocation, of adjusting the allocation of resources and the structure of economic activity to the possibilities and the demands of the new market framework. A critic of the course of economic integration must argue that some other policy could increase the upside of the integration dividend, bring the dividend sooner and/or lower the adjustment costs. This still leaves plenty of room for substantive disagreement concerning the "fair" division of the costs and benefits of economic integration between East and West or young and old.

An aspect of the GDR economy not sufficiently appreciated in the nostalgia one occasionally hears about economic life under the old system is that for at least a decade GDR economic planners had neglected the seed corn required for maintaining living standards.[3] Investment in the GDR had been sacrificed to maintain consumption levels for most of the 1980s so that the east German economy entering unification resembled the British economy after the Second World War—the capital stock had been worn down, through intensive use for an extended period of time without sufficient replacement investment. Besides the unavoidability of rebuilding the capital stock, there was yet another liability faced by the GDR economy in the form of the cumulative damage to the forests, waters, and air of east Germany. The scale of the environmental damage thus far discovered has shocked even the most cynical critics of the GDR. Together the badly worn capital stock and the devastated environment meant that relative living standards at the end of the Honecker era were simply *not* sustainable. One of the uncounted blessings of economic integration has been that east Germans were spared that inevitable crash in consumption without even the promise of a prosperous long run.

Hyperprotectionism is an accurate description of the structure of the GDR economy that is relevant both for understanding the current unemployment problem and as one very significant source for productivity growth in the new states. Under central planning, goods were largely produced by monopolies that were coordinated through the nonmarket system of material balances. With the monetary, economic, and social union of July 1990, east German households became completely free to choose. The initial impact of this move to a system of free trade amounted to a virtual boycott of eastern goods. Industries identified with so-called key technologies that had been vigorously promoted by the economic leadership of the GDR were precisely those branches to find themselves the most vulnerable to open competition. They were not alone. Nonpriority branches such as textiles and automobile production were likewise swamped by competitors from beyond the borders of the old GDR. With relative wage costs in east Germany far above relative productivity (more about this below), downsizing and respecialization became the central elements of restructuring the economy in order to increase productivity.

Like other centrally planned economies, the GDR had produced a little bit of everything but not much very well. Following monetary and economic union, east German producers have become forced to specialize in far fewer products to generate cost reductions from improvements in the division of labor of the kind associated with Adam Smith's pin factory. A second source of gains in productivity from economic integration will be the cost savings on intermediate products that enterprises were once forced to acquire from domestic monopolies or exclusive suppliers in the Council for Mutual Economic Assistance (CMEA).

As mentioned above, the east German capital stock had been kept on a starvation diet for almost a decade, with some factories acquiring greater antiquarian value as working museums of industrial technology than economic value as productive assets. In such a situation, similar in many ways to Germany in the early postwar years, the productivity of initial investment projects will be extremely high, as critical bottlenecks are expanded and new plants are built using technologies that not long ago had been completely off-limits to east German enterprises either because of Cocom restrictions on high-tech imports from the West or the scarcity of hard currency. As roads, railway lines, and telecommunications are repaired, modernized, and expanded, the productivity of existing and newly installed capital will grow as well.

Another reason to expect dramatic growth in productivity during the adjustment process is that market incentives matter enormously for individual behavior. The relatively undifferentiated structure of wages and salaries in the GDR will change. A dramatic reduction of sick days even *before* the start of monetary and economic union was reported. Those sick days used to contain a significant portion of a socially accepted form of time theft known as a "social insurance vacation." A modest increase in work effort can easily have the impact of a doubling of the east German capital stock.[4]

Three basic sources for the integration dividend have been identified in this section: gains from trade and specialization; high returns to public and private investment in the early phase of integration; and the impact of market incentives on the intensity of economic activity. An important feature should be mentioned that distinguishes the east German case from the other economies in the process of transition from socialist central planning to private market allocation. Macroeconomic stability has never been a serious question in the German case. Both the fiscal (including the social security system) and monetary systems of the old Federal Republic have been able to expand to

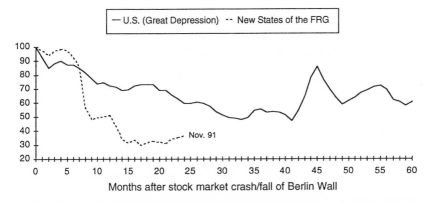

Fig. 1. The collapse of industrial production. (*Source:* United States: Federal Reserve Board index of daily industrial production; East Germany: Industrial commodity production [November 1989 to November 1990], Index of net manufacturing output [July 1991 to November 1992].)

incorporate the new states. Within a framework of macroeconomic stability (understood as stabilization of the prices and real living standards), markets can indeed handle the structural adjustments required of the east German economy in the process of economic integration.

Getting Through the Tunnel: The Collapse of the East German Economy and the Safety Net of the Social Union

In the last year of the centrally planned socialist economy of the GDR, it cost on average 4.4 East German marks to earn 1 DM of exports on Western markets. Were all current costs in GDR marks to be converted into DM at 1:1, it should have been obvious to most people that it was going to be quite impossible to make any money selling goods for 1 DM that cost 4.4 DM to produce.[5] Thus it should have come as no surprise that a significant consequence of entering the monetary, economic, and social union with an greatly overvalued currency would be what macroeconomists call a strong negative demand shock, which is to say that the bottom would fall out of the market for east German–produced goods. And did it ever.[6]

To put the collapse of east German production into historical perspective, figure 1 displays two indexes of industrial production. The index for the United States begins with October 1929, the month of the crash of the stock market, and the index for east Germany begins with November 1989, the fall of the Berlin Wall. Both indexes have been normalized to 100 for those historical months. The collapse of industrial production in east Germany has been deeper and faster than the drop that took place during Great Depression in the United States. We must postpone to the next section the question whether the 1:1 conversion of wages and salaries could or could not have been avoided. The miracle of the bloodless political revolution that took place in east Germany was followed by no less an economic miracle—a deep depression in production occurred without a corresponding fall in real consumption in the new states—indeed average real consumption has increased in the new states of the Federal Republic (table 1)![7]

Another way to quantify the impact of the economic revolution in east Germany on economic life there is to estimate the number of persons who have experienced a fundamental change in their work lives (table 2). To construct a lower bound for the proportion of the labor force that has experienced a significant change as a direct consequence of the collapse of the old regime and the economic integration with west Germany, we begin with 9.9

TABLE 1.   Selected Consumer Expenditures in East German Families with Two Adults and Two Children, Price Changes and Implicit Quantities

	1989 (marks per month)	1990 July-Dec (DM per month)	Price change		Implicit quantity change
			Variant 1	Variant 2	
Washing machines	6	8	- 67 %	- 67 %	+ 300 %
Overstuffed furniture	15	18	- 7 %	- 54 %	+ 70 %
Color televisions	25	37	- 78 %	- 82 %	+ 640 %
Automobiles	43	233	- 31 %	- 64 %	+ 890 %
Gasoline	82	110	- 27 %	- 23 %	+ 80 %
Spirits	33	17	- 54 %	- 49 %	0 %
Coffee	42	12	- 78 %	- 83 %	+ 40 %
Total consumption expenditure	1802	2407	Price level approximately unchanged		+ 34 %

Note: The expenditure data come from family budget diaries for wage and salary employee households of two parents and two children. Statistisches Amt der DDR, Abteilung Lebensniveau und Bevölkerungsbefragungen, *Statistik des Haushaltsbudgets 1989: Arbeiter- und Angestelltenhaushalte.* Statistisches Bundesamt, *Einnahmen und Ausgaben ausgewählter privater Haushalte im Gebiet der ehemaligen DDR 2. Halbjahr 1990,* Heft 15 der Schriftenreihe Ausgewählte Arbeitsunterlagen zur Bundesstatistik. The price-change data come from detailed, unpublished individual price comparisons from the economic research institute of the former GDR Ministry of Finance and the German Institute of Economic Research in West Berlin. Variant 1 assumes that the difference between December 1989 East and West German prices equals the change in prices (GDR Ministry of Finance data). Variant 2 is calculated from DIW individual price comparisons 1989 East Berlin to July 1990 East Berlin and July 1990 East Berlin compared to July 1990 West Berlin. The implicit quantity increased is calculated using the mean of the two price variants. The consumer price index for the new states was used for all family expenditures (*Jahresgutachten 1991/92 des Sachverständigenrates zur Begutachtung der gesamtwirtschaftlichen Entwicklung,* Deutscher Bundestag, 12. Wahlperiode, Drucksache 12/1618, 18 November 1991).

million persons employed in the GDR in 1989. According to estimates by the German Council of Economic Experts, by the last quarter of 1991 the east German labor force was reduced by almost 300,000 workers who had migrated to the West. Approximately a half million east Germans were commuting to western jobs. Early retirements have led to almost three-quarters of a million withdrawals from the labor force. Approximately 160,000 workers have left the labor force for full-time retraining.[8] Withdrawals from the labor force for all other reasons totaled over 200,000, presumably with a relatively higher proportion of women. Registered unemployment during the last quarter of 1991 was almost 1.1 million workers (estimated to average about 1.4 million for 1992).

Altogether, by the fourth quarter of 1991 these changes amounted to a drop in employment in the new states of nearly 3 million (30 percent of employment in 1989). In addition, 1.2 million employees were working reduced hours (on average a reduction of 57 percent) with 360,000 working in the public employment program (ABM).[9] There are 375,000 new self-employed people. All in all, at least half of the east German labor force had experienced a major change in labor force status by the end of 1991. The actual proportion must be significantly higher, since it does not include changes associated with internal restructuring of existing enterprises or with changing employers.[10]

The retired population of east Germany has, at least statistically, come through German unification very well treated. For a standard old-age pension (forty-five insurance years, average income), a retiree in the new states as of 1 January 1992 receives 993 DM—56.7 percent of the standard pension in the old states. Before the monetary, economic, and social union went into effect 1 July 1990, an employee who had forty-five insurance years and participated in the voluntary supplemental pension insurance plan received a monthly pension of 520 marks.[11] This nominal increase of 90 percent is at

TABLE 2.   Changes in the East German Labor Force, 1989–91 (in thousands)

Employment in 1989	9,860
Moved to west Germany	295
Commute to jobs in west Germany	495
Early retirement	735
Participation in full-time retraining program	160
Out of labor force, n.e.c.	210
Unemployment	1,055
Employment in the fourth Quarter 1991	6,910
of which	
Short-time workers	1,200
Public employment projects (ABM)	360
New self-employed	375

least twice the size of the increase in the cost of living for average east German pensioners over the same period.

It is difficult to identify any class in the new states that has suffered a major deterioration in its standard of living compared to the status quo ante. What is simply astounding is that this is true at a time when the east German economy still finds itself in the trough of a deep depression. This is only possible due to the enormous transfers from west Germany to east Germany, now running on the order of over $100 billion annually. The social union was extended by west Germany in good faith as matter of constitutional obligation. East German voters now represent what is arguably the largest single special interest in German politics today.[12] With the right to vote in German parliamentary elections, citizens in the new states are in a position to enforce that obligation. Thus we can be reasonably confident that the social safety net, made in west Germany, will continue to hold in the East. One can easily imagine how the scale of U.S. aid to the reconstruction of the CIS would be affected were voters there allowed to vote in the presidential election of 1992.

Getting Off on Both the Right and the Wrong Foot

The state treaty to create a monetary, economic, and social union of the two Germanys went into effect on 1 July 1990. On that day both monetary and fiscal sovereignty were effectively transferred to the Bundesbank and the Ministry of Finance of the FRG. A four-month-old east German institution—the Treuhandanstalt (THA)—was transformed into a public corporation with the purpose of privatizing the vast bulk of east German economic assets under its control.

The decision to quickly transplant the legal order of the social market economy of the Federal Republic and to create a monetary union of east and west Germany was not surprising, given the positive experience with currency reform and west German postwar reconstruction. There are three major differences that significantly complicate the early years of reconstruction that distinguish the present east German case. In 1948 the old Federal Republic began with an established governmental administration (virtually intact at the local level) and a court system with judges and lawyers experienced in German property and contract law. On 1 July 1990 such system-specific human capital was extremely rare in east Germany—a lawyer trained for a planned economy is simply not interchangeable with a lawyer trained for a market economy. Thus it should not really surprise anyone that government at the state and local levels and the administration of justice in east Germany have not worked particularly well during these initial years of German unification. On the other hand, it should take no more than a few years to accumulate enough system-specific human capital to make a visible improvement in the workings of governmental administration and the legal system in the new states. A second complication that distinguishes the reconstruction of east Germany from postwar west Germany has been all the difficulties associated with the reestablishment of private property rights in the former. The initial emphasis of the principle of property restitution as opposed to indemnification was an unfortunate policy error that is discussed below. The third fundamental difference is that in 1948 west German businesses were able to enter the DM era as lean, mean, value-adding machines. In contrast, virtually every economic organization in east Germany, including public service, has been forced into major reductions in staffing. Part of the downsizing, to use that fashionable euphemism, would have been the inevitable part of the adjustment to an open economy from a position of hyperprotectionism. However, the rate of old-job destruction and rate of new-job creation are not constants but variables influenced by the terms of the original monetary conversion and the past and future course of wage setting in east and west Germany.

There are two fundamentally distinct aspects in any monetary conversion: 1) the conversion rate(s) for the value of financial assets and liabilities in the wealth accounts of households, businesses, and governments and 2) the conversion rate(s) for terms of existing contracts for labor, housing rentals, etc. in the respective income/expenditure accounts. In principle there could be an enormous range of possible variation, for example, all debt might be forgiven (including that of banks to depositors, i.e., bank accounts wiped out) while existing contracts could be moved to approximate parity with west German levels. Each possible combination of rates has significant macroeconomic and microeconomic implications. In point of fact, the actual public debate actually turned out to bear a striking resemblance to a scholastic discussion of the "just price" rather than an informed policy debate. However, discussion of the ethical dimension of German unification must be postponed to the following section.

Monetary conversion can have an impact on either the aggregate demand or the aggregate supply sides of the macroeconomy. The rate of conversion of assets and liabilities, in particular household bank accounts, which constitute an important component of the stock of money, could affect the aggregate price level. Both the Bundesbank and the German Council of Economic Experts analyzed the conversion from the perspective of the simplest quantity theory of money. The quantity of new money created by the monetary union was compared with estimates of the new production potential from the economic union. The concern, especially of the Bundesbank, was that a 1:1 conversion of GDR marks into DM would increase the monetary stock by a greater proportion than east German production would increase

German national product. Somewhat more sophisticated was the awareness that a mistake in the initial conversion of existing wage contracts would ultimately be corrected in the labor market but that any mistake in the conversion rate of east German money would have long-run effects on the price level—in fact, rather small potatoes macroeconomically speaking. The conversion rate for wages in existing employment contracts can affect the supply side of the economy depending upon whether labor costs are matched by labor productivity. On this point west German policymakers were fairly clear, as the known data on the domestic cost of earning a DM from exports to the FRG clearly indicated that a 1:1 conversion of labor contracts would destroy the competitiveness of the bulk of east German industry on 1 July 1990.

It is not surprising that the quantity theory of money was the last thing on the minds of east German wealth holders when it came to the issue of converting the family savings into DM. Bigger bank accounts are better bank accounts from an individual's perspective. It is also not surprising that east German workers saw the problem of the conversion of labor costs from the opposite perspective, namely labor earnings and ultimately wage parity with the West. A bigger paycheck is a better paycheck, again from an individual's perspective. Indeed the situation was more complex than a matter of contrary perspectives because the logic of the socialist planned economy's system of subsidies and taxes, further confounded with shortage, made the very notion of *a* purchasing power of the GDR mark exceedingly problematic.[13] The purchasing power of the mark in a retired couple's savings account was in a certain sense higher than the purchasing power of the mark in a young family's account waiting to purchase a car. A thousand marks could certainly buy the connected Stasi officer a better "market" basket than the average consumer could acquire.

While the west German policymakers' concern with aggregate demand and aggregate supply shocks that could result from an inappropriate conversion of savings and wages could not be faulted on principle, however imperfect the particular estimates of money demand and productivity gaps might in fact have been, the microeconomic view of a representative East German desiring to start unification with a larger bank account and a higher wage was fundamentally flawed, even if from a statistical point of view the conversion rate 1:1 was not so outrageously different from the difference in *average* purchasing power of the two marks. What was involved is an example of the classic fallacy of composition. If east German wages after monetary union exceeded productivity, other things (especially employment) would not remain equal. If east German savings were to be converted at 1:1, then somewhere in the banking system's balance sheets, assets would likewise have to be increased (i.e., either at the expense of debtors, in the first instance east German businesses, or the federal government).[14]

The eventual parameters of monetary union involved a conversion of private bank accounts at an average rate of 1.8 M/DM, business debt at 2 M/DM, with the difference offset by a new debt of the federal government, and a 1:1 conversion of current wages, pensions, and other contractual payments. The stiffer resistance to east German demands on the wealth account was due to a relatively strong west German Ministry of Finance, well aware of the long-run implication of this conversion for future government finances, rather than an overriding concern with a one-time upward blip in the German price level. Unfortunately there was no willingness in east Germany on the part of management to take a strong public stand on the issue of the conversion of wage rates, much less actively resist. West German unions have regarded the prospect of cheap east German labor with as much suspicion as the UAW regards free trade with Mexico and has pushed for rapid wage parity for the East. With several elections to come, there was also no political party willing to deny the unmistakable will of the east German electorate. Thus the 1:1 conversion of wage costs has turned out to be a significant, though neither the first nor last, step in a rush to wage parity.[15] Even now in the trough of a depression, wage-parity considerations appear to rank as high as employment considerations in east German public opinion. The aggregate-supply shock that has accompanied economic unification was tragically inevitable given the eastern demand for wage parity and the constraints of democratic politics.

What some hoped would begin the great capital race into east Germany, has turned out instead to be a steeplechase of marathon proportions. Compared to privatization, the conversion to the deutsche mark and the extension of the west German social safety net to break the fall of an economy carrying 16 million people were relatively straightforward logistical and administrative challenges successfully met by German organizational genius. Thus privatization in east Germany has involved all the practical and moral difficulties in reassigning property rights for an entire economy with two important complicating factors: a growing unemployment problem and a stock of legitimate property claims accumulated over more than one-half century of expropriations—Nazi, Soviet, and SED.

Besides abortion law, the resolution of claims for expropriated property has proved to be one of the thorniest questions posed in German unification. The general principle of restitution of property to original owners rather than payment of compensation was agreed upon about one month after the signing of the treaty on monetary, economic, and social union and two weeks before the treaty officially went into effect. The joint statement of the FRG and the

GDR regarding the settlement of unresolved property questions[16] was regarded as sufficiently important to be later included as an appendix to the unification treaty.[17] The resulting 2.5 million outstanding property claims have posed the largest single obstacle to the rapid privatization of the east German economy. In the first months of German unification, property claims could block privatization deals pending the final determination of ownership. The chaotic state of public-property records in East Germany made it extremely difficult to establish clear title to much east German property, even in the absence of a claim. Bank credit was impossible for a management buy-out team to obtain until clear title to the company's property acquired from the THA could be established.

As it became increasingly clear that a fundamental bottleneck for the flow of investment into east Germany was the pace of privatization, major course corrections were attempted in a flurry of legislation in the spring of 1991 and in the summer of 1992. Under the so-called Investment-Obstacle Law, the principle of restitution rather than payment of compensation was not abandoned, but a number of important exceptions were allowed. In particular, the THA received the authority to sell companies or land to bona fide investors even against the expressed wishes of owners with legitimate claims who have filed claims for restitution. The THA also obtained the same right to sign long-term leases with investors. The sales revenue would go to the legitimate owner as financial compensation. Original owners have the possibility of appealing a decision of the THA or the local governments in such cases, but such court appeals would *not* block investment from taking place. Another important change in the law was the suspension of Section 613a of the Civil Code (BGB) for east Germany through the end of 1992. That regulation protects employees from dismissal as a consequence of one company being taken over by another. For an investor hoping to restructure an east German company this was a significant handicap. The new regulations also expanded the possibilities of freeing investors from liabilities due to both known and unknown environmental hazards on acquired sites. Finally the so-called Splitting Law granted the THA much greater authority to break up east German companies into economic units that better correspond to west German companies.[18] The second revision of the property rights law passed in early summer 1992 has further chipped away at the priority of property restitution for the same purpose of facilitating the transfer of property to investors. Optimistically expressed, the spring 1991 and summer 1992 legislation indicate the learning capacity of German policymakers. On the other hand, it is by no means clear that all these new laws together will still be sufficient to undo the initial, misplaced priority of property restitution over compensatory payment.

Sources of East German Anxiety and Anger

Perhaps it is due to the peaceful nature of the political revolution that took place in East Germany that one is prone to overlook the fact that the process of economic unification involves an economic revolution as well. Every revolution has its winners and losers.[19] The former first secretaries of local party committees, most employees of the old Ministry for State Security, and professors of Marxism-Leninism can certainly be counted among the losers of the political and economic revolutions in east Germany. Short of a restoration of the SED to power, there is little that could ever make them happy again. At the same time, there are clearly identifiable winners in the revolution—medical doctors, plumbers, and theologians-turned-politicians just to name some obvious examples. However, the vast majority of the east German population has entered the process of economic integration with considerable uncertainty, at least with respect to the timing of the personal advantages and disadvantages to accrue. For some there is even uncertainty whether the personal advantages from economic integration will outweigh the personal disadvantages in the end. This fear is strongest among the working population over forty-five years of age, for whom the interval between the loss of their present jobs and the start of the retirement pensions could be filled with an alternating series of odd jobs and spells of unemployment. The fear is also strong among those employees whose accumulated system-specific (e.g., accounting and law) and industry-specific (e.g., electronics, textiles) human capital of experience and training has been almost completely devalued by the change in system and increase in competition.[20]

Neither the obvious winners nor losers pose a challenge to our understanding; what they saw *ex ante* is what they'll get *ex post*. The uncertain majority located between the clearly identifiable winners and losers from economic unification is the seat of east German anxiety. Had this profound anxiety remained the private concern of millions of east Germans, policymakers could afford to ignore it and wait for the historical sorting of winners from losers to occur during the course of economic integration. The problem should go away by itself, assuming the validity of the arguments for a dividend from integration.[21] However, political competition between the parties in the new states will focus on the median voter located somewhere in that anxious majority. The potential danger for the process of economic integration is that legitimate concerns about the social consequences of the economic transformation will find expression in demands for industrial policies and regulatory controls that will hamper the structural adjustments needed in the east German economy.

What was lost in the transformation from planned socialism to the social market economy was the nearly absolute security of economic status. Under the old economic system, the socialist state owned and controlled the vast bulk of physical capital that, together with the power to tax, provided the means to protect, indeed to guarantee individual economic status.[22] Economic security was reasonably complete. This expectation can be characterized as a social asset on household balance sheets, quite similar to the claim for protection that the feudal serf had on the lord of the manor. With the collapse of the socialist economic order, the east German population has been in effect released from an overpriced insurance policy. Continuing the insurance analogy, the east German population canceled its economic status insurance but is still waiting for the dividend to arrive in the mail.[23]

This is not to say that the east German population was left naked and defenseless to cope in a cold capitalist world. The social union of the Germanys had been introduced simultaneously with the monetary and economic union. Helmut Kohl took a further step by promising both East and West Germans that economic unification would be (in the jargon of welfare economics) a Pareto improvement. The exact words of Helmut Kohl in his speech during the Bundestag debate on the unification treaty express the distributive ethic of liberalism in the European sense.

> I can say to the German people in the GDR what Minister President de Maizière has emphasized as well: no one will be worse off than before—and many will be better off. For the German people in the Federal Republic: no one will have do with less because of German unification. The point is to put at the disposal of our countrymen and women in the GDR a portion of our economic growth over the coming years as help for self-help. I believe this moral obligation of national solidarity to be self evident.[24]

In effect Helmut Kohl promised a floor to *both* East and West Germans: no one will have a lower material living standard as a consequence of German unification. From this statement it is also clear that Kohl implicity assumed that west German economic growth would be sufficient to guarantee the floor promised to east Germany. It is an interesting exercise to calculate the minimum and maximum transfers from west to east Germany that would be consistent with Kohl's promise. The maximum transfer is assumed to be the entire increment of economic growth compared to the base year of 1989. The minimum transfer is calculated as the increment of growth in the west German economy above the long-run trend growth rate.[25] These calculations are presented in tables 3 and 4 in both absolute and per capita terms. Thus for Helmut Kohl to have kept his promise, the actual amount of transfers should fall in the range 51–109 billion DM in 1990 and 72–190 billion DM in 1991.

Two numbers help to put these figures in perspective. The gross national product of the new states in 1991 amounted to 193.1 billion DM, which indicates just how small the east German economy had shrunk compared to the west German economy. Table 5 reports public transfers, both gross and net, from west Germany to east Germany as calculated by the Council of Economic Experts in their annual report on the state of the German economy. The net public transfer of 113 billion DM that took place in 1991 is well within the range estimated in tables 3 and 4, falling about one-third of the distance between the low and the high estimates.

In table 4 the aggregate figures are converted into per capita terms for west and east Germany, respectively. Consumption in the new states in 1991 was 12,200 DM (which slightly exceeded nominal GNP per capita). From table 5 we can calculate that the net transfer from west to east was roughly 1,800 DM per capita with respect to west Germany and 7,000 DM per capita with respect to east Germany. Thus we see that transfers from west to east have been very substantial. It would appear that Helmut Kohl was right. There is a slight problem, however. Many, if not most, east Germans believe that they are being treated unfairly by their Landsleute in the West.

The inter-German dialogue over the past two years has revealed a fundamental clash in notions of distributive justice held by east and west Germans. Most west Germans rightly view the relatively low productivity and correspondingly low living standards in east Germany as not the fault of the old Federal Republic and that the higher living standard of west Germans was not achieved at the expense of east Germany. Hence west Germans view their own obligation as limited to getting the social market economy up and run-

TABLE 3.   West German Economic Growth Increments, 1990 and 1991
(all figures in constant 1991 DM)

	Difference between Actual GNP and 2.4% Annual Growth, Minimum	Difference between Actual GNP and 1989 GNP, Maximum
1990	51 billion	109 billion
1991	72 billion	190 billion

TABLE 4.   West German Economic Growth on per Capita Basis, 1990 and 1991
(all figures in constant 1991 DM)

	Per Capita from Old States		Per Capita to New States	
	Minimum	Maximum	Minimum	Maximum
1990	800	1,700	3,200	6,800
1991	1,100	3,000	4,500	11,800

ning in the East and to provide advances for social insurance and infrastructural investment.

The east German view is usually summed up in a play on words that translates as "overcoming division through sharing" (Die Teilung durch Teilen überwinden). The reasoning that leads to this view is roughly the

TABLE 5.   Public Transfers to East Germany in 1991 (in billion DM)

	Federal govern- ment	State and local gov- ernments, West Ger- many	German Unity Fund	European Commu- nity, European Recovery Program	Federal Labor Office	Total expendi- tures/ receipts
Unification-related expenditures						
Payments to state budgets in the new states	18	5	35	1	—	59
Transfer payments directly to the population	24	—	—	9	30	63
Other expenditures in the new states, technical and personnel	47	3	—	—	—	50
Gross payments to east Germany	89	8	35	10	30	172
Unification related receipts	—	4	3			7
Taxes and social insurance contributions from new states, narrowly defined	30	—	—	—	6	36
Other receipts from east Germany	3	—	—	—	1	4
Net payments to east Germany, broadly defined	56	8	31	7	23	125
Unification related receipts, broadly defined						
Increased tax receipts attributed to a 1 percent increase in real economic growth in the West	3	3	—	—	—	6
Savings of division- related expenses	4	—	—	—	—	4
Saving from division- related tax breaks	1	—	—	—	—	1
State government share of debt service of the fund	1	—	—	—	—	1
Net payments to east Germany, narrowly defined	47	5	31	7	23	113

Source: *Jahresgutachten 1991/92*, table 36, p. 136.

following: all Germans lost the Second World War, and centrally planned socialism in the GDR is an economic consequence of that war; having been locked behind a wall in an economic system they had not freely chosen, east Germans have borne a disproportionate share of the burden of that war; ergo, east Germans are now entitled to transfers from west Germany in a grand final act of postwar burden sharing.[26] The gap in living standards, the gap in labor earnings, the gap in pensions are viewed as evidence of continuing injustice.[27] Hence we observe a circle of mutual recrimination between Ossi and Wessi. Financial transfers that most west Germans believe are generous expressions of solidarity with their eastern cousins are viewed as tightfisted by east Germans. This reaction unsurprisingly invites a countercharge of ingratitude.

Much to the chagrin of the Communist leadership of the old GDR, the east German population has always measured its living standards against prosperity made in west Germany. The gap in living standards between the GDR and the rest of eastern Europe was hardly consolation for the east/west gap in life chances. This fundamental orientation has not been altered by the process of German economic integration. The fact that the conditions for the transformation of the east German economy to the social market economy of the expanded Federal Republic of Germany are much easier than in any of the other reforming economies of eastern Europe does not console those whose greatest fear is that when the winners are separated from the losers in German unification, they will be condemned to an old east German standard of living with no west Germany to flee to.

One recalls the bitterness felt by those who saw their life savings destroyed by hyperinflation in the twenties and had memories of the humiliation of the Versailles treaty. Uncertainty compounded by a sense of moral betrayal could be socially explosive now. But the root causes are the shock of the uncertainty of life in the market following the hyperprotectionism of the socialist economic order and the clash of an internalized socialist distributive ethic with the liberal ethic of the new order, *not* a fundamental failure in economic policy. One can be an optimist about the course of economic integration and still worry plenty about the politics of the present situation.

The Vital Signs of German Economic Integration

When an economist refers to the long run, it is *not* meant as an inevitable conclusion of history but always as prediction of future economic developments *conditional* on today's starting point and expected future developments. Historically speaking, Germany is still much closer to its division than its economic integration. Thus it is appropriate to close this optimistic case with an indication of the vital signs to monitor for continued optimism.

Monetary union alone could not bring about the rise in living standards needed to keep the east German population in east Germany. Only a massive inflow of capital and management from west to east will ultimately close the intra-German productivity gap that remains the root cause of the gap in living conditions between the old and new states of the FRG. Substantial private investment will only follow substantial privatization. Hence the privatization process–investment link is critical. The chapter closes with a few examples of unlikely but possible events that could put the optimistic scenario in jeopardy.

One can imagine a major court ruling that certain exceptions to the restitution principle for property expropriated under the GDR are inconsistent with the Basic Law of the FRG. The relative independence of the THA from direct political manipulation could change, especially as a consequence of electoral outcomes in 1994 or even in anticipation of that election year. By the end of 1993, THA should be moving into its final phase of privatization. If the endgame for the THA does not start by 1994, one could begin to doubt that it will soon get out of the restructuring business. Should the dissatisfaction in east Germany grow, one could imagine a major series of strikes or even civil disturbances that would succeed in obtaining the government's attention but only further inhibit private investment, not unlike the effect of a riot in an American city.

But rather than close with such pessimistic thoughts, it is better to recall the quotation with which this chapter began. The economic reconstruction of the new states is a difficult task that will necessarily take time. Sometimes optimism demands patience.

NOTES

1. The bottom line perceived at the time was typically expressed as "Lieber eine Ende mit Schrecken als ein Schrecken ohne Ende," i.e., a horrible ending beats a neverending horror.

2. Indeed, one could go farther and simply deny that most east and west Germans, and not just those who strongly supported immediate economic unification, had any idea what was actually involved in economic integration, in particular that far more than Stasi jobs would disappear. While it is the ultimate sign of good fortune to be right for the wrong reasons, nonetheless it should shake the confidence of those whose beliefs have completely flipped from euphoric optimism to deepest pessimism. Perhaps most Germans still don't quite understand. In any event one hears *no* voices in the new states calling for the restoration of the old order, in contrast to the CIS, where voices for reaction are still loud enough to be heard.

3. For more information on the last decade of the GDR economy see Irwin L. Collier, Jr., "The GDR Five-Year Plan 1986–1990," *Comparative Economic Studies*

29 (1987): 39–53; "Cutting Costs and Macroeconomic Adjustment: The GDR in the 1980's," in *Pressures for Reform in the East European Economies,* vol. 2, U.S. Congress, Joint Economic Committee (Washington, D.C.: U.S. Government Printing Office, 1989), 256–90; and "GDR Economic Policy during the Honecker Era," *Eastern European Economics* 29 (1990): 5–29.

4. In a Cobb-Douglas model of production with a capital elasticity of 1/4 and a labor elasticity of 3/4, a 26 percent increase in labor input, holding capital input constant, is equivalent to a 100 percent increase in capital input, holding labor input constant. A 26 percent increase in effective labor input due to increased effort on the job does not seem an impossibility given the difference in work incentives between the two economic systems.

5. Examining coefficients of domestic cost of DM exports, disaggregated by Kombinat and for 183 individual enterprises that sold over 10 million DM worth of goods in Western markets, Akerlof et al. concluded that only 8.2 percent of east German firms had been viable in the sense that short-run variable costs could be covered by sales revenue at the observed wages in east Germany. See George A. Akerlof, Andrew K. Rose, Janet L. Yellen, and Helga Hessenius, "East Germany in from the Cold: The Economic Aftermath of Currency Union," *Brookings Papers on Economic Activity* 1 (1991): 1–87.

6. Making matters worse, the collapse of the CMEA trading arrangements resulted in another adverse demand shock.

7. According to a study by the DIW that examined real household income between May 1990 and May 1991, on a per capita basis real household income increased by 12 percent (including those households that either moved to the West or commute to jobs in the West). The increase was 9.7 percent for all households that remained in the new states and did not commute to a western job. 60 percent of all private households were estimated to have experienced an increase in real income. For a household in which the principal earner was unemployed household real income was estimated to have fallen only 1.5 percent. For the worst case, in which both husband and wife were unemployed, real household income dropped an average of 15 percent (*Handelsblatt,* 23 January 1992).

8. Another 240,000 were involved in part-time retraining programs.

9. With the expiration of certain special provisions for short-time work in the unification treaty at the end of December 1991, short-time workers dropped to 520,000 in January 1992. The next big wave of dismissals of short-time workers occurred in July 1992.

10. Examples of major career changes would include a research physicist in Robotron computers transferred into sales, a bureaucrat from the state planning commission in the Treuhandanstalt division for public relations, an economist from the Central Institute for Economics of the Academy of Sciences teaching mathematics for a private management retraining school in east Berlin.

11. *Handelsblatt* 6 January 1992.

12. The two striking examples of that potential to influence policy (not necessarily for the better), the decision of conversion of wages and salaries at 1:1 and the decision to move the Hauptstadt of the Federal Republic to Berlin, were decisively influenced

by the extremely homogenous and strongly felt views on these issues held by east Germans.

13. For an introduction to the technical literature on purchasing power in socialist economies, see Irwin L. Collier, Jr., and Manouchehr Mokhtari, "Comparisons of Consumer Market Disequilibria in Hungary, Poland, Romania, Yugoslavia and the German Democratic Republic," in *East Germany in Comparative Perspective* ed. David Childs, Thomas A. Baylis and Marilyn Rueschemeyer (London: Routledge, 1989), 137–62.

14. This is less of a distinction given the not unusual Treuhand practice of *privatizing* an east German enterprise while *nationalizing* some or all of its debt to the banking system.

15. In anticipation of unification, significant wage and salary increases had been granted throughout the east German economy.

16. The statement also affirmed the irrevocability of the expropriations that occurred under Soviet occupational authority (1945–49).

17. In his book assembled from interviews during his recovery from a failed assasination attempt, then Interior Minister Schäuble writes that he considered a major contribution of his was to keep the word *Entschädigung* (indemnify) out of the statement, and include instead *Ausgleichsleistungen* (compensation payments). The distinct impression one gets from reading Schäuble's book is that ultimately fiscal considerations played at least as great a role in the west German positions as did the formal constitutional guarantee of property. See Wolfgang Schäuble, *Der Vertrag* (Stuttgart: Deutsche, 1991), 251–64.

18. This package of laws was heavily commented upon in the financial press, for example the three-part article published successively April 8, 9, and 10 in *Handelsblatt* written by one of its principal authors in the Ministry of Justice, Herbert Biener.

19. The famous promise by Helmut Kohl that there would be no losers is discussed below.

20. There is most likely a residual "signaling" value. Employers might presume someone with a doctorate in chemistry would be easier to retrain than an assembly-line worker.

21. Before the next scheduled parliamentary elections at the end of 1994, there is much time for more sorting to take place. Anxiety will be lower, though the bitterness of those who find themselves with Wessi tastes on an Ossi budget will be quite intense and concentrated.

22. With the important exception of citizens who were perceived as threats to state security through their political dissent or desire to emigrate. This claim is also subject to the reservation that east German consumption levels at the end of the 1980s were not sustainable.

23. For a paper that takes the insurance analogy quite literally, see Wolfram Schrettl, "Transition with Insurance: German Unification Reconsidered," *Oxford Review of Economic Policy* 8 (1992): 144–55.

24. Federal Chancellor Helmut Kohl, speech in the Bundestag, 21 June 1990, *Texte zur Deutschlandpolitik,* Reihe III/Band 8a-1990, 396.

25. Real GNP growth averaged 2.4 percent annually for the previous decade.

26. For example, from an interview between deputy chair Wolfgang Thierse (SPD) from east Germany and editors from the west German weekly magazine *Der Spiegel*, 25 February 1991, 27–30:

The fundamental expectation in general was the following: our rich brothers and sisters in the West are not going to leave us hanging; after all they are Germans just like us; we and they lost the war together.

27. In the German television network ZDF monthly poll (Politbarometer) for January 1991 (sample of 1,155 east Germans), 83 percent of those polled characterized the difference in income levels between east and west as "extremely unfair." 82 percent felt that the federal government had done too little to equalize living conditions in the two parts of Germany (*Handelsblatt,* 29 January 1991).

PART 4

Women, Politics, and Society

One of the greatest successes of forty years of state socialism in the former German Democratic Republic was the protection of women in the economy. The network of support for and encouragement of women's participation in the economy was truly impressive, particularly in light of the treatment of women in the West. As Hanna Schissler notes in the first contribution, it is surprising that the opportunities for women opened by the Second World War were closed so swiftly in the Federal Republic. The explanation rests in the aggressiveness with which West German parties and churches reasserted their dominance in the debate over sex roles, and in the lack of effective organization on the part of women exhausted by the war and its aftermath. Schissler demonstrates the economic and social consequences of this state of affairs: women were relegated to the "Pink Ghetto" after the war, where they were compensated for their work at a fraction of the rate of men. And as economic pressures forced more and more women into the work force, social pressures on women grew. Schissler notes that these cross-pressures on women, to be both homemakers and wage earners, are common in industrial societies. Andrei S. Markovits explores the factors leading to the rise of the new women's movement in West Germany, including the radicalization of the student movement during the 1960s and 1970s, and the controversies over West German abortion law. The inclusion of more and more women into the movement, however, seems to have come at the cost of its coherence.

The next two essays, by Christiane Lemke and Jeremiah A. Riemer, examine the implications of German unification for women's politics in unified Germany. In the first essay, Lemke compares the development of women's movements in both the former GDR and the FRG. Whereas the women's movement in the West was highly developed if somewhat fragmented, the strictures of state socialism prevented the growth of an independent women's movement in the East until very late in the game. Significant portions of the western women's movement were shaken by the collapse of socialism in Eastern Europe and the Soviet Union, whereas the eastern movement was instrumental in rejecting "patriarchal socialism." Lemke adds that differences in life experiences have led to misunderstandings between women in the East and the West, leaving Lemke to conclude that the future of the women's movement in unified Germany is uncertain. Riemer examines the issue of German abortion law. At unification, one of the key issues dividing the two Germanys was abortion law. In the East, abortion was available on demand. In the West, abortion was limited by the state and the churches. Initially, it seemed that abortion law might be one of the few areas where east German experience would prevail over west German preferences, particularly as most Germans, east and west, support abortion on demand. Yet as Riemer argues, the center-right coalition that dominated unification and won the first postunification election in December 1990 seems bent upon imposing its wishes on the East as well as the West. The abortion debate may well be disappearing into the maw of technical debate and policy-making in the German Bundestag.

Women in West Germany from 1945 to the Present

Hanna Schissler

In 1945, not only had Germany brought death and destruction to Europe and the world, but to itself as well: more than three million men had been killed or were prisoners of war. Immediately after the war, the German population consisted of 7.3 million more women than men. The ratio of women to men in the population between twenty and forty years old was in particular to women's detriment.[1] Young women had lost their husbands or fiancés; women who wanted to get married and have families could no longer find suitable husbands. (Interestingly enough, this uneven relation has since been labeled an "abundance of women"—as if women were responsible for the state of affairs—instead of a "lack of men," which would be a more accurate description of the immediate impact of the war.)[2] In 1950 nearly *one-third* of the 15 million households were headed by single women: war widows, single mothers, and divorced women.[3]

One of the most remarkable and, from a feminist point of view, distressing aspects of West German history is how quickly after the collapse of Germany at the end of the Second World War traditional gender relations were restored, despite the demographic discrepancies. This chapter explores the ways in which women were returned to their subservient role. Since unification has been achieved along primarily west German lines, the patterns established after 1945 in the West are particularly relevant to understanding gender politics in postunification Germany.

Women's Roles after the Second World War

To understand gender politics in the postwar period and determine which factors were decisive in rebuilding West German society, we must consider, first, factors specific to German history and, second, factors resulting from the immediate postwar situation and the emerging cold war.

Historical Dimensions

Germany's unconditional surrender in 1945 and the end of the Nazi regime offered the chance for a new beginning in gender politics. In dealing with women and gender relations in Germany it is important to keep in mind the ambivalent legacies of the Nazi regime and of the Second World War: women who were supposed to be housewives and mothers, according to the official Nazi ideology, were toward the end of the war increasingly recruited into the labor force.[4] As an American intelligence report stated in 1947, it was Hitler, after all, who "gave women an importance, even though subject to Nazi ideology, which they had not enjoyed heretofore in German life."[5] It was women who removed the rubble of the destroyed cities and with all their skills tried to bring their families through the hardships of hunger and, frequently, homelessness. In 1945 it looked as if Germany's future rested on the shoulders of its women: "The crux of the problem in Germany is that as women go, the country goes," wrote the American columnist Anne O'Hare McCormick in 1948 in the *New York Times*.[6] As in the First World War, women's position was strengthened through the war. Yet, only for a very short time did it look as if women had gained some ground.[7] As Barbara Willenbacher has argued, their position was strengthened in their traditional spheres, namely as caretakers of the family and as homemakers, since families' survival rested mainly on women's capacity to obtain food, to repair clothing, to sew new clothes from old pieces.[8]

Not only was the survival of their families largely dependent on women's skills and energy, but the western parts of Germany were flooded with refugees from the East (12 million by 1950), and there was a severe shortage of housing. Women also—particularly in the East—had to endure rape and other forms of violence, a fate many tried to escape through suicide. Women had to face the economic, political, and moral consequences of the lost war and the atrocities of the Nazi regime. Men who came back from the war or prison camps frequently were broken. Men had difficulties reintegrating into family life: they were not used to the independence women had gained during their absence. Patterns of authority in families, especially over teenage children, were not easily reconstituted, partly because children would no longer accept their fathers' authority or in many cases because men's worldview was shaken, triggering doubts about the male role. Divorces reached an all time high in 1948.[9]

In 1942 the Office of Strategic Services had already identified women as a group particularly hurt by the Nazis, like Jews, foreign workers, and decisive Catholics or Protestants and had recommended that after the war special attention be paid to women's position in society.[10] Americans trying to understand why Germans had followed Adolf Hitler in such great masses emphasized the "German authoritarian tradition." This assumption carried over to gender as well as family relations.[11] In 1948 the American Occupation Forces founded a Women's Affairs Section in order to help women's groups to organize and articulate themselves politically, to find their place in a new democratic society, and to overcome the legacy of national socialism. Considering the vagueness of its conceptions about women's place in society, assumptions about German women's submissiveness, a very small budget, and vague political guidelines, we should judge with skepticism the effectiveness of the enterprise of the Women's Affairs Section. The section was less creative than reactive—especially to the Soviets' thorough political approach in women's policies—in redefining women's social and political role in a Western society that was about to be rebuilt from scratch, in theory offering unique opportunities for social engineering.[12]

It was widely felt that the hardships suffered by women during the war and the postwar period would and should have political consequences and entitle women to the same rights as men in the rebuilding of the defeated country. But when the Parliamentary Council convened to deliberate a new constitution for the new Federal Republic in 1949, it was not easy to convince members that mere political rights, as codified in the Weimar Constitution, would not suffice and that women should be granted full social and civic equality with men. Mainly due to the endeavors of Elisabeth Selbert, a member of the SPD, including a massive mobilization of women's public opinion, the West German Basic Law finally established that "Men and Women are equal."[13]

This provision meant that the Civil Code had to accommodate the requirements of gender equality, but political leaders were not in a hurry to oblige. Not until 1953 were all laws that discriminated against women suspended. It was not at all clear what precisely was meant by equality between men and women. Some, in particular the churches, believed it meant partnership under men's authority and legal hegemony, a "separate but equal" formula. Others, primarily the Social Democrats, thought it meant legal equality between men and women but a continuance of women's ascribed positions as caretakers of the family. The latter was the dominant position and gained the broadest political and social support. The churches and the Social Democrats, then, took opposite positions in shaping gender and family policies.[14]

In restructuring West German society virtually no one could imagine full social and economic equality between men and women. There were two major barriers in realizing women's equality that emerged from immediate experience with the Nazis and from the threat of Communism. First was the question of how much the state should interfere in society. After the experiences of the Nazi period, this was a particularly sensitive issue, underlined in its importance by the developments in the Soviet zone of occupation. In the West, the relationship of men and women, as well as women's place in society, was perceived as private and thus beyond the state's control. This conviction worked against women in the labor market in crucial ways. There was an inherent tension between the principle of gender equality and the principle of freedom of contract, which was guaranteed by the Basic Law to both employers and workers and which was one of the pillars of stability and social peace in West Germany.[15] The legal and the political systems strengthened the principle of freedom of contract and intervened only if the impact of the freedom of contract was too obviously damaging to women, for example when they were pregnant.[16] Second, the Basic Law, while proclaiming gender equality, also put the family under its special protection. Therefore, it created tension between women as independent human beings and women as those traditionally responsible for the well-being of their families.

It was widely agreed that the state should define general norms but should intervene as little as possible in the freedom of contract, in the economy, and in family arrangements. The state thus abstained from implementing women's legal equality socially, economically, and politically, which would have required a whole range of legal as well as political actions. It would have required insight into the problems of women's lives and the nature of the sexual division of labor in late industrial societies—an insight that in the fifties and sixties was hardly developed in West Germany (or in any other industrially developed Western country). Equality would have required active state intervention, which in the postwar period no one in West Germany was willing to exert or accept.

The Cold War and the Postwar Situation

The ways in which women's lives in East Germany were reshaped functioned as a powerful deterrent to restructuring in West Germany from the late forties up to the sixties. Communist convictions and the regime's desperate need for laborers assigned women in the East a place very different from their place in the West. The differences became obvious in the immediate postwar period. In 1948, the *New York Times* stated:

> Nobody but the Russians seem to give due weight to this pregnant fact [the heavy loss of male lives during the war]. Except in the Soviet Zone the Occupying Powers apparently assume the traditional attitude of German men toward women. . . . The more intelligent among the women, worried by their responsibility in a country where the male minority is

in general too old or too young to shoulder even half of the burden, feel ignored and undervalued by the Western Powers as well as by the German administration.[17]

In the Soviet zone of occupation women were granted full legal equality with men, and they were fully integrated into the labor force, a step observed with suspicion in the West and condescendingly labeled "forced emancipation." The beginning of the cold war thus had an impact on how women's policies were defined, making it all too easy to abstain from implementing gender equality by pointing to the "forced emancipation" of women in the East. Claims for equality by women could be easily dismissed, and traditional female roles proclaimed as what women were really striving for in a free society: the right to stay home and take care of husband and children.[18]

Conservative politicians and churches thus encouraged the return to a supposed state of normalcy. In the early fifties the sociologist Helmut Schelsky praised the family as the last haven of stability in a world in which the individual was severely uprooted.[19] The CDU, the governing party in the fifties and sixties, hesitated before the notion of a gender equality that would, as leading members of the CDU perceived it, be detrimental to mothers and children and thus endanger family life.[20] Through rhetoric as well as political measures, such as campaigns against two wage earners, laws to regulate women's work, and a system of family allowances (Kindergeldgesetz), as well as firm establishment of the male family wage, politicians and major social forces tried to keep women at home.[21] As the historian Robert Moeller has pointed out, the ruling Christian Democrats wanted to "protect" women and the family by enabling women to stay at home as mothers and house-wives, and the Social Democrats and the unions wanted to make sure the family was adequately supported by increasing male wages and by fighting for the male family wage. But virtually no one challenged basic assumptions about this conception of the sexual division of labor and women's place in society.[22] It was not at all unusual for a woman to be dismissed as soon as she got married. And such dismissals happened not only in factories, but were common practice also in the civil service. The revised Civil Service Law of 1950 went so far as to legalize this practice: "A female civil servant can be dismissed if she marries."[23] As Moeller points out, policies in the forties and fifties that "ostensibly protected the family were in fact policies that defined the social and political status of women" in society.[24]

At the same time, a long-standing, fundamental difference divided the middle-class portion of the women's movement, which emphasized separate but "equal in value" spheres for men and women, from the socialist women's movement, which stressed equality in all realms of society, especially in the labor force and in politics. The latter notion could be put into effect only by forceful political and economic regulation. The debate in West Germany was decided in favor of the former position, in part as a reaction to developments in the East.[25] Thus the legal status of women was adjusted, while at the same time politicians tried to preserve as many traditional elements in the social and economic positions of women as possible. Nobody at the time had a clear notion of what women's equality meant. The relatively tame Deutsche Frauenring, a newly founded umbrella organization including the Association of German Housewives and German female academics, was not very success-ful in fighting for women's rights.[26] The idea prevailed that there should be "true partnership between men and women," not mechanical equality, and that women, if they were active in the public sphere, should adhere to some form of "motherly policy."[27] Even a socialist woman like Käte Strobel, who became Minister for Family Affairs and Health in the 1970s, elaborated on women's special mission and motherly qualities:

> In particular, it is women with socialist convictions who demand gender equality in all fields, which does not require a physically-conditioned reserve or forbearance of women [eine körperlich bedingte Zurückhaltung und Schonung der Frau]. . . . Female particularity, which is founded in our bodily and in our psychological constitution, does not need to suffer from this. In fact, it should not suffer; neither should our tasks, which we have to fulfill as housewives and, in particular, as mothers. On the contrary, it is this necessary appreciation of women's original tasks that constitutes at the same time a demand for equality.[28]

It was not until 1957 that family law was amended by the Act on Equal Rights for Men and Women (Gleichberechtigungsgesetz). Men's legal pre-ponderance in most issues of marriage was abolished.[29] Women had the right in principle to engage in paid work (previously they had had to ask for their husband's permission). The husband's right of disposal over the wife's prop-erty (the legacy of the Civil Code of 1900) was also abolished. But Articles 1356 and 1360 of the Civil Code stated that women's contribution to the support of their families consisted mainly of doing the housework, and that women were only allowed to go out to work if this decision did not interfere with their duties as mothers and wives. The Act on Equal Rights for Men and Women of 1957 legalized what came to be called the "housewife mar-riage."[30] It took until 1977 for a new family law under the Social Democratic-Liberal coalition to free arrangements between husband and wife about who should be doing what within the family economy (the partnership mar-riage).[31]

Women's Responses: The Pink Ghetto and Beyond

Although women's work was discouraged, discriminated against, undervalued (through unequal pay and, later, so-called light wages), and regulated with questionable measures,[32] and although the return to domesticity was officially praised by churches and politicians, women were not kept from going out to work. The massive downward mobility of the middle classes in the forties (about half of all teachers were dismissed in the process of denazification) was in part alleviated by women seeking employment.[33] Economic need at first, then rising expectations and a favorable economic climate during the "economic miracle" in the 1950s and 1960s, encouraged many women to continue to work after they married and had children. Between 1950 and 1975 the rate of female employment increased from 47.4 percent to 54.0 percent.[34] Even more striking is the change in the internal structure of the female labor force. First, the share of *married* women in the labor force rose constantly from 25 percent in 1950 to 42 percent in 1982.[35] Interestingly, men's employment decreased in the same period, falling from 63.2 percent to 59.1 percent.[36] Nearly 90 percent of women married to an industrial worker were in gainful employment outside the home. This clearly shows the class character of the debate on women's work. In the 1950s overall wages were very low. Only a third of the families had incomes higher than 600 marks, a fourth of the families had an income between 250 and 400 marks, and 11 percent made less than 250 marks. And since female wages were especially low—in the fifties female industrial wages were 45.7 percent lower and female white-collar wages were 43.7 percent lower than respective male wages—families headed by women were especially badly off.[37] The second major change that occurred was a shift in the sectors in which women were employed. Between 1950 and 1985 the percentage of women working in agriculture declined from 34 percent to 7 percent, and the percentage in the service sector (industries and professions) rose from 12 percent to 32 percent, while the percentage in manufacturing industries remained stable at 25 percent.[38]

In the 1950s and 1960s, it was hard for married women to pursue gainful employment. This contributed to women's feelings of failing their families as well as their jobs (if they managed to combine both). Yet living according to the proclaimed gender stereotype—as mothers and homemakers—triggered feelings of uselessness (the so-called housewife syndrome).[39] All these circumstances show how little the clause of the Basic Law ("Men and Women are equal") meant in social reality, and how easy it was to hold norms that conflicted with women's claims for equal rights, such as freedom of contract between employers and employees and family norms. Women were caught between two difficult alternatives. If they chose to go out to work they were accused of neglecting their families and blamed for all kinds of societal ills. If they chose to stay home, women seemed to be supporting existing gender roles. Frequently the decision to depend on the male breadwinner revealed its consequences late in life, when marriages ended in divorce, often after as many as twenty-five years. Women who had chosen to be housewives then realized what a dependent life really meant, financially as well as emotionally. Not only did they themselves feel undervalued as well as underemployed within the marriage, not only did they risk serious injury in case of divorce, but women were increasingly expected to find at least part-time employment, especially if the children were no longer young.[40] Gender norms were neither consistent nor livable for women, and they caused severe friction in women's (and thus also in men's) lives.

In the 1950s and 1960s, traditional social norms on gender were in mounting discord with the social reality of women's work. What was supposed to be normal was in more than one way questionable. Hundreds of thousands of women had to live their lives without a male breadwinner. Single women were marginalized in an atmosphere where social stability was equated with the nuclear family. Single women, whose condition was directly caused by the war—either they had lost their husbands or fiancés during the war or they could not marry because potential husbands were no longer available—had to struggle hard for social recognition and to make ends meet. They felt left out. They were the stepchildren of the economic miracle.[41] Against all odds, women increasingly, in fact, went out to seek gainful employment.[42] They did so quietly, and if they had small children to take care of, they did so mostly as supplementary breadwinners. The stability of traditional gender relations underwent a silent erosion, a process that was not acknowledged until the 1970s.

Women were trapped in every regard. Economic necessity or the wish to do better urged them to work outside the home, yet family and gender ideologies made it hard for them. Children who had mothers working outside the home were targets of the nation's pity as neglected Schlüsselkinder and thus constantly played on womens' conscience. Pediatricians pointed at the detrimental effects, especially on small children, if their mothers went to work. The journal *Der Kinderarzt* attached labels such as "maternal deprivation," "disturbed families," "irresponsible child neglect" to the effect of working mothers.[43] It was a no-win situation for women. They faced severe stress, either in the form of double burdens or in the form of dependence upon a working husband. Many suffered from depression. The feelings of inadequacy never left women in the fifties and sixties, whatever model they chose or were pushed to choose. Only in the last twenty years have women found some reprieve, when the new women's movement found a language for women's concerns and the awareness of gender inequality increased.

Thus a multiplicity of female life courses emerged in West Germany. There were women who obliged and lived according to traditional gender ideology and stayed at home to become homemakers. There were women who chose the typical three-phase model: working before marriage and until the first child is born, staying at home until the children are older, and reentering the work force at a low level or on a part-time basis. There were of course women with full-time jobs who faced job discrimination, including low wages and lack of promotion. Additionally, there were single women who worked because they did not have the chance to get married, and single women (mostly divorced, but also widowed or never married) with dependent children, who worked to make ends meet. Finally, there were women who chose not to have children and who pursued careers. Each of these choices had its price, a price working men did not have to pay.

The multiplicity of female life patterns in West Germany was decisively different from female life patterns in the GDR, where women reached the highest degree of employment. In the GDR, employment was an essential part of every woman's life, whether she was married or single, with or without children.[44] The duty to work in the GDR did not relieve women from their burden of housework, but it certainly relieved them from constant doubts about whether going to work was the right thing to do. Female employment was a matter of fact in the former GDR and did not need special legitimizing efforts as in West Germany. So, with German unification, considerable friction in women's self image can be observed alongside the economic hardship that affects women in particular.

How do the changes in women's employment in West Germany fit into the gender ideology and the self perception of women and men in the 1950s and 1960s? How does the continued expansion of women's, and especially married women's, labor coincide with what at the time was again labeled as the "natural *destination* of woman"? The notion of female work as only *supplementary* to the family income enabled a constant expansion of female work outside the home, without endangering the stability of traditional role models and, in fact, without questioning the sexual division of labor.[45] This also explains how major changes could take place without being noticed as structural changes. It also explains why major changes in the social organization of work and new employment patterns could be perceived and discussed as a "woman's dilemma"[46] and the notorious "woman's question," and how some fundamental social changes that were under way could be ignored until the seventies, when they entered the public debate.[47]

Gender and Industrial Society in Germany

According to the sociologist Helge Pross, women in west Germany have legally gained equal rights in practically all domains since the late 1970s,[48] but this legal equality does not yet mean equal chances.[49] The labor market in west Germany (as elsewhere) continues to be sex segregated. Women are concentrated in the "pink ghetto," where they earn less than men.[50] Women today are still more likely than men to interrupt their work outside the home to care for small children. But between the early 1950s and today, the length of time women withdraw from the labor market in order to tend small children has decreased, on average from fifteen to eight years. The west German social structure deters mothers' work outside the home: day-care centers are missing, schools end at midday, and women still are expected to organize the necessities of the family. One or more breaks in her working career are still a common experience for a woman in west Germany.[51] Part-time jobs are highly favored among women who at the same time have to take care of their families. If women drop out because of their familial duties, it is difficult to return to and compete successfully in the job market. Usually women have to accept lower positions than they had previously held, if indeed they manage to return to the labor force at all.

The centers of power continue to be in men's hands, be it in economics, politics, or educational institutions. Only a few women make it to the top, and successful careers are rarely made in part-time jobs. The social system is strong enough to keep women in "their place," the low end of income levels and fluctuating between home and labor market. In times of economic recession, when women compete directly with men, women are still the ones who are worse off. They are more often affected by unemployment than men—not the least because many employers think that women do not need to work or perceive women as a higher employment risk. Although public services, the service sector in general, indeed the entire economy can no longer exist without the female labor force, male labor continues to be more easily marketable.[52]

Today, combining work and family is more often taken for granted, at least that combination is what more and more women, especially young women, aim at. (Men also do not prefer the pure housewife marriage any longer, though many of them still think women should stay at home for a few years when small children have to be cared for. And as much as they might favor women's work, they are not too happy if women compete with men directly.)[53] A woman's choice to combine work and family still is not easy, but it is less loaded with guilt than in the fifties and sixties. The rising life expectancy of women and technical improvements that reduce household work together mean that household tasks no longer fill out women's whole lives. Although women continue to carry the double burden, the solution of earlier times, dropping out of the labor force as soon as a family is founded, is no longer an acceptable alternative for women in west Germany, as the increase of married women between thirty and fifty in the labor force makes clear.

The equal rights clause of the Basic Law was an important accomplishment—an accomplishment for which women in the United States are still striving—but in west Germany it did not and does not reflect social reality. The political will to deal with gender inequality has increased markedly, partly because the ambivalences in women's lives reached intolerable proportions, partly because a look at other European countries shamed and embarrassed the Federal Republic.[54] Developed industrial societies can afford to deal with issues beyond mere economic survival and can address questions of life quality, gender relations, and injustice. On the other hand, social movements like the women's and the ecological movements point out the limits and fundamental problems of developed industrial societies. More awareness of gender inequality, however, does not automatically lead to improvements in women's situation. Its immediate impact is to make the inequality between men and women more painful, thus arousing all kinds of reactions of discontent, insecurity, resentment on all sides, and often outright hostility. Structural problems of society are painfully felt in women's and men's private lives and dealt with in people's personal relations, where the dynamic of what tears people apart is rarely understood, instead of in the social, economic, and political field.[55] According to Ulrich Beck, the situation in west Germany can be characterized by a raised awareness of gender injustice, paralleled by the unchanged situation of women, especially on the labor market and in their family obligations. This situation mocks the gains women have achieved in education, where they have become virtually equal with men.[56]

In public debates it is meanwhile acknowledged that combining children and families with work is an unresolved structural problem of society, although it frequently still is addressed as the "woman question." Increased public awareness of gender inequality certainly is a direct outcome of the new women's movement, and it is partly due to the impact the Greens had on formulating political issues in the last ten years. The Greens forced the gender question onto the political agenda and triggered activities in the other political parties (the quota regulation in the SPD, the "partnership between men and women" party congress of the CDU, the founding of a women's ministry and equality offices). For several years political activities to improve the situation of women have been under way in all political parties and hotly debated among women politicians.

Since unification, a new challenge has arisen. The ideological split of the cold war that divided Germany also had a lasting impact on different paths in women's place in society, east and west. It is widely acknowledged that women will be the main losers of unification, since west Germany does not know a "right to work," and no market economy has endowed women with as many protections as did the former GDR.[57] The adaptation of the GDR to the market will follow the multiplicity of west German models, which means a painful forcing of women in the former GDR into the patterns of west Germany. Since unification, one of the burning questions is how will women in the east adjust to a situation in many ways much harder than the patriarchalism of state socialism, which after all guaranteed women the right to work, income, job security, legal abortions, and day-care facilities.[58]

The situation of women in Germany has been contradictory over the last forty years. Not only did the division of Germany mark decisively different paths of development for women in East and West Germany, but in West Germany the many ambivalences and contradictions were not easily understood. Although the Second World War seemed to question men's prerogatives, the restoration of traditional sex roles in the 1950s in West Germany took place without overwhelming protest from the affected women, who were exhausted and longed for what most of them perceived as a return to normality—an interesting case of "false consciousness." In the early 1950s, the longing for peace and economic security prevented further demands and major protest from women, who with few exceptions all too willingly accepted their roles as housewives and at best supplementary wage earners.[59] Maurice Godelier has stated in his book *La Production des Grands Hommes:* "Men's greatest strength lies not in the exercise of violence but in women's consent to their domination; and this consent can only exist if both sexes share the same conceptions, which here legitimize male domination."[60] Godelier could well have had in mind the reinstitutionalization of traditional gender roles in West Germany in the 1950s.

The gender division of labor is fundamental to industrial societies. Since industrialization, men have been forced to work outside the house. Women have been assigned to the family work inside the house without pay, *and* they have been forced to work outside the house, particularly if they belonged to the working class. The bourgeois ideal of gender division of labor has never functioned, nor has it ever been consistently applied, although it has for much of the nineteenth as well as the twentieth century saturated women's as well as men's minds. As Jerry Z. Muller stated (with a hint towards the 1992 presidential elections in the United States):

> The ideal of the two-parent family—grounded in heterosexuality, codified into law, based on fidelity, with a partial but essential division of labor between men and women and geared toward the raising of

children—came into existence around 1950 and disappeared around 1965, and is now insisted upon by fanatics intent upon imposing their arbitrary values on a diverse nation.[61]

Women in West Germany and elsewhere are in a difficult situation. They are neither fully integrated into the labor force, nor are they really protected by the system they were and are assigned to, the family. One of the fascinating questions of present society is whether this inherent conflict, which is so very clearly seen in the question of gender inequality, can be solved politically, and if so in which ways.

The status of an adult in our society is defined by work—work outside the house, paid labor. Work in our society has its special rules. It presupposes the readily available individual and tends to singularize and individualize people. Consequently, a society of highly mobile individuals would best meet the requirements of modern economies. The reproduction of humankind is solved in another subsystem of society, the family, which follows different rules. The ways in which work and family are constructed lie in permanent and inherent conflict with one another. This conflict can be *eased* by political measures, but as far as I can see it has nowhere yet been *solved*. The ones who are most affected by this socially constructed conflict are women. Because of the ways in which the reproduction of humankind has historically been shaped, women are subjected to the rules of both subsystems: work and family at the same time, while men clearly are expected to follow the rules of work outside the house. That is why looking at women and their struggle to reconcile work and family, to participate fully in public life, to obtain an equal share in the chances, as well as sharing the costs of modern life, offers such fascinating insights into the functioning of society.

Conclusion

Despite the liberalizing forces unleashed by the Second World War, relationships between men and women in West Germany in the 1950s returned to a rather conventional (although somewhat modernized) model: men working outside the home and women being responsible for the house and the children. But this model was slowly undermined by the growing participation of women, especially married women, in the labor force, and by an erosion of patriarchal positions within the families. Gender relations have undergone major changes in the last forty years, with the position of women changing most dramatically and consequently affecting men's position as well. As in all western industrial societies, forms of living in Germany have diversified. The obligatory strength of marriage has declined. Fewer people marry, and the ones who do marry tend to have fewer children (the tendency is clearly toward the one-child family). Single parent families are on the increase. This puts additional stress on women's lives, since women in most cases are the ones who carry the real double burden of raising children and working outside the house. Arrangements between men and women have become more complex; choices have increased dramatically, for women as well as for men. At times people try to solve the problems that the complexities of modern life and the closure of the labor market pose for women by strengthening traditional behavior and traditional role models. In times of rising divorce rates, the housewife marriage, though it continues to be rewarded by the German tax system (Ehegattensplitting), no longer provides women with economic security. For the time being, women face the difficult fact that traditional marriage no longer guarantees security. But neither are they able to lead a fully independent life because the tightening labor market pushes them into menial jobs. Additionally, society has not paid sufficient attention to the contradictory demands on women's lives, has not provided models of reconciling work and family for both women and men. The consequence is that women experience the dangers of both realms, family and work, that historically have been so poorly balanced in modern industrial society. Women are the ones who at present are falling through the net of an individualized life-style.[62]

Much has been done in recent years, and much remains to be done in the question of equal chances for men and women. Gender inequality is frequently treated as a relic of past times, which should and could be overcome, but things are more complicated: the crucial question for the future of gender equality and equal chances for women is, whether activists who fight for women's equality will succeed in changing the framework of society in a way which would allow more equality, not only juridical equality but equal chances in economic, political, and social life. This is difficult to achieve, since, as I have tried to show, we live in a society where the inferior status of women not only has a long tradition but is in a peculiarly contradictory way built into modern industrial society.

NOTES

1. In the three Western Zones in 1946 there were 167 women for every 100 men in the age group twenty to thirty years, and 151 women for every 100 men in the age group thirty to forty years. Gerhard Baumert and Edith Hunniger, *Deutsche Familien nach dem Kriege* (Darmstadt: E. Röther, 1954), table, 15.

2. The publicist Walter Dirks, well known as the editor of the critical journal *Frankfurter Hefte,* a forum for Left Catholic and Christian socialist ideas, stated in 1951 that the abundance of women made women cheaper as potential marriage part-

ners, according to the laws of supply and demand. He worried whether this did not imply a temptation to make a "bad choice" on both sides. "Was die Ehe bedroht: Eine Liste der kritischen Punkte," *Frankfurter Hefte* 1 (June 1951): 22, quoted in Angela Vogel, "Familie," in *Die Geschichte der Bundesrepublik Deutschland: Gesellschaft,* ed. Wolfgang Benz (Frankfurt am Main: Fischer, 1989), 40.

3. Adelheid zu Castell, "Die demographischen Konsequenzen des Ersten und Zweiten Weltkriegs für das Deutsche Reich, die Deutsche Demokratische Republik und die Bundesrepublik Deutschland," in *Zweiter Weltkrieg und sozialer Wandel,* ed. Waclaw Dlugoborski (Göttingen: Vandenhoek & Ruprecht, 1981), 117–37. For the general situation of women after the war, see Ute Frevert, *Women in German History: From Bourgeois Emancipation to Sexual Liberation* (Oxford: Berg, 1988), 253ff.; Eva Kolinsky, *Women in West Germany: Life, Work and Politics* (Oxford: Berg, 1989), 24ff.; Vogel, "Familie," 35ff; Robert G. Moeller, "Reconstructing the Family in Reconstructing Germany: Women and Social Policy in the Federal Republic, 1949–1955," *Feminist Studies* 15, 1(1989): 140; Barbara Willenbacher, "Zerrüttung und Bewährung der Nachkriegsfamilie," in *Von Stalingrad zur Währungsreform: Zur Sozialgeschichte des Umbruchs in Deutschland,* ed. Martin Broszat et al. (Munich: Oldenbourg, 1989): 595ff.; Annette Kuhn and Doris Schubert, eds., *Frauen in der deutschen Nachkriegszeit,* 2 vols. (Düsseldorf: Schwann, 1984–86); Sibylle Meyer and Eva Schulze, *Wie wir das alles geschafft haben: Alleinstehende Frauen berichten über ihr Leben nach 1945* (Munich: Beck, 1984); Sibylle Meyer and Eva Schulze, *Von Liebe sprach damals keiner: Familienalltag in der Nachkriegszeit* (Munich: Beck, 1985); Klaus-Jörg Ruhl, ed., *Frauen in der Nachkriegszeit 1945–1963* (Munich: Deutscher Taschenbuch, 1988); Klaus-Jörg Ruhl, *Unsere verlorenen Jahre: Frauenalltag in Kriegs- und Nachkriegszeit, 1939–1949* (Darmstadt: Luchterhand, 1985); Anna E. Freier and Annette Kuhn, eds., "'Das Schicksal Deutschlands liegt in der Hand seiner Frauen': Frauen in der deutschen Nachkriegsgeschichte" in *Frauen in der Geschichte,* no. 5 (Düsseldorf: Schwann, 1984); Annette Kuhn, "Power and Powerlessness: Women after 1945, or the Continuity of the Ideology of Femininity," *German History* 7 (1989): 35–46.

4. On women in Nazi Germany and during the war, see Claudia Koonz, *Mothers in the Fatherland: Women, the Family, and Nazi Politics* (New York: St. Martin's, 1986), critically reviewed by Gisela Bock, *Bulletin of the German Historical Institute London* 5, 1(1989): 16–24, and Koonz's response, "Erwiderung auf Gisela Bocks Rezension von 'Mothers in the Fatherland'" *Geschichte und Gesellschaft* 18 (1992): 394–99; Renate Bridenthal, Atina Grossmann, and Marion Kaplan, eds., *When Biology Became Destiny* (New York: Monthly Review Press, 1984); Timothy Mason, "Women in Germany, 1925–1940," *History Workshop Journal,* (1976): 74–113 and (1976): 5–32; Ludwig Eiber, "Frauen in der Kriegsindustrie: Arbeitsbedingungen, Lebensumstände und Protestverhalten," in *Bayern in der NS-Zeit,* ed. Martin Broszat et al., vol. 3 (Munich: Oldenbourg, 1981): 570–644; Annemarie Tröger, "German Women's Memories of World War II," in *Behind the Lines: Gender and the Two World Wars,* ed. Margaret Randolph Higonnet et al. (New Haven: Yale University Press, 1987), 285–99.

5. *ODI Weekly Intelligence Report,* no. 83, 13 December 1947, "Women's politi-

cal organizations in Bavaria," n.p., Record Group 260, Box no. 149, Folder 5/297-1/
1, Washington National Record Center (Suitland); see also Nori Möding, "Die Stunde
der Frauen? Frauen und Frauenorganisationen des bürgerlichen Lagers," in Broszat et
al., *Von Stalingrad,* 642f.

6. Office of the Director of Intelligence, Comment to Memorandum No. 348, 15,
Records of the Work of the Youth Activities Section, including Women's Affairs
Section, RG 260, Box 149, Folder 5/297-1/1, Washington National Record Center
(Suitland).

7. Nieves Kolbe, Domenica Rode, and Ingrid N. Sommerkorn, "Chancen und
Grenzen der Emanzipation von Frauen in der Nachkriegszeit," *Frauenforschung* 6
(1988) 13–32; Ilona Ostner, "Ideas, Institutions, Traditions: West German Women's
Experience 1945–1990," *German Politics and Society,* no. 24–25 (1991– 92): 87–99.

8. Willenbacher, "Zerrüttung," 605f.

9. Frevert, *Women in German History,* 251f.; Willenbacher, "Zerrüttung," 599f.
On the change in the relationship between parents and children see Yvonne Schütze,
"Zur Veränderung im Eltern-Kind-Verhältnis seit der Nachkriegszeit," in *Wandel
und Kontinuität der Familie in der Bundesrepublik Deutschland,* ed. Rosemarie Nave-
Herz (Stuttgart: Enke, 1988): 95ff.; and Reinhard Sieder, *Sozialgeschichte der Familie*
(Frankfurt am Main: Suhrkamp, 1987): 236ff.

10. "Current German Attitudes and the German War Effort," 19 March 1942,
Record Group 226, Office of Strategic Services, Research and Analysis Branch,
Psychology Division, Box 2, Folder: Washington PS-OP-7, no. 437603, Report no.
16: National Archives, Washington, D.C., 25.

11. See, for example, Bertram Schaffner, *Father Land: A Study of Authoritarianism in the German Family* (New York: Columbia University Press, 1948), chapters
about "The German Father" and "The German Mother," 15ff. and 34ff; more differentiated than Schaffner is Howard Becker, "German Families Today," in *Germany and
the Future of Europe,* ed. Hans Morgenthau (Chicago: University of Chicago Press,
1951), 12–24. In 1944 German family structures were discussed at length at a conference at Columbia University, where psychiatrists, anthropologists, and sociologists
investigated the German national character, in order to be prepared for reeducating the
Germans after the war. See "Report of a Conference on Germany after the War, called
by the Joint Committee on Post-War Planning," Columbia University, 29–30 April,
6, 20–21 May, 3–4 June 1944, Record Group 260, Box 149, Folder 5/297-1/1,
Washington National Record Center (Suitland).

12. See Henry P. Pilgert, *Women in West Germany, With Special Reference to the
Politics and Programs of the Women's Affairs Branch,* Historical Division, Office of
the Executive Secretary, Office of the U.S. High Commissioner for Germany, 1952;
Hermann-Josef Rupieper, "Bringing Democracy to the Frauleins: Frauen als
Zielgruppe der amerikanischen Demokratisierungspolitik in Deutschland 1945–1952,"
Geschichte und Gesellschaft 17 (1991): 61–91. See also the critical comment on
Rupieper's article by Rebecca Boehling, *Geschichte und Gesellschaft,* forthcoming.

13. Basic Law, Article 3, sec. 1; see also Frevert, *Women in German History,*
264; Kolinsky, *Women in West Germany,* 41ff.; Moeller, "Reconstructing the Family"
141f.; Angela Vogel, "Frauen und Frauenbewegung," in Benz, *Geschichte der Bun-*

desrepublik, 162ff. The Christian Democratic party had introduced a "separate but equal" formula into the deliberations on the status of women that then was defeated through massive mobilization of groups within the parliament as well as the general public; Vogel "Familie," 162.

14. "It is the Social Democratic anticlericals who are really important in the development of family patterns that significantly diverge from those adhered to by the clerical group" (Becker, "German Families Today," 17).

15. Christiane Homann-Dennhardt, "Gleichberechtigung via Rechtsnorm? Zur Frage eines Antidiskriminierungsgesetzes in der Bundesrepublik" in *Frauensituation,* ed. Uta Gerhardt and Yvonne Schütze (Frankfurt am Main: Suhrkamp, 1988), 166f.

16. Robert G. Moeller, "Protecting Mothers' Work: From Production to Reproduction in Postwar West Germany," *Journal of Social History* 22 (1989): 413–37.

17. See note 6 above.

18. See Hanna Schissler, "The Effects of Anti-Communism and the Cold War on the 'Woman's Question'" (Paper delivered at the Annual Meeting of the Southern Historical Association, Fort Worth, Texas, 14 November 1991).

19. Helmut Schelsky, *Wandlungen der deutschen Familie in der Gegenwart,* 5th ed. (Stuttgart: Enke, 1967), 63.

20. Ruhl, *Frauen in der Nachkriegszeit,* documents 52, 55.

21. Ruhl, *Frauen in der Nachkriegszeit,* 107ff.; Moeller, "Reconstructing the Family"; and Moeller, "Protecting Mothers' Work".

22. Moeller, "Reconstructing the Family," 157.

23. Civil Service Law, sec. 63/1; quoted in Kolinsky, *Women in West Germany,* 47. The condition under which a married woman could be dismissed was that the husband had to be a civil servant too and had to have pension rights.

24. Moeller, "Reconstructing the Family," 137.

25. Rosemarie Nave-Herz, *Geschichte der Frauenbewegung in Deutschland,* 3d ed. (Hannover: Niedersächsiche Landeszentrale für politische Bildung, 1989); Renate Wiggershaus, *Geschichte der Frauen und der Frauenbewegung in der Bundesrepublik Deutschland und in der Deutschen Demokratischen Republik nach 1945* (Wuppertal: Peter Hammer, 1979); Möding, "Die Stunde der Frauen?" 619–47; Vogel, "Frauen und Frauenbewegung."

26. Möding, "Die Stunde der Frauen?" 633ff.; Vogel, "Frauen und Frauenbewegung," 180ff.; Nave-Herz, *Geschichte der Frauenbewegung,* 61ff.

27. Möding, "Die Stunde der Frauen?" 640ff.

28. Käte Strobel, "Gleiche Rechte! Gleiche Pflichten!" in *Frauenbuch,* ed. Lisa Albrecht and Hanna Simon (Offenbach: Bollwerk-Verlag Karl Drott, 1947), 41.

29. Frevert, *Women in German History,* 281f.

30. Sec. 1356 stated: "The woman runs the household in her own responsibility. She is entitled to take on paid employment, as far as this can be combined with her duties in marriage and family." And Sec. 1360a stated: "Should the husband be unable to make an adequate living, the wife is obliged to seek paid employment in addition to her regular housework duties." See also Kolinsky, *Women in West Germany,* 43. The Act on Equal Rights for Men and Women, which finally revised some of the worst regulations of the Civil Code of 1900, still allowed men to go to court if their wives

identified "too much" with their work outside the home. Moreover, they could go to court if men felt that the family was neglected and if women's enthusiasm for their work went beyond the motive of merely *contributing* to the family income. Such court action might not have happened frequently, but men were legally entitled to do so. See Vogel, "Frauen und Frauenbewegung," 176.

31. Frevert, *Women in German History*, 286; Kolinsky, *Women in West Germany*, 50ff.

32. In 1952 working mothers (married as well as unmarried) were protected by law (the Maternity Protection Act). Robert Moeller has pointed out the ambivalence of this law, which on the one hand protected working mothers and guaranteed them paid time before and after childbirth, but on the other hand enabled employers to regulate women and make pregnancy an issue in working contracts. Factory inspectors who had to enforce the law pointed out that some employers tried not to hire women of childbearing age because of the costs and the restrictions the law imposed upon them. The Maternity Protection Act was designed to regulate what was considered a deplorable exemption rather than a rule. The lawmakers had in mind women who were forced to work outside the home because of material scarcity. Hardly anybody to be found at the time perceived this to be a question of free choice. See Moeller, "Protecting Mothers' Work"; see also Kolinsky, *Women in West Germany*, 54ff.

33. Willenbacher, "Zerrüttung," 610f., 615.

34. Castell, "Demographische Konsequenzen," table 10, 137. This increase seems moderate if we compare it to the GDR, where female employment increased from 52.4 percent to 81.5 percent between 1950 and 1975 (Erwerbsbeteiligung von Frauen im Alter von 15–59 Jahren, table 7, 135).

35. Statistisches Bundesamt, ed., *Datenreport: Zahlen und Fakten über die Bundesrepublik Deutschland* (Bonn: Bundeszentrale für politische Bildung, 1983), 84; Statistisches Bundesamt, ed., *Frauen in Familie, Beruf und Gesellschaft* (Stuttgart: Kohlhammer, 1987), 62f.; see also Kolinsky, *Women in West Germany*, 151ff.

36. Statistisches Bundesamt, *Datenreport*, 84 (Erwerbsquoten: Anteil der Erwerbspersonen an 100 Männern, bzw. Frauen).

37. Vogel, "Familie," 53, 59; numbers from Frevert, *Women in German History*. In 1981 female wages in industry still were 31.2 percent lower than males' wages. Between 1960 and 1980 the male-female wage differential in the lowest paying ranks in industry decreased from 31.2 to 20.6 percent, but in 1980 56.3 percent of the male blue-collar worker were still in the highest paid category, while only 5.4 percent of women reached that level (*Women in German History*, 277, 280).

38. Kolinsky, *Women in West Germany*, 160.

39. Helge Pross, *Die Wirklichkeit der Hausfrau* (Hamburg: Rowohlt, 1975), 220ff.

40. Ibid., 13; see also Frevert, *Women in German History*, 273.

41. Sibylle Meyer und Eva Schulze, "Von Wirtschaftswunder keine Spur: Die ökonomische und soziale Situation alleinstehender Frauen," in *Perlonzeit: Wie die Frauen ihr Wirtschaftswunder erlebten*, ed. Angela Delille and Andrea Grohn (Berlin: Elefantenpress, 1985), 92–98.

42. Castell, "Demographische Konsequenzen," table 10, 137, Entwicklung der Erwerbsbeteiligung in der BRD 1950–1975. The Erwerbsbeteiligung of women in-

creased as follows: 1950: 47.4 percent; 1955: 51.8 percent; 1960: 54.1 percent; 1965: 54.0 percent; 1970: 53.8 percent; 1975: 54.0 percent.

43. Frevert, *Women in German History,* chap. 18.

44. Female employment in the GDR was by the mid seventies nearly as high as men's, see Castell, "Demographische Konsequenzen," table 7, p. 135; the situation of women in the GDR and their life patterns are described in Hildegard Maria Nickel, "Women in the German Democratic Republic and in the New Federal States: Looking Backwards and Forwards," *German Politics and Society,* no. 24–25 (1991–92): 34–52; and in Dorothy Rosenberg, "Shock Therapy: The Effect of Unification on Women in Germany," *Signs* 17 (1991): 129–51.

45. Frevert, *Women in German History,* 269f.

46. Schelsky, *Wandlungen,* 335ff.

47. The most profound discussion in the seventies, in my opinion, is to be found in Marie-Luise Janssen-Jurreit, *Sexismus: Über die Abtreibung der Frauenfrage* (Frankfurt am Main: Fischer, 1976); and in the many works by Helge Pross. In English the only available work by Helge Pross that I can find is "West Germany," in *Women in the Modern World,* ed. Raphael Patai (New York: Free Press, 1967), 247–66. More recently in the works of Ulrich Beck und Elisabeth Beck-Gernsheim, especially *Das ganz normale Chaos der Liebe* (Frankfurt am Main: Suhrkamp, 1990); for the United States, Kate Millett, *Sexual Politics* (New York: Simon and Schuster, 1969); Peter Filene, *Him/Her/Self,* 2d ed. (Baltimore: Johns Hopkins University Press, 1986); and innumerable books and articles thereafter. Two recent books on women and gender in an international perspective are Karen Offen, Ruth Roach Pierson, and Jane Rendall, eds., *Writing Women's History: International Perspectives* (Bloomington: Indiana University, Press 1991); therein is the article "Historical Research on Women in the Federal Republic of Germany," by Ute Frevert, Heide Wunder, and Christina Vanja, 291–31; and the article "Historical Research on Women in the German Democratic Republic," by Petra Rantzsch and Erika Uitz, 333–53; and Gisela Kaplan, *Western European Feminism* (New York: New York University Press, 1992).

48. Helge Pross, "Von der Rechtsgleicheit zur Gleichberechtigung," *Aus Politik und Zeitgeschichte* B45 (1981): 14–25.

49. This is particularly pointed out by authors such as Barbara Willenbacher "Thesen zur rechtlichen Stellung der Frau," in Gerhardt and Schütze, *Frauensituation,* 141–65, and Jutta Limbach, "Wie männlich ist die Rechtswissenschaft," in *Wie männlich ist die Wissenschaft?* ed. Karin Hausen and Helga Nowotny (Frankfurt am Main: Suhrkamp, 1986), 87–107.

50. Statistisches Bundesamt, *Frauen,* 68, 82f.

51. Kolinsky, *Women in West Germany,* 153ff.

52. Ulrich Beck, "Freiheit oder Liebe? Vom Ohne-, Mit-, und Gegeneinander der Geschlechter innerhalb und außerhalb der Familie," in Beck and Beck-Gernsheim, *Das ganz normale Chaos,* 27ff., 36ff.

53. Helge Pross, *Die Männer* (Hamburg: Rowohlt, 1978) 165ff.; and the follow-up study by Sigrid Metz-Göckel and Ursula Müller, *Der Mann* (Weinheim: Beltz, 1986).

54. Kaplan, *Contemporary Western European Feminism,* 107ff.

55. A poignant description of these things is to be found in Lillian Rubin, *Intimate*

Strangers: Men and Women Together (New York: Harper and Row, 1984); see also Beck, "Freiheit oder Liebe?"

56. Ulrich Beck, *Risikogesellschaft: Auf dem Weg in eine andere Moderne* (Frankfurt am Main: Suhrkamp, 1986), 162.

57. See Rosenberg, "Shock Therapy," and Nickel, "Women."

58. On this whole issue, which I cannot explore here thoroughly, see Rainer Geißler, "Soziale Ungleichheiten zwischen Männern und Frauen—Erfolge und Hindernisse auf dem Weg zur Gleichstellung in den beiden deutschen Staaten," *Sozialwissenschaftliche Informationen für Unterricht und Studium* 19 (1990): 181–96; Rainer Geißler, "Soziale Ungleichhheit zwischen Frauen und Männern im geteilten und im vereinten Deutschland," *Aus Politik und Zeitgeschichte* B14–15 (1991): 13–24; Hanna Schissler, "The Effects of Unification on Women's Issues" (Paper delivered at the University of Maryland, Baltimore County, March 1991); Dorothy Rosenberg, "GDR Women in Transition: Side Effects in the Unification Process," and Joyce Mushaben, "Ohne Frauen ist kein Staat zu machen: The Political-Economic Status of Women in the New Germany" (Papers delivered at the meeting of the German Studies Association, Los Angeles, 27 September 1991); and the pessimistic outlook by Ute Gerhard, "German Women and the Social Costs of Unification," *German Politics and Society,* no. 24–25 (1991): 16–33.

59. For more information and some thoughts on the question of whether the postwar period indeed provided a real chance for women's emancipation, see Kolbe, Rode, and Sommerkorn, "Chancen und Grenzen," as well as Ostner's opinion on that issue, "Ideas," 90.

60. Maurice Godelier, *The Making of Great Men* (Cambridge: Cambridge University Press, 1986), 148.

61. Jerry Z. Muller, "The Health of Nations: Adam Smith's Family Formula," *Washington Post,* 27 September 1992, sec. C.

62. Beck and Beck-Gernsheim, *Das ganz normale Chaos;* and Beck, *Risikogesellschaft.*

The New Women's Movement

Andrei S. Markovits and Philip S. Gorski

Like so much else, the new women's movement had its roots in the contradictions of Außerparliamentaristic Opposition (extraparliamentary opposition, or APO) and the German student movement. It began abruptly and with symbolic flourish on 13 September 1968, at the Twentieth SDS (Sozialistischer Deutscher Studentenbund, or German Association of Socialist Students) Delegate Conference. The podium made dismissive remarks on a speech by Helke Sander of the newly founded Berlin Action Committee for Women's Liberation (Berliner Aktionsrat zur Befreiung der Frau).[1] Outraged, "comrade" Sigrid Rüger angrily hurled a tomato into the face of SDS theoretician Hans-Jürgen Krahl. Directly thereafter, the first Broads' Committee (Weiberrat)—so self-named, partly in irony, partly as a polemic—was established in Frankfurt. In 1969, Broads' Committees from the entire Federal Republic met in Hannover under the slogan, "Liberate the socialist eminences from their bourgeois dicks!" Yet these women remained socialists first and women second. For them, as for August Bebel in his *Women and Socialism* published nearly one hundred years before, capital's struggle with labor was still the "main contradiction" subsuming all other "contradictions," including those concerned with gender, as "secondary." "Since under capitalist relations of production all regions of social and private life are marked by class antagonism, the theory and practice of the women's movement also has a class character."[2] Tellingly, the Frankfurt Broads' Committee filed en masse into the German Communist party (Deutsche Kommunistische Parti, DKP), and the Berlin women's group renamed itself the "Socialist Women's League of West Berlin."[3] These conformations had the character "more of Marxist school courses for women than emancipation groups. The women were supposed to receive tutoring in political economy in order to elevate them to the men's level of knowledge."[4]

The "autonomous" or "radical feminist" current of the German women's movement, as opposed to its Marxist counterpart, first emerged in the summer of 1971 on the wave of protest against the antiabortion clause of the

German criminal code known as Paragraph 218. "Action 218" and women's liberation were thrust into the public eye through a spectacular media event organized by journalist and publicist Alice Schwarzer, since then arguably contemporary Germany's best known and most controversial feminist. Following the example of the Parisian Mouvement de la Libération de la Femme, Schwarzer assembled 374 women, some prominent, some ordinary, whose names, photos and signatures appeared in the 1 June cover story of the German weekly *Stern,* entitled "I had an abortion!"[5] The publication of the *Stern* article mobilized support and activity well beyond the narrower intellectual avant-garde and socialist university milieu, irreversibly altering the women's movement's direction, membership, and concerns. In the same month, the first delegate conference of Action 218 took place in Düsseldorf.[6] A scant six weeks after the appearance of the *Stern* article, 2,345 additional women publicly reported their abortions, and 86,000 declarations of solidarity had been received.[7] In Ute Frevert's words: "That things did not remain in the realm of theory in the academic ghetto and that a women's movement with its own action program and political goals developed, was essentially on account of the . . . debate about Paragraph 218."[8]

There are several reasons why the Paragraph 218 debate was so formative. In contrast to, say, wage discrimination (one of the empirical cornerstones of the orthodox socialist analysis),[9] which affects women severely but not exclusively, the issue of abortion revealed a *gender-specific* oppression "without class content." It was a matter not of inequality in production but of regulation of reproduction, here, significantly, in the most individual, literal, and physical sense. It is important to see how the character of the abortion issue spawned the new women's movement. First, for socialist women it potently challenged Bebel's and Engels's "secondary contradiction" theorem, confronting them with the choice of being principally "socialist" or "feminist," and propelling women in many cases towards a conversion to radical feminism and a switch over to Sponti or autonomous women's groups.[10] Second, the abortion issue harbored vast potential for protest, because it ultimately touched all women, not just students but otherwise "apolitical," "average" housewives as well.

Throughout the 1980s, abortion remained a major catalyst for feminist politics in the Federal Republic. Opposition to Section 218 of the penal code helped to activate the women's movement. Indeed, abortion became one of the most contentious issues surrounding unification in 1990. This was the case because abortion was completely legal in the former East Germany. The continued legality of abortion in the five new east Länder of Germany was perhaps the only instance where a former East German arrangement was not dismantled by or adapted to West German conditions. It led to the awkward situation whereby a woman could have a completely legal abortion in one state, say Saxony, and be liable to criminal prosecution in another, say Bavaria. This anomalous situation was resolved in June 1992, when the Bundestag voted to adopt a modified version of the East German arrangement for the Federal Republic as a whole. As can be expected, conservative forces have mobilized to have this legislative decision reversed by the courts.[11]

Through this shift in perspective, introduced by Paragraph 218, a cluster of discriminatory practices, long unproblematic and imperceptible, emerged markedly: sex-specific oppression in the sphere of social reproduction. This politicization of the private, that is, sensitization to problems in home life and to issues related to sexuality and child raising, opened a vast and unexplored area for thought, discussion, and action in the discourse of West Germany's politics.

The first Federal Women's Congress held in March 1972 in Frankfurt ushered in the new women's movement and a phase of feverish and innovative political activity. Four work groups were organized: "reasons for the self-organization of women"; "the situation of employed women"; "the function of the family in society"; "action paragraph 218."[12] An extensive catalog of demands was drafted, including part-time work for men and women, equal wages for equal work, a "baby year" of paid leave for both mother and father, and the creation of autonomous—that is, men-excluding —women's organizations.[13] The target of the measures was the "double burden" of domestic responsibilities and career. Attention was focused especially on discussing "liberation" through paid employment without liberation from traditionally unpaid duties at home. Activity quickly left the congress hall and spread to the street. Provocative and attention-grabbing demonstrations were the order of the day. Beauty pageants were disturbed, entrances to pornography shops walled shut, church membership publicly renounced en masse, pig tails (Schweineschwänze) distributed to doctors at the Hartmann League Convention (the West German medical association). "Behind the slogans, 'together, women are strong' and 'the personal is political,' an entirely new understanding of organization and politics was concealed."[14]

The spring of 1972 also saw the emergence of the first women's magazine and handbook in the Federal Republic: Grunhild Feigenwinter's *Witch's Press* (*Hexenpresse*) and a *Women's Handbook* published by the Berlin Bread and Roses group. West German women, comparatively late in starting their own movement, also devoured translated imports from the already sizable stock of American feminist literature.[15]

Although various new topics in feminist politics began germinating at this time, most activities in 1973–74 remained centered around Paragraph 218. After the safer, more efficient suction method of abortion had been demonstrated in the Federal Republic for the first time at a women's congress in Munich on 11 February 1973, this method itself became a subject for agitation.[16] In 1974 the social-liberal coalition presented its draft for a reform of Paragraph 218 in the form of the so-called term-solution (Fristenlösung). This proposal was to permit abortions within the first three months of pregnancy under certain (bureaucratically defined) conditions. In response, the women's movement established Action—Last Chance (Aktion letzer Versuch) and proclaimed 16 March a national day of protest. To present graphically their plight and status, women throughout the Federal Republic marched wearing the garb of deceased victims of illegal abortion clinics, bandaged their mouths shut or wore papier-mâché ball and chain. In characteristic turn of phrase, *Der Spiegel* proclaimed an "uprising of the sisterhood."

Yet even before the SPD/FDP abortion reform bill passed the Bundestag in 1974, substantially chilling feminist agitation in the Federal Republic in the process, harbingers of the new women's movement's second phase, the so-called introspective turn (Wende nach innen), had already emerged. In 1973, women students in Heidelberg established the first of what would eventually become many "crs" (for conscious-raising) or "self-experience" groups.[17] On 3 March 1974, the first women's festival, the ROCKfest im Rock (Rockfest in skirts), took place on the campus of Berlin's Technical University, attracting, not the expected 200 women, but 2,000, for an evening of all-women's dancing, drinking, and socializing.[18] As women discovered women socially and sexually and phrases such as "the new tenderness" and "women love women" made the rounds, two lovers, Judy Andersen and Marion Ihns, went on trial for murdering the latter's husband. Slanderous press sensationalism and shoddy legal procedure let lesbianism become the real issue for both sides.[19] This ugly confrontation with patriarchal power strengthened the stream of lesbians out of the closet, kindled tense but productive disputes among and between hetero- and homosexual women about sexual politics, and sparked the experiments of "movement" lesbians. Beginning in 1974 at Berlin's Free University, permission to have women's study groups, seminars, and professorships were wrested from the (usually resistant) university administration. By the spring of 1974, some twelve women's centers had been established in the Federal Republic,[20] for the exchange of information and experiences, holding meetings, and dispensing medical advice.[21]

In 1975 the UN proclaimed an "international year of the woman," and Alice Schwarzer published the first women's lib best-seller in the Federal Republic, entitled *The Little Difference and Its Big Consequences* (*Der kleine Unterschied und seine grossen Folgen*). The book focused on the patriarchal appropriation of female sexuality as a means of controlling reproduction. The positive public exposure stimulated by the book and an unparalleled baiting campaign by the press against Schwarzer drew mass attention to the women's movement for the first time. During the second half of the 1970s, increased media exposure, combined with the introspective turn away from agitation, lured droves of hesitant "moderate" and "unpolitical" women into the movement.[22] In contrast to the veteran APO-68ers, feminized ex-Communists, and "flipped-out" anarcho-Spontis, these women brought no political experience to the movement with them; instead they mostly wanted to talk about everyday problems, their problems. Not being interested in nor knowledgeable about Marx, these women sought a suitable forum for their problems in the crs and self-experience groups. Proceeding from their own very subjective concerns (Betroffenheit), they typically addressed themes such as childhood, sexuality, career, family life, relationships, identity, and feelings toward other women.[23] But when these women were "talked out," they often disappeared again. The cr-/self-experience groups therefore had transient memberships with high turnover and very short life spans, few of them lasting over a year.[24]

The threads of a feminist public emerged in this phase of the women's movement. In 1976, the first women's publishing house, Women's Offensive (Frauenoffensive) was founded in Munich, to be followed by half a dozen others throughout the country in short order.[25] Women's book stores in Berlin and Munich also opened their doors that year.[26] And in 1977, two national women's magazines, *Emma* and *Courage,* appeared on the shelves at newsstands, and together quickly reached a circulation of over 200,000. Moreover, every year since 1976 a Women's Summer University has been held in Berlin. Each year had its own theme: "Women and Science" (1976), "Women as Paid and Unpaid Labor-power" (1977), "Women and Mothers (1978), "Autonomy and Institutions" (1979).[27]

But the development of the women's movement differed from that of other alternative movements in one significant respect: organization. The women's movement had attained dimensions that could no longer be coordinated through the personal contacts of activists. At the same time, it possessed no umbrella organizations equivalent to the Sozialistisches Büro or Netzwerk (much less to those in the ecology, peace, and antinuclear movements), nor were national meetings, congresses, and demonstrations organized, which would have promoted an expansion of informal networks. There were two principal causes for this: first, the fact that all problems related to the reproductive sphere came to be, by necessity, thematized on the level of the personal and nonpolitical, both of which were inherently contradictory to any conventional strategy of mass agitation; and second, that the principal of autonomy, which opposed contact to other, typically patriarchal, political organizations, impeded concrete steps towards the formation of cross-gender solidarism.

These deficiencies did not necessarily emanate from the nature of feminist politics per se; they can perhaps best be understood with the help of a comparative example, in this case the American women's movement's engagement through the National Organization for Women (NOW) in the battle for the Equal Rights Amendment. Regardless of the concrete outcome of the struggle, which in the ERA's case resulted in an actual defeat for NOW and American women's rights, NOW succeeded in mobilizing a huge number of America's women, who became part of the women's movement even if they never developed an active feminist consciousness. The flexibility and tolerance of the American political system allowed an antinomian challenge to that system with a much broader range than was the case in Germany. Briefly put, their different respective environments and histories made organizing for similar causes a fundamentally different experience for women in the United States and the Federal Republic.

The women's movement's comparative deficit in formal organization in relation to other new social movements, especially the ecological/antinuclear movements, did not per se prevent the transmission of its concerns into the alternative parties. But it did contribute to a constellation in which the heterogeneous concerns of the new social movements were organized under the banner of a "green" party and were thereby burdened with an ecological identity not always in line with the problems and interests they sought to represent—such as women.

In the period from 1977 to 1980, the women's movement's main attention, like that of other new groups, was focused mostly on project-related undertakings. In part, the projects provided the foundation for an expanding feminist counterculture. In addition to the efforts toward creating a feminist public through the publishing houses, magazines, and bookstores mentioned above, women's bars, restaurants, psychotherapy centers, and even driving schools were opened. A code of clothing and insider slang allowed feminists to identify one another. And for gay and straight alike, women's communes enjoyed a brief flourishing, beginning in 1976.

Next to publicity work, so-called women's houses were perhaps the most widespread variety of project during this period. By offering shelter, support, and therapy for battered women and their children in a communal environment, these houses not only aided victims but helped to rend the veil of silence previously cast by the authorities over violence in the home. The first West German women's house was opened in Berlin in 1976, and by 1979 women's houses already existed in fourteen cities in the Federal Republic.[28] Women's health centers sought to work against the estrangement of women from their own bodies through self-examination, gynecological education, and counseling.

Active and aggressive campaigns against rape and violence towards women, organized, propagated, and discussed with an intensity reminiscent of Action 218, complemented these self-help projects. Showings of the porno hit *The Story of "O"* were blocked, and *Emma* took *Stern* to court for its all-too-often insulting and chauvinist cover pictures. On 1 March 1977, women in Berlin took to the streets to protest a rape/murder, and on 30 April, Walpurgis Night, in the first "take back the night" march, bands of women armed with pots and pans careened and clattered through the streets. The first rape-crisis hot line also appeared that spring.[29] The theoretical capstone was laid by the publication of the German edition of Susan Brownmiller's feminist critique of rape, *Against Our Will.*

Beginning in 1979–80, the women's movement cautiously searched for commonalities with the other new social movements. In a declaration, "Violence Against Women," drafted at its second national conference on 6–7 October 1979 in Düsseldorf, the Democratic Women's Initiative drew connections between sexual violence against women, "structural violence" in the workplace, the arms race and ecological destruction.[30] Other groupings, such as Women for Peace (Frauen für den Frieden), addressed pressing global issues from the women's perspective.[31] At the Women's Congress against Nukes and Militarism on 15–16 September 1979, Sibylle Plogstedt spoke of the "man against man battle mentality" (Mann gegen Mann Kampfdenken), making the connection between violence and patriarchy yet more explicit.[32]

Concurrent with this seeming repoliticization, a new constellation, gravitating around phrases such as "new motherliness" and "new femininity," polarized the ideological fronts within the women's moment. In a representative text of the sort published in the *Women's Yearbook '77*, Eva-Maria Stark argued that "the desire for a child can come from deep within one's belly," and praised the strengths of motherhood, the "peaceful mother-child relation," "the affection and willingness to sacrifice," and the "needs and rhythms of our bellies."[33] Four years later, Monika Jaekel reemphasized in yet more unambiguous language that motherhood was the essence of womanhood:

> Women long to affirm and live that which concerns and comprises them. . . . We women want to begin unfolding the social potential of being a mother as part of a strong and unified women's movement.[34]

In certain respects this romanticization of the corporeal dimension of motherhood and the menstrual cycle represented the search for "equality with difference," the attempt to reclaim a feminine identity from the desire for absolute equality. The dangers immanent within the "new femininity" manifested themselves most dramatically in the brief popular renaissance of witchcraft, moon-cults, paganism, and other pre-modern spiritualist and irrationalist tendencies. Radical feminists aimed their attacks above all at the new femininity's patent biologism, its equation of female needs with hormonal drives. Radical feminists perceived this new femininity as providing an apolitical picture of women that played all too easily into the hands of traditional male conservatives. Moreover, they argued, new femininity was too deeply biologistic, thus ignoring socialization in the shaping of sex roles.

The women's movement in the late seventies proffered a contradictory complexion. On the one hand, signs of politicization were evident in the unfolding antiviolence and antirape campaigns. Attempts to center feminist theory and praxis within an overarching "revolt of the reproductive sphere against the conditions of the productive sphere,"[35] and a "greening" of the women's movement, beginning in 1979, emerged in organizations such as the German Women's International and Women for Peace. This was also the first time that future Green politicians such as Petra Kelly emerged as activists in the feminist, peace, and ecology movements. In the eyes of many feminists, particularly in the radical camp, the chief obstacle to a unified, politicized women's movement was the lack of a "concrete utopia," an imaginative vision of a future feminist society, which could serve as a horizon for the orienting of everyday politics. The mysticist, spiritualist revival was alas not serviceable as a concrete utopia, an imaginative dramatization of long-range political ideals. Much more, it revealed a latent antimodernist tendency present in all the new social movements that made them susceptible and attractive to certain rightist, reactionary politicians. This antimodernism was to resurface later in the fundamentalist wing of the Greens as well. Above all, the complexity of the latter once again reaffirmed the immense difficulty of formulating a viable reformist politics in defense of the reproductive arena.

NOTES

Editor's Note: This chapter is based upon Andrei S. Markovits's forthcoming book *The German Left: Red, Green and Beyond* (London and New York: Oxford University Press).

1. Alice Schwartzer, *So fing es an! Die neue Franuenbewegung* (Munich: Deutscher Taschenbuch, 1983), 13.

2. See Gisela Brandt, Johanna Kootz, and Gisela Steppke, *Zur Frauenfrage im Kapitalismus* (Frankfurt am Main: Suhrkampf, 1973).

3. Herrad Schenk, *Die feministische Herausforderung. 150 Jahre Frauenbewegung in Deutschland* (Munich: C. H. Beck, 1981), 22.

4. Ibid., 85.

5. See a facsimile of the declaration in Schwartzer, *So fing es an!*, 124.

6. Schenk, *Die feministische Herausforderung,* 87.

7. Ute Frevert, *Frauengeschichte. Zwischen bürgerlischer Verbesserung und neuer Weiblichkeit* (Frankfurt am Main: Suhrkampf, 1987), 278.

8. Ibid.

9. See especially Brand, Kootz, and Steppke, *Zur Frauenfrage im Kapitalismus.*

10. Schenk, *Die feministische Herausforderung,* 86.

11. For a superb discussion of the issue of abortion and other subjects pertaining to gender politics in the two Germanys as well as the united Germany, see the articles in the double issue of *German Politics and Society* entitled "Germany and Gender," 24–25 (1991–92). See also Jeremiah M. Riemer's essay in this volume.

12. Schwarzer, *So fing es an!,* 28.

13. Frevert, *Frauengeschichte,* 280.

14. Ibid., 281.

15. Brandt, Kootz, and Steppke, *Zur Frauenfrage im Kapitalismus,* 131.

16. Schwarzer, *So fing es an!,* 35.

17. Ibid., 37.

18. Ibid., 52.

19. Ibid., 54–55.

20. Ibid., 41.

21. Schenk, *Die feministische Herausforderung,* 88.

22. Ibid., 89 and 92.

23. Ibid., 91.

24. Ibid.

25. Ibid., 101.

26. Ibid.

27. See ibid., 100 and 102.

28. Ibid., 99.

29. Schwarzer, *So fing es an!,* 75.

30. See reprint in H. Billstein and K. Naumann, eds., *Für eine bessere Republik. Alternative der demokratischen Bewegung,* (Cologne: Pahl-Rugenstein, 1981), 220–21.

31. See FfdF-Aufruf in Billstein and Naumann, *Für eine bessere Republik,* 220–21.

32. Ibid., 225.

33. Reprinted in Schwarzer, *So fing es an!,* 188–92.

34. Reprinted in Schwarzer, *So fing es an!,* 193–94.

35. Schenk, *Die feministische Herausforderung,* 216.

Old Troubles and New Uncertainties: Women and Politics in United Germany

Christiane Lemke

The unification of the Federal Republic of Germany (FRG) and the former German Democratic Republic (GDR) on 3 October 1990 marked a watershed for women in Germany. The merging of the market-based, democratic western Germany with the formerly Communist-ruled eastern part of the country has no precedent in modern political history. Likewise unprecedented is the merging of two countries in which women had assumed very different social and political roles.[1] Therefore, there is a high degree of uncertainty about the medium- and long-term consequences of unification for women's social and economic life as well as for their political role in society. While it has become obvious now that the economic costs of unification are enormous and exceed most predictions made in the year of unification, opinions differ widely about how this will affect different social groups.

Among the many paradoxes produced by the collapse of Communist rule throughout eastern and east-central Europe is the fact that political liberalization did not enhance women's role and status in society, let alone their political influence, at least not immediately. While the East German case is special because of the rapid unification with the FRG, women are now faced with conditions drastically different from those in which they were raised and on which they oriented their lives. While the collapse of the Communist regime certainly opened new and unexpected opportunities for women, it also represents a crisis of tremendous proportions for most women in the short run.

Already during the turbulent months marking the collapse of the Communist regime, the goals, aspirations, and expectations of women's groups, activists, and professional politicians in charge of women's affairs differed in the FRG and the GDR, foreshadowing some of the difficulties of the

147

inner-German dialogue among women in united Germany. While the lives of women in the five new states of east Germany changed more dramatically than that of women in the old FRG, unification has clearly posed a great challenge to the women's movement in the West as well. This chapter will analyze the impact of unification on women as a political force in Germany. The main thrust of my argument is that the different histories of the postwar women's movement in the FRG and the GDR have shaped women in the two parts of Germany and will shape future policies in the country. Unification has not eliminated old troubles women were facing in society, but it has added new uncertainties.

This chapter will begin with a brief description of the major policies concerning women as outlined in the Unity Treaty of 1990, then address the two different worlds of women in the former GDR and the FRG, and finally analyze women's political activities and participation in the two parts of Germany.

Women in the Process of Unification: The Unity Treaty

In the first set of agreements between the GDR and the FRG, the treaty on economic, monetary, and social union, which established the currency union between the two states on 1 July 1990, fiscal and economic policies were at the core. Policies affecting women's roles in society were barely touched upon. The major document concerning the policies toward women in the five new states and in united Germany is the Unity Treaty, which was to establish the political unification of the GDR and the Federal Republic on 3 October 1990. Due to pressure from a number of women activists and politicians, Article 31 of the treaty formulates policy goals regarding (1) equal rights, (2) reconciliation of work and family life, and (3) child care, as well as regulations concerning the different abortion laws in the FRG and the GDR.

The article reads as follows:

(1) It shall be the task of the all-German legislature to develop further the legislation on equal rights for men and women.

(2) In view of different legal and institutional starting positions with regard to the employment of mothers and fathers, it shall be the task of the all-German legislature to shape the legal situation in such a way as to allow a reconciliation of family and occupational life.

(3) In order to ensure that day care centers for children continue to operate in the territory specified in Article 3 of this Treaty (the former GDR- C. L.), the Federation shall contribute to the costs of these centers for a transitional period up to 30 June 1991.

(4) It shall be the task of the all-German legislature to introduce regulations no later than 31 December 1992 which ensure better protection of unborn life and provide a better solution in conformity with the Constitution of conflict situations faced by pregnant women—notably through legally guaranteed entitlement for women, first and foremost to advice and public support—than is the case in either part of Germany at present. In order to achieve these objectives, a network of advice centers run by various agencies and offering blanket coverage shall be set up without delay with financial assistance from the Federation in the territory specified in Article 3 of this Treaty. The advice centers shall be provided with sufficient staff and funds to allow them to cope with the task of advising pregnant women and offering them necessary assistance, including beyond the time of confinement. In the event that no regulations are introduced within the period stated in the first sentence, the substantive law shall continue to apply in the territory specified in Article 3 of this Treaty.[2]

A major point for women in the unification process was maintaining the different abortion laws until the end of 1992. The abortion law in the former GDR is less restrictive than the law in the old FRG. Women hoped that unification would enable them finally to introduce a more liberal abortion law with German unification.[3]

Despite this achievement, German unification was a highly controversial theme among women.[4] While East German women welcomed the fall of the authoritarian Communist regime in their country, many have remained critical of the rapid pace and the policies of unification. The tremendous speed of the unification left women little time to mobilize their resources. Those in the West who were critical about the path chosen for unification, including prominent West German Social Democrats and leaders of the West German unions, pointed to the mounting social tensions and economic hardships devolving from increasing unemployment and fiscal constraints due to unification, some of which would affect women negatively. West German feminists were above all concerned that the emphasis on nationalism and unity by the government would strengthen conservatism and paternalism, creating an unfavorable climate for women's rights.

Given the need for new policies while integrating the east German states, politically active women have tried to use this watershed in German history to promote more progressive policies for women and to push for effective political improvements. But so far, few measures have been taken and the policy guidelines remain weak, especially on the national level, reflecting the overall conservative approach of the current government. For example, the coalition agreements of the newly elected CDU/FDP government of united Germany include several statements concerning equal-rights and child care.[5] The agreements, which basically outline the direction of policies in this legislative term, call for a law on equal rights (Artikelgesetz) regulating the promotion of women, the competence of equal-rights officers in the federal administration, and other mechanisms to promote women in industry. With respect to the labor market, women are to be included in retraining and job creating programs according to their share among the unemployed. The governing parties also intend to work with the states on regulations granting a right to public child care. Providing public child care has been a particularly pressing issue in east Germany, where the percentage of working mothers has traditionally been higher than in the FRG, but it was also one of the major deficits in the old FRG. Fiscal constraints may undermine the provisions for child care, however, since the states have to provide the finances. The new states will continue to be poor for the foreseeable future, restricting their choices even if they wish to maintain existing child-care facilities after subsidies granted by the national government in the transition period expire within the coming months.

The Two Worlds of Women: Work and Family East and West

The controversies over the policies of unification clearly reflected the different social and economic roles and the contrasting experiences of women in both parts of Germany in the past forty years. Recent comparative scholarship has found the Federal Republic to be a "conservative welfare state."[6] In fact, even though women in the FRG are very well educated and well trained, participation in the labor force has increased only modestly over the past decade and is lower than in the United States, France, or Denmark, for example (1989: 57 percent). Ilona Ostner finds west Germany to be a "strong male breadwinner" model when compared to other European countries, with women and families largely depending on men's earnings.[7] Since women are largely responsible for child rearing, their life-cycle pattern differs from that of men; women are more likely to interrupt their professional careers.[8] Given the insufficient provision of child-care facilities, in particular in urban areas, and the unfavorable school hours per day, the "choice" between work and family—one of the policy goals of the CDU/FDP government—depends mainly on whether a family with two earners can afford child care for themselves. It should therefore not come as a surprise that Germany's birth rate is among the lowest in Europe (only Italy has a lower rate).

    In the former GDR, paid employment outside the home was the rule for women and men, even for the elderly, who were among the poorest group in the country. The Communist SED regime mobilized women to participate in the labor force due to a chronic labor shortage and provided an extensive net of child-care facilities. Thus women's employment increased steadily. In 1989, 83 percent of all women between the age of sixteen and sixty worked outside the home.[9] This lifetime-work model for women had a number of consequences for social policies.[10] Wages were generally low, since family income was based on the earnings of two partners and a whole range of noncash benefits, subsidies, and services supplemented the modest cash income. There was a restricted range of wages and incomes (with the exception of high-ranking party functionaries), but women often accepted work below their level of qualification if they had children or worked part-time. Pensions of women were lower than those of men (and certainly much lower than in the FRG), but they did not differ as greatly from each other as in the FRG, since they were based on the years worked, and not, as in the FRG, also on previous earnings, highly differentiated in the FRG. Furthermore, in another difference from West Germany, East German women very seldom received financial support from their former husbands in case of a divorce, since it was assumed that they would work to sustain themselves.

As a result of the different social and economic systems, women's economic role and significance for the household economy differed fundamentally in the two states. According to data published by the German Institute for Economic Research (DIW), women in East Germany contributed 40 percent to the average household's income before unification, whereas West German women's average contribution was only 18 percent.

Yet, women did not fare well under the SED regime and faced a number of disadvantages and discriminatory practices at work. Despite the official governmental rhetoric of equal rights, discrimination against women existed in the GDR and, as some east German activists claim, increased in the 1980s as the SED regime reemphasized mothering, or "mommy politics."[11] Data collected during the last years of the Communist regime revealed that women's wages among industrial and construction workers were 12 percent lower than that of men, even if they performed the same tasks.[12] A significantly higher proportion of women was grouped in the lower and lowest wage groups. Extra benefits and wage supplements for overtime additionally increased male workers' income. The report also points to a number of discriminatory procedures in hiring and promotion. Due to the lack of data and valid empirical material in the former GDR, the extent of discrimination may never be fully uncovered, but women have become deeply skeptical about the practices of the former regime.

The restructuring of the east German economy has hit both women and men, but certain groups of women have faced greater uncertainties more quickly. Since women in the GDR were more often employed in the least efficient and competitive industries, such as textiles, or worked in less socially secure positions, they were the first hit by unemployment after the currency union. Industrial production fell by 40 percent in the first half of 1990, and unemployment skyrocketed after the economic and currency union in July 1990. Early in 1991 about 40 percent of the area's work force of about 8.5 million were unemployed or on "short work with zero hours," meaning that they report to work to draw part of their wages for a few months.[13] Unemployment among women has risen steadily from 54 percent in December 1990 to 57 percent by October 1991. The highly sex-segregated training and employment patterns limit women's choices more than men's, and women over forty-five have little chance of finding a new job. Furthermore, family responsibilities and lower mobility disadvantage women. For example, only a very small percentage of those who currently commute to west Germany to work (approximately 200,000 workers) and those who migrate west (still 20,000 per month) are women. Hardest hit by the restructuring are single mothers and mothers with small children, since they often have difficulties even participating in one of the retraining programs.

Contrasting Experiences: The Two Women's Movements West and East

The Federal Republic of Germany, as a result of unification, now contains two distinctly different women's movements. The women's movements in the East and in the West of Germany are both shaped by the different political histories of the old FRG and the former GDR. Moreover, the hostile ideological confrontation between the two states until the opening of the GDR separated women of the two societies, leading to ignorance and misperception about each other's aspirations, aims, and activities.

Traditionally German women have aligned with organizations pressing for social reforms, in particular with parties on the left and with unions, but Nazism had eradicated socialist, liberal, and radical roots of the women's movement and left a generation of women more concerned with rebuilding their shattered lives than with organizational or elite-level politics. The roots of the contemporary west German women's movement are twofold: first, there is the small group of traditional women's rights activists in the refounded political institutions of the FRG, and, second, there is the radical new women's movement that formed in the early 1970s outside of established institutions. In East Germany, a distinct political women's movement did not emerge until the final collapse of the Communist regime in 1989, but its roots date back to the early 1980s, with the formation of small oppositional civil rights and peace groups. As a result, radical feminism flourished in West Germany as one new approach to women's issues, but it was absent in East Germany. Postmaterialist values and new politics were prominent in the West German movement, whereas in East Germany feminism was often closely intertwined with civil rights issues. Socialist feminism, once an attractive concept in East Germany, and—embracing pluralism and democracy—also in West Germany, has suffered a severe setback due to the failure of socialism throughout east-central Europe.

West Germany: Traditional and New Women's Movement

Previous comparative research on the German women's movement had maintained that the movement was rather weak, especially when compared to the United States.[14] This weakness was traced back to the weakness of political liberalism in German history and the devastating policies of national socialism, which eradicated feminism in Germany. In contemporary Germany, the lack of coherence, the problems of coalition building, the absence of an influential national women's organization such as NOW in the United States, as well as the marginal role of pressure and lobby groups, were taken as indicators of the weakness of the German movement. More recent scholarship has found, however, that the peculiar institutional and structural features of the German political system provided a different setting for women's political activities.[15]

The west German contemporary women's movement is characterized by the dual structure of women's political activity. On the one hand, there are the grass roots–oriented projects and activities, mainly run by radical feminists or women with an anti-institutional and antistatist approach. On the other hand, activities on behalf of women's rights and feminist policies have become part of the institutionalized political system, in particular on the local and state levels, from women's ministries to equal opportunities offices. Movement-oriented and institutional politics often influence each other, but they differ in strategies, priorities, and resources.

In the immediate postwar decades, only a small number of women were active in politics. Politically, they represented the "traditional" women's movement of the pre- and postwar generation of women activists, working mostly through the social or liberal democratic parties, voluntary organizations, and, in part, the unions. As in other West European countries, the United States, and Canada, the early 1970s saw an increasing mobilization of women, most prominently in the emergence of the new women's movement evolving from the student movement in the late 1960s. The social-liberal coalition coming to power in 1969 proposed a wide range of social reforms, in areas such as family and divorce law, education, and abortion policy. This new reform space encouraged grass-roots mobilization with its slogan "dare more democracy." Public actions to legalize abortion drew nationwide attention in the early 1970s. But frustration about the failure to legalize abortion, the overall slow pace of change, and the inflexibility of large traditional organizations such as the SPD and the labor unions, led many women to believe that only independent new organizations could enhance women's influence and status in society. Thus fundamental conflicts arose between those women activists who sought political change through institutionalized politics—in particular through the Social Democratic party, the unions, and some professional organizations—and radical feminists striving for "autonomy." The term autonome Frauenbewegung, or autonomous women's movement, clearly reflects the antistatist and anti-institutional approach of radical feminists who saw the movement as different and above all independent from conventional political institutions.

Radical feminists concentrated on grass-roots activism and local projects such as shelters for battered women, cultural centers, bookstores and cafes, or summer universities for women. Radical feminism aimed at creating a women's culture, based on communitarian values. It flourished in particular in the university environment, in urban areas, and among well-educated women, but it found little support from working-class women. Throughout the 1970s the movement was prone to splintering and remained a rather weak political force on the national level. The federal structure of Germany provided for great differences between the states, with some, mostly those governed by Social Democrats and Liberal Democrats, taking the lead to implement new policies. Some support was mobilized from those employed in the educational, health, and cultural sectors as well as from public administration. Slowly, several projects and initiatives that had their origins in the radical feminist counterculture of the autonomous women's movement, such as the shelters for battered women or self-help groups, managed to become part of German public life. Even government officials today recognize the innovative capacity of these projects, half of which are run by "autonomous" groups. Feminists have generally rejected the control and regulation of state bureaucracies, but in order to survive financially they have found it necessary to cooperate with municipal and state governments and with the federal ministries. Meanwhile, most of the projects and centers receive some local and state funds, but they are often poorly endowed and financially insecure.[16]

One of the major results of women's increasing mobilization and political engagement is the establishment of an entire network of political institutions pursuing women's policies. A new generation of women, influenced and often trained by their experience in the women's movement, has entered politics in the 1980s, in particular on the state and local levels. Women gained more public visibility and influence through women's ministries in the executive branch of government or women's offices. First initiated in 1979, all Länder, or states, had women's offices by the end of the 1980s. In the new east German states such offices were created along with the reestablishment of the Länder in 1990. Women's ministries were established in lower Saxony and Schleswig-Holstein, while others have joint ministries, such as Berlin and Hesse. In some states independent authorities were established (Hamburg, Bremen), while others opened women's offices assigned to the minister-presidents (Baden-Württemberg, Bavaria). Of the five new Länder only Brandenburg established a ministry for women joined with other departments. At the federal level, a Federal Ministry for Women was finally established in 1986 (from 1979 to 1986 there was a Directorate on Women's Affairs) as part of the Ministry for Youth, Family, Women, and Health. After the 1990 elections the Ministry was restructured to become the Ministry for Women and Youth. At the local level there were some 900 equal-rights offices (Gleichstellungsstellen) in 1991 in the old Federal Republic, and, by March 1991, about 330 such offices had been established in the new east German states.[17] These new branches of government and administration have given women more voice in policy-making and some resources to pursue women's rights policies, even though many feminists feel that their power and influence is not sufficient.

Women's political mobilization has not only changed the institutional and administrative structure of the German political system. It had a major impact on the competition and policies of the political parties, the major political actors of the parliamentary system. The ascendancy of the Greens in 1983, the first new party to enter national parliament for decades, provided new opportunities for women in the 1980s. Radical feminists and women's activists were major supporters of the grass roots–oriented Greens. Along with the environmental and peace movements, second-wave feminism was in fact a driving force in the Green party. The "antiparty" party approach as well as the emphasis on new politics based on nonhierarchical communitarian philosophies has been particularly attractive to women of the new women's movement.

Throughout the 1980s the Greens were instrumental in generating public discussions on feminist issues, even though their radical stand was controversial. They were the first to openly address sexism in parliament, for example. Antidiscrimination legislation has been another major issue of the Greens. Moreover, their bold approach to increasing the political representation of women in parliaments has had a major impact on the German party system. Due to the electoral competition, the other major parties started to redesign their policies towards women voters and to increase the number of women in their organizations. Thus despite the overall conservative political climate on the national level throughout the 1980s under the CDU/FDP government coalition, issues of women's rights and women's public visibility increased.

While women's representation in political parties is still significantly lower than that of men, it almost doubled between 1971 and 1981.[18] In 1988, women made up 25.6 percent of members in the largest party, the Social

Democratic party (1976: 19.9 percent), 22.5 percent in the Christian Democratic party (1976: 18.5), 14.2 percent in the Christian Social Union (1976: 11.1), 24.0 percent in the Free Democratic party (1976: 19.1), and 37.5 percent in the new Green party. However, women are still underrepresented in leading party positions. In the parties' executive committees at the federal level, women's representation is largest in the Green party (1988: 54.5 percent), followed by the Social Democratic party (35.0 percent), the Free Democratic party (21.2 percent), the Christian Democratic party (20.0 percent), and the Christian Social Union (9.7 percent).

Pressure to increase the number of women at decision-making levels in political parties and in parliaments came in particular from intraparty women's groups, such as the Working Group of Social Democratic Women (ASF) in the SPD and the Women's Union in the CDU. In recent years, women's representation in decision-making bodies became an issue itself with much of the debate centered around inflexible hard quotas or soft "goal" quotas.[19] Studies have shown that women are confronting both individual and institutional barriers to their participation in conventional forms of politics.[20] Even though public attitudes towards women in politics have changed significantly, women find it much harder to engage in politics. Marriage and especially motherhood are the most influential factors hindering women from seeking a political career in Germany. Typically, women in higher political positions are single, whereas only few of the male politicians are unmarried. Women with children find it almost impossible to be politically active while having a family and a job, especially since the general conditions for making job and family life compatible are worse in the Federal Republic of Germany than in other European countries.

While earlier scholarship was largely based on a deficiency hypothesis that women as women were not as well prepared or suited to pursue a political career, institutional barriers within the organizations themselves have become another focus of attention in recent years. The organization, structure, and political life in political parties make no allowances for the specific living conditions of women. Structured during the period when women were largely absent from these institutions, the female life-style and life cycle are usually not taken into consideration, and, as Robert Michels observed long ago, large bureaucratic organizations once established develop a life of their own that is hard to change.

Because women are so drastically underrepresented in the leading bodies of the political parties, some form of quota regulation within the party enjoys wide support among women in the parties. The quota discussion reflects the increasing impatience of women. Under the pressure of women, the parties favored different measure and policies, reflecting their parties' ideologies and traditions. The Social Democratic party decided in 1988 to establish an initial quota of 33 percent, followed in 1992 by a 40-percent quota for candidatures and offices. In 1988 the Christian Democratic Union introduced a flexible goal that women be represented in offices and mandates proportionate to their membership. The Free Democratic party adopted a similar resolution, under which women were to be represented at all levels and, for the next five years, according to their membership proportion, even though the party has been reluctant to introduce ways to enforce this policy.

Due to the mobilization of women in the past decade and policies adopted by the Greens, the SPD, and—less forcefully—by the CDU, women's political representation in parliament has increased. While the proportion of female delegates in the Bundestag, or national parliament, had fluctuated between 6.8 percent in 1949 and 9.8 percent in 1983, the proportion jumped to 15.4 percent in 1987. This was due above all to the high proportion of women in the Green faction in parliament. Even though the West German Greens are now no longer represented in the national parliament, the first all-German elections to the Bundestag, on 2 December 1990 brought the highest number of women into the legislature of the Federal Republic since the postwar years, due to the parties' strategies to increase the number of women on party lists. Women comprise 20.4 percent of the representatives in the national parliament, 135 in absolute numbers.[21]

Even under the current CDU/FDP government, four cabinet positions were filled with women, the highest number in postwar history. Typically, however, women hold the less powerful, less endowed, and low-prestige ministerial posts, such as Women and Youth (Angela Merkel, CDU), Family and Senior Citizens (Hannelore Rönsch, CDU), Health (Gerda Hasselfeldt, CSU), and Development, Construction, and Housing (Irmgard Adam-Schwaetzer, FDP), thus reproducing the typical pattern of the male-dominated political world.

While it is still unclear how an increasing number of women in parliaments and decision-making bodies will influence and change political decisions and policies in a given country, since the number of cases is still so small, women have gained more public visibility. On a symbolic level of politics this may, however, be an important feature for modern democracies.

Women's Mobilization in East Germany: From Oppositional Activity to the "Civic Revolution" of 1989

The women's movement in the former GDR emerged only late, in 1989, but women had been active in small oppositional or informal groups for almost a decade before the collapse of the Communist regime. The first groups of women emerged as part of the unofficial peace movement. Activists have reported organized meetings of women as early as 1978.[22] In 1982, a pacifist group, Women for Peace, was formed protesting a new draft law that provided for the drafting of women in case of a national emergency. Some of the activists, like Bärbel Bohley, Katja Havemann, Ulricke Poppe, or Vera Wollenberger, later took leading roles in the opposition. Women were also part of the emerging human-rights groups, such as the Initiative for Peace and Human Rights, formed in the mid-1980s, as well as environmental or informal women's groups that formed mostly under the shelter of the Protestant church in the 1980s.[23] Because of the rigid policies under the Communist regime, several of these activists were harassed by the secret police, the Staatssicherheit (or Stasi), expelled from the country, or imprisoned.

In the West, very little was known about these activities, mostly by the handful of interested experts on the GDR, and the history of the East German women's movement has yet to be written. For the early activists, peace and civil and human rights issues were crucial, while feminist thinking was marginal to these broader political and societal concerns. The only area in which women's concerns and some feminist thinking was expressed publicly, beginning already in the 1970s, was GDR literature. In fact, novels, poems, and an increasing body of documentary literature provided open and subtle forms of criticism of the official SED policy towards women, which, as women have maintained, far from "liberating" women, served to instrumentalize women to preserve the power of the SED.[24] In addition, some cultural transfer of feminist literature took place in the past decade due to the common German language, primarily in academic circles, while feminism was officially taboo.

Women's political mobilization increased throughout the year of 1989, reaching its peak in December of 1989 with the formation of the Independent Women's Association, an umbrella organization for a variety of oppositional women's groups. By May 1989, several months before the massive migration to West Germany that triggered the political crisis of the SED regime, about 200 women from several local groups met in Jena to share feminist ideas. Dissatisfaction with the growing gap between official rhetoric of gender equality and their everyday life experience of overwork and the double burden of work and children, as well as the blockage of reforms by the SED, fueled women's criticism.

In the fall of 1989, shortly before the Berlin Wall opened on 9 November, several women's groups sprang up. Women activists have described the mood of this period as "euphoric," and mobilization was highest in the months shortly before and after the regime collapsed. On 3 December 1989, 1,200 women met in Berlin to found the Independent Women's Association, the Unabhängige Frauenverband (UFV).[25] The activists sharply criticized the failures of the Communist regime and set themselves apart from the official Communist party–dominated Women's Federation. Liberation through socialism was criticized as a "myth." "Patriarchal socialism" had rather strengthened male-dominated power relations in society.

The Independent Women's Association demanded in its first statements that the GDR should establish a viable democracy while embracing some of the achievements of the former regime. In particular, it insisted that the right to work and the provisions for public child care had to be guaranteed by a future democratic government. Because of their criticism of Western capitalism, the new Independent Women's Association originally rejected the idea of German unification, which had become increasingly popular after the opening of the Berlin Wall. In their own words, women from the association favored an ecologically concerned, grass-roots democracy with communitarian values.[26] For the first time in GDR history, an equality commission was formed on the national level, and Tatjana Böhm, a member of the UFV, became a member without portfolio of the "reform" cabinet under Prime Minister Hans Modrow.

Because of mounting popular pressure in November and December 1989—mass demonstrations drew up to 500,000 participants in these months—the government, still led by the Communist party under Modrow, now renamed the PDS (Party of Democratic Socialism), finally agreed to enter talks with the opposition. Following similar arrangements in Poland and Hungary in the transition period from Communist rule, a roundtable was established in Berlin. Fourteen different groups and parties met from 7 December 1989 until the freely elected GDR government was formed after elections in the spring of 1990 to discuss and prepare the transition to a democratic polity. The Independent Women's Association was at first excluded from the roundtable, but after fierce protests it was finally represented along with other grass-roots and oppositional groups, such as the prominent New Forum. The constitution for a new reformed East German state, which included equal rights provisions for women and men, never came into effect because the GDR government moved swiftly to unify with the FRG over the summer of 1990.

One of the puzzles of the unification process is the fact that women and the first independent GDR women's organization, the UFV, were increasingly marginalized even before the first free elections in the GDR and even more so in the process of unification. This is even more surprising since the collapse of the Communist regime had given rise to an increasing political mobilization of women. Several observers, including GDR women activists themselves, have blamed the increasing domination of the political discourse and decision making by established political parties from the Federal Republic of Germany,[27] but this is only a partial explanation.

There are at least three other reasons for this marginalization of the women's movement in the former GDR in 1989–90. First, its marginal position reflects the legacies of Communist rule. After all, feminism had been silenced under the SED regime, and the concept of an independent women's group did not enjoy widespread support. The Women's Association never had mass appeal, but represented a fairly small group of active women, largely concentrated in the urban environment of Berlin and some other cities in the former GDR. Another major reason for the increasing marginalization may be seen in the unfavorable climate for a separate GDR state. Given the economic squeeze of the country due to a failing economy, women found it nearly impossible to argue convincingly that their demands for a reformed state were not only desirable but also workable. The vast extent of economic and ecological problems, part of which were for the first time publicly revealed by a government report published in December 1989, shocked the population. As mass migration to the West continued and the state's economy deteriorated, many East German citizens viewed unification with the affluent Federal Republic as the only way to cope with these problems. Finally and probably most importantly, similar to other post-Communist societies, the powerful push toward a market-based economy contradicted women's demand for state regulation of jobs, job guarantees, and extensive child-care benefits.

The elections on 18 March 1990 were disappointing for the women who had been active in the oppositional women's groups.[28] The Independent Women's Association, which ran together with the Green party, enjoyed little support, receiving only 2.0 percent of the votes. Since women had failed to press for top ranks on their coalition party list, they were not even able to send one of their representatives to parliament. Almost half of all women had voted for the conservative, CDU-led Alliance for Germany, which won 48 percent of all votes. Women's representation in the GDR parliament, the Volkskammer, decreased from 32.5 to 20.5 percent.

As a result many activists of the association have questioned the significance of national and party politics, shifting their attention to projects on the local level.

Coming to Terms with Past and Present

The contrast between the recent history of the West and East could not be greater. In the FRG, women became more demanding, self-assertive, and professional in politics, whereas GDR women until very recently were forced to adapt to a paternalistic, rigid political system. The radical feminist approach that had become part of the discourse among women in the FRG was confusing for many East German women, whereas women in the FRG found it difficult to relate to the previous experience of GDR women and their demands. East German women took pride in their participation in the civic revolution and sought to "bring something into united Germany," but west German women often criticized their sisters from the East because of their lack of experience and their "gender-blindness."[29]

Conflicts also arose over the evaluation of life experiences. For example, motherhood was an essential part of the lives of east German women activists, who usually had children early in their lives; their demand to secure and improve child care was rooted in their experience as working mothers. While the demand to provide public child care was widely supported by Social Democratic and union women in the FRG, west German feminists often shunned the emphasis on motherhood and family life. This, in return, was unacceptable for east German feminists. As one activist observed: "GDR women never get around to expressing the contradictions in their history while West German women forget they live in a sick society whose fundamental values they carry around with them in their thinking and behavior. West German feminists ride the hobby horse of twenty years in the women's movement since they are well practiced in analyzing patriarchal structures. Yet it still costs DM 900 to reserve a place in nursery school in the West!"[30]

Women in both parts of Germany still find it difficult to "speak the same language," because of their different pasts and presents. Language reflects this different cultural and political context and is often telling. One example is the different perception of the term *Pflichtberatung*, or mandatory counseling, in the abortion debate. As one east German feminist explained, many east German women perceive the term *Pflicht* as an obligation for the state to offer women some counseling and advice about abortion, something they had not had under the Communist regime. West German women, on the other hand, read the term *Pflicht* as *Zwang* (*Zwangsberatung*), or forcible counseling, which they see as patronizing of women.

The clash of values has created new fault lines among women as a political force. Different experiences, expectations, and political cultures in the two parts of Germany will continue to influence women's political thinking. At a time when women in the former GDR were confronted with dramatic changes in their economic situation, social status, and cultural environment, women in west Germany had difficulties relating to these experiences. Not surprisingly, prejudice often turned into mistrust, alienation into frustration.

Because of German unification, women in the Federal Republic are now facing a number of new and immediate challenges. Old concepts have been discredited, such as socialist feminism, while radical as well as liberal feminism may be insufficiently equipped to cope with the complex challenges posed by merging two fundamentally different social, economic, and cultural systems. The task is not easier but more complicated, because the FRG now contains two different women's movements with different priorities and expectations. In any case, there are no quick and no simple solutions for the problems facing women in Germany today.

NOTES

1. For a useful overview of the situation of women in the old Federal Republic see Federal Ministry for Youth, Family, Women, and Health, *Frauen in der Bundesrepublik Deutschland* (Bonn, 1989). In English see Eva Kolinsky, *Women in West Germany: Life, Work, and Politics* (Oxford: Berg, 1989). A useful resource text about the situation of women in the German Democratic Republic is Gunnar Winkler, ed., *Frauenreport '90* (Berlin: Die Wirtschaft, 1990). See also selected proceedings of the workshop "Women and Unification," Harvard University, Center for European Studies, 18–19 May, 1991 published in "Germany and Gender: The Effects of Unification of German Women in the East and the West," *German Politics and Society*, no. 24–25 (1991–92).

2. *Treaty between the Federal Republic of German and the German Democratic Republic on the Establishment of German Unity (Unification Treaty),* Article 31 "Family and Women" (English translation by the German Information Center, New York, 1990).

3. See the article on abortion by Jeremiah Riemer in this volume.

4. In fact, there was a widespread feeling among women in the East that they would be the losers of German unification. Thus the impact of unification was a hotly debated issue among women in the summer of 1990. See, for example, Christiane Lemke, "Frauenpolitische Optionen und Kontroversen im deutschen Vereinigungsprozeß," in *Die Politik zu deutschen Einheit,* ed. Ulrike Liebert and Wolfgang Merkel (Opladen: Leske und Budrich, 1991), 243–58.

5. See "Auszüge aus der Koalitionsvereinbarung: Schwerpunkte der Politik in den nächsten vier Jahren," *Das Parlament,* 1 February 1991, 7–8. Women outside of parliament have also been active. For example, five hundred professional women met in October 1990, sponsored by the city of Frankfurt's Commission for Women, to call for a revised constitution for united Germany along the lines of "freedom, equality, and sisterhood." "Women Seek More Rights through New Constitution," *The Week in Germany,* ed. the German Information Center, 2 November 1990, 6.

6. Gösta Esping-Andersen, *The Three Worlds of Welfare Capitalism* (Cambridge, Mass.: Polity, 1990).

7. Mary Langen and Ilona Ostner, "Gender and Welfare," in *Towards a European Welfare State?* ed. Graham Room (Bristol: SAUS, 1991), 127–50.

8. Studies have shown that women still face various obstacles in pursuing their careers. Women are highly concentrated in so-called female jobs, which are often low in pay because they are performed by women. Three-fourths of girls and young women concentrate in only 20 professions out of 350 tracks offered in vocational training. In addition, despite their skills, professional opportunities often remain inaccessible for women. Studies show that doors that have been opened for women in the educational sector are slammed shut in the labor market. See Federal Ministry, *Frauen in der*

Bundesrepublik, 32–38. Despite pressure from professional women, students, and some professional organizations, German universities continue to be a strongly male-dominated domain. The number of female students in universities and colleges in the (old) Federal Republic has increased over the past two decades to 38 percent in 1987, but the share of female professors remains low. Only some 5 percent of all university and college professors are women. The situation in the former GDR was not much better; while about 50 percent of the students were female, only 4.3 percent of the professors were women. See Federal Ministry, *Frauen in der Bundesrepublik,* 28; "Deutsch-deutsche Gemeinsamkeiten: Kaum Frauen an der Spitze: Frauenanteil an den Universitäten der Bundesrepublik und der DDR," *Der Spiegel,* 19 February 1990, 150.

9. The significance of paid employment in east German women's lives and the different life expectations in the West and the East are well documented in the first empirical survey in Infas, *Frauen in den neuen Bundesländern* (Bonn: INFAS). See also Bundesministerium für Frauen und Jugend, *Materialien zur Frauenpolitik 11/ 1991,* Dokumentation, (Bonn, 1991).

10. See, for example, Ute Gerhard, "German Women and the Social Costs of Unification," *German Politics and Society,* no. 24–25 (1991–92): 16–33.

11. This term is used by Myra Ferree, "The Rise and Fall of Mommy Politics: Feminism and Unification in (East) Germany," (1991, photocopy). It refers to the use of the east German phrase *Muttipolitik.*

12. Winkler, *Frauenreport '90,* 121.

13. Russell J. Dalton, "Politics in the New Germany" (1991, Photocopy), 30; *Wirtschaftswoche,* 21 December 1990, 52. See also "German Privatization in East Mired in Hard Times," *New York Times,* 12 March, 1991, sec. A.

14. See Myra Marx Ferree, "Equality and Autonomy: Feminist Politics in the United States and West Germany," in *The Women's Movements of the United States and Western Europe,* ed. M. Katzenstein and C. Mueller McClurg, (Philadelphia: Temple University Press, 1987), 172–95.

15. A good example is Myra Ferree, "Institutionalizing Gender Equality: Feminist Politics and Equality Offices," *German Politics and Society,* no. 24–25 (1991–92): 53–66.

16. Of the 200 shelters for battered women in the (old) Federal Republic more than half are run by "autonomous" women's groups; the others are supported by various welfare or church organizations. After the collapse of the Communist regime, several shelters were opened for women in the territory of the GDR. An estimated 4 million women per year in the region of the old Federal Republic are abused by their husbands. According to one survey, rape occurred in one out of five marriages at least once. Matrimonial rape is not yet a criminal offense in the Federal Republic. See Federal Ministry, *Frauen in der Bundesrepublik,* 69.

17. *Pressemitteilung des Bundesministeriums für Frauen und Jugend,* no. 32, 18 April 1991. See also "Gleichstellungspolitik in der DDR und der BRD" (report about a conference held at the Humboldt Universität, Berlin, 17–19 September 1990, Type-script).

18. Federal Ministry, *Frauen in der Bundesrepublik,* 80. Some 460,000 women

in the Federal Republic were members of one of the parties before unification, or about 1.7 percent of the female population over eighteen years.

19. Federal Ministry, *Frauen in der Bundesrepublik,* 79.

20. See the study by Beate Hoecker, *Frauen in der Politik* (Opladen: Leske und Budrich, 1987).

21. The largest share are Social Democratic women with sixty-four members (27 percent of the party's faction), followed by the CDU/CSU, the strongest faction in parliament (forty-four women, or 14 percent of the faction), the FDP (sixteen women, or 18 percent), and the two small parties, the PDS (eight women) and the Alliance '90/Greens (three women). In Länder, or state parliaments, the proportion of women varies between 9 and 29 percent. It is usually higher in states with a left-of-center majority (SPD, Greens), such as Hamburg or Schleswig-Holstein, whereas in the CDU and CSU-governed states, such as Baden-Württemberg, Saxony, or Bavaria, the proportion is smaller.

22. Petra Streit, "Raising Consciousness," *German Politics and Society,* no. 24–25 (1991–92): 10.

23. Bärbel Bohley ("mother of the revolution") became the major spokeswoman for the New Forum, the most popular oppositional group. Ulrike Poppe is an active member of Democracy Now. Vera Wollenberger is a founding member of the east German Green party and member of the German parliament for the Greens.

24. On earlier feminism in the GDR see Christiane Lemke, *Die Ursachen des Umbruchs 1989: Politische Sozialisation in der ehemaligen DDR* (Opladen: Westdeutscher, 1990), chap. 4.

25. The Independent Women's Association (Unabhängiger Frauenverband) was founded on 3 December 1989, in Berlin. See "Aufbruch der Frauen gegen die 'mittelmäßigne Männer," *Tageszeitung,* 4 December 1989; "Die Frauenbewegung braucht einen großen politischen Anspruch," interview with Ina Merkel, *Tageszeitung,* 6 December 1989. Clearly, earlier activities—often severely curtailed by the secret police, or Stasi—fed into the movement of 1989–90. In respect to the emergence of an informal network of women in academia in the GDR, see "Atemschwelle: Versuche, Richtung zu gewinnen," *Feministische Studien* 1 (1990): 90–106. Professional women in academic institutions published a statement in an official journal in November 1989, "Geht die Erneuerung an uns Frauen vorbei?" *Für Dich* 46 (1989). A Center for Interdisciplinary Women's Research was also established at the Humboldt University, Berlin. See Irene Dölling, "Situation und Perspektiven von Frauenforschung in der DDR," *Bulletin No. 1,* ed. Zentrum für interdisziplinäre Frauenforschung, Humboldt Universität Berlin (Berlin, 1990), 1–25.

26. When it became obvious early in 1990 that the GDR would move towards closer cooperation with the FRG, the association defined itself as a women's organization in "Germany." Winkel, *Frauenreport '90,* 204. For an elaboration on the early goals and policies of the new association, see Ina Merkel, "Frauen in der DDR: Vorschläge für eine Kultur der Geschlechterverhältnisse," in *Aufbruch in eine andere DDR,* ed. Hubertus Knabe (Reinbek: Rowohlt, 1989), 90–97.

27. This view is partly echoed by some American feminists. See, for example,

Dorothy Rosenberg, "Shock Therapy: The Effect of Unification on Women in Germany," *Signs* 17 (1991): 129–51.

28. The first free elections in the GDR brought the following results: Alliance for Germany (CDU, DSU, DA) 48 percent; SPD 21.8 percent; PDS 16.3 percent; Liberals 5.3 percent; Alliance '90 (New Forum and other civic groups) 2.9; Greens (with Independent Women's Association) 2.0; others 3.2 percent. A simple proportional system was used in the elections.

29. One example of the different approaches is the debate over male and female nouns and professional titles (*Berufsbezeichnungen*). Because of the feminist critique and pressure from women's groups in the (old) FRG, job advertisements have to address both male and female candidates (e.g., *Professor/in*) and there is a greater sensitivity about excluding women in addresses, newspaper, articles, and the like by using male nouns only. In the former GDR, on the other hand, only male titles were used and women would refer to themselves as *Dozent* (not *Dozentin*) or *Mechaniker* (not *Mechanikerin*). Among west German feminists and women's rights activists this is widely criticized as lack of consciousness, whereas east German women regarded the debate as superficial.

30. Streit, "Raising Consciousness," 14.

Reproduction and Reunification: The Politics of Abortion in United Germany

Jeremiah M. Riemer

The Open-and-Shut Case

In the summer of 1990, West German women in favor of reproductive choice found that unification with East Germany provided them with their first real opening on this issue in fifteen years.

The initial closure on abortion rights began in 1975, when the Constitutional Court in Karlsruhe overturned provisions in a recently enacted reform of Germany's century-old Penal Code that had substantially—and briefly— liberalized abortion throughout the old Federal Republic. Unlike the situation in the United States at the time of *Roe v. Wade,* the politics of abortion in West Germany pitted a left-liberal national legislature against a conservative court. By passing a law amending Paragraph 218 of the Penal Code, the ruling coalition of Social Democrats and Free Democrats in Bonn had tried to legalize abortions undertaken during the first three months of pregnancy. The only stipulation was that each operation be performed by a licensed physician after consultation. The 1974 regulation was immediately challenged by the Christian Democratic opposition and Länder under their control. As a the result of Karlsruhe's ruling, the Bundestag was forced to pass a more restrictive measure, which went into effect in 1976.[1]

In place of the 1974 measure's Fristenlösung ("term" or "periodic" model, roughly comparable to the trimester standard of *Roe v. Wade*), the 1976 law now substituted an Indikationslösung: abortions could be granted only if one of four specified criteria known as *indications* (such as rape or incest, danger to the mother's life, severe deformities in the fetus, or social hardship) were met. The role of counselors and doctors changed from advising pregnant women about a free decision before a deadline to determining which women would be eligible for an abortion. Doctors (who were barred from simultaneously performing any abortions they might approve) and counselors had to act in conformity with administrative guidelines set up by the different Länder, who under the German system implement federal laws. In practice it proved easier to obtain a favorable indication from counseling centers and doctors in the Protestant north than in the Catholic south. The north-south divide was paralleled by a division between de facto liberalization and de jure restrictions. Owing largely to the permissive attitude of authorities in the northern Länder, the number of abortions increased dramatically over the next decade and a half. But there was a legal backlash centered in conservative Bavaria. In 1988 Bavarian state attorneys put on trial a doctor from the town of Memmingen who had performed numerous unauthorized abortions for years. The highly publicized Memmingen case brought out intimate details about pregnant women's private lives in an atmosphere that feminists and sympathetic journalists were quick to call a "witchhunt" and "crusade."[2]

Meanwhile, during its last two decades as a separate state, Communist East Germany became a place where abortion during the first trimester had become a guaranteed right.

A lively public debate in July and August 1990 seemed to portend a new opening for reproductive choice in a uniting Germany. As the result of one state treaty that had gone into effect on 1 July, the German Democratic Republic was already joined to the Federal Republic in a currency and economic union. The two governments were now trying to work out the details of a second state treaty that they hoped would complete political unification by autumn, just in time to prepare for all-German elections in December. One of the most troublesome snags in the hurried negotiations turned out to be the abortion issue. There were several reasons for this.

One factor was public opinion. East Germans had voted overwhelmingly for conservative parties allied to Kohl's CDU in the Volkskammer election of March 1990, agreed to let West Germans run a trustee agency to privatize their industries, and had just exchanged their old currency for the deutsche mark in July. But they were by no means eager to give up their more liberal abortion law. Polls also showed that most West Germans favored either a liberal Fristenlösung or complete decriminalization of abortion; only a minority agreed with the Indikationslösung of 1975 or wanted something more severe.[3] An extension of the West German regulation into East Germany was not desired in the East; one could even argue that East German reproductive rights represented the only instance of a "socialist accomplishment" that most West Germans wanted for themselves.

Just as important as public opinion was the political constellation facing the negotiating parties. Though both German governments were now headed by Christian Democrats, only Chancellor Helmut Kohl was bound to the antiabortion position of the western CDU and its largely Catholic constituency. Kohl's East German counterpart, Lothar de Maizière, had stated that his government was committed to bringing an East German component into unification. De Maizière had also looked forward to making both Germany and his Christian Democratic party "more Protestant." The eastern Christian Democrats came mostly from the Evangelical church. In contrast to the United States, where an evangelical Protestant is often an activist against abortion rights, the term in Germany refers to the established Lutheran church, whose opposition to abortion has never been as strong as for the Catholic church. (Among German Protestants, only a minority of Lutheran pietists or members of free congregations have protested against abortion as militantly as American evangelicals.) Furthermore, the governing East German CDU headed a "Grand Coalition" including Social Democrats and Liberals, while the Christian-Liberal coalition in Bonn depended on the opposition SPD for majorities needed to approve the constitutional changes that were to accompany the unification treaty. All these factors gave pro-choice forces a stronger voice than they would have had under conditions of routine politics.

The negotiations on the unification treaty made it look as though the proponents of liberalized abortion rights might be able to test their chances in this more fluid political climate. An impasse over Paragraph 218 during the negotiations led to a compromise in the final document (ratified at the end of the summer) that promised to keep the issue open for as long as another two years. But within a year after unification, the issue seemed to be heading for a second closure along the familiar lines of routine politics. Three dimensions of this special "open-and-shut" case are worth examining: the state (its territorial jurisdiction and institutions), the parties (and their role in the political process), and the public policy discourse.

1. Unification involved a territorial extension of West German federalism eastward to five Länder that had only a brief existence in the GDR before coming under the direct rule of East Berlin. Postwar German federalism as practiced in the West for forty years has always combined a minimum of centralism with a maximum of *subsidiarity*, the principle of relying on local government as much as possible. It is the extensive civil services of the Länder, rather than the small central government in Bonn, that implement and enforce most federal laws. All levels of governments, in turn, often delegate administration to quasi-autonomous (or *parapublic*) institutions.[4] The extension of subsidiarity and cooperative federalism to the new Länder posed several unique and difficult questions in the abortion case: If the east Germans and their

west German supporters insisted on keeping a separate regulation in the new Länder, what principles of jurisdiction would apply to German citizens who resided in the old Federal Republic but availed themselves of the more liberal east German abortion law (or who—to put the same point another way—"violated" west German law while on east German territory)? Given that the five new Länder were not equipped with trained public administrations and parapublic institutions to carry out the provision of the unification treaty requiring advising centers for pregnant women, how would the federal government set up these centers on the east Germans' behalf? Finally, how would different political forces with a say on questions of jurisdiction and institution building—opposition parties with veto power over ratification of the unification treaty, coalition partners in the East and Federal German governments, and a chancellor with broad powers to allocate ministerial posts—affect the extension of German federalism to the East where the abortion issue was involved?

2. Political parties dominate the legislative process in Germany in a way that makes it difficult for independent political actors to build alliances cutting across party lines or to bypass parties altogether. Activists in the women's movement have had the choice of working *within* parties that have other priorities or of protesting *against* parties from the outside; appealing to individual legislators (even those elected from constituency districts) is not a routine option. However, the special circumstances of German unification led to stalemates on a few issues (such as abortion and the choice of a working capital city) that forced the architects of unification (themselves heads of parties or party strategists) to suspend party and coalition discipline on these isolated issues. Even so, the tendency for party control to reassert itself was strong once the initial reasons for stalemate (in this case, the need to gain quick Four Power approval of the unification treaty) disappeared. After unification, legislators who were formally free to vote their consciences on the abortion issue still knew that their careers depended on party loyalty.

3. Whereas in the United States the abortion debate has aptly been described as a "clash of absolutes"[5] between competing definitions of rights, in Germany the public-policy discourse is characterized by what looks like a compromise incorporating values of family and community.[6] The American debate has pitted advocates of abortion rights, defined as a matter of personal freedom and privacy ("freedom of choice"), against "right-to-life" crusaders who frequently invoke the family while opposing publicly supported education about birth control and family planning. By contrast, there seems to be a widespread con-

sensus in Germany about the desirability of reducing the number of abortions and the important role that social-welfare measures and family policy have to play. During the unification process, some middle-of-the-road politicians believed that this social consensus might form the basis for a "third way" between East Germany's liberal policy and West Germany's more stringent regulation. Even after the deadlock on abortion became apparent, all political parties continued to highlight the social dimension by paying special attention to the importance of advising centers for pregnancy counseling. Yet the apparent consensus on family welfare could not conceal a conflict on the existential stakes of the abortion question as deep as in the United States. The abortion compromise imposed by Germany's Constitutional Court is one that the six competing partisan proposals for a new regulation seek variously to simplify, harden, appease, or challenge. How the social dimension is emphasized by politicians says more about the different parties' strategies for coping with the court's ruling than it does about their acceptance of the court's reasoning. That reasoning, in turn, is partly based on an interpretation of Nazi policies on abortion and civil liberties that is by no means the most persuasive reading of Germany's past.[7]

State Institutions and Jurisdiction

1990—The Two-State Solution

Until the summer of 1990 West German conservatives in the CSU and CDU were insisting that an all-German regulation on abortion law follow the general pattern of unification: here, as in other fields, they wanted East Germany "annexed" to the Federal Republic. A more liberal group around Bundestag President Rita Süssmuth (who as Health and Family Minister had stood down conservatives in her party on AIDS) still hoped to find some kind of compromise—a third way—between the West's restrictive Indikationslösung and the East's permissive Fristenlösung. But as the deadline for ratification loomed, the chief negotiator of the treaty on the West German side, Interior Minister Interior Wolfgang Schäuble, received instructions from Chancellor Kohl not to let the treaty founder on the abortion issue. In order to expedite unification, Schäuble and his East German counterpart, Günther Krause, settled on what amounted to a two-state solution. Each territory would retain its original law.

Both unitary solutions—either extending West German law to the new Länder or trying to find a third way—proved to be so fraught with complications that Schäuble made sure that they were ruled out by July. But the two-state solution for abortion within the framework of a single state created problems all its own. Two of these snags held up negotiations at the last moment in August. One question that needed to be answered was how long the interim solution of two regulations would last. The other was how to treat abortions sought by residents of the original West German Länder in what would soon be the "former GDR."

Conservatives were only willing to accept a short transition period before the Federal Republic's law (or something stricter) became applicable in the East. Kohl and Schäuble took their side because the chancellor and his negotiator worried that an interim of up to four years might keep the abortion issue alive for the elections of 1994. The CDU was already looking forward to solid victories in most of the new Länder soon after unification, and Kohl was confident of becoming confirmed as the first all-German postwar chancellor at the polls in December 1990. The party's long-term electoral strategy depended on using these windfall mandates to see the eastern part of Germany through tough economic times; extraneous issues like abortion only distracted from this single-minded task.

For precisely the opposite reasons, and because they hoped that a viable model of choice in the new Länder might set a positive example for the entire country, the SPD and others on the left side of the abortion issue sought a longer tenure for the separate regulation obtaining in the soon-to-be former GDR. Ultimately, the SPD settled for a two-year period, but only after the Social Democrats and the Free Democrats extracted a concession from the CDU on the other outstanding issue—jurisdiction.

In August the Liberal cabinet ministers and higher civil servants working with Kohl and Schäuble on the unification treaty raised a last-minute objection to the principle of jurisdiction favored by the CDU. Like their Christian Democratic colleagues, the male leaders of the FDP were originally inclined to treat abortion as a marginal issue. But pressured by the women in their ranks, the Liberal party leaders sided with the SPD on changing the principle of jurisdiction from residency (Wohnortprinzip) to site of occurence (Tatortprinzip).

There was no small irony in the designations endorsed by the two sides in this subsidiary debate. In German, Tatort also means "scene of the crime." (Anyone who has watched German television knows that Tatort is also the name of a popular police detective series.) Those in favor of decriminalizing abortion thus had to employ legal language implying that it was indeed a crime. The Tatortprinzip meant that west German prosecutors and courts would be helpless to prevent abortions undertaken by west German women who picked a clinic east of the Elbe as the "scene of the crime." This principle was written into the treaty in spite of conservative anxieties that it would promote "abortion tourism" in the east.

The unification treaty charged the Bundestag with finding a single regulation for all of Germany by the end of 1992. If parliament could not meet that deadline, the GDR's "material law" would continue to be valid. The new regulation would have to guarantee "the protection of prenatal life" and commit the government to helping "master conflict situations in accordance with the constitution" by giving women "legally secure claims to advising and social assistance." These guarantees had to be "better than what currently prevails in both parts of Germany." In order to bridge the temporary gap between the two jurisdictions, the government was also required to set up an extensive network of advising centers for pregnant women in the former GDR. These advising centers had to be "personally and financially equipped so that they could fulfill their task of advising pregnant women and providing them with necessary assistance—beyond the point of birth as well."[8] As with the agreements on the tenure and jurisdiction of the two-state solution, the provisions for advising centers reflected a compromise between the CDU, which emphasized the passages on "better" protection for the fetus, and the SPD, which insisted on broad social assistance addressing a variety of situations affecting pregnant women and new mothers.

1991—Divide and Conquer

After its victory in the federal election on 3 December 1990, the Kohl government pursued a divide-and-conquer strategy on the abortion question by adminstrative means. At Kohl's disposal were the established institutions of the Federal Republic's "chancellor democracy" and the new advising centers mandated by the unification treaty. Having acquired new constituencies in the east—non-Catholic workers and women accustomed to abortion rights—the CDU now put both old and new institutions to work in order to counteract a consequence of its own electoral success.

   Within the limits of coalition government, the federal chancellor has broad constitutional powers to shape a cabinet, including the power to create and consolidate ministries. In constructing his first all-German government, Kohl used these powers to give the appearance of strengthening women's influence while actually diluting their power. Before leaving the cabinet for the presidency of the Bundestag, Family Minister Rita Süssmuth had occasionally been a forceful liberal voice on women's issues inside the Kohl government of the 1980s. Her successor, Ursula Lehr, was less outspoken but inherited a post that put her in charge of a nominally wide range of issues—youth, family, women, and health. Now Kohl proposed to split Lehr's ministry in three. He thereby increased the number of female faces in the cabinet, including an east German who was put in charge of women's policy. But the real impact of this change was to contain, rather than amplify, the voices of east German women on abortion policy.

The division of assignments and the degree of experience among the three cabinet ministers revealed what was really at stake in the reorganization.[9] Of the three new ministries (Health, Family and Seniors, Women and Youth), only the Health Ministry headed by Gerda Hasselfeldt of the CSU was given any real power when it acquired (from the Welfare Ministry) responsibility for setting policy on the health insurance funds, now being extended to the East. The west German woman put in charge of the Ministry for Family and Seniors, Hannelore Rönsch, claimed that responsibility for Paragraph 218 belonged on her tiny department's turf because "abortion is a family matter." Her strong views on abortion policy were not merely procedural. She criticized the "assembly-line morality" of women who abort too readily ("200,000 abortions per year are too many") and looked forward to establishing advisory centers in the former GDR, where "they haven't even reflected on the subject heretofore."[10]

These advisory centers aside, real responsibility for Paragraph 218 lay with the man appointed to the Justice Ministry by the Liberals. The new head at Justice, Klaus Kinkel, had only recently decided to join the Free Democratic party. In his previous post as State Secretary in the Justice Ministry he had occasionally seemed willing to compromise on such classically liberal issues as privacy or reproductive choice where the civil libertarian position clashed with priorities like administrative uniformity and public security. During the unification treaty negotiations, Kinkel had originally sided with Schäuble on the Wohnortprinzip, ostensibly on constitutional grounds.[11]

This left Angela Merkel, a soft-spoken Lutheran pastor's daughter, as the sole defender of an east German woman's perspective in the cabinet. Thirty-six years old at the time of her appointment, Merkel had the least political experience of any cabinet member and owed her quick political rise to Chancellor Kohl. (Her only previous post was as press spokesperson to de Maizière, whom she would later replace as the token easterner on the CDU executive.) Her mini-ministry, Women and Youth, had little control over abortion policy. Whereas Rönsch's Family Ministry claimed some administrative responsibility for the issue, Merkel's department was given other assignments, such as child and day care. The rationale for this division of labor was provided by the chief administrative deputies to both ministers. Rönsch's state secretary, Roswitha Verhülsdonk, insisted that the CDU's new thinking on women transcended outworn categories: "We no longer put women in boxes—60% family mother, 40% worker." Her counterpart in Merkel's ministry, Peter Hintze, formulated the same point as a rhetorical challenge to feminists: "Now women and family aren't mentioned in the same breath—is that emancipation, after all?"[12]

During the short-lived intra-German dialogue on Rita Süssmuth's proposed third way in July 1990, Roswitha Verhülsdonk had commented on how difficult it was to persuade her GDR colleagues in the CDU about the superiority of the western regulation on abortion: "Under socialism they were never able to reflect on ethics."[13] Using the appointment powers of the chancellory was one technique for isolating east German Protestants and women within a predominantly Catholic and western party that looked on their new citizens from the East as people who had grown up in an ethical wasteland. The new advising centers for pregnant women that Family Minister Rönsch was setting up in the new Länder provided the Christian Democrats with another opportunity for moral education in conservative reproductive ethics. As in other areas of policy, social welfare and family planning in the Federal Republic are carried out by parapublic institutions that range from communal organizations to church groups.[14] Vague administrative guidelines allowed Rönsch's Family Ministry to implement the unification treaty's call for "an extensive network of advising centers of different carriers" in a way that favored conservative institutions over centers that might also provide information on birth control. In West Germany, most women with unwanted pregnancies could avail themselves of advice from Pro Familia, an organization similar to Planned Parenthood. But the federal Family Ministry awarded hardly any east German slots to Pro Familia and gave far more advising centers in this overwhelmingly secular and Protestant region to the Catholic charitable organization Caritas.[15]

Parties and Process—Release from Party Discipline?

Virtually all votes in the Bundestag take place along strict party lines. Party control makes it nearly impossible for groups with interests that cross partisan boundaries, such as women, to form alliances on single issues of supreme importance to them. In cases like abortion, party discipline can also erect a barrier against translating public attitudes commanding a majority into public policy. But on two issues that threatened to hold up the unification process in the summer of 1990—abortion and the choice of a working capital city (Berlin or Bonn)—arrangements were made to release the parties from their customary discipline. During the last-minute wrangling between government and opposition in August 1990, which produced the compromise of Tatortprinzip plus a two-year separate regulation for the East, the Social Democrats tried to extract a formal commitment from the CDU that party discipline would be suspended when it came to an all-German parliament's vote on a new abortion law. Chief negotiator Schäuble, insisting that the concept of party discipline had no constitutional standing, refused to put any such promise in writing.[16] But informal talks among the parties, together with the FDP's strong showing in the 3 December elections, led to a coalition agreement between the Christian Democrats and Liberals that freed delegates from both governing parties to vote their consciences on a reform of Paragraph 218.

One year into unification, the upshot of unbinding the parties from coalition discipline appeared to be a hardening of partisan positions. The new legislative term began with promises to find common ground. In January 1991 the highest-ranking woman member of the FDP, Irmgard Adam-Schwaetzer, vowed to introduce a measure by February. Her proposal was a compromise slightly to the left of Süssmuth's third way and similar to the Social-Liberal government's law of 1974. Adam-Schwaetzer's formula was Fristenlösung plus Zwangsberatung—the term model after obligatory advising. But the Bundestag waited until a commission of Christian Democrats came up with its recommendation before debating six separate bills, two for the CDU and one for every other party caucus represented in the Bundestag, on 26 September.

The CDU majority, in line with the party commission's report, foresaw a simplification of the prevailing west German Indikationslösung, with two indications (medical and psychosocial emergency) replacing the current four and with stricter criteria for approval of abortions by doctors. A minority in the CDU/CSU favored toughening the law by striking every indication except medical cause. The SPD came out for a term model with generous provisions for voluntary advising, while the FDP introduced a measure based on the Adam-Schwaetzer formula (term model with *obligatory* advising). The two small parties representing only east Germans, the PDS and the Alliance '90 grouping affiliated with the Greens, both wanted to get rid of Paragraph 218 altogether, with the PDS additionally favoring a constitutionally guaranteed right to abortion. After a first reading and debate of all six bills, a Bundestag commission was set up to study the matter further.[17]

The press was full of talk about a workable compromise, based on speculation that the SPD and FDP would settle their differences on the requirements of advising and be joined by Christian Democrats who were indicating that they could live with a term model. Such a compromise depended on enough Christian Democrats breaking ranks with their party and joining liberals like Walter Wallmann, a member of the CDU Presidium and ex-minister-president of Hesse, who published an essay in the weekly news magazine *Der Spiegel* advocating a term regulation as the only practical solution.[18] But no matter what individual Christian Democrats said to the media, the legislative process itself sharpened party lines. The sole example of dissension from party leadership in the Bundestag, the two-way split among the Christian Democrats, showed that the largest parliamentary group was divided not on how to compromise but on where to draw the line between the Christian Democratic position and that of the other parties. Leaders of the CDU/CSU and FDP did try to reach agreement on the financial provisions of abortion legislation by advancing the argument that the coalition agreement freeing members of parliament to vote their consciences on Paragraph 218 applied only to the reform of the criminal code and that "shifting majorities" were otherwise undesirable. Had this argument won the day, it would have greatly strengthened the hand of Finance Minister Theo Waigel (CSU). But this coalition side agreement, apparently approved by the Liberals' chairman and parliamentary leader, was indignantly rebuffed by others in the FDP (notably by the party's general secretary, a woman, and a former interior minister with strong liberal convictions).[19]

The Public Policy Discourse—The Shadow of the Court and the Shadow of the Past

The third way on abortion that Rita Süssmuth had introduced into the public debate in 1990 was something of a misnomer. Traditionally, the concept referred to the possibility of a middle position between free-market capitalism and Soviet-style Communism. Its points of reference were the Scandinavian welfare state, interwar ideals of worker self-management later revived by the New Left, or the vague postwar hopes for a synthesis of social democratic and Christian social teachings that were displaced by the ideological battle lines of the cold war. Süssmuth's slogan of the third way referred to a more concrete possibility, that of compromise between East German abortion rights and West German abortion restrictions. In fact, the substance of the Süssmuth compromise (an Indikationslösung so loose as to approach the Fristenlösung plus Zwangsberatung later proposed by Schwaetzer) was slightly more conservative than what East Germany already had and what most West Germans probably wanted. What really mattered was the procedural message conveyed by the Bundestag president's use of the term third way. She wished to signal (above all to the women in the East German CDU) that, despite their smaller numbers and minimal bargaining clout, the views of her East German colleagues would carry weight in the negotiation process.

The distinction between substance and procedure is helpful in understanding exactly how East German views figured, more passively than actively, in the all-German discourse. Procedurally, the chief East German contribution was catalytic: the mere presence of an East German negotiating party allowed the abortion debate to be reopened—until such time as it could be settled along West German lines. Substantively, what mattered most was the effort West German politicians made to strengthen the "social" component of public policy toward pregnant women, ostensibly as a gesture toward their new East German constituents.

By 1990 even the most conservative politician could recognize that many East Germans worried about losing such "socialist accomplishments" as child care and kindergarten even as they rushed to embrace capitalism. None of the established parties wanted these themes to be monopolized by the PDS, the successor party to the SED. It was not surprising that the SPD should have been emphasizing state-provided care for mothers and infants. Nor was the stress on family policy unusual for the Christian Democrats. Conservative family values (indeed the very concept of family) were at the core of the CDU's identity from its inception, when they helped Adenauer integrate much of the once fractured German Right into a successful catchall party during the 1950s.[20] A Christian Democratic innovation in the 1980s was the creation of a federally funded foundation, Mother and Child—Protection of Unborn Life, to assist pregnancy counselors.[21] But why was the FDP—a market-oriented party with virtually no working-class backing and an attitude toward the welfare state best described as one of begrudging acceptance—insisting on social assistance to pregnant women? And why was it the SPD, rather than the Free Democrats, that seemed to be occupying the more liberal (small *l*) political space where abortion was defined as a personal decision free from political interference?

All three parties would have agreed with Maria Michalk, the East German Christian Democrat appointed to head the CDU's commission on Paragraph 218, that social assistance had to be the core of any abortion law.[22] But the centrality of the social dimension meant different things to different parties. In each of these meanings, the question of how to deal with the Constitutional Court was paramount, while incorporating East German concerns was secondary or incidental. The CDU/CSU adopted a strategy of conversion to forestall legal action by its own right wing, the FDP opted to play it safe by second-guessing the court, while the Social Democrats appeared willing to risk testing the court and demonstrate the desirability of constitutional reform.

The essentials of the CDU's strategy, using the Family Ministry to set up counseling centers as agents of moral education in the new Länder, has already been mentioned. It only remains to be added that this was a two-front strategy within the CDU/CSU itself. On the eastern front, the party made sure either to appoint East German Christian Democrats (*a*) whose potential advocacy for a liberal regulation (as expressed in the eastern CDU's 1990 party program)[23] could be isolated within the party or (*b*) who were more like western Catholics than eastern Lutherans. Angela Merkel, who as late as the spring of 1991 was reiterating her support for decriminalization and freedom of conscience, was an example of the former.[24] Maria Michalk, who became chair of the CDU's internal commission and a vice-chair of the party's parliamentary group, was an example of the latter; as a representative of the

East German Sorbs, an ethnic Slavic minority, she was one of the few Catholics in the eastern CDU.[25]

The second frontline creating problems for the CDU/CSU was south of the Main river rather than east of the Elbe. Even before unification, the government of Bavaria (home of the Memmingen trials) planned to go before the Constitutional Court and challenge the permissive implementation of abortion policy in other Länder and the use of health-insurance funds to pay for abortions. Early in 1991, Kohl hoped to postpone having the CDU/CSU take a position on a new abortion law until the court had dealt with the Bavarian case. However the Constitutional Court would not accommodate Kohl's schedule. With an overload of new cases (many pertaining to unification) crowding its docket, the court signaled that it would rather wait for the Bundestag to pass a new law before it passed on the Bavarian government's complaint about current practice.[26] In July, after the CSU staked out its hardline position at a party conference in Ansbach, the Bavarians renewed their threat of constitutional action.[27] Since the CSU's chairman, Theo Waigel, was also federal Finance Minister, the Bavarians had a certain leverage over CDU moderates. (A promise to increase family allowances and guarantee a kindergarten slot for every child by 1995 was part of the CDU/CSU package.)[28] So it was not surprising that the CDU/CDU commission on abortion thereupon tried to accommodate the Ansbach Declaration.[29] Even this move to the right did not prevent the conservative Werner Group (named after an MP from Ulm) from introducing a minority draft banning all abortions except ones based on a strictly defined medical indication.[30]

Neither the SPD nor the FDP had to contend with conservatives or litigious dissenters inside their parties. But the Liberals did not want a replay of the Constitutional Court's 1975 decision overturning the 1974 law. The FDP, with its formula of trimester model plus obligatory counseling (a three-day moratorium before obtaining an abortion during the first twelve weeks), decided to stay on the safe side of compromise, even seeking advice from a law clerk (Referentin) at the Constitutional Court.[31] The SPD's legal experts were less worried about second-guessing the court because they were more willing to consider the option of constitutional amendments if their preferred solution (a trimester regulation with optional counseling) failed to pass the test of constitutional review. More than the other established parties, the Social Democrats liked the idea of using German unification as an opportunity to craft a new constitution modifying the nominally provisional Basic Law of 1949.[32] The SPD hoped that this more permanent constitution would enumerate new personal rights (such as a right to employment) and "state goals" (such as a public commitment to ecology). During the summer 1990 debate on abortion, some Social Democratic jurists specifically proposed anchoring a "right to self-determined pregnancy" in the constitution.[33] Regardless of their strategic differences, all the major parties claimed to be guided by the principle of Hilfe statt Strafe, aid instead of punishment. The parties argued over the size, content, and meaning of social assistance. The CDU portrayed its proposal as more family oriented, while the SPD accused the CDU of patriarchal policies that insulted women facing a difficult decision with small financial incentives to bear children.[34] But all agreed that the social dimension was vital to gaining the Constitutional Court's approval of any law. Where they disagreed was over the question of whether providing assistance to pregnant women made punishment unnecessary altogether. Here, too, the vital question was how to read the message of the Constitutional Court.

Critics of the Constitutional Court's 1975 decision, such as the League of Women Lawyers, have pointed out that the court is not bound to reject a new law for the same reasons today.[35] Nevertheless, a review of the majority and dissenting decisions in the 1975 case conveys an impression of the constraints felt by legislators making decisions about how far abortion might be decriminalized.

In 1975 the court majority had held that provisions in the Basic Law guaranteeing everyone "the right to life and to the inviolability of his person" extended to the fetus and required the legislature to "protect . . . developing life" where necessary by "strengthen[ing] the expectant mother to accept the pregnancy as her own responsibility and to bring the fetus to full term." In considering the balance between criminal penalties and social measures, the state could "not forget that nature has entrusted the protection of the developing life to the mother" and that its "principal goal . . . should be to reawaken and, if required, to strengthen the maternal will to protect [the unborn child] where it has been lost." The court admitted that "the use of criminal law gives rise to special problems which result from the singular situation of the pregnant woman." The state was not required to use criminal sanctions where social measures like counseling would work better. However, the majority stated that "in all other cases the termination of a pregnancy remains a wrong deserving of punishment" and that the legislature could only "dispense with criminal sanctions . . . under the condition that another, equally effective legal sanction was at its command which would permit the clear recognition of this act as a wrong (disapprobation by the legal order) and which would prevent abortions as effectively as a penal provision."[36]

If the majority viewed punishment as an indispensable last resort, the two dissenters (including the court's only woman) took the view that the Basic Law could not compel the legislature to use criminal sanctions. "According to the freedom-oriented character of our Constitution," the dissenters wrote, "the legislature must have a justification for punishing but not for abstaining from punishment." The dissenters faulted the majority for failing to exercise judicial self-restraint and for misunderstanding (indeed reversing) the constitution's theory of fundamental rights. Whereas the dissenters saw the Basic Law guaranteeing "the citizen *defensive rights* vis-à-vis the state," the majority believed in a "more extensive meaning of fundamental rights as *objective value decisions* . . . which the state must continually implement through affirmative measures."[37]

Related to the philosophical disagreement over punishment and rights was a historical dispute over the relationship between Article 2, Section 2 of the Basic Law (right to life and inviolability of the person) and Germany's Nazi past.[38] The majority pointed out that this section of the Basic Law "may be explained principally as a reaction to the 'destruction of life unworthy to live,' the 'final solution,' and 'liquidations' that the National Socialist regime carried out as governmental measures." In Article 2 (2) and in another article outlawing the death penalty, the Basic Law affirmed "the fundamental value of human life and of a state concept which emphatically opposes the view of a political regime for which the individual life had little significance and therefore which practiced unlimited abuse in the name of the arrogated right over life and death of the citizen."[39] To protect life in the womb, argued the Court, was to oppose the logic of the Holocaust.

The dissenters questioned the majority's abstract reasoning, offered a more contextual reading of this chapter in German history, and came to a diametrically opposite conclusion about the implications of the Nazi past for the relationship between the state and reproductive choice. The Basic Law's reaction against the inhumane ideology and practice of national socialism, wrote the dissenters,

> referred to the mass extermination of human life by the state in concentration camps and among the mentally ill, to officially ordered sterilization and forced abortions, to medical experiments with humans against their will and to countless other state measures expressing disregard for individual life and human dignity.
>
> To draw conclusions about the constitutional evaluation of a killing of the fetus undertaken not by the state but by the pregnant women herself or with the volition of a third party is even more misplaced when one considers that the National Socialist regime itself adopted a very rigorous standpoint on this issue corresponding to its biological-demographic ideology.[40]

The two dissenting justices pointed out that the Third Reich enforced statutes against abortion more strictly than had been done in the Weimar era. Tougher penalities, including penitentiary sentences, were meted out to those assisting in abortions and to pregnant women who aborted on their own. In cases where abortion (in Nazi terminology) "infringed upon the continued vitality of the German people" the death penalty was introduced. Given that these "gruesome and excessively high penalities" were still on the books while the Basic Law was being framed, and were only removed by intervention of the Allied occupation forces, the dissenters argued that "the reasons leading to Article 2, Section 2 of the Basic Law could hardly be invoked in favor of a constitutional obligation to punish abortions." If any lesson was to be drawn from the Basic Law's "decisive rejection of the totalitarian National Socialist state," they concluded, it had to be one enjoining "restraint from the use of criminal penalties."[41]

To the extent that the 1975 dissent was any indication of how the court might rule differently on a more liberal abortion law in the 1990s, proponents of choice could hope that decriminalization and a stress on individual rights might win out over the conservative interpretation of fundamental rights obliging punishment as a last resort against violations of state goals. What the advocates of choice could not count on was a *Roe v. Wade*–like defense of abortion as a right to privacy, which even the Court's two dissenters in 1975 had said "would be going too far."[42] Political advocates of abortion rights usually stressed that they shared the conservatives' goal of reducing the number of abortions. Pointing out that the abortion rate in both parts of Germany was roughly the same, in spite of the different regulations, they rejected punishment partly because it was less effective than social assistance. One of the reasons why the debate was crowded with statements looking askance on abortion, with pragmatic arguments about the ineffectiveness of punishment, and with positive references to counseling and social assistance as a more hopeful alternative was the hope that all these sentiments would impress a court about the conservative intent of the most liberal legislation. Placing "child-friendly" statements in the legislative record provided legislators worried about judicial review with a paper trail from Bonn to Karlsruhe.

Conclusion

Although the West German women's movement helped put abortion reform on the political agenda in the 1970s, feminist demands for the repeal of Paragraph 218 became increasingly isolated in subsequent decades or were moderated in the name of political pragmatism and concessions to fetal protection.[43] Unification with East Germany, where women took stronger abortion rights for granted, did not bring the fortification of feminist power some expected, in part because women in the two halves of Germany soon discovered that they inhabited very different worlds.[44] Some women's groups, notably the League of Women Lawyers, entered into the debate on abortion and unification, especially in July of 1991, when a trimester regulation or "third way" for all of Germany seemed possible.[45] But the jurists who mattered most in the debate were the in-house lawyers hired by the parties and the state.

As with every other aspect of German unification, the abortion question was caught between reason of state (Staatsräson) and the logic of party government (Parteienräson). The abortion case was opened because parties held the statesmen negotiating the unification treaty hostage to a demand that the negotiators considered secondary. The case began to shut when party politics reasserted itself after unification. By the end of 1991 some movement away from the parties' rigid positions and toward a workable majority in the Bundestag was detectable as increasing numbers of Christian Democrats (including a few east Germans anticipating the party congress in Dresden) contemplated abandoning their "unification chancellor" for common ground with the Liberals.[46] Such a reopening of reproductive choice (with the attendant risks of conservative judicial rejection) could be attributed to party politics *on behalf of* women inside and outside the new Länder. But there could be no talk of an east German "contribution" to unity or of an autonomous women's politics.

NOTES

A grant from the German Marshall Fund of the United States to observe the March 1990 Volkskammer election helped to initiate research on this and other aspects of German unification. The author also wishes to thank Deidre Berger, Abby Collins, Catherine Epstein, Michael G. Huelshoff, Peggy Knudson, Andy Markovits, Wendy Mink, Michaela Richter, Steve Sokol, and Felix Zwoch.

1. On the legislation and judicial review of the 1970s, see Donald P. Kommers, "Abortion and Constitution: United States and West Germany," *American Journal of Contemporary Law* 25 (1977): 255–85; Hartmut Gerstein and David Lowry, "Abortion, Abstract Norms, and Social Control: The Decision of the West German Federal Constitutional Court," *Emory Law Journal* 25 (1976): 849–78.

2. Gisela Friedrichsen, *Abtreibung: Der Kreuzzug von Memmingen* (Frankfurt am Main: Fischer, 1991).

3. A poll undertaken by Emnid for *Der Spiegel* found 23 percent of West Germans and 43 percent of East Germans in favor of complete decriminalization, with 33 percent of West Germans and 35 percent of East Germans preferring a trimester regulation. See "Wie ein Gong: Die Union will in dieser Woche über einen eigenen Entwurf zur Reform des Abtreibungsparagraphen 218 abstimmen," *Der Spiegel*, 16 September 1991, 24. Another poll commissioned by the illustrated magazine *Neue*

Revue found that 89 percent of those interviewed (1,574 men and women between sixteen and sixty years old) favored one of two term models; those interviewed were evenly split between favoring no restrictions (with the offer of counseling) and non-binding restrictions (obligatory counseling) during the first trimester. See "89 Prozent für Fristenlösung," *Frankfurter Rundschau*, 20 September 1991.

4. Peter J. Katzenstein, *Policy and Politics in West Germany: The Growth of a Semi-Sovereign State* (Philadelphia: Temple University Press, 1987), chap. 1.

5. Laurence H. Tribe, *Abortion: The Clash of Absolutes* (New York: Norton, 1990).

6. See Mary Ann Glendon, *Abortion and Divorce in Western Law: American Failures, European Challenges* (Cambridge: Harvard University Press, 1987).

7. For a more differentiated reading of German legal traditions, emphasizing the contrast between the court majority's "authoritarian liberalism" and the dissenting opinion's "classical liberalism of parliamentary supremacy," see Douglas G. Morris, "Abortion and Liberalism: A Comparison between the Abortion Decisions of the Supreme Court of the United States and the Constitutional Court of West Germany," *Hastings International and Comparative Law Review* 11 (1988): 159–245. The instrumentalization of the national socialist legacy for the Federal Republic's debate is fully explored in Catherine Epstein, "Abortion in Germany: The Political Uses of the Nazi Past" (Harvard University History Department, photocopy).

8. Article 31, Paragraph 4 of the Unification Treaty, reprinted in *Der Vertrag zur deutschen Einheit* (Frankfurt am Main: Insel, 1990), 78.

9. Werner A. Prager, "Ein Kabinett für den Alltag," *Die Zeit,* 1 February 1991, North American edition, 6.

10. "Ministerinnen: Ein bischen zuständig. Im aufgesplitterten Gesundheitsministerium haben jetzt gleich drei Frauen wenig zu sagen," *Der Spiegel,* 18 February, 1991, 73.

11. Wolfgang Schäuble, *Der Vertrag: Wie ich über die deutsche Einheit verhandelte* (Stuttgart: Deutsche, 1991), 238.

12. "Ministerinnen," 73.

13. "Wie Pusteblumen: in Gesamtdeutschland gibt es zunächst zwei Abtreibungsgesetzte: Vier Jahre soll die DDR-Fristenlösung fortgelten," *Der Spiegel,* 2 July 1990, 70.

14. Katzenstein, *Policy and Politics.*

15. "Leicht übergangen: Beim Ausbau der Schwangerschaftsberatung in der Ex-DDR bevorzugt Bonn konservative Organisationen," *Der Spiegel,* 22 April 1991, 81.

16. Schäuble, *Der Vertrag,* 238.

17. See *Frankfurter Allgemeine Zeitung,* 27 September 1991, for a summary of the debate and drafts. The full debate is reprinted in *Das Parlament,* 4–11 October 1991.

18. "'Für die Fristenlösung': CDU-Präsidiumsmitglied Walter Wallmann über Abtreibung und die Grenzen des Strafrechts," *Der Spiegel,* 16 September 1991, 26–30.

19. See "Zweifel an einheitlicher Linie der Union im Parteien-Streit über den Paragraphen 218," *Frankfurter Allgemeine Zeitung,* 19 September 1991; "Zwischen Union und FDP zeichnet Streit ab," *Frankfurter Allgemeine Zeitung,* 20 September

1991. On the importance of the financial package, see "Risiko des Scheiterns: Die im Einigungsvertrag vorgesehene Reform der Abtreibungsregelen in Ost und West könnte an Geldmangel scheitern," *Der Spiegel*, 5 August 1991, 22–23.

20. Claus Leggewie, *Die Republikaner: Phantombild der neuen Rechter*, 2d ed. (Berlin: Rotbuch, 1989), 33–43.

21. Bundesministerium für Jugend, Familie, Frauen, und Gesundheit, *Frauen in der Bundesrepublik Deutschland* (Bonn, 1989), 96. This report on the status of women and what the federal government was doing for them was one of several publications available from the Bundeszentrale für politische Bildung, which stationed trailers outside places like the Brandenburg Gate and the department store Kaufhaus des Westens in 1990 so that East Germans could learn about how the West German system worked.

22. Charima Reinhardt, "Streit um §218-Kompromiss: Union vertagt Entscheidung/Keine Einigung über soziale Hilfen," *Frankfurter Rundschau*, 18 September 1991.

23. The draft program of the CDU in the GDR printed a day before the 18 March 1990 Volkskammer election stated:

Protecting unborn and born life places great responsibility on society and parents.

Helpful assistance accompanying applications for abortions must precede this decision of conscience. Society has to create conditions under which the life of the child will be chosen and can be conducted in the framework of good, humane relations.

Prohibitions on abortion and threats of punishment are no aid to life.

Reprinted in *Die aktuelle Programmatik von Parteien und politischen Vereinigungen in der DDR: Dokumentionen* (Berlin: Wahltreff 90—Zentrum für politische Information und Dokumention, 1990), 27.

24. Günter Bannas, "Die Jüngste in Kohls Kabinett raucht noch in der Öffentlichkeit: Angela Merkel zeigt kein Ministergebaren," *Frankfurter Allgemeine Zeitung*, 3 April 1991.

25. Another East German Catholic, Claudia Nolte, was made speaker of the Working Group on Women and Youth and appointed to the CDU parliamentary group's commission on Paragraph 218 along with Michalk. See "Vernünftige Lösung: Kanzler Kohl will verhindern, dass die ostdeutsche Fristenlösung auf Westdeutschland übergreift," *Der Spiegel*, 11 March 1991, 128–29.

26. "Sachverstand geborgt: Die FDP wird offensiv: Abtreibung bis zur zwölften Woche soll straffrei bleiben," *Der Spiegel*, 14 January 1991, 33–34.

27. Peter Fahrenholz, "CSU droht mit Verfassungsklage: Parteiausschuss lehnt jede Fristenlösung bei Abtreibung ab," *Frankfurter Rundschau*, 15 July 1991.

28. Charima Reinhardt, "Streit um §218-Kompromiss: Union vertagt Entscheidung/Keine Einigung über soziale Hilfen," *Frankfurter Rundschau*, 18 September 1991.

29. Paul Hoffacker, a CDU deputy who favored a less-than-extreme right position requiring women to justify abortions based on the "social distress indication" before a commission (see "Das zerreisst die Partei," *Der Spiegel*, 13 May 1991, 20), was hopeful that the Ansbach Declaration could command a majority in the CDU/CSU. See "Union auf Ansbacher Kurs," *Frankfurter Rundschau*, (dpa), 1. However, Merkel

had reservations about the CSU's insistence that doctors document their approval of abortions in writing. See Günter Bannas, "Nach 'Ansbacher Erklärung' noch kein Einvernehmen der Union über Abtreibung," *Frankfurter Allgemeine Zeitung,* 16 July 1991.

30. Charima Reinhardt, "Mehrheit in Union billigt Gesetzentwurf zum 218: Minderheit beharrt aber auf einer Verschärfung," *Frankfurter Rundschau,* 20 September 1991.

31. "Sachverstand geborgt."

32. The Social-Liberal debate is brought out in an interview with the parties' constitutional experts: "'An den Grundlagen nicht rütteln': Herta Däubler-Gmelin (SPD) und Justizminister Klaus Kinkel (FDP) über eine neue Verfassung," *Der Spiegel,* 13 May 1991, 80–94.

33. Tina Stadlmayer, "SPD-Frauen: 'Ihr laßt euch einseifen,'" *Tageszeitung,* 12 July 1990. The theme of this report on an intra-German conference of Social Democratic women was that while the West Germans confidentally spoke up for new constitutional rights like "self-determined pregnancy," their East German counterparts had difficulty persuading the men in the SPD Volkskammer caucus to go along. In the East German CDU, it was reported, the situation was even more discouraging: there the entire CDU faction in the Family Committee caved in to the western position and voted against the Fristenlösung.

34. See the articles in the *Frankfurter Allgemeine Zeitung,* 27 September 1991.

35. Ursula Nelles, "Abortion: The Special Case—A Constitutional Perspective," *German Politics and Society,* no. 24–25 (1991–92): 119.

36. 39 BVerfE 1 (1975), translated in Donald P. Kommers, *The Constitutional Jurisprudence of the Federal Republic of Germany* (Durham, N.C.: Duke University Press, 1989), 347–48, 352, 353, 355.

37. Ibid., 359, 357.

38. An excellent discussion of the use and abuse of the Nazi past in parliamentary debates and judicial opinions may be found in Epstein, "Abortion in Germany."

39. Kommers, *Constitutional Jurisprudence,* 349.

40. Wiltraud Rupp-v. Brünneck and Helmut Simon, "Zitate aus dem Urteil des Bundesverfassungsgerichts (Abweichende Meinung . . . vom 25. Februar 1975)," from *BVergGE,* vol. 17, reprinted in *Die Bundesrepublik Deutschland: Entstehung, Entwicklung, Struktur,* ed. Wolf-Dieter Narr and Dietrich Thränhardt, 2d ed. (Königstein/Ts.: Athenäum, 1984), 165–66 (translation by J.R.).

41. Ibid., 166.

42. Kommers, *Constitutional Jurisprudence,* 359.

43. See Margarethe Nimsch, "Abortion as Politics," *German Politics and Society,* no. 24–25 (1991–92): 118–34.

44. See the report by Betinna Musall, "Viele dachten, die spinnen," *Der Spiegel,* 18 March 1991, 68–84.

45. See "Zustimmung und Kritik für Vorschlag Rita Süssmuths zum Abtreibungsrecht," *Tagesspiegel,* 25 July 1990; also Claudia Burgsmüller, "'Dieser Preis ist zu hoch.' Rita Süssmuths §218-Vorschlag mach den Embryo zum

Rechtssubjekt." *Tageszeitung*, 31 July 1990. (Burgsmüller is editor of the feminist law publication *Streit*.)

46. See "Wille zum Absprung: In der Debatte um den Paragraphen 218 tendieren immer mehr CDU-Abgeordnete zur Fristenlösung," *Der Spiegel*, 11 November 1991, 41.

Note: This article is rendered tentative by the Constitutional Court's projected ruling in April 1993.

PART 5

Inter-German Relations, the Demise of the GDR, and the Politics of Unification

These essays analyze the dramatic events of 1989–90 in Germany. In the first essay, A. James McAdams explores the seeming stability that had developed between the two Germanys right up until the collapse of the (former) German Democratic Republic. He notes the peculiar special status of German-German relations prior to 1989, and the ways growing superpower tensions in the 1980s pushed the two sides together. Yet, as McAdams argues, neither explanation is complete: ultimately, the improvement in German-German ties during the 1980s was due to domestic politics and innovation, particularly changes in the West German domestic political environment that led conservative West German politicians to seek contacts with the GDR. In contrast, the GDR's leadership was unable to make reciprocal gestures domestically to match those offered by the FRG. Once the superpowers returned to detente, Soviet pressures for reform grew, and the West German political environment turned against the GDR (as conservative politicians reignited inflammatory anti-GDR rhetoric to shore up their right wing, and Social Democratic politicians expressed dissatisfaction with the results of the decade-long SPD-SED dialogue), Honecker and his allies returned to old and increasingly irrelevant policies and politics. The collapse of the SED, then, is to be found in its inability to cope with these pressures, and their reverberations in the GDR's domestic politics. The very rigidity that held the SED and the GDR together for so long led to their collapse.

The politics of this collapse, and the events leading to the first all-German election since 1933, are analyzed in the next contribution. Arthur M. Hanhardt, Jr., explores the politics of collapse in the GDR. He argues that changes in the international system, particularly revived détente, the "new thinking" emanating from Moscow, and the opening of the Hungarian portion of the iron curtain pressured the SED to reform. These developments in the international system were resisted by the SED with a surprising feebleness and its normal inflexibility. The ineffectualness of the SED opened the political game to several grass-roots organizations to articulate and popularize opposition to the state, which in turn were swept aside by a rising tide of frustration and anger. As Hanhardt notes, these domestic developments, helped along by conservative West German politicians, quickly overwhelmed those articulating a "third way" for the GDR. While it was not clear at the time, the opening of the Berlin Wall was the end of the GDR in any form. Domestic pressures pushed unification, and on West German terms. The Four Powers were unable and unwilling to shape German unification.

Finally, John D. Ely explores one of the unexpected outcomes of German unification, the reemergence of right-wing extremism. He argues that the collapse of right-wing political groups, including the Republikaner, with German unification was widely misunderstood among analysts of German politics. Rather, the transformation of the German economy, coupled with the economic distress in eastern Germany, has created a core of support for right-wing parties, and that they are likely to remain a fixture in German politics in the near future. He then analyzes their goals.

Explaining Inter-German Cooperation in the 1980s

A. James McAdams

The 1990s have become the decade in which inter-German relations have literally melded into true *intra*-German ties. Following the collapse of East Germany's Socialist Unity Party (SED) in the fall of 1989 and with the emergence of a broad public consensus in early 1990 that East Berlin could no longer hope to resolve its massive economic problems without outside assistance, the foundations were laid for the absorption of the German Democratic Republic into a unified German nation-state. Importantly, it was not Bonn that had to compromise with its neighbor on the final form that such a state would take, but instead the GDR that was forced to shed its socialist trappings and finally cast off all pretensions to a separate and distinct East German identity.

Only one-half decade ago, few observers would have thought that such a spectacle—German reunification—was conceivable in any form. Indeed, for all of the GDR's well-known troubles, most would have predicted quite the opposite. Not only were both of the German states entering into the fifth decade of their separation, but even more intriguing, relations between the GDR and the FRG *as autonomous states* had acquired a noteworthy momentum throughout the 1980s, even a kind of "normalcy," that had surprised and impressed students of German affairs.[1] In the first decade following the signing of the inter-German Basic Treaty (1972), the two states had frequently struggled to find issues of substance on which to expand their relations. But in the 1980s, contacts between Bonn and East Berlin had really taken off, beginning with Helmut Schmidt's first official visit to the GDR in the late fall of 1981 and leading up to Erich Honecker's breakthrough trip to the FRG in September 1987.

Equally striking about this period, Germans of all political persuasions seem to have reached a tacit consensus about the necessity of promoting such ties. While there had always been narrow circles in both countries that lobbied for the cause of greater inter-German understanding, most notably in the FRG, on the left wing of the West German Social Democratic party (SPD), the remarkable change in the 1980s was that even the old critics of German-German accommodation seem to have concluded that there was no viable alternative to good relations between the two states. Who was not astonished at the seeming transformation of orthodox East German communists, like Honecker, into outspoken advocates of improved ties? Or who was prepared for a similar metamorphosis in the behavior of West German conservative leaders, like Helmut Kohl and Franz-Josef Strauss? At that time, it was as if the GDR and the FRG were finally positioned to square the circle of achieving both the benefits of a meaningful rapprochement while preserving their existence as separate entities simultaneously!

By itself, the recognition alone that this phase of inter-German accommodation ultimately fell through is enough to make one wonder what made it possible in the first place. In retrospect, it seems almost inexplicable that so much could have been accomplished over years of hard negotiations between East Berlin and Bonn, for all of these gains suddenly to have been proven so fleeting. Was there ever any substance to the Germanys' relations in the 1980s, one might ask, or did the twin East German crises of the summer and fall of 1989—the advent of the refugee crisis and the problematics of the Honecker succession—expose the relationship to have been much shallower than outside observers had ever suspected?

In their efforts to interpret the motives of the GDR and the FRG in the past, western scholars have already provided many of the clues that we need to account for the behavior of the two German states over the past decade. But as I shall contend, there is still one factor, the domestic context of policy-making in East Berlin and Bonn, that needs to be taken more fully into account if we are to decipher both the Germanys' motivations and gain some additional insight into the reasons for the GDR's abrupt fall.

Inter-German Relations as a Special Case

Most accounts of the transformation in the inter-German relationship in the 1970s and 1980s begin, quite rightly, with the intractability of the basic issues that always separated the GDR and the FRG.[2] As contending parts of a divided nation, the Germanys clearly had to wrestle with problems throughout their histories that no other European state had to face. Moreover, the formal preconditions that each state placed upon the resolution of inter-German differences themselves often proved to be inimical to any sort of cooperative arrangement.

For example, even after signing the Basic Treaty, the West German government continued to insist that its long-range goal remained the "completion of the unity" of the German nation; it reserved for itself the right to pass judgment on the domestic policies of the East German regime, and to offer the GDR's citizens West German passports, in short, to do everything possible to preserve the "special" character of the inter-German relationship. Yet, for its part, the East German SED insisted that there was nothing at all that was unique about its contacts with the FRG; any and all attempts by Bonn to interfere in the GDR's internal affairs would be treated as outright violations of the Basic Treaty's prescription that the Germanys should develop "normal, good-neighborly relations with each other on the basis of equal rights."

If there was an odd twist to the difficult negotiations that took place between the Germanys in the 1970s, however, it was that had the FRG and the GDR in fact been any other European countries, with equally strong animosities and equally checkered pasts, the two states probably would have made no effort at all to work on even the rudiments of their ties. The impediments to dialogue would have just been too great. The claims of the one side (the FRG) to a special interest in its counterpart's internal affairs would have been enough to quash even its adversary's most idealistic dreams about the virtues of any cooperative arrangement. Conversely, the determination of the other side (the GDR) to seal itself and its population off from many routine political, cultural, and economic contacts with the other Germany might have also made the costs of cooperation for any normal partner prohibitive.

In these respects, ironically, the two German states could be thankful that they were not entirely typical. So long as Bonn and East Berlin could agree after signing the Basic Treaty about the fruitlessness of policies that were designed to gain the upper hand over their rivals by ignoring them or trying to isolate them—so-called policies of strength, which both states espoused in the 1960s—the leaders of the FRG and the GDR were also compelled to recognize that their ability to achieve even some of their most heartfelt priorities was contingent, almost paradoxically, upon the tacit cooperation of their adversaries.

On the one side, the West Germans seem gradually to have recognized that their desire to keep the dream of reunification alive was at least partly dependent upon some form of regular interaction with East Berlin. A GDR that was cut off from the West, as had been the case throughout the 1960s, was also a GDR that was lost to West German influence and whose population was most likely to lose all hope for the survival of common national aspirations. Read within the context of the Basic Treaty, this was not just a philosophical agenda for those who believed in the transcendental unity of the German nation, but also an immediate, practical challenge. In effect, one needed the GDR's cooperation in order to implement all of those policies that were designed to keep German commonalities alive: the facilitation of inter-German travel, the upgrading of roads and railways, the improvement of postal services and telecommunications, and, as Günter Gaus, Bonn's first permanent representative to the GDR found, above all, the maintenance of the delicate series of understandings surrounding the status of West Berlin.[3]

On the other side, the GDR's complementary objective was to use the framework of the Basic Treaty and every subsequent negotiation with the FRG as a way of gradually whittling down Bonn's claims about the special character of the inter-German relationship.[4] As East Germany's leaders recognized during the 1970s, it was one thing for the SED to tell its population, as it did on a regular basis, that the GDR was a state like any other, but even more beneficial if it could get West German authorities to convey the same message, if inadvertently, simply by demonstrating that they took the GDR seriously as an equal negotiating partner.

As numerous analysts have shown, the GDR's leaders were also not oblivious to the substantial economic benefits to be had from any improvement in relations with Bonn. In this case, one must be careful not to read factors into East Berlin's calculations that had been a part of the inter-German relationship well before the 1970s, such as the special Swing credit used to finance overdrafts in the GDR-FRG trade balance or the GDR's indirect ties to the EEC. Such advantages could be had *even if* the political climate between the two states remained strained. But on a host of other counts, ranging from the FRG's payment of road-use fees to visa charges, from its support for communications services to the numerous financial agreements relating to West Berlin, it is also true that the East German economy became the beneficiary of continually growing subsidies throughout the decade. By 1979, according to even the most conservative estimates, these gains exceeded DM 1 billion annually.[5]

The consequence of such overlapping interests was revealing. While East and West Germany's maximal positions during the 1970s may have had an air of irreconcilability to them, there was always at least a fine line of mutual advantage on which the two states could cooperate. Nevertheless, the puzzle that we still have to explain is how the Germanys could go from the modest successes that they were able to register during this decade to the qualitative leap in their interactions of the 1980s. For despite their early successes, there were also numerous instances in which the FRG and the GDR were practically stalemated.

In part, the problem lay with the limitations of the Basic Treaty itself. For example, partly because the inter-German agreement was never clear on the point, the two states were continually at loggerheads over Bonn's rights and responsibilities under the 1971 quadripartite agreement over Berlin.[6] Was West Germany entitled to expand its political ties with the city, as Western interpretations of the four-power accord implied, or was the Soviet and East German reading of the document, favoring a much looser bond between the FRG and the city, the appropriate guideline? The two sides' inability to find a common ground on this seemingly tangential issue alone meant that many inter-German agreements for which there was already substantial support in both capitals (e.g., a proposed treaty on cultural exchanges) were held up until well into the 1980s.

But even if the Basic Treaty had been a better agreement—which West German conservatives (and even some of their East German counterparts) often insisted was desirable, without always specifying how this might have been feasible—the chief problem for those representatives charged with the day-to-day management of the inter-German relationship was that their efforts to resolve outstanding problems were never very far removed from the loftier political considerations of their governments. Experts like Gaus and his East German counterpart, Michael Kohl, might have known all along what was necessary to make negotiations work; one could not expect the other side to change too quickly, one had to anticipate occasional setbacks in order to maintain the flow of contacts between the Germanys.[7] But, the authorities back home in Bonn and East Berlin also had other agendas.[8]

All too often in the 1970s, the Germanys' representatives found that there was nothing cumulative about their individual successes. Indeed, progress in one domain, far from being a guarantee of further gains in others, was often an open invitation for one or the other German government to take advantage of its counterpart's willingness to compromise.[9] An accord would be reached on a matter of specific interest—say, the 1978 agreement on the Berlin-Hamburg Autobahn—but the quality of German-German understandings in general would be scarcely improved. The East German government could pocket the considerable financial gains to be made as a result of an agreement, but in other areas, such as the treatment of West German journalists working in the GDR, its restrictive practices would remain much as in the past. In like manner, the West German government could benefit from East Berlin's readiness to allow for limited undertakings enhancing the FRG's access to West Berlin, but such a gain would scarcely prevent West German politicians from making speeches that called into question the legitimacy of the East German regime.

Clearly, additional considerations were necessary to provide the two states' governments with the impetus which they needed to regard inter-German cooperation as something more than just the management of a complex relationship.

Geography, Geopolitics, and Inter-German Cooperation

It is in this light that a second group of scholars and many German participants point to the role that external factors played at the turn of the decade in providing politicians in Bonn and East Berlin with just such an incentive.[10] It was not so much that the German governments were suddenly able to settle their old disputes, proponents of this perspective contend—many of these continued, largely unabated during the 1980s—but instead the two powers' growing awareness of a shared geopolitical predicament at the time that tended to neutralize the impact of such differences. Perhaps no other European states were as closely integrated into their respective security alliances as the Germanys. But at the same time, given the fact that the FRG and the GDR were, by virtue of their central European locations, precariously exposed along the battle lines of capitalism and socialism, Bonn and East Berlin were also the first to feel the impact of even the slightest altercation between the superpowers.

To be sure, there was nothing new about the Germanys' geographic fate. Yet, it is hard to disagree that there was something special about the unstable situation that descended in the 1980s. This was not only a period in which the member states of both blocs were challenged by successive international crises over Afghanistan, Poland, and above all, the drawn out battle over INF. But in addition, precisely because of their great dependence upon their superpower allies, both German states had reason to recoil at the clumsy and sometimes heavy-handed manner in which the Americans and the Soviets managed these crises.[11] Whether in the Federal Republic or in the GDR, one could not watch the modest gains in East-West relations of the 1970s being put at risk only a decade later without wondering about the wisdom of tying one's fate too closely to the whims of the big power. Why, many West Germans could ask themselves, did their American allies fail to appreciate the value of the limited but very practical exchanges that Bonn had negotiated with its eastern neighbors? Or as many East German leaders wondered at the time, why was Moscow oblivious to the economic and political gains that the GDR too had made in its dealings with the West?

Thus, an archetypical Atlanticist like Helmut Schmidt surprised many western policymakers in the wake of the Soviet invasion of Afghanistan with his outspoken calls for a German alternative to the, in his words, "speechlessness" that had descended upon the superpowers. And even more startling for the Soviets, Honecker, who had always seemed to be the embodiment of unquestioning loyalty to Moscow, used the altercation over West Germany's INF deployments in 1983 and 1984 to carve out his own country's distinctive defense of détente between the blocs.[12]

Does this mean that the Germanys' shared desire to "minimize the damage" (to use Honecker's words) already done to East-West relations was the driving force behind Bonn's and East Berlin's decision to upgrade their ties in the 1980s? This seems to be what analysts had in mind at the time when they appealed to concepts like "the Europeanization of Europe," the "Germanization of détente," and the "rebirth of central Europe" to account for the Germanys' displays of foreign-policy autonomy in the early parts of the decade.[13] Moreover, officials in both Bonn and East Berlin themselves frequently lent support to such observations by anthropomorphizing the record of East and West German relations with their allies. "We once occupied the role of subservient children in our relations with our superpower guardians," policymakers in both capitals explained, with a remarkable consistency. "But we have come of age, and now that we are the equals of our partners, it is reasonable that we should speak up in times of uncertainty to protect ourselves."[14]

Nevertheless, while the FRG and the GDR were undoubtedly united in their hopes of finding ways to ameliorate tensions between the superpowers, there are at least two reasons why such motivations, while undeniably an important part of the puzzle of inter-German cooperation, still provide us with an incomplete understanding of these developments. The first potential pitfall is simply the danger of romanticizing relations between the Germanys and their allies at any point, since German assertiveness, East and West, was hardly as new as it might have seemed at times. Even in their early decades, when both the FRG and the GDR were most dependent upon the good will of the superpowers, the two states struggled with their allies constantly over what they considered to be the latter's insufficient attention to German priorities. In many instances, moreover, the self-assurance of such early leaders as Konrad Adenauer and Walter Ulbricht proved to be, not a stimulus for detente, but instead a major obstacle in reducing tensions between the blocs.

But second, even if one agrees that the FRG and the GDR came to similar conclusions in the 1980s about their central European fate, which one prominent West German analyst has labeled the "new German question," the "almost desperate desire for peace by the German people in West and East,"[15] who is to say that this revelation had to lead to better *inter-German* ties? It is true that there were those, both in the East German government and in leading West German political parties, like the SPD and the Greens, who came to view inter-German cooperation as an effective way in which Bonn and East Berlin could contribute to better East-West relations. One thinks of Honecker's appeals for an inter-German "community of responsibility" and of subsequent discussions between the SED and the SPD about chemical and nuclear-weapons-free zones in central Europe.

But on the other hand, at least on the West German side, many of those who advocated an inter-German security partnership did not need to be converted to the idea that FRG-GDR ties should be assigned a higher priority. They were already believers. The same could not be said, however, for most members of the Christian Democratic Union/Christian Social Union (CDU/CSU), much of the Free Democratic party (FDP), and Helmut Schmidt's supporters on the right wing of the SPD. Whatever their differences with the United States, and these were undeniably great, Schmidt and his successors in the Christian-Liberal coalition of 1982 also numbered among the most articulate supporters of policy positions which East Berlin had the greatest reason to decry, above all, NATO's INF deployments.[16] But at the same time, these very same figures also began during the 1980s to reassess the way in which the GDR fit into West German priorities.

Similarly, one must also be wary about concluding that security questions alone were at the heart of East Berlin's behavior. There can be no doubt that the peace issue was taken quite seriously by both the East German government and its population. But there was also a great deal about Honecker's emphasis on inter-German security dialogue that was not as new as it appeared. Since the GDR's founding, in fact, all of the country's leaders had routinely emphasized both Germanys' moral responsibility for European peace ("that war should never again spring from German soil"). But as often as not, East Berlin's invitations to discuss security questions with Bonn were simply a sophisticated way of getting the FRG to recognize the GDR's equality under international law. Yet, there was still something very new about Honecker's willingness to promote dialogue with the FRG at this point, because he also incorporated so many other themes on which the Germanys had run aground in the past—cultural ties, travel, emigration, and even questions of ideology. Here too, while the two states' location between the blocs was undoubtedly important, some additional factor seems to have helped to facilitate cooperation between them.

Domestic Politics and Innovation in German Foreign Policy

This missing variable in East and West Germany's calculations is to be found in the ways in which the two states' contrasting political systems both helped and hindered their relations over this period. For only a focus on the domestic politics of policy-making in the Germanys can account for both the timing of the dramatic improvement in FRG-GDR ties in the 1980s and the almost simultaneous transformation of so many of the old critics of the policy into supporters of inter-German détente.[17]

Most analysts agree that the GDR and the FRG were always extremely cautious innovators.[18] The kind of caution that their policymakers exhibited, however, tended to vary directly with their respective political systems. Because of the way in which policy was made in the GDR, where foreign-policy decisions were tightly linked to a broad range of domestic social and economic priorities, East German politicians consistently proved reluctant to entertain major shifts in any single policy direction which might have entailed comparable shifts in others. But precisely because of the high degree of centralization involved in coordinating such a system—indeed, most decisions of consequence were frequently reserved to the SED general secretary himself—the GDR's leaders at least had the advantage of being able to show a great degree of tactical finesse toward Bonn, adapting specific policies as they saw fit to the demands of the moment.

Conversely, in West Germany, where the emphasis on reaching consensus within a governing coalition and, ideally, among all of the major parties had come to play a central role in shaping what governments would and would not dare to undertake, policymakers were generally not able to make day-to-day adjustments with the ease of their adversaries; hence, West German diplomats like Gaus repeatedly bemoaned Bonn's inability to make decisions quickly as a clear weakness in all negotiations with the East.[19] But where the West Germans did excel, in part because of the rise of modern parties in the FRG (so-called Volksparteien) put a premium on showing political flexibility over time, was in gradually changing the way in which they pursued long-term foreign-policy objectives. This, as we shall see, turned out to be a telling advantage over the GDR.

How do such considerations help us to understand the options of the East and West German regimes in the early 1980s? First, it is crucial to note that Honecker's government never went through the wrenching reevaluation of priorities that would have constituted a fundamental shift of its foreign policy at this time. In fact, in the country's first four decades, we can only point to one period—in the early 1970s, with Ulbricht's downfall and the new Honecker government's striking reassessment of all of the SED's social and economic policies—when such a change definitely took place. Instead, throughout the 1980s and even up to Honecker's fall, the East German leadership stuck to the position that it had maintained in the previous decade: that it was willing to open the GDR and its citizens to more frequent contacts with the West only after Bonn *first* showed its recognition of and respect for East German sovereignty. Where the GDR's leaders did show signs of moderating their behavior—and this needs explaining—was in the greater self-assurance with which they pursued their established policy at this particular juncture, sending the FRG simultaneously signals about the negative consequences that would come from a failure to cooperate and, conversely, the positive gains that could be made by meeting the GDR at least half way.[20]

The evidence suggests that the East German regime's newfound confidence was in large part a response to a more fundamental shift in *West German* policy toward the East, which came with the rise of the Christian-

Liberal coalition in 1982. It is nothing new to say that the CDU/CSU began at this time to advocate many of the same principles in furthering inter-German relations—"small steps" and menschliche Erleichterungen—for which it had constantly criticized its Social Democratic predecessors in the 1970s. But more germane to our emphasis on the impact of the West German domestic system, it was not simply the case that the conservatives learned only after coming to power that they had no alternatives to pursuing such practical policies ("eine Politik des Machbares," as Helmut Kohl frequently put it). The learning experience was already behind them. Although it was not common knowledge at the time, prominent members of both the CDU and the CSU (including even Franz-Josef Strauss) had had numerous informal contacts with East German officials throughout the 1970s and into the early 1980s. They understood all along that were they to come to power, a businesslike relationship with the SED could only be sustained by toning down the nationalist rhetoric of the past and respecting the sovereignty of the GDR.[21]

Rather, the more telling change in the 1980s was the way in which purely political considerations, far removed from the abstract "German question" and from the vagaries of international affairs, practically compelled such leaders to compromise with East Berlin. Whereas in the 1970s, it had often made political sense for the CDU/CSU to take the Social Democrats to task for impairing chances for national reunification by recognizing the authority of the East German leadership, in the 1980s, for very similar, largely electorally determined reasons, it made equally good sense for Kohl's government to prove that it too could pursue a viable Deutschlandpolitik: its new coalition partners in the FDP, themselves having moved significantly to the left on foreign-policy issues, demanded it; the weakness of the CSU, following Strauss's abortive bid for the chancellorship in 1980, allowed it; and the West German electorate seemed to expect it as well. Furthermore, there is good reason to think that the CDU/CSU chose to take, for it, innovative stands on this single issue, notwithstanding occasional attacks from its right wing, because leaders like Kohl and Strauss gambled that there were always other scores to be found—fiscal policy, unions, crime and punishment—on which the Union parties could maintain their conservative credentials.[22]

Let us note, this was not just any shift in the political winds from the GDR's perspective. Having a "realistic" conservative government in power was potentially even more beneficial for East Berlin than dealing with Schmidt's SPD. First, it meant that the East Germans could count on any deal which they struck with the new coalition gaining approval in the Bundestag, since the CDU/CSU, unlike its predecessors, had to worry much less (assuming the cooperation of the FDP) about selling this particular priority to its parliamentary opponents. This advantage was perhaps never better demonstrated than in the Kohl government's readiness in 1983 and 1984 to guarantee two sizeable private bank credits (of DM 950 million and 1 billion, respectively) to the GDR, at a time when the Polish crisis had constricted East German access to international capital markets and East Berlin faced a sudden shortage of hard currency to pay off its debts.[23]

Second, the fact that the SPD was driven into opposition meant that the East German regime could benefit more than ever before from the consequences of interparty competition in the FRG. As the Social Democrats sought to regain voters lost to the Greens in the early 1980s and as they found their own Ostpolitik overtaken by the Union forces, those figures within the SPD (such as Egon Bahr and Willy Brandt) who had always called for a more active relationship with the East found their positions automatically strengthened. They then quite logically began to look for ways (e.g., dialogue with the SED on common ideological values) in which the SPD could regain its leading role in promoting ties with the GDR.

The significance of these shifts in the West German party scene was that, in many respects, the GDR did not need to come to the FRG. Both figuratively and literally, the West Germans came to the GDR—Länder presidents running for reelection, mayors of West Berlin seeking an independent profile for their city, SPD parliamentarians exploring arms-control opportunities, and conservative notables establishing credibility in the new politics with the East. Of course, West Germany did not come away empty handed; quite the contrary, as a spate of agreements on cultural exchanges, environmental problems, and above all, inter-German travel and emigration clearly show. FRG officials may even be right when they insist that on balance they were able to obtain more from such deals than was the GDR.[24] The point is only that changes in the domestic politics of the FRG, and not in East Germany, seem to have provided the primary stimulus that both Germanys needed to upgrade their relations at this particular time.

Domestic Politics and the Fate of the GDR

This focus on the domestic roots of foreign-policy change would be of interest only to academics were it not for the fact that even before the massive outflow of refugees from the GDR in 1989 and the outbreak of spontaneous demonstrations in the country, relations between East and West Germany had already showed signs of noticeable deterioration. No doubt, part of the problem was due to the paradoxical consequences of events transpiring *outside* of the two states: the abatement of U.S.-Soviet tensions in the later years of the Reagan administration and, of course, the consolidation of Mikhail Gorbachev's reformist government in Moscow. If differences between the superpowers had given each of the Germanys a common theme to discuss, the signing of the INF treaty in December 1987 demonstrated just how thin the veneer of commonality was between Bonn and East Berlin.

Accordingly, Germans on both sides of the national divide wondered what their new contribution was to be. Were specifically inter-German channels of communication between the blocs still a vital necessity once Washington and Moscow proved capable of conducting responsible arms-control negotiations? And where, after all, were such initiatives as the narrow SPD-SED security dialogue to go once the big powers had again jumped onto the bandwagon of détente?

But in addition, it is equally significant that the domestic forces in West Germany that had provided such an important impetus to German-German cooperation in the 1980s also showed signs of shifting against the GDR at this juncture. By 1987 and 1988, as the Social Democrats began to grapple with the difficult challenge of regaining voter confidence for the upcoming national elections of 1990, prominent members of the SPD were already weighing the priority of their party's relations with the GDR. On the whole, the SPD leadership could agree about the importance of maintaining continuity in inter-German ties. But among the party's rank-and-file, there were also indications of rising frustration that friendly ties with the SED regime had done nothing to alter the slow pace of internal change within the GDR; younger members called upon the party to balance its talks with the SED elite with a greater attention to East German out-groups, such as the Lutheran church and dissident artists and intellectuals.[25]

Even more consequential, however, was the CDU/CSU's changed position by the end of the decade. For unlike 1982–83, when the Union forces had had to prove to the West German electorate that they would not spoil the fruits of the SPD's Ostpolitik, by the end of the 1980s, with numerous inter-German accomplishments to bolster their credibility, the conservatives could afford to proceed much more cautiously. Thus, despite the good spirits which accompanied Honecker's 1987 trip to the FRG, Kohl repeatedly put off plans to make his own visit to East Germany, and by late 1988 he had begun regularly to express his indignation at the SED's internal politics.[26] By the spring and summer of 1989, with the rise of the ultraright Republikaner and accompanying signs of disarray within the CDU/CSU leadership, the Union parties' flagging electoral fortunes actually pressed their leaders to return to tougher themes in their Deutschlandpolitik, as they groped for ways of reasserting their conservative credentials.[27] In this context, it cannot have been too surprising that by the end of the summer, spokesmen for both the CDU and the CSU seem to have rediscovered the hoary theme of German reunification, as if oblivious to its potentially damaging impact upon relations with the GDR. Ironically, without really thinking about the substantive issues involved, the Union leadership was preparing itself for the tumultuous events of late 1989.

In this light, even before the autumn crisis of East Germany's party leadership, it is not hard to see why the SED should have found itself abruptly thrust into a disadvantaged position. While it had grown accustomed to having Bonn make accommodating moves in its direction for almost a decade, the Honecker regime was unprepared, both psychologically and institutionally, for making the kinds of reciprocal gestures (e.g., changes in its treatment of dissidents; even more liberal emigration laws) necessary to neutralize growing criticism from the FRG. Indeed, the fact that East Berlin perceived itself at the time to be fighting a battle on all fronts—against Bonn's supposed interference in its internal affairs, against manifest reformist pressures from its principal allies in Moscow, and increasingly against its own citizenry—seems to have brought the party leadership to conclude that it had no other choice but to rally around old policies and old postures. It feared that innovation in any one domain would necessarily lead to an unraveling of its entire formula for maintaining socialism in the GDR. Evidently, while the SED's centralized institutions made it disinclined to adapt to its new circumstances, the party's leaders at least had the short-term advantage of using these mechanisms to erect a wall of noncompliance between themselves and the outside world.

Against this background, it is fair to say that such issues as the refugee crisis exposed latent, long-standing fissures in the inter-German relationship. But they certainly did not cause them. Instead, for reasons that were at least in part domestic and not entirely related to the German question itself, those factors that had promoted a high level of cooperation between the FRG and the GDR in the 1980s—one might even say, an *artificially* high level—had simply eroded, exposing the fragile architecture of relations between the two states.

Of course, the inter-German relationship was only one of several domains in the 1980s in which East Berlin was able to profit greatly from its counterparts' readiness to engage in compromise; other areas included the Honecker government's relations with its cultural community, its churches, and for a short while at least, even the Soviet Union, where the SED was able to strike similar, if also equally fleeting bargains with its adversaries.[28] Yet, while the party leadership may eventually be judged to have skillfully capitalized on the opportunities presented to it at this time, it does seem as though many of the old regime's successes, in the inter-German relationship as elsewhere, were like castles built in the sky. They were impressive to look at so long as the external supports remained in place to prop them up, but also fated to collapse with the passing of the favorable circumstances that had given rise to them in the first place.

NOTES

For their helpful comments on earlier versions of this paper, I am grateful to Gerard Braunthal, Wolfgang Danspeckgruber, Jameson Doig, Gerald Garvey, Wolfram Hanrieder, Gerhard Loewenberg, and the participants in the DAAD seminar on Political Science and German Studies. I am also thankful for the financial support that I received for undertaking this study from the International Research and Exchanges Board, the Fulbright-Hays Commission, the Alexander von Humboldt Stiftung, and the Center of International Affairs, Princeton University.

1. See for example, Gebhard Schweigler, "Normalität in Deutschland," *Europa Archiv* 6 (1989): 173–82.

2. For representative accounts, see for example, Ernst D. Plock, *The Basic Treaty and the Evolution of East-West German Relations* (Boulder, Colo.: Westview, 1986); Joachim Nawrocki, *Relations between the Two States in Germany* (Boulder, Colo.: Westview, 1986); and Wilhelm Bruns, *Deutsch-deutsche Beziehungen* (Opladen: Leske, 1982).

3. Cf. Günter Gaus, "German-German Relations from the Point of View of the German Democratic Republic," *German Studies Newsletter* 3 (1984): 12–13.

4. Author's interviews, East Berlin. Also, Barbara Vogel, "Die SED und die Verhandlungen über den Vertrag über die Grundlagen der Beziehungen zwischen der DDR und der BRD" (Akademie für Gesellschaftswissenschaften, GDR, photocopy).

5. Cf. Jeffrey Michel, "Economic Exchanges Specific to the Two German States," *Studies in Comparative Communism* 20, no. 1 (1978): 73–83. However, a common misconception is that these economic benefits necessarily made the GDR more dependent upon the FRG. For two excellent critiques of this position, cf. Hanns-D. Jacobsen, "Sonderfall Innerdeutsche Beziehungen," in *Wirtschaftskrieg oder Entspannung,* ed. R. Rock and H.-D. Jacobsen (Bonn: Neue Gesellschaft, 1984), 136–43; and Sandra Peterson, "Inter-German Relations: Has the Cost Risen for the West?" in *Germany Through American Eyes,* ed. G. Mattox and J. Vaughan (Boulder: Westview, 1989), 47–65.

6. An addendum to the Basic Treaty notes that inter-German agreements can be applied to West Berlin "in conformity with the quadripartite agreement." But the FRG and the GDR were never able to agree on what this meant in practice, since the Berlin accord of 1971 specified both that ties between West Germany and West Berlin might be "maintained and developed" but also that the city was not a "constituent part" of the FRG.

7. Author's interviews with Gaus and many of his and Kohl's colleagues from the 1970s, Bonn and East Berlin.

8. On this theme, see the provocative piece by Robert Putnam on "two-level games" in international politics, "Diplomacy and Domestic Politics," *International Organization* 42 (1988): 427–60.

9. The situation which the Germanys' representatives encountered in the 1970s has many of the attributes of a "prisoner's dilemma." On this, cf. Kenneth Oye, ed., *Cooperation under Anarchy* (Princeton: Princeton University Press, 1986); and Robert Axelrod, *The Evolution of Cooperation* (New York: Basic Books, 1984).

10. Among these scholars, see Jonathan Dean, "Directions in Inter-German Relations," *Orbis* 29 (1985): 609–32; Renate Fritsch-Bournazel, "The Changing Nature of the German Question," in *The Two German States and European Security,* ed. F. Stephen Larrabee (London: Macmillan, 1989), 30–52; and M. Jopp et al., "Deutsch-deutsche Beziehungen im Ost-West Konflikt," in *Die beiden deutschen Staaten im Ost-West Verhältnis,* ed. Ilse Spittmann-Rühle and Gisela Helwig (Cologne: Wissenschaft und Politik, 1982), 22–37. On the GDR in particular, see Ronald D. Asmus, "The Dialectics of Detente and Discord," *Orbis* 28 (1985): 743–74; Christiane Rix, "Ansätze fur eine neue Sicherheitspolitik der DDR," *Hamburger Beiträge zur Friedensforschung und Sicherheitspolitik* 10 (December 1986): 7–32; and Gerd Meyer, "The GDR's *Deutschlandpolitik* in the Early 1980s," in Larrabee, *Two German States,* 129–55. For a representative East German account, see the argument by Max Schmidt, "The Two German States and European Security," in Larrabee, *Two German States,* 106–28.

11. For a West German perspective, see especially Harold Müller and Thomas Risse-Kappen, "Origins of Estrangement: The Peace Movement and the Changed Image of America in West Germany," *International Security* 12 (1987): 52–88. On the United States-FRG relationship in general, see the definitive study by Wolfram Hanrieder, *Germany, America, Europe: Forty Years of German Foreign Policy* (New Haven: Yale University Press, 1989). I too have argued along these lines about the GDR. Cf. A. James McAdams, "The New Logic in Soviet-GDR Relations," *Problems of Communism* (1988): 47–60.

12. Erich Honecker, *Reden und Aufsätze,* vol. 10 (Berlin: Dietz, 1986): 16.

13. For example, Eric Frey, *Division and Detente: The Germanys and Their Alliances* (New York, Praeger, 1987), 75–87; Klaus Blömer, "Freedom for Europe, East and West," *Foreign Policy* 50 (1983): 23– 38; and Egon Bahr, *Was wird aus den Deutschen?* (Hamburg: Rowohlt, 1982). For the book that anticipated it all, see Peter Bender, *Das Ende des ideologischen Zeitalters* (Berlin: Severin und Siedler, 1981).

14. I paraphrase here a parent-child metaphor that I repeatedly encountered in the FRG's Foreign Office and in the GDR's Ministry of Foreign Affairs alike.

15. Richard Lowenthal, "The German Question Transformed," *Foreign Affairs* 63 (1984–85): 314.

16. The novel development for such parties as the CDU and the CSU in the 1980s was that they began to *discuss* security questions at all with the GDR—during Honecker's 1987 visit to Bonn, for example, their conservative Bundestag *Fraktion* leader, Alfred Dregger, even found that he shared some of his East German guest's concerns about nuclear "singularization." But in interviews with Dregger and other CDU/CSU and FDP parliamentarians in 1987 and 1988, I found scant support for the idea that the FRG and the GDR had common security interests.

17. Ralf Dahrendorf's insight about the German "cartel of anxiety" still captures the mood involved in the making of foreign-policy decisions in both the GDR and the FRG. Cf. his *Society and Democracy in Germany* (New York: Doubleday, 1969), 192. However, I know of no comparative study of foreign policy-making that deals with the Germanys in particular. My thoughts about this question have been informed by reading the classic comparison of U.S. and Soviet policymaking by Zbigniew

Brzezinski and Samuel Huntington, *Political Power: USA/USSR* (New York: Viking, 1963).

18. On the FRG, cf. Gebhard Schweigler, *West German Foreign Policy: The Domestic Setting,* Washington Papers no. 106, vol. 12 (New York: Praeger, 1984), 86–87; and Hans Peter Schwarz, *Die gezähmten Deutschen* (Stuttgart: Deutsche, 1985), 53. On the GDR, cf. my *East Germany and Detente* (Cambridge: Cambridge University Press, 1985); and for relevant institutional considerations, cf. Thomas Baylis, "Leadership Structures and Leadership Politics in Hungary and the GDR," in D. Childs, T. Baylis, and M. Rueschemeyer, eds., *East Germany in Comparative Perspective* (London: Routledge, 1989), 34–59; and Gert-Joachim Glässner, "Bureaucratic Rule: Overcoming Conflicts in the GDR," no. 13 (Vienna: Research Project, Crises in Soviet-Type Systems, 1986), 39–61.

19. Author's interview with Gaus, Bonn. Also, cf. Günter Gaus, *Wo Deutschland liegt—Eine Ortsbestimmung* (Hamburg: Hoffmann und Campe, 1983), 184.

20. For an example of a "threat," consider the raising of the GDR's mandatory currency exchange requirement (the *Mindestumtausch*) for foreigners in 1980; for an example of inducements to cooperation, consider the post-1983 overtures to the SPD or the radical liberalization of East German requirements for emigration and short-term travel to the West.

21. Author's interviews, Bonn and East Berlin. For example, I was surprised to learn from East German officials that they met with Strauß on a regular basis from the mid-1970s onward; he told one of my discussion partners that the major problem with the Basic Treaty was that he himself had not negotiated it! For an important study of the evolution of CDU/CSU policy on these issues, cf. Clay Clemens, *Reluctant Realists: The CDU/CSU and West German Ostpolitik* (Durham, N.C.: Duke University Press, 1989), esp. chap. 7.

22. A similar point can be made about CDU/CSU tactics in the 1970s. At least in part for electoral reasons, the conservative parties (and particularly the CDU) chose to adopt innovative stands on social policy questions at this time, while in contrast to the 1980s, it was the *Deutschlandpolitick* which was used to enhance the Union's conservative credentials.

23. On the GDR's economic calculations, see the insightful piece by Thomas Baylis, "Explaining the GDR's Economic Strategy," *International Organization* 40 (1986): 381–420.

24. Author's interviews, Bonn.

25. Author's interviews with members of the SPD Bundestag *Fraktion,* Bonn.

26. See his December 1988 State of the Nation address, in *FBIS/WEU,* 1 (December 1988): 4–5.

27. On pressures for a tactical turn of course within the CDU, see, for example, Gunter Hoffmann, "Nachruf gefällig: Der Streit um den Kurs der Union dauert an," *Die Zeit,* 7 July 1989, 4.

28. For some speculation on this theme "before the crisis," see my "The GDR at Forty: The Perils of Success," *German Politics and Society* 17 (1989): 14–26.

The Collapse of the German Democratic Republic and Its Unification with the Federal Republic of Germany, 1989–90

Arthur M. Hanhardt, Jr.

My thesis here is that the orthodox Communist political system of the GDR collapsed—or "imploded"[1]—under a combination of internal and external factors that had been present and essentially manageable for years, but that became suddenly overwhelming in 1989. This was the year in which the Soviet Union terminated the support it historically provided orthodox Communist regimes under Stalin after World War II and, later, as part of the Brezhnev Doctrine. At the same time, the forces of reform and opposition within the GDR were too weak, uncoordinated, and unpracticed to enable them to redirect the GDR along a "third path" between the capitalist West and failed socialist models of the East. Absent external props and effective internal alternatives, the GDR was driven by a popular demand to unite with the Federal Republic of Germany (FRG). This occurred on 3 October 1990 and was politically confirmed in the victory of Chancellor Kohl and his pro-unification coalition in the Bundestag election of 2 December.

The SED Regime and the Forces of Change in the 1980s:
External Factors before 1989

Pressures on the GDR regime came from external and internal sources during the 1980s. From without, the GDR was exposed to reforms initiated by Mikhail Gorbachev in the Soviet Union after 1985 and tolerated, if not encouraged, in Eastern Europe with the end of the Brezhnev Doctrine.[2] The East German leadership firmly—and correctly, from their point of view—resisted Gorbachev's "New Thinking" policies of perestroika and glasnost as inapplicable and, indeed, inimical to the GDR as an orthodox Communist political, social, and economic system. To have accepted perestroika and glasnost would have meant questioning the supremacy of the ruling Socialist Unity party (SED), thus putting its future and that of the state into serious doubt.

Tension between the GDR and the Soviet Union grew in the second half of the 1980s. The aging GDR leadership initially viewed Gorbachev as an inexperienced youngster who could be manipulated by his more experienced elders and betters.[3] This attitude changed to alarm as New Thinking produced views that could be interpreted as a severe threat to a continuation of the orthodox status quo in Eastern Europe. A "Gang of Four"—Erich Honecker (GDR), Gustav Husák (Czechoslovakia), Todor Zhivkov (Bulgaria) and Nicolae Ceausescu (Rumania)—joined Soviet conservatives such as Igor Ligachev in opposing the liberal reformists that included Aleksandr Yakovlev and Eduard Shevardnadze. Although Gorbachev's position was ambivalent until at least 1988 and perhaps as late as 1989,[4] the reigning uncertainty encouraged the East European conservatives to heighten their resistance while encouraging domestic liberals to maximize what they saw as an opportunity to assert themselves with Gorbachev's support.

Certainly the New Thinking papers and ideas emanating from the Moscow think tanks were disseminated throughout East Europe and within the GDR. The work of Oleg Bogomolov and Viatcheslav Dashitchev was widely circulated. Both wrote about the Soviet future in East Europe, stressing the importance of national self-determination and sovereignty.[5]

Clearly, improved relations between the United States and the Soviet Union were adding to the external pressures felt by the GDR leadership.[6] In 1988 it was becoming apparent that the Soviet Union under President Gorbachev might not be relied upon to come to the aid of the SED in time of internal crisis, as it had in the past.

Internal Pressures before 1989

Internally, the leadership of the SED had been masters at utilizing interbloc cold war hostility for domestic political purposes. This was demonstrated during the workers' uprising of 17 June 1953 and the construction of the Berlin Wall on 13 August 1961. In both cases the Soviet Union intervened to support the SED regime, then led by Walter Ulbricht. Cold war conditions enabled the SED to perfect a surveillance state that rewarded a Nomenklatura and other elites concerned about keeping their privileges. The development of a comprehensive welfare state was largely motivated by the demands of a labor-intensive economy that had to compensate for increasingly obsolescent plant and equipment by enlarging the work force and encouraging the working class to work ever harder.

The domestic economy of the GDR became a model and even a source of envy in the Soviet bloc. With the accession of the Honecker regime in 1971 the outlines of a modus vivendi between the SED and the people of the GDR was established. For their part, the SED would guarantee stable prices for basic commodities along with low-cost housing, public transportation, and comprehensive social services. For its part the people of the GDR would not openly oppose the sociopolitical status quo and the dominant position of the SED.

This understanding between the SED and the people of the GDR held through the inflationary pressures occasioned by the oil shocks of the 1970s. By the 1980s, the GDR economy was paying dearly for the subsidies needed to keep prices stable. Neglect of the industrial infrastructure and the environment were major costs of an increasingly desperate effort to keep the domestic situation under control by preserving its implied, but crucial modus vivendi. The full extent of the environmental and economic disaster in the GDR went largely unnoticed in the West, which was also pumping subsidies into the GDR system in an effort to stabilize the economy and "humanize" the regime. Ironically, the West was also using the territory of the GDR to dump its own environmentally unacceptable wastes: the GDR was quite willing to trade environmental degradation for hard currency. Only with the availability of data such as that published in the *Sozialreport '90* did the full extent of the actual situation in the GDR become apparent.[7]

Implicit in the modus vivendi described above is an essentially schizophrenic situation between a publicly formalistic, indeed hypocritical, accommodation to the SED regime and its concomitant illusion of public approval. This illusion became a reality for the SED leadership. Stated differently, the political quietude in the GDR became a misleading warrant of the legitimacy of the GDR regime and leadership. When this warrant was required for the survival of the regime in 1989, it was found seriously wanting.

Two aspects of the domestic situation of the GDR from the beginning of the 1980s are particularly important in this context: unofficial political groups and the failure of political socialization. Although the understanding described above precluded overt political opposition to the SED regime, political activity away from the officially sanctioned forum was possible in the interstices of what came to be known as the Nischengesellschaft, or society of (private) niches in the GDR. Within these spaces, such as those provided by the Lutheran church, political groupings were formed on such issues as the environment, human rights, and peace.[8] The state security apparatus, known as the Stasi, was fully informed of the activities of these groups, but usually intervened only when they went out into the public. One such occasion came January 1988 in East Berlin during the annual commemoration of the murders of Rosa Luxemburg and Karl Liebknecht.

Unofficial and uninvited demonstrators unfurled banners proclaiming Rosa Luxemburg's view that "true freedom is the freedom of those who think differently." This led to the arrest of the 120 "unofficial" demonstrators.

In one sense the Stasi can be said to have succeeded in its efforts to stymie opposition in the GDR: state and Stasi always had the option of imprisoning and exiling those who refused to be silenced. Thus the potential leaders of an indigenous opposition—as, for example, the balladeer Wolf Biermann, who was expatriated in 1979—were relatively easily gotten rid of in the West. Dissent in the GDR rarely appeared in public until well into 1989, when sheer numbers guaranteed individual safety.

In her comprehensive study, Christiane Lemke discusses the limited effectiveness of political socialization in the GDR.[9] Lemke shows that the political socialization effort in the GDR led to a "dual political culture" (politische Doppelkultur). One aspect demonstrated a spurious "official" political culture that, while insubstantial, nonetheless provided the regime with an illusion of legitimacy and of a "GDR national identity and culture." The illusion was so strong that Margot Honecker, the GDR Minister of Public Education, claimed in a speech before the Pedagogical Congress of the GDR in June 1989 (!) that "our youth is prepared to defend the socialist achievements of the GDR—if necessary by force of arms."[10]

The other, contradictory aspect of this dual political culture represented the reality of the meager results of decades of political socialization in the GDR. Thus the socialized political support that the GDR regime presumably came to rely upon as a distinct socialist political culture, with a socialist personality and a GDR national identity, was as substantial as the fabled emperor's clothes.

Thrown upon their own devices by the growing accommodation between the United States and the Soviet Union in the second half of the 1980s, the SED and its domestic allies were literally out in the cold. Sensing this, thousands of East Germans preferred taking their chances in the competitive Ellenbogengesellschaft (elbow society) they knew primarily from West German television and comparatively wealthy relatives. Those choosing to remain in the GDR—the overwhelming majority—gradually lost their fear of the SED and the Stasi, turning the streets into a venue for a "political culture of demonstrations." Once this happened in 1989, the GDR was, in effect, doomed as a state independent of the Federal Republic of Germany.

1989: The Year of Change—External Pressures

External pressures on the SED became acute in 1989.[11] Gorbachev's initial ambivalence gave way to a clearer policy of accommodation with Europe in a "common European house" and with the United States. The GDR leadership had to be concerned about what room of that house it might occupy between capitalist Western Europe and a reformist Eastern Europe set adrift by Gorbachev's Soviet Union. The Gang of Four was still in place, but its members were unable to offer much in the way of concrete mutual support.

To add insult to perceived injuries, Gorbachev visited the FRG for four days beginning on 12 June, shortly after President Bush had offered the FRG a role "as partners in leadership" during his visit to West Germany at the end of May.[12] The "Gorbymania" exhibited by the West German government and people startled foreign observers, who openly worried about the possibilities of a West German–Soviet détente. More significantly the joint declaration issued by President Gorbachev and Chancellor Kohl spoke of the right of every state to choose its own political and social system. This could only be interpreted as threatening by the leadership in East Berlin.

The liberalizing states of Eastern Europe, Poland, and Hungary were gradually turning against the GDR in the late spring and summer of 1989. Hungary ostentatiously pulled down the Iron Curtain on 2 May, opening the prospect of escape for thousands of vacationing GDR tourists illegally crossing the "green border" into Austria and thence on to West Germany. On 10 September Hungary significantly increased the external pressure on East Germany by announcing that after midnight, East German citizens were free to depart Hungary for third countries of their choosing even if they had no valid travel documents. This decision and its implementation caused outrage in East Berlin, which was now confronted with even larger numbers of East Germans heading for West Germany as Übersiedler by way of Hungary and Austria.

The action of the Hungarian government and its foreign minister, Gyula Horn, was based on humanitarian concerns (conditions among the thousands of East German "campers" were becoming intolerable), a profound dislike for the GDR leadership in Budapest, and the prospect of West German economic assistance. East Germany responded swiftly and with harsh rhetoric. The Hungarians were accused of violating the 1969 Vienna Convention on Treaty Rights, of ignoring "reasonable" offers to solve the problem, and of engaging in "trafficking in human beings" in exchange for western money.[13]

Along with the out-migration through Hungary, the East German government was also confronted with the phenomenon of its citizens seeking exit by occupying the West German embassies in Warsaw and Prague. As was the case in Hungary, the embassy occupations received a great deal of attention in the West German media. With an eye on Bonn, the liberalizing Polish government sought a "humanitarian" solution to the would-be East German immigrants and refused either to expel East Germans or to hinder East Germans' freedom of movement in Poland. Czechoslovakia, as a mem-

ber in good standing of the Gang of Four, tried to hold the line by attempting
to seal off the West German embassy. When hundreds of East German
occupiers became thousands, conditions rapidly deteriorated.

As the crisis built two things became clear:

1. The East German government was unable to respond effectively
and
2. Something had to be done to forestall a debacle on 7 October, the
fortieth anniversary of the founding of the GDR.

That the gerontocrats in charge of the East German government were
nearing their biological end was common currency. Guessing about the political succession was a preoccupation among GDR specialists. Conventional
wisdom predicted leadership renewal sometime between the fortieth anniversary and the twelfth Party Congress of the Socialist Unity party, scheduled
for the spring of 1990. No one could predict that the aging leadership would
stay at the helm until the East German system sank beneath the waves of
popular discontent. No successors could be found who were capable of
steering the GDR along a reform course between the temptations of the
capitalist, market model represented by West Germany and the threats posed
by the reforms and changes swirling through Eastern Europe and the Soviet
Union.

The ineffectiveness of the East German government's response to the
pressures emanating from Hungary, Czechoslovakia, and Poland was abun-
dantly demonstrated during the last days of September and the beginning of
October. With hundreds of East Germans in the West German embassy in
Warsaw and with the utter collapse of sanitary conditions among the thousands of East Germans in the Palais Lobkowicz (the West German embassy)
in Prague, the Honecker government decided to allow the refugees free
passage to the Federal Republic. The refugees were accused of "betraying
their homeland," were considered "expellees," and were put on trains that
passed through the GDR during the night from 30 September to the 1 October. ADN, the East German news agency, commented that the East Germans
in transit had "through their behavior trampled moral values and had banished
themselves from our society. Not a single tear should be shed because of
them." Nonetheless, East Germans attempted to jump aboard the trains as
they passed through, causing disturbances at major train stations.

By 2 October the West German embassies in Prague and Warsaw were
once again overwhelmed with East Germans. East Berlin accused Bonn of
provocations on the eve of the fortieth anniversary celebrations. Negotiations
ensued and on 4 October chartered trains of the GDR Reichsbahn once again
rolled through the GDR with some 7,600 Übersiedler on board. This time

stations and tracks were cleared to prevent the previous demonstrations and desperate attempts to board the trains in transit.

These cases illustrate the East German government's helplessness and ineffectuality. While clearly wanting to get rid of thousands of people who represented an embarrassing problem at an embarrassing time, the GDR leadership nonetheless insisted that people leaving the country pass through East Germany, thus adding insult to the injury felt by those East Germans who wanted to leave, as well as those wishing to remain in the GDR. People in the first category wondered why they too were not allowed to leave, while many of those wanting to stay wondered about internal reforms needed to stem the outflow of valued and needed citizens.

In addition to the external aspects affecting the East German response to pressures in the late summer and autumn of 1989, the actions of the Federal Republic of Germany must also be considered (if briefly). While it is no doubt an exaggeration to say that the West German government was aggressively destabilizing the GDR, Bonn did nothing to ease the immediate situation in East Germany once it became acute. Perhaps the most insistent and insinuating West German intervention was television.

ZDF and ARD, the two West German state television networks, covered events in East Germany over, through, and around GDR efforts to hinder TV reporting. Often the story was that no story could be gotten. What did get through affected attitudes in both Germanys. This was particularly the case in West German reporting on East Germans in the East European embassies and the reception that Übersiedler got upon arrival in the FRG. For example, news reports showed footage of East Germans frantically attempting to enter the FRG embassy grounds in Prague. In addition, the dramatic announcement by Hans-Dietrich Genscher and Rudolf Seiters that East Germans in the embassy would be allowed free passage to West Germany and the nearly hysterical receptions at Helmstedt and Hof were emotionally charged moments on West German television. These reports no doubt encouraged the second wave of emigrants that left on 4 October.

West German TV reports on dissent spreading throughout East Germany also had their effect. A growing number of demonstrations and demonstrators spread across the GDR toward the end of September. ZDF and ARD efforts to cover these events had predictable consequences, usually ending with the familiar "hand-over-the-lens sequence." Since none of this was reported on GDR television, the customary pattern of East German viewers learning from West German TV was reinforced.

It can also be argued that in the autumn of 1989, West German TV reporting had its credibility reinforced through the gradual reform of GDR television. East German TV had begun changing its look earlier in 1989 with an expensive revamping of "Elf99," a youth-oriented program featuring a mix of rock music, snazzy sets, and SED political orthodoxy. By the end of October and with increasing frequency after 9 November, "Elf99" became critical in its political commentary. On 25 November, "Elf99" produced a show on the life-styles of the politburo in the East Berlin suburb of Wandlitz (also known as Volvograd). East German television, through the magazine program "AK-Zwo," began producing investigative reports along with critical talk and call-in shows.

An increasingly critical and credible East German television underscored the credibility of West German TV: East German TV was now showing essentially the same things as FRG TV. Whether or not this was justified cannot be addressed here, but East German doubters, fence sitters, and true believers were now getting from their own media information that confirmed what had for years come only from the West.

1989: The Year of Change—Internal Pressures

Only a selection of the internal events, movements, and people affecting political changes in the GDR during the autumn of 1989 can be dealt with here. Two events that occurred in May and June took on great significance as the summer passed. Both involved Honecker's heir apparent, Egon Krenz, and were later to make it virtually impossible for him to effectively assume the leadership of either the SED or the GDR state apparatus.

The communal elections of 7 May 1989 produced the usual results: with 98.77 percent of eligible voters participating, 98.85 percent voted for the candidates of the National Front. These figures were down slightly from the 1984 communal elections. Citizens' initiatives (Kirche von unten and others), sensing public dissatisfaction and dissent, observed the balloting and demanded an open accounting of negative ballots. Their demands were denied, leading to charges of fraud and obfuscation.

The Ministry for State Security (MfS or Stasi) documented potential opposition stemming from the electoral protest. Stasi reports dated 8 and 19 of May contain a veritable who's who of persons who were to play political roles in the autumn of 1989 and after.[14] It can certainly be argued that the stonewalling through which the party and state apparatuses sought to inhibit criticism only spurred the ardor of those who sought a public accounting of what had actually happened.

In the event, it was Egon Krenz, the chairer of the election commission, who certified the official results. From then on Krenz was widely identified with what to many seemed egregious and unnecessary lying. Four months later, on 7 September, Stasi forces broke up a demonstration protesting electoral fraud in the Alexanderplatz. Coincidentally, "Beijing Days in Berlin" were opened on the same day in celebration of the fortieth anniversary of the founding of the Peoples Republic of China (PRC).

Relations between the PRC and the GDR leadership became particularly close between the Tiananmen massacre and the demonstrations in East Germany. *Neues Deutschland,* on 6 June, lavished praise on the determination of the Chinese leadership in dealing decisive blows against the "counterrevolutionary rioters" while restoring peace and order. This line was followed by Egon Krenz, who happened to be visiting Oskar Lafontaine in Saarbrücken at the time. (Later, in his memoirs, Krenz pleads that he was only following his leadership and was totally unaware of the background of the Beijing events.)[15]

The message of the SED leadership was clearly understood by the East German people: misbehavior in the form of unsanctioned public demonstrations will be subject to the "Chinese solution." Marlies Menge, in "Ohne uns Läuft Nichts mehr," writes of the outrage and fear felt among East Germans who saw a clear connection between students in China and their plight in the GDR.[16]

Perhaps the most important internal development in the late summer and autumn of 1989 was the political culture of demonstrations in the GDR. From time to time unauthorized political demonstrations had occurred in the GDR—as in the Liebknecht-Luxemburg demonstration cited above. These were relatively small and easily dealt with by state security forces. As in 1988, the first demonstration of 1989 took place in Leipzig on 15 January, the seventieth anniversary of the murders of Karl Liebknecht and Rosa Luxemburg. The Stasi report on this demonstration is an example of detailed information security forces had to act upon should they be ordered to by the political leadership. The principal participants were named with short biographies, their motives were analyzed, and their activities outlined: the Stasi demonstrably knew everything.[17]

Protest demonstrations took place in East Berlin on 7 June and 7 September, with arrests of 120 and 80 persons, respectively. On 11 September, 50 demonstrators were arrested following a Monday evening service at the Nikolaikirche. They were sentenced to four-month prison terms. Monday demonstrations continued in September. On the twenty-fifth about 5,000 demonstrators took to the streets of Leipzig and staged a sit-in at the Leipzig train station. The police and state security forces did not intervene in this, the largest demonstration of the summer. The tradition and practice of Monday-night demonstrations was thus firmly established. As the fortieth anniversary of the GDR came ever closer, events were moving toward a climax that would end SED rule and, ultimately, dissolve the GDR.

To assure an orderly celebration of 7 October, a massive police buildup sealed off much of central East Berlin. In spite of this activity, demonstrations broke out and were brutally beaten down, not only in East Berlin and Leipzig, but also in Arnstadt, Dresden, Ilmenau, Jena, Karl-Marx-Stadt,

Magdeburg, Plauen, and Potsdam.[18] The cycle of demonstration and repression continued through Sunday, 8 October.

The next day attention concentrated on Leipzig and what was promising to become a massive and violent confrontation between security forces and tens of thousands of citizens at the Monday demonstration. There is still some confusion about the sequence of events on 9 October and the roles of various actors. Egon Krenz credits his friend Walter Friedrich of the Central Institute for Youth Research in Leipzig with making him aware of the demands of the demonstrators and leading him to order restraint on the part of security forces under his control.[19]

Others attribute the peaceful course of events on the ninth to a committee of Kurt Meier, Jochen Pommert, Roland Wotzel (SED district secretaries), Kurt Masur (Gewandhaus Orchestra), Pastor Peter Zimmermann, and Bernd Lutz Lange (cabaret artist). Under pressure of developments that looked highly confrontational, these six formulated a statement that was broadcast on the afternoon of 9 October to gathering demonstrators.

The intensity of the situation cannot be overstated. Kampfgruppen, paramilitary units from local factories, were mobilized to support Leipzig police and state security forces. From the Nikolaikirche and three other churches the masses moved to the Karl-Marx-Platz along the Georgiring to the Hauptbahnhof. As the crowd grew it called for "Democracy NOW" and chanted the now-famous "Wir sind das Volk"—"We are the People!"

The security forces were held back on side streets. The Kampfgruppen were confronted by demonstrators who engaged them in discussions about the political situation. Aside from directing traffic, the police did not interfere as the 70,000 participants made their point in a most compelling manner.

On the subsequent Mondays, the demonstrations grew. On the sixteenth there were 120,000 demonstrators, on the twenty-third 300,000, and on the thirtieth 200,000.[20] The numbers are the most common estimates, but the relative masses are no doubt nearly correct. Several characteristics of these demonstrations are worthy of mention:

1. The demonstrations spread to all parts of the GDR.

2. The demonstrations demanded changes in policies and personnel.

3. The demonstrations produced political results. For example, the Oberburgermeister of Dresden, Wolfgang Berghofer, began a dialogue with a Group of 20 citizens resulting in a Ten Point Catalog of reforms, including press freedom, freedom to travel, and the free expression of opinion. This example was followed elsewhere.

4. Finally, German unification played virtually no role during the October demonstrations.

In East Berlin changes came rapidly between 9 October and the beginning of December. On 18 October Erich Honecker resigned, citing bad health. Egon Krenz, long-time heir apparent, became general secretary of the SED Central Committee; six days later he added the titles of chairman of the Council of State and chairman of the National Defense Council.

The high point of the October demonstrations actually came on 4 November in East Berlin. In a massive demonstration carried live on GDR TV, leading figures in art, literature, and politics spoke; Christa Wolf, Christoph Hein, Stefan Heym, and many others made memorable statements. Christa Wolf received enthusiastic applause when she said, "Imagine, a socialism where no one runs away." Christoph Hein accused Erich Honecker of being responsible for a society that had little to do with socialism, but rather one characterized by bureaucracy, demagogy, domestic spying, and abuse of power. Stefan Heym caught the mood by saying, "It is as if someone had thrown open the windows."

Not everyone was greeted with cheers and applause. General Markus Wolf, former chief of GDR espionage, was booed when he tried to defend the Stasi. The head of the Berlin SED, Gunter Schabowski, barely completed his remarks against the whistles and cat-calls of the massive audience.[21]

A poignant moment came during the address of Pastor Friedrich Schorlemmer, a founding member of Demokratisher Aufbruch. Schorlemmer appealed to people to "stay here [in East Germany], we need everyone and everybody." The fact was that thousands were leaving the GDR every week. And those who from then on articulated their views at demonstrations called for German unification.[22] During the month of November, the dominant slogan at demonstrations changed from Wir sind DAS Volk (We are THE People) to Wir sind EIN Volk (We are ONE People) and Deutschland einig Vaterland (Germany united fatherland). The Leipzig Monday night demonstrations of 20 and 27 November clearly showed the trend: speakers arguing against reunification and in favor of reforming the GDR were shouted down. The reformist fervor of October had diminished between the opening of the Berlin Wall and the promulgation of Chancellor Helmut Kohl's ten-point plan for the future of the two German states on 28 November.[23]

On 1 December the Volkskammer struck the leading role of the SED from the GDR constitution, ending the virtual identity of party and state in East Germany. Two days later the entire politburo and central committee of the SED resigned, ending the brief and unlamented Krenz era.

New political organizations were severely handicapped. The rulers of the GDR had, for years, gotten rid of dissidents and reformers simply by arresting and imprisoning them. Since the early 1970s, the FRG was prepared to purchase the freedom of imprisoned dissidents and reformers from a GDR ravenous for hard currency to prop up its increasingly ailing economy.

While moving from the GDR to the FRG was often a hardship, the pain was eased by the fact that these people were going from one Germany to another. Language and culture in the FRG were not "foreign," even though the forced or voluntary emigrants sometimes had problems adjusting to a different society.[24] Moreover, given the freedom of expression in the FRG, the dissidents from the East could continue developing their critical ideas. Often these people became integrated into left-wing "critical" or Green politics in the FRG. A case in point is that of Rudolf Bahro, who was imprisoned in the GDR in 1977 for his Marxist, but critical book *Die Alternative,* had his freedom purchased in 1979, and thereafter became a founder of the Greens in the FRG.

In contrast to the situation for Poles, Czechs, and Hungarians, the East German opposition had another Germany where they could continue their work. This sapped the potential strength of an indigenous GDR alternative, which, caught between Stasi and emigration, could not organize in a systematic way until the SED regime began losing its grip in the summer of 1989. By then it was too late for people such as Jens Reich, Rolf Henrich, and the Brie brothers' Sozialismusprojekt at the Humboldt University to construct or implement a third way model appealing to a public opting for West Germany.[25]

GDR Groups, Parties, and the March 1990 Election

The revolution in the GDR produced a number of groups and movements, forced the transformations of the SED and the bloc parties, and led to the founding of new parties in East Germany between the summer of 1989 and the Volkskammer election in March 1990. The rapidity of change was often meant poor documentation. Here are profiles of some of the more important organizations.

Political Groups

From the spring of 1988 and into 1989 a network named Die Arche (The Ark) coordinated church-based organizations in East Berlin and throughout the GDR.[26] The election fraud of May 1989 gave strong impetus to its groups seeking to implement measures encouraging East Germans to stay and work for reform rather than joining those seeking to leave.

Three of the many political groups that played significant roles in the GDR during the fall of 1989 and on into 1990 are:

Neues Forum — New Forum
Demokratie Jetzt — Democracy Now
Vereinigte Linke — United Left

Neues Forum

Neues Forum (NF) was founded on 10 September 1989 by painter Bärbel Bohley, the attorney Rolf Henrich, and Jens Reich, a molecular biologist on the staff of the Academy of Sciences of the GDR. Ms. Bohley resumed her activities after returning from political exile in Great Britain. Rolf Henrich, an attorney from Eisenhuttenstadt, was banned from practice after publishing his book, *Der vormundschaftliche Staat (The Tutelary State)*, in West Germany.[27] Jens Reich advocated reform from within the GDR.

A report of the Stasi, dated 19 September, presents a detailed picture of the founding participants of NF.[28] What emerged is a loose coalition of groups such as Doctors for Peace, Women for Peace, Freedom and Justice, and Christian Women for Peace. Indeed NF was founded as an organization or "political platform" functioning "below the level of the political party."[29] NF grew rapidly in September and by the end of October some 100,000 signatures were carried on supporting lists.

Shortly after its founding, NF formally applied to the East German Ministry of the Interior for official recognition as a political organization according to Article 29 of the GDR Constitution.[30] State response was swift: NF was banned as anticonstitutional group "hostile to the state."[31]

The idea of an oppositional or reformist group asking the state for legal status may seem a bit strange. Nonetheless this position was entirely consistent with its goal of seeking a constructive dialogue with the powers of party and state in the GDR. NF sought to effect change without overthrowing the system.

What NF sought was a third way between those symbolized by the two Germanys: by retaining the benefits of a humane socialism while securing on the advantages provided by a market economy. Nowhere was a third way clearly charted.

NF adopted a program and statute at its meeting on 27 and 28 January 1990. NF reaffirmed its commitment to grass-roots organization without becoming a formal political party. Earlier, on 3 January, NF had joined five other parties and groups—Social Democratic party, Demokratischer Aufbruch, Demokratie Jetzt, Vereinigte Linke, and the Initiative Frieden und Menschenrechte to form the Wahlbündnis '90 to prepare for the Volkskammer election.[32]

Demokratie Jetzt

Demokratie Jetzt (DJ) issued a "Call to Interfere in Our Own Affairs" and "Theses for a Democratic Restructuring of the GDR" on 12 September 1989. Leaders of this movement sought to bring together Christians and critical

Marxists to create a democratic socialism. Among the founding members of DJ were the physicist Hans-Jurgen Fischbek, the translator and mathematician Ludwig Mehlhorn, the historian and cofounder of "Women for Peace" Ulrike Poppe and her husband Gerd Poppe, the theology professor Wolfgang Ullmann, and Konrad Weiβ, a documentary filmmaker. DJ is an organization of intellectuals with strong ties to the Evangelical church and an equally strong desire to realize a democratic, humane socialism.

There was little that distinguished DJ from NF. Perhaps the most important difference concerned the SED. While NF considered at least part of the SED capable of reform, DJ claimed that the best way to reform the SED was to have it go into the opposition in a newly elected Volkskammer. In the early days, DJ also had a better defined ecological program than NF, demanding that environmental data held secret be released and that an open discussion of waste disposal and energy policy begin.

Vereinigte Linke

Vereinigte Linke (VL) issued its Böhlener Plattform early in September 1989, calling for a united Left in the GDR. Its membership drew heavily on the same sources as NF and DJ: students, union members, and intellectuals affiliated with the Evangelical church. Ex-SED members were numerous among supporters of the VL.

As a political group, VL campaigned for a renewal of socialism in the GDR based on councils, public ownership of the means of production, and a multiparty system along with civil and human rights guarantees. VL also spoke of a third way between capitalism and Stalinism, labeled, without much elaboration, as "self-governing socialism"—Selbstverwaltungssozialismus.

The three groups sketched above shared many things: commitment to socialism, GDR sovereignty, dedication to human and civil rights, grassroots politics, respect for the environment, and concern for the Third World. Yet the fact that these three groups were joined by a half dozen others on the left side of the political spectrum in the GDR (e.g., Initiative Frieden und Menschenrechte, Die Nelken, Grüne) revealed a badly fragmented East German Left.

An effort to overcome divisions on the Left through the Wahlbündnis '90 was only partly successful. This alliance of six parties and groups proved unworkable and led to the splitting of NF: some members went over to the Social Democratic party, others founded a market-oriented Deutsche Forumpartei (DFP) that allied itself with the Bund Freier Demokraten. Later, on 7 February 1990, three groups, NF, DJ, and Initiative Menschenrechte und Frieden formed Bündnis '90—Alliance '90 (B90). B90, which considered itself to be an alliance of groups and platforms, not a party, had no partners in West Germany and attempted to present a self-confident and independent GDR element in the Volkskammer election campaign. The VL found itself unable to join B90 and instead allied with Die Nelken, a Marxist group appealing to Marxists without a party—predominantly former SED members. The alliance was called Aktionsbündnis Vereinigte Linke.

Political Parties

The East German political party landscape had three elements:

1. The SED and its successor, the PDS;
2. The former block parties: Christian Democratic Union of Germany (CDU), Liberal Democratic party of Germany (LDPD), Democratic Farmers party (DBD), and the National Democratic Party of Germany (NDPD); and
3. The new and reconstituted parties: Social Democratic Party of Germany (SPD), Democratic Awakening (DA), German Social Union (DSU), Liberal Democratic party (LDP), Communist Party of Germany (KPD), Greens, Independent Womens Federation (UFV), Independent Social Democratic Party of Germany (USPD) and others.

The SED/PDS

As the events of autumn 1989 unfolded, the question of what to do about the SED became increasingly insistent. The nomenklatura, the privileges, the party-Stasi connection, the devastated economy and ecology joined to discredit the SED. Yet a party of 2.8 million members with a highly developed organization and extensive properties and assets was a force, even in decline. The question was: can a Stalinist party that has been in power for forty years be reformed? The overwhelming answer was no.

Nonetheless, by 11 October, even the hardline SED chief of ideology, Kurt "Tapeten" Hager was speaking of "necessary renewal" in the GDR.[33] Once this need was recognized, the SED party leadership tumbled.

At the tenth meeting of the SED central committee on 8 November, virtually all of the remaining old guard were relieved of their duties. Hans Modrow, the popular district first secretary in Dresden chaired the Council of Ministers and played a key role in attempting a renewal of the SED while head of the transitional government that served until March 1990.[34]

Following Krenz's ouster from party and state offices early in December, the way was open for an attempted SED renaissance under Gregor Gysi, supported by Hans Modrow, Wolfgang Berghofer, and Manfred Pohl as vice-chairers. They were elected to their offices during a lengthy session of an extraordinary SED party conference on 8 and 9 December. On 16 and 17 December, Gregor Gysi called for renewal and pluralism and the party gave itself a new name: SED-Partei des Demokratischen Sozialismus—(SED-Party of Democratic Socialism).

Even the popular Gysi could not prevent the SED-PDS from declining to about 800,000 members in January and February of 1990—a loss of two million. Egon Krenz was expelled in January and the party expunged the widely despised "SED" from its name early in February. Neither measure helped brake the party's decline, although the party did better than expected in the March election. Nonetheless, the PDS continues to have difficulties dealing with its past—Vergangenheitsbewältigung.[35]

The Block Parties: CDU, LDPD, DBD, and NDPD

The block parties had a common problem in the late summer and early autumn of 1989: if they were to survive, they must shed their past close association with the SED. The block parties had recognized the leading role of the SED for four decades. They had been financed by the SED. They had also served in the Volkskammer as loyal members of the National Front. The key to their dissociation from the SED would lie in how convincingly they could separate themselves from the SED without appearing to be unacceptably opportunistic.

The CDU began distancing itself very cautiously from the SED in October 1989. The process went neither easily nor quickly. This was indicated in the two drafts of a CDU position paper that appeared on 28 October and 25 November in *Neue Zeit,* the CDU party newspaper. While the CDU was a "socialist party" in the first draft, this was modified considerably in the second (November) draft, which spoke of a vaguer socialism based on a "Christian understanding" of the term.

The position of the CDU was made particularly difficult by the role the Lutheran church had played in nurturing the various oppositional groups. Thus the party's position on ecology, human rights, and peace had to be drawn very carefully during the run-up to the Wende. Once Lothar de Maizière became party chairer on 10 November, the CDU could move forward under a respected church leader and attorney who took the CDU out of the block on 4 December.[36]

At its party convention on 15 and 16 December, the CDU broke decisively with the SED. The CDU called for an end to "socialist experimentation," a return of state property to its original owners, a market economy, and German reunification.

With the GDR election campaign heating up, the CDU withdrew its cabinet ministers from the Modrow government at the end of January. At the same time, the CDU in the GDR moved closer to the CDU of the FRG. Finally, on 5 February, the CDU joined with Demokratischer Aufbruch and the Deutsche Soziale Union (DSU) to form the electoral Allianz für Deutschland.

The LDPD, under its chairer, Manfred Gerlach, was the first of the block parties to carefully move away from the SED in September 1989. In a speech commemorating the fortieth anniversary of the GDR, Gerlach announced programmatic changes for the party and stated that the GDR must ask why the people, most of whom are "Children of the Revolution," were leaving East Germany.[37]

Although it left the block on 5 December and gradually moved away from its long support for the SED to embrace the tenets of liberalism, the LDPD had difficulties in making the transition. For example, it took the LDPD a considerable time to move away from its support for a centrally planned economy. This reluctance contributed to the split in East German liberal forces with the Deutsche Forumpartei (DFP) East German Freie Demokratische Partei (FDP). Nonetheless, support for the LDPD, as indicated by its membership figures, increased by about 8,000 in the fall of 1989. The final transition to traditional liberal positions came in the LDPD party convention on 2 February 1990. The party changed its name to simply LDP, and Rainer Ortleb replaced Manfred Gerlach as party chairer. Following these changes, the liberal parties, DFP, FDP and LDP joined in a Bund Freier Demokraten—Federation of Free Democrats to continue the Volkskammer election campaign.

The Democratic Farmers party and the National Democratic Party of Germany were created in 1948 by the SED to extend its appeal, by way of the block, to the agricultural sector, minor Nazis, Wehrmacht veterans, and the nationalist bourgeoisie. The minor role of these parties declined in the last years of the GDR and, when faced with the Wende, clearly had no future. Other parties refused to ally with them for electoral purposes, and, unlike the other block parties, they had no feasible allies in the Federal Republic.

The New and Reconstructed Parties

The list of new parties that accompanied the events of 1989–90 in the GDR is extensive and includes the Deutsche Biertrinker Union (DBU), which, although concerned with serious matters, such as the Reinheitsgebot, was not seriously political even though it was a duly certified party. Two new parties and one reconstituted party will be examined here: the Demokratischer Aufbruch (Democratic Awakening, DA), the Deutsche Soziale Union

(German Social Union, DSU), and the Sozialdemokratische Partei Deutschlands (Social Democratic Party of Germany, SPD).

Democratic Awakening began as an initiative to move grass-roots protest out of the churches of the GDR to appeal to a broader public on the basis
of a Christian socialism. As it developed in the summer of 1989, DA became
an effort to involve critical church voices in the reform of the East German
political system. Their concerns were given urgency by the falsification of
the communal election results in May and the unwillingness of state authorities to engage in dialogue.[38]

Although an earlier meeting had been broken up by police,[39] a conference of some 200 delegates of DA was held in East Berlin on 30 October
1989 and resolved to form a political party that would work for new electoral
laws in the GDR, achieve a productive industrial society that would also
provide for ecological and social needs, and press for a multiparty political
system that would also separate party and state. At the same time major
industries would remain under state ownership, although smaller businesses
and crafts might be in private hands under market conditions that would
protect the weak in society and protect the environment.[40]

The establishment of DA as a political party took place in Leipzig on
16 and 17 December. Internally, the party soon had to deal with a schism.
The attorney Wolfgang Schnur and Pfarrer Rainer Eppelman gradually had
taken positions favoring German reunification and a market orientation for
the East German economy. Pastor Friedrich Schorlemmer and others held
that the GDR needed a leftist party of sufficient strength to keep the SED/PDS
from making a comeback. Consequently they switched from the DA to the
SDP/SPD.

Following the split, DA struck "the vision of a socialist society" from
its platform and later entered into the electoral Allianz für Deutschland with
the CDU and DSU. The party was dealt a severe blow just prior to the
election when it turned out that its chairer, Wolfgang Schnur, had worked
for years as an informer for the Stasi. Following Schnur's resignation, Rainer
Eppelmann chaired the party.

The German Social Union (DSU) was founded on 20 January in Leipzig.
The DSU brought together eleven Christian, liberal, and conservative oppositional groups under the leadership of Pfarrer Hans-Wilhelm Ebeling of the
Thomas-Kirche. Present at the founding was the West German minister of
development assistance, Jürgen Warnke of the Christian Social Union (CSU)
of Bavaria.[41] Warnke's presence was not accidental, for the DSU was considered to be the East German branch of the CSU.

At the first party congress of the DSU, held in Leipzig on 18 February
1990, Ebeling called for immediate German reunification according to Article

23 of the West German Basic Law immediately after the Volkskammer election.[42] The DSU joined the Allianz für Deutschland in spite of some programmatic differences.

The reconstitution of the Social Democratic Party of Germany (SPD) was not an easy matter. The party had been forcibly united with the Communist Party of Germany to form the SED in April 1946. Relations between the SPD (West) and the SED were complex and difficult.[43]

When it became clear that the SED might not survive the turbulence of the autumn of 1989, the SPD (West) faced a quandary. Should it abandon its earlier course and drop efforts to effect change though dialogue with the SED, or should it abandon the SED and support indigenous efforts aimed at resurrecting social democracy in East Germany? As was often the case in 1989–90, events drove policy. On 7 October 1989, the Sozialdemokratische Partei in der DDR (Social Democratic Party in the GDR, SDP-DDR) was founded under conspiratorial conditions in Schwante near Oranienburg.

Four pastors of the Evangelical church, Helmut Becker, Martin Gutzeit, Markus Meckel, and Arndt Noack, along with the Berlin historian Ibrahim Böhme, had prepared the way for the SPD-DDR in the summer of 1989 by creating an Initiativgruppe with the aim of eventually establishing a social democratic party. Their goal was an "ecologically oriented social democracy" that would institute a rule of law with a division of powers, parliamentary democracy with party pluralism, a market economy forbidding monopolies, the recognition of civil rights, and the continuation of two separate German states.[44] Thus the SDP-DDR was ready to come forward with a program in Schwante that was well elaborated compared to those of other new GDR parties.[45]

As Willy Brandt had declared in another context, it was inevitable that "what belongs together, grows together." At the SDP-DDR delegates' conference from 12 through 14 January 1990, the party name was changed to simply the Sozialdemokratische Partei Deutschlands (Social Democratic Party of Germany, SPD).[46] The SPD (East) came out for a united Germany and generally aligned itself with the SPD (West) in preparation for the Volkskammer election campaign.

At the first SPD (East) party congress on 24 and 25 February 1990, Ibrahim Böhme was elected party chair, and Willy Brandt became the honorary chairer of the party. It was clear that the party had expanded both in terms of membership and organization. In fact, on the basis of faulty survey data, the SPD (East) expected to garner 45 percent of the vote on 18 March.[47]

This rapidly changing political landscape was confusing to an electorate that was for the first time confronted with wide range of choices. As a result, the outcome was very much in doubt.

The Volkskammer Election of 18 March 1990

As results came into the television studios hastily installed in the Palast der Republik it was clear that the expectations of the SPD were dashed and that the parties of the Allianz für Deutschland were headed for victory. The Allianz parties gained 48 percent of the vote to 21.9 percent for the SPD. The PDS came in with a surprisingly strong showing of just over 16 percent. The liberal Bund Freier Demokraten managed just over 5 percent.

What accounted for the electoral outcome that gave victory to the conservative Allianz on territory that had been widely considered to be a social democratic stronghold? The most compelling explanation is that of Dieter Roth.[48] Drawing on Anthony Downs's *An Economic Theory of Democracy* and electoral and public opinion data from the Forschungsgruppe Wahlen, Roth shows that GDR voters wanted speedy unification with the FRG. These voters were thus "rational" in supporting those parties that were perceived as hastening the unification process. Since the Christian Democratic parties dominated the governing coalition in Bonn and were also now committed to rapid unification, it made sense for East German voters to support their GDR equivalents and partners.

There are other, supplementary explanations of the outcome. Perhaps the most important was the massive presence of the Christian Democratic parties in the East German election campaigns. In addition, the negative association connected with "socialism" among East Germans no doubt helps account for the relatively poor showing of the SPD. Finally, East Germans wanted change. Many felt that change could be expected with greater certainty from the Right than from a Left that, justly or not, was identified with the former regime.

The Politics of Unification

While it was clear after the Volkskammer election of 18 March that Germany would be unified, questions remained regarding how and under what domestic and international conditions. Domestically, the questions concerned the legal framework to be applied to unification. Internationally, the Two Plus Four talks quickly devolved into one (the Soviets) versus the rest. Since the Soviets expressed strong security concerns, and given that they had some 340,000 troops stationed in the GDR, the Soviets could not be ignored. The international conditions for uniting Germany revolved around ways to reassure the Soviets of their security, and to buy them off.

The domestic battle over unification had two elements: the form of economic unification, and the form of political unification. Economic unification entailed both the extension of the West German mark to the GDR (the East German mark was nonconvertible, and had no prospects of future convertibility), and the extension of western social and economic benefits to the East. Economic unification was driven by the continuing waves of East Germans leaving for the West, even if in somewhat lessened numbers after the March election. Additionally, the fall of the Wall revealed the bankruptcy of the East German economy, and demands for a leveling of standards of living in East and West were growing. Bonn, which had campaigned in the East on improving economic conditions, was forced to deliver.

The debate about the form of economic union was sharp. Oscar LaFontaine, the SPD's chancellor candidate for the elections scheduled for December 1990, argued that unification had to be slowed, until it could become clear what the costs would be for West German taxpayers. Kohl was able to deflect this criticism by contending that unification would be relatively cost free, since east German firms could continue to export to eastern Europe. Kohl also appealed to the need to meet East German demands for better standards of living, and the emotionally charged, historic drive to unify the divided nation.

Kohl was unable to resist the pressures exerted by the Bundesbank. Bank president Karl-Otto Pöhl feared that Kohl's earlier pledge to exchange East and West marks at 1:1, coupled with higher federal borrowing to pay for reconstruction and social programs in the East, might touch off inflation in the German economy. Kohl adroitly reduced the Bundesbank's influence by naming Pohl the head of the group to unify the economies of the Germanys, where Pohl would be the first to blame if economic unification was too slow. To apparently placate the powerful head of the independent Bundesbank, Kohl agreed to tighten Germany's stance on European monetary integration along lines proposed by Pohl. The treaty on monetary, economic, and social union between the two Germanys was signed on 18 May, and on 1 July economic union was effected.

Politically, the two Germanys could be united either by formal treaty between the two sovereign states (Article 146 of the West German Basic Law), or by the dissolution of the GDR and the application of its constituent parts to join the FRG (Article 23). The former was preferred by the West German Social Democrats, and much of the Left in the East. This strategy would have slowed unification, and improved their chances in the December 1990 election. Legally, the two states would have had to be unified by August to hold a united election. Unification via Article 146 was not supported by many West German conservatives. Unification via Article 23 seemed to be quicker, provided a cleaner break with the GDR's past, and maintained the important democratic elements of the Basic Law. It also improved the likelihood that Kohl could win the first national election in the newly unified Germany, since Kohl was more popular in the East than in the

West. Buttressed by a strong showing in the May communal elections in the GDR, and despite criticism from the Left, East-West negotiations were conducted on the basis of Article 23.[49] After long and occasionally acrimonious bargaining, with key points of contention such as abortion laws deferred, a treaty unifying the two Germanys was signed on 31 August 1990.

Technically, German economic and political union was not possible as long as the Four Powers maintained their rights in Germany. The large number of Soviet troops on East German soil was a reminder that unification was contingent upon external developments. Yet the internal, domestic pressures for unification were so strong, and the Soviet military and political position so weak, that the Soviets could at best slow unification. The efforts of the Western powers, led by the United States, were directed at getting the Soviets to graciously and quickly bow out of the GDR, while saving face and assuring Soviet security. The Western powers followed two tracks to convince the Soviets to support quick German unification.

Multilateral negotiations constituted the first track of the Western strategy. In the course of the Two Plus Four talks, and later at the London NATO Summit on 5–6 July 1990, the Western powers sent clear signals to Moscow that they considered the cold war to be over, that future NATO strategy would not take advantage of collapsing Soviet influence in eastern Europe, and that German unification was imminent. The second track focused upon bilateral assurances to the Soviets, especially during the U.S.-Soviet summit in May–June 1990. Kohl and Foreign Minister Genscher also sought to reassure the Soviets, in February during a visit to Moscow, and in June during meetings in Copenhagen, Brest, and Munster. The Soviets tried vainly to either neutralize Germany, or keep both parts in their respective blocks. With the Warsaw Pact rapidly disintegrating, these efforts lacked credibility.

Kohl's visit to Gorbachev on 14 through 16 July finally broken the logjam. The Soviets and Germans agreed that the Soviets would withdraw their troops gradually from the GDR, that until the Soviets were gone no NATO Bundeswehr units would be stationed in the East, and that after the Soviets left no non-German NATO troops would be deployed in the East. The Germans also agreed to extend economic support to the Soviet Union, and construct housing for the soldiers returning home. Soviet-German friendship was formalized in a treaty between the two signed on 9 November 1990.

Much has been made of the Kohl-Gorbachev talks of July 1990. These discussions seemed to push along an understanding on the part of the Soviets that Germany was fully dedicated to peace, and that war would not begin in Germany again. Yet the agreement itself only constituted Soviet recognition of long-standing Western positions in the Two Plus Four talks. The Soviets had few options, economic unification had been achieved, and the pressures for quick political unification were rising. The Soviets undoubtedly held out for the best deal they thought they could get, but it was a far cry from past Soviet demands.

With the Soviets on board, and the economic and political treaties signed, all that was left was for the Four Powers to suspend their rights over Germany. This was unceremoniously accomplished on 1 October 1990. Amid public celebrations and fireworks, the Germanys were formally unified on 3 October 1990.

The First Bundestag Election in a United Germany

The Bundestag election of 3 December 1990 involved the traditional politics of the Federal Republic with an admixture of the groups and parties that had played a role in the East German revolution. The changes of the past year conspired to make the event anything but politics as usual.

Most affected by the changes were the political fortunes of the SPD. SPD chancellor candidate Oskar Lafontaine represented an attitude and a generation within the West German Left that had treated the GDR as a foreign land. German unification was never a high priority for Lafontaine. Indeed contacts between the SPD and East Germany tended to be through the SED establishment and aimed at a long-term change through rapprochement (Wandel durch Annäherung) between the Germanys.

It was natural then that Lafontaine was a persistent critic of German unification in 1989–90. Lafontaine preferred discussing difficult truths involved in unification to pandering to the popular mood favoring a rapid anschluß of the GDR to the FRG. Lafontaine and his party paid dearly for an attitude that was widely interpreted as arrogant—a quality frequently associated with Lafontaine.

In any event, SPD policies and personalities, with the exception of former chancellor Willy Brandt, left the field to the Christain Democratic and liberal parties. In the former GDR this meant essentially that the Volkskammer election results of March 1990, along with the communal and state elections that followed, were repeated on 2 December. In the West, the Christian Democratic and Liberal parties' positive position on unification and perceived competence in dealing with its economic consequences carried the day.[50] CDU/CSU plus FDP garnered 54 percent of the vote, keeping the SPD in the opposition with 33.5 percent. The Greens, who failed to ally themselves with their Eastern counterparts, missed the 5 percent hurdle with a showing of 3.9 percent. Thanks to a separate accounting of votes in the five new states of the FRG, the PDS/LL (Leftist List) and B90/Grünen made it into the twelfth Bundestag, which consists of six parties.

The results of the election added up to strong support for Chancellor Kohl. His understanding of the events of 1989–90 for Germany boosted his popularity after the currency, finance, and social union of 1 July 1990. His skills as a public figure in the autumn of 1990 carried him and his political allies to victory at the polls. Before him and his colleagues stood the awe-inspiring complications and costs of the unification they had so ardently sought.

NOTES

Much of this is the product of a sabbatical year (1989–90) in what was then West Germany. I should like to thank the Deutsche Akademische Austausch Dienst (DAAD), Radio Free Europe/Radio Liberty, The United States Information Service (USIS), and Deutsche Welle for providing support. None of these institutions is responsible for my views and possible errors. Neither is Botschafter a.D. Gustav A. Dräcker, who generously read and commented upon an earlier draft of this manuscript. An earlier version of this chapter was delivered as a paper at the 1990 meetings of the American Political Science Association in San Francisco.

1. This term is used by Fred Oldenburg in his BIOSst report no. 10/91, *Die Implosion des SED-Regimes Ursachen und Entwicklungsprozesse* (Cologne: 1990). This term is also used by Uwe Thaysen in *Der runde Tisch oder: Wo bleibt das Volk?* (Opladen: Westdeutscher, 1990), 186ff.

2. Difficulties between the GDR and the Soviet Union were apparent even before Gorbachev came to power. A foretaste of GDR problems came during the theater nuclear forces buildup in central Europe resulting from Soviet SS-20 deployments and NATO counterdeployments in 1983. The GDR took a position between the fronts. GDR leaders were clearly unhappy with the mounting nuclear deployments and in their way resisted the Soviet moves. See Arthur M. Hanhardt, Jr., "The Prospects for German-German Detente," *Current History* 88 (1984): 380ff. At the same time the GDR leadership firmly suppressed an "unofficial" domestic peace movement that also sought to inhibit nuclear deployments.

3. See Jens Kaiser, "Zwischen angestrebter Eigenstandigkeit und traditioneller Unterordnung," *Deutschland Archiv* 24 (1991): 478–95. A similar attitude vis-à-vis the Soviet leadership led to the downfall of Honecker's predecessor, Walter Ulbricht, in 1971.

4. Fred Oldenburg in *Die UdSSR und der Zusammenbruch des Kommunismus in Osteuropa* (BIOst report no. 62/1990, Cologne, 1990) stresses Gorbachev's ambivalence in the matter of Soviet control in Eastern Europe through the spring of 1989. Nonetheless this ambivalence was sufficient to cause the Eastern European conservatives to "dig in" domestically and thus to heighten internal tensions.

5. For example, Dashitchev declared in 1988 that the Brezhnev Doctrine was no longer applicable even if that was not yet the official position of the Soviet government. He caused a minor sensation in West Germany in June 1988 by suggesting that the Berlin Wall and the borders of the GDR were remnants of the cold war "that would have to disappear in due time." Cited in *Die Welt,* 9 June 1988.

6. Wolfgang Pfeiler, "Sowjetische Deutschlandpolitik und sowjetisch-amerikani-

sche Beziehungen" in *Die USA und die Deutsche Frage 1945-1990,* ed. Wolfgang-Uwe Friedrich (Frankfurt am Main: Campus Verlag, 1991).

7. Gunnar Winkler, ed., *Sozialreport '90* (Berlin: Die Wirtschaft, 1990). Also important in this regard are the essays of Heinz Kallabis published as *"Realer Sozialismus"—Anspruch und Wirklichkeit* (Berlin: Treptower, 1990).

8. Robert F. Goeckel, *The Lutheran Church and the East German State* (Ithaca: Cornell University Press, 1990).

9. Christiane Lemke, *Die Ursachen des Umbruchs 1989: Politischen Sozialization in der ehemaligen DDR* (Opladen: Westdeutscher, 1991).

10. Margot Honecker on GDR TV, 14 June 1989.

11. Parts of the following sections are drawn from Arthur M. Hanhardt, Jr., "Demonstrations, Groups, Parties, and the Volkskammer Election: Aspects of Political Change in East Germany" (Paper delivered at the Annual Meeting of the American Political Science Association, San Francisco, 30 August–2 September 1990).

12. The role of the United States in the runup to German unification is easily underestimated. For a comprehensive treatment of this relationship see: Wolfgang-Uwe Friedrich, "Demokratische Realpolitik: Die Deutsche Frage als Problem der deutsch-amerikanischen Beziehungen 1949-1990," in Friedrich *Die USA,* 29–38. For a U.S. view on Gorbymania, see Andrew Nagorski, "Seducing the West: After Gorbachev: Have the Germans Lost Their Hearts—and Their Heads?" *Washington Post,* 18 June 1989, sec. A.

13. The irony of the last point was lost on no one familiar with the long-standing East German practice of exchanging political prisoners for hard currency payments from Bonn.

14. Armin Mitter and Stefan Wolle, eds., *Ich liebe euch doch alle! Befehle und Lageberichte des MfS Januar-November 1989* (Berlin: BasisDruck, 1990), 34–39 and 42–45.

15. Egon Krenz, *Wenn Mauern fallen. Die friedliche Revolution: Vorgeschichte, Ablauf-Auswirkungen* (Vienna: Paul Neff, 1990), 132–34.

16. Marlies Menge, *Ohne uns läuft nichts mehr* (Stuttgart: Deutsche, 1990), 87–88.

17. Mitter and Wolle, *Ich liebe euch,* 11–16.

18. Christoph Links and Hannes Bahrmann, *Wir sind das Volk: Die DDR im Aufbruch. Eine Chronik* (Berlin: Aufbau, Wuppertal: Peter Manner, 1990), 7–19.

19. Krenz, *Wenn Mauern,* 134–37.

20. See the figures in Ronald A. Francisco, "Leadership and the Crisis of State in the GDR" (Paper delivered at the Annual Meeting of the American Political Science Association, San Francisco, 1990).

21. In contrast with the self-serving memoirs of Egon Krenz, Gunter Schabowski's books covering the period are thoughtful reflections on the decline and fall of the GDR. See Günter Schabowski, *Das Politbüro* (Hamburg: Rowohlt Taschenbuch, 1990) and *Der Absturz* (Berlin: Rowohlt, 1991).

22. See Urszula Kozierowska, "Frieden vor Einheit," interview with Friedrich Schorlemmer in *Träumen Verboten,* ed. Peter Neumann (Gottingen: Lamuv, 1990), 45–56.

23. "Zehn-Punkte Programm zur Überwindung der Teilung Deutschlands und Europas/Rede von Bundeskanzler Kohl vor dem Deutschen Bundestag am 28. 11. 1989 (Auszuge)," *Umbruch in Europa: Die Ereignisse im 2. Halbjahr 1989. Eine Dokumentation* (Bonn: Auswätiges Amt, 1990), 111–20.

24. Barbara Grunert-Bronnen, *Ich bin Bürger der DDR und lebe in der Bundesrepublik* (Munich: R. Piper, 1970).

25. See as examples Gregor Gysi, *Wir brauchen einen dritten Weg,* ed. Andrè Brie (Hamburg: Konkret Literatur, 1990) and Rainer Land, ed., *Das Umbaupapier (DDR)* (Berlin: Rotbuch, 1990).

26. See Gottfried Timmel, "Eine 'Arche'—viele Noahs," *Frankfurter Allgemeine Zeitung* 6 November 1989.

27. Rolf Henrich, *Der vormundschaftliche Staat—Vom Versagen des real existierenden Sozialismus* (Hamburg: Rowohlt, 1989).

28. Mitter and Wolle, *Ich liebe euch,* 154.

29. Rolf Henrich, "Die DDR zwischen Ausbruch und Aufbruch" in *Jetzt oder Nie—Demokratie, Leipziger Herbst '89,* ed. Neues Forum Leipzig (Leipzig: Forum 1989, Munich: Bertelsmann, 1990), 15.

30. "DDR-Oppositionsgruppe 'Neues Forum' beantragt Zulassung als politische Vereinigung," *Süddeutsche Zeitung,* 20 September 1989.

31. "'Neues Forum' will Gerichte anrufen," *Süddeutsche Zeitung,* 23–24 September 1989.

32. The SPD and Demokratischer Aufbruch left Bündnis '90 prior to the Volkskammer election.

33. "SED-Chefideologe Hager spricht sich für 'erforderliche Erneuerung' in der DDR aus," *Süddeutsche Zeitung,* 12 October 1989. The appelation *Tapeten* ("wallpaper") comes from Hager's dismissal of glasnost and perestroika as unneeded in the GDR: "Just because the neighbors changed their wallpaper did not mean that we must change too."

34. For Modrow's view of events see Hans Modrow, *Aufbruch und Ende* (Hamburg: Konkret Literatur, 1991).

35. See, for example, Walter Janka, *Schwierigkeiten mit der Wahrheit* (Hamburg: Rowohlt, 1990); and, Hermann Rudolph, "Eine Partei die sich nicht stellt," *Süddeutsche Zeitung,* 16 August 1990.

36. De Maizière's Stasi past as an "informal associate" caught up with him after unification, forcing his departure from politics.

37. "DDR-Politiker fordert Reformen," *Frankfurter Allgemeine Zeitung,* 21 September 1989; full text in *Der Morgen,* 20 September 1989, 3.

38. Monika Zimmermann, "Die Protestanten in der DDR gehen aus der Kirche auf die Straße," *Frankfurter Allgemeine Zeitung,* 27 October 1989.

39. "Neue Oppositionsgruppe in der DDR gegründet," *Süddeutsche Zeitung,* 3 October 1989.

40. "DDR-Liberale stellen Führung der SED in Frage: Kritik am Wahlsystem: Oppositionsgruppe 'Demokratischer Aufbruch' strebt Parteigründung im nächsten Jahr an," *Süddeutsche Zeitung,* 31 October–1 November 1989.

41. "Deutsche Soziale Union in Leipzig gegründet," and "Selbstverwirklichung mit Fernsteuerung," *Süddeutsche Zeitung*, 22 January 1990.

42. "Ein Neuanfang mit der 'Allianz für Deutschland'/Schäuble und Waigel beim DSU-Parteitag in Leipzig," *Frankfurter Allgemeine Zeitung*, 19 February 1990.

43. See Ann L. Phillips, *Seeds of Change in the German Democratic Republic: The SED-SPD Dialogue* (Washington, D.C.: American Institute for Contemporary German Studies, 1989).

44. Albrecht Hinze, "Zaghafte Bewegung im erstarrten Land," *Süddeutsche Zeitung*, 21 September 1989.

45. The text of the document can be found in Gesamtdeutsches Institut, "Analysen, Dokumentation und Chronik zur Entwicklung in der DDR von September bis Dezember 1989" (Bonn, 1990, Typescript), 46–68.

46. "Die Sozialdemokraten in der DDR bekennen sich zur Einheit," *Frankfurter Allgemeine Zeitung*, 15 January 1990.

47. Albrecht Hinze, "DDR-SPD beschließt 'Fahrplan zur Einheit,'" *Süddeutsche Zeitung*, 26 February 1990; and Martin E. Süskind, "Der schwierigste Balanceakt steht noch bevor," *Süddeutsche Zeitung*, 26 February 1990.

48. Dieter Roth, "Die Wahlen zur Volkskammer: Der Versuch einer Erklärung," *Politische Vierteljahresschrift* 31 (1990): 369–93.

49. See Wolfgang Schäuble, *Der Vertrag: Wie ich über die deutsche Einheit verhandelte* (Stuttgart: Deutsche, 1991).

50. See Forschungsgruppe Wahlen, *Bundestagswahl 1990* (Mannheim, 1990), 22.

The "Black-Brown Hazelnut" in a Bigger Germany: The Rise of a Radical Right as a Structural Feature

John D. Ely

Germany's New "Republicanism": A Danger in a United Germany and Nationalist Europe?

For those with a historical memory, perhaps nothing in the recent past is more disturbing than new images of neo-Nazi gangs in the streets of Germany and unexpected radical Right electoral victories. In the former GDR, the towns of Hoyerswerda, Rostock, and Mölln have become national symbols of rising neo-Nazi persecution of refugees and foreign-born residents of Germany. In the old part of the Federal Republic the new Right parties and formations such as the "Republicans" (REPs), the National Democratic Party of Germany (NPD), and the German People's Union (DVU) have demonstrated not only that antidemocratic tendencies are still alive in Germany, but that they are politically powerful. In 1991 alone, there were some 1,500 reported attacks on "foreigners," a five-fold increase over the previous year. The fall of 1991 was characterized by a particular rash of attacks, and this autumn again such attacks, not merely on refugees but also on dark-skinned persons in general, whatever their legal status, were daily occurrences filling the newspapers. Particularly in the new federal states, such violence has made it difficult for nonwhite people to travel, work, and live in Germany. Some sixteen people died in 1992 from outbursts. Outbursts of chauvinistic nationalism and racial violence and the emergence of fascistic conceptions of community, state, and ethnos have not only plagued Germany, but other parts of Europe as well, recalling a past epoch. Jörg Haider and Jean-Marie Le Pen are making headlines in Austria and France respectively, Pamyat and other right-wing nationalisms are growing in Russia, with increasing ties inside the military and old Communist establishment. These phenomena are developing alongside strong-arm, nationalist talk in Poland and Romania; nationalist-fascist leaders among the Croats and Serbs are playing important political and military roles in the new Balkans. Combined with threatening economic conditions, all these events recall a Europe more like the twenties than any period following World War II.

Germany is once again becoming a major, indeed, great power in Europe. Its de facto role in foreign policy is evident since the catalyzing role of Germany in supporting its old interests in the area in the Yugoslavian breakup. More important still is the economic opening provided by the end of the East bloc. Here, too, we see a situation similar to that earlier in this century. In such a context, the reemergence of a radical Right in the elections of September 1991 in the German city-state of Bremen and of April 1992 in the German states of Schleswig-Holstein and Baden-Württemberg, where Gerhard Frey's German People's Union and Franz Schönhuber's Republicans have made stunning gains, can only be a cause for alarm. The less cautious had predicted Schönhuber's decline and a crisis for the Republicans following the disappointing showing in the 1990 Bavarian state elections; but the party surprised everybody once again with 11.6 percent of the vote in Baden-Württemberg in 1992. Indeed, in the new historical climate, the following question seems pertinent: does Germany's Right pose a danger to the liberal democratic state in Germany or, indeed, the stability of Europe? Schönhuber's earlier preunification successes in the Berlin and European Parliament elections of 1989, the threat of the DVU in Bremerhaven, and the successes of the NPD in Frankfurt focused on xenophobia, an attack on the Left, the call for a return to Germany's "true" (1937!) borders, and a violent antipathy to planned European unification in 1992. These themes have been picked up in various ways and reworked, in both the old and new German federal states, since unification; and it is these issues, above all xenophobic antagonism to "foreigners," that have led to renewed electoral successes. Estimations of antidemocratic voter potential in Germany have recently risen alarmingly. Possible new coalition arrangements—especially if troubles continue for Chancellor Kohl's CDU—also harken back to situations that prevailed in a period most had thought long overcome: the possibility of a "great coalition" of the democratic parties compelled by the *weakness* of a democratic Right rather than the strength of the Left, a situation that characterized the instability of the Weimar Republic. To view such circumstances, particularly with an overstressed economy and a situation where the radical claims of the Greens fall on deaf or even antagonistic ears, suggests the weakness of a "red-green" alternative to the CDU.[1]

The social composition of those regions where the new radical Right has had successes in Germany are also cause for concern. Success has occurred particularly in run-down housing projects and declining areas of heavy industry long ruled by SPD governments elected by traditionally oriented voters, voters who are increasingly using their "rational" or "protest" votes to elect the new Right. Such areas are typically depressed economically, and the perspective among the youth one of hopelessness.[2] But we do not just see evidence of direct transfer of larger numbers of voters from the SPD to the new Right. We also see the breakdown of urban areas (even in "postindustrial" and "modern" cities like Frankfurt) into *core* areas of high employment, wages, and levels of education, along with clear governmental presence and industrial policy, on the one hand, and *marginal* areas of structural unemployment, poor education and opportunity, and government neglect. This follows the projected split of the post-Fordist industrial state into a core of highly educated, well-paid intellectual workers, and a large marginalized population of cheap service labor for this core ("new class") sector.[3] In Frankfurt am Main, as Eike Hennig observes, this division into a core and periphery is part of a "dialectic of the modern" that Leftist concerns with "civil society" and abstract conceptions of communication and "posttraditional" society fail to grasp conceptually.[4] Remarking ironically on the sense of "polite" in the German use of *Zivil,* Hennig and other commentators have noted that, under the notions of "ideal speech" and the "civil society," everyone in Germany is so interested in the most "modern" elements and a conception of affluence that they were conceptually unequipped to deal with new Right successes. While the SPD and the "realist" Greens have been focusing on "speech communities" and posttraditional civil society,[5] this apparent manifestation of earlier forms of political life fits into an aspect of the new world order such intellectual models do not address. Indeed, in the sense that such conceptions of civil society seek to reintroduce a socialist conception of bourgeois society in German discourse without a critique of capitalism, we see the new constitutional position of the Left resting on a concept of the public sphere that is explicitly detached from any institutional moorings.[6] Not only does such an attitude ignore what Tocqueville among others noted of American civic associations, namely their participatory moment, but it provides a focus on political speech within a narrow conception of political action; it is thus surprising that it would fail to predict new Right radical successes or understand that they rest on something other than "posttraditional" values.

These developments constitute at the very least a frustrating set of developments for which no obvious policy response from liberal or Left perspectives is self-evident. The development of the new Right and the nationalistic, antisocial, antisocialist, post–cold war context in which it is occuring will lead to changes in the character of the German state in response. Already we see a de facto change in the order of "legitimate violence" in the country. This has occurred because the disciplining effect on foreign labor that neo-

Nazi gangs and their popular supporters have created in the new federal states has occurred with apparent tacit support of law enforcement. The development of an internal state of fear for nonethnic Germans combined with a viable electoral politics of xenophobia will affect both German foreign policy and upcoming debates on the German constitution. Indeed, it is part of an apparent change in the character of the German polity. If the Greens at the beginning of the eighties signified the rise of a viable and influential radical Left after the delegitimation of German Communism, the new-Right parties, especially the "Republicans," signify the establishment of a structurally significant radical Right. This is part of a changing complexion in Germany's political culture as a whole. Even so simple an issue as the peacefulness of Marlene Dietrich's funeral would have been unthinkable in the Federal Republic of a few years earlier. Similarly plans to commemorate the V-2 ballistic missile by firing one in a commemorative ceremony, as proposed in the fall of 1992, would have been as unimaginable in the old "Federal Republic" as it is unsurprising in the new "Germany." Nationalist historians' claims that Germany has already "mastered" its past seem confirmed, at least in this sense. Kohl's openly nationalist federal campaigns in 1987 and 1989–90, the "adjustments" and adaptations that conservatives have continually made in response to radical Right propaganda, the "historians' debate," the Renaissance of scholarship and influence by the conservative jurist, Carl Schmitt, and the open cultivation of a cultural or ethnic nationalism have been characteristics of a new kind of national conservative spectrum which has been developing in the past decade, a development which has been accelerated by the unification process. This is an part of a general change in tenor.[7] Even the normally antipopulistic lobby group for German capital, the FDP, has experienced a change in complexion due to the recent official meetings of its leading figure, Otto Lambsdorff, with the Austrian radical Right leader Jörg Haider, who represents a radical nationalist, even neo-Nazi revival of that country's Free Democrats. Unlike their German colleagues, the Austrian Free Democrats had always been more "national" than "liberal," but prior to Haider's leadership, they went through a brief liberal period under the aegis of Norbert Steger.

Despite the manner in which the development of the radical Right will change the character of Germany, it is unlikely that it is a major threat to the "basic democratic order," the liberal constitutional and parliamentary state. As Andrei Markovits and Simon Reich argue, here we see a general institutional rationality of Germany's progressive and democratic integration in the European system, marking a clear contrast to the integration Germany achieved in the twenties and thirties.[8] The new institutional power of the liberal state at this level clearly dwarfs and largely absorbs a threat posed by the new Right.[9]

Nonetheless, the expansion and extensiveness of new right violence in 1991–92 has caused many commentators to talk about the "fragility" of German democracy.[10] The manner of responses to such rightist violence reflect the weaknesses upon which they thrive. Chancellor Kohl himself deployed a Schmittian language of an "emergency state," Staatsnotstand, though Kohl here referred to the excess of asylum applicants and the violence as the circumstances causing the emergency. Meanwhile, leftists talk openly of leaving Germany; comparisons to Weimar have become commonplace. While danger to the liberal democratic state per se is perhaps not serious, the rise of the radical Right, its xenophobia and violence, are clearly a part of the important transformation of the "Federal Republic of Germany" to plain, old "Germany."

Comparison with the past is thus important for understanding the new radical Right and its threats. The new radical Right, seen in historical perspective, is *not particularly new*. Whether in comparison with the NPD successes of the sixties, the virulent, revanchist, intolerant, and protofascist ideologies and passions from Arthur Moeller Van der Bruck, or the fascisms of Central Europe in the twenties and thirties, we see a striking consistence among the most recent "populistic" or fascistic new Right groups like the REPs or the DVU to the older patterns.[11] To be sure, there is some postmodern ornamentation on the old model. As Bill Buford has suggested, while skinheads are a reaction and adaptation to the counterculture, they do constitute a novel form of political action developing from punkers and football hooligans in England and spreading to other industrial nations.[12] The terminology *scene* and *scenerie* to describe new Right youth milieus, the role of heavy metal culture, even the name of nightclubs such as Am Richterplatz (Judge's Square), underscore this new element.[13] In a sense, perhaps, the yuppie props of the new Right charisma, Haider's clean-cut look or David Duke's face-lift, underscore this as well. These effects are largely issues of "style." Good looks are just a feature of the mass media in a TV environment, while utilization of mass media in whatever form is as old as fascist politics itself.

The central features of Right populism or the radical Right have remained unchanged. Not only the use of mass media, but the entire physiognomy of fascist and radical Right politics are evident in this most recent incarnation: one sees charisma and the leadership principle. Xenophobia and radical nationalism are central, interspersed with racist, social Darwinist, and mythological ideological elements. Political integration rests on populist mobilization. We see an absence of a substantive vision and a reaction to successes of the Left combined with the parasitizing of leftist issues or forms of action. The important role of border areas and economically depressed but socially dissociated regions so characteristic of xenophobic and fascistic movements in general is found in these groups. Rootedness ideologies, support for social issues for low income groups, revolutionary assault on the state, and strict conservative defense of political and social conformity and uniformity are features as evident today as they were decades ago. While this fascistic or radical Right has not taken up a permanent historic space forged during an era in which it emerged, it does have an overall character as recognizable today as it was seventy years earlier.

Who Are These Guys? Beer Drinking Bavarians or Real Neo-Nazis?

> The likelihood that the Federal Republic will be defeated by a totalitarian enemy who grows an easily recognizable mustache and prefers brown shirts is exceptionally slight. There will be no second Hitler to test the Bonn state, no imitation bringing the people under his spell. It'll be an unmistakable original whose appearance is trimmed to its time and corresponds to its needs. At best the enciphered similarities will be evident to the experts.
>
> —Franz Schönhuber, *Trotz allem Deutschland*
> (*Germany despite Everything*)

Despite the fact that they are the least neo-Nazi of the recently successful radical Right, the "Republicans" are clearly the most influential of these groupings. They bring the issues raised above into a clear perspective. The REPs were founded by Franz Schönhuber and a couple of other prominent conservative dissidents from the Bavarian Christian Social Union (CSU) in November 1982, three auspicious months before the federal elections that brought the conservative-liberal coalition to power and seated the first Greens in the Bundestag.[14] Schönhuber, a charismatic "people's tribune" in the style of Franz-Joseph Strauss with a background in the Waffen SS of which he is exceedingly proud, has been the unquestioned ruler of this party since he became chair in 1985. A vague and disconcerting mixture of conservative Bavarian beer-hall politics and neo-Nazi elements characterized Schönhuber's development and impregnated the party he founded. For years host of a popular and populist Bavarian politics talk show (a kind of Donahue with the politics of George Wallace), he was fired in 1982 after the publication of his autobiographical memories of life in the Waffen SS. With a fat pension and book proceeds, Schönhuber went into politics.

The book, *Ich war dabei* (*I Was There Too*), in its eighth printing in 1989 (one hundred and eighty thousand copies), is a classical example of fascist myth building.[15] *Der Spiegel* emphasized the voyeuristic and pornographic aspects of the book but did not focus on the medium for such voyeurism, Schönhuber's stories of liaisons with, among others, young *Polish* peasant girls during World War II (57f.). Populist applause for the international units in the SS is mixed with attacks on the leaders of the national socialist movement, who largely betrayed the rank and file. Schönhuber thus constructs an "internationalist" version of the "stab in the back" legend, with heroes like SS Colonel Steiner, who desperately defended Germany against the Russian hordes with SS units composed of French soldiers, "the great grandchildren of Napoleon." "If everyone had fought," writes Schönhuber, "as gallantly as the French volunteers defending Hitler's bunker, world history might have run differently" (135). Next to such tidbits, the most striking moment in the book is Schönhuber's description of his "republicanism"— written at least two years before the party was founded. Schönhuber's father, a Bavarian butcher (Schönhuber emphasizes the same craft-anchored background as Strauss, whose father was also a butcher), joined the populist and "antimonarchist" SA brownshirts. These brownshirts were opposed to the aristocratic and monarchistic elements in the German general staff and the Nazi party and hence here, in Schönhuber's view, the republican element. With a quick historic lie drowned out in a book dripping with Bonapartist flourishes, Schönhuber emphasizes the manner in which the SS took over the populist traditions of the SA. The implied result, republican = SS, has a distinctively Orwellian feel (29f.). (I have chosen to use *REPs* rather than either *Republicans* or *"Republicans"* for the remainder of this article, since this term helps prevent Schönhuber from injecting his brown views into the meaning of *republican*.)

Though Schönhuber has always sought to keep the REPs from being tainted by openly neo-Nazi doctrines, the major successes of the party in Berlin in 1989 revealed again and again the brown-encoded elements in the REPs.[16] The chair of the REPs in West Berlin until he resigned under indictment on felony theft charges a few weeks after the election, a police officer named Bernhard Andres, proclaimed on election night that the party was for "German order and cleanliness (Sauberkeit)."[17] Schönhuber does not shy from terms like "Western decadence" or "poison injected by intellectuals" and told *Der Spiegel* that he would personally make sure that any "anti-Semite" left the party, "but by and by, one has the impression as a German that the Central Council of the Jews is the fifth occupying force on German soil."[18] Given anxiety about Turkish membership in the European Community, one notes as well an increasing focus on the demonization of Islam in REP rhetoric.[19]

The REPs' political *Program of Basic Principles* (1983)—though not as obviously as either the NPD's or the DVU's—gives evidence of elusive brown elements beneath a black conservative facade and Bavarian beer-hall settings.[20] These elements are packaged so neatly that they just fit within the "basic democratic order"; but their overall character is formed by two

related issues: xenophobia and fear of Überfremdung (roughly, "excess for-
eignization") on the one hand, and an ethnic nationalism on the other. This
latter, it must be emphasized, is connected with revanchist conceptions of a
greater Germany—a mainstay of the party since the beginning. The call for
a greater Germany, alluding above all to the borders of Germany in 1937
including Eastern Prussia, while always couched in "democratic" phrasing,
evokes the imperialist and fascistic expansion of Germany earlier in this
century.

In this respect, one can only note a strange and unsettling conjuncture
between the rise of the Right and the process of German unification occuring
just afterwards. The REPs, proclaims the program in near volkish terms,
strive for a "community of German patriots." They are a "free national party
with strong social and ecological obligations." The array of "brown-green"
rhetorical fragments so unceremoniously left in shards earlier by the Greens
has been collected and pieced back together: "We strive for the preservation
of the German people and its ecological Lebensraum; this includes both the
protection of unborn life and the environment."[21] In Schönhuber's calls for
"rotation" and "ecological obligations" we see a distinctive feature of authoritarian populism, whether of the new Right or the older fascisms: the parasiti-
zation of ideas and slogans from the Left—in the case of the REPs, from the
Greens and from the ecology and new social movements.[22] Quasi bioregion-
alist "ecological" ideologues like Henning Eichberg, who once attempted to
influence the Greens, now find ideas such as "ethno-pluralism" (which seeks
to preserve ethnic homogeneity in their specific "natural" regions or territories) have great resonance among the radical Right. In the ex-GDR among
the skinheads and neo-Nazi gangs, one also notes this parasitizing—from the
techniques and styles of street fighting to signs, for instance, declaring Hoyerswerda to be a "Foreigner Free Zone" or neo-Nazi groups with names like
"Citizen Initiative for Democracy and Identity."

While Schönhuber develops a concept of "life" with influences from
contemporary ecological discussions, the more disturbing brown element in
the REPs rhetoric of "life" is the revanchist talk of requiring more Lebensraum for the German people. Schönhuber considers all those who do not
strive for the 1937 German borders (i.e., the old Wilhelminian Empire plus
Austria but missing the Sudetenland) as "traitors."[23] Schönhuber adds as
well a strongly anticlerical element, slyly playing off CSU leader Theodor
Weigel's true "black" Catholicism against the deceased Franz-Joseph
Strauss, who was never so "dark black." Party programs and statements carry
a decisively antiyuppie, antielitist tone. Ex-NPD member and Frey press
executive editor, Harald Neubauer, who served as Bavarian REPs chair during the period of its initial successes, told some four hundred people in

Nuremberg during a 1989 campaign rally that the REPs opposed the "Schiki-micki society" and supported "respectable industrious citizens."

Here one sees the street fringe of extreme nationalism that Schönhuber seeks to suppress and that has recently become important for the Right in the new federal states. From the beginning, such an overlap between these beer-drinking Bavarians and the neo-Nazi fringe and skinhead scene has been evident. When Neubauer would speak for the REPs, upwards of 2,000 skins would protect the hallways. Neubauer's rhetoric, like Schönhuber's, charac-teristically encodes brown images in a highly plebeian, black language: "pure wurst without chemicals" and an end to Germany as the "welfare office for the whole world."[24] For Schönhuber, the German "hosts" ought to determine the conditions under which the foreign "guests" will be treated. This mixture of frenetic "patriotism" (in an ethno-nationalist sense), xenophobia, and anti–European Community rhetoric has been carried over into the process of unification; and it was reflected in the recent successes in April 1992 due to opposition to the Maastricht (1991) and Schengen (1990) agreements on European unification and alignment of border and immigration policies.

Finally, and crucially, Schönhuber is the absolute and charismatic leader of the party. One notes the internal fighting in the party between individual mini-charismatics all struggling for the best subordinate leadership positions, characteristic of Right-radical parties. But Schönhuber remains in command and is unquestionably the most brilliant speaker and mind in this party.[25] A typical REP electoral gathering (e.g., at a "Fireman's Festival") is one short introduction and a two-hour intense charismatic performance by the leader largely bringing down the tent.

A thick black constitutional veneer over the wooden core appears in various political positions, as in the rhetorical tact that Schönhuber shares with earlier neo-Nazis in the Federal Republic. His writings have, in this respect, a Bonapartist flavor, and this "internationalist" or "universalist" movement overlaps with his version of ethno-pluralism; he praises the great-ness and uniqueness of each national culture as long as they maintain their integrity and do not mix.[26] Support for the death penalty is too much for him (in contrast to the French National Front or the Austrian followers of Jörg Haider). His vacation house in Turkey caused a minor scandal. And indeed, the "internationalist" tones in *Ich war dabei* (heroics of French and Ukrainian volunteers in the SS, the stylized foreign legion as well as Schönhuber's affairs with Polish maidens during World War II) is a novel element in typical Right-radical credos.[27] To this point, despite Schönhuber's reference to the republicanism of the brownshirts and the thuglike appearance of his body-guards, there has been no attempt by the REPs to initiate an even faintly paramilitary element for the party. Uniforms have yet to appear.[28]

The REPs and the Police

Fascism has characteristically had an important symbiotic relation to the conservative political biases of existing elements of the security state.[29] In the case of the REPs, the bridge is not to the courts, but to the institutions of law enforcement. This is a crucial factor in understanding the early successes by the party, both in West Berlin and in Bavaria, though this issue has proved less decisive with the subsequent decline of the German new social movements during the unification period. Continuing brutal confrontations between the West Berlin police and the radical elements of the new social movements (the house squatters and the Autonomen) have been a trying feature of West Berlin life since the early 1970s with almost no respite—from the near civil-war conditions of the house squatter movement to the 300 injured policemen of the last May First riots of this year. It was an open secret that in the January city-state elections there, entire units of the police voted en bloc for the REPs; and the Berlin party chair, Andres, was a police officer.[30]

Underpaid and overworked, and rapidly becoming the supposedly nonpartisan scapegoat for the government's unpopular policies—as true for the ruling CDU today as for the SPD governments of the 1970s—the police are finding their own political means to express their discontent. Young men drawn in large part from small outlying and rural areas by the allure of the civil-servant status that the police enjoy are unaccustomed and unhappy when the German (party) state deploys them to defend unpopular housing policies and unpopular big industrial projects or guard unpopular state visitors—policies that are first made possible by the impermeability of the German state and party system to the manifold elements in German society that do not support such projects.[31] The German police, wanting themselves to keep their de jure, nonpolitical status as defenders of the population against criminals, become de facto political tools. The criminalization of citizen initatives and popular movements leads boomeranglike to the politicization of the police. Confronted with the political violence of young anarchists living (not by coincidence) in the Turkish neighborhoods of West Berlin or being handed bags full of stones by elderly women or farmers (to a general chorus of "fascist pigs" and "Nazis out") violently opposed to the Wackersdorf project in upper Bavaria, the police strike out for an identity to fill the vacuum left by the discrepancy between their alleged status and the actual work they are given. Schönhuber has very carefully exploited this structural contradiction between the German state and civil society with his support for the police, but the contradiction has not been his discovery.[32] Nonetheless, such developments are cause for alarm. While rightist influence in the courts is not as pronounced as in the Nazi past, it is still evident, as is the role of conservative jurists in the school of Carl Schmitt.[33] The antipathy to the Left and rightist bias of the Berlin police has been evident since the house-squatter struggles of the late seventies, as has the slowness of the state to respond to rightist violence in the past two years. Indeed, in some areas of the new federal states, as in Freiburg bei Dresden, the police have themselves attacked political refugee applicants in their homes with billy-clubs, knocking down their children, with liberal epithets such as "asylum filth" (Schiessasylant) and "foreigners out."[34]

The REPs, the New Right, and the Other Parties

Prediction of REP and new Right successes on the part of other German political parties has generally been poor, and reaction to successes mixed.[35] In the important Berlin elections of January 1989, the REPs were not a theme. The reaction of the Frankfurt conservatives in the wake of the surprising West Berlin results was more striking. Burdened by bribery scandals and terrified by polls (which remained in the filing cabinets) predicting a solid defeat and much Right-radical electoral potential, the CDU carried out what was probably the first strategically designed xenophobic, antiforeigner campaign with a noticeable anti-Semitic tinge in the history of the Federal Republic.[36] For the most part, while conservative responses have been reactive and adaptive, they have not demonstrated acceptability of the REPs as a democratic party or a potential coalition partner.[37] With notable exceptions such as Alfred Dregger, who simply repeats Schönhuber's "host" and "guest" analysis word for word to the Springer newspapers, the CDU and CSU have quickly distanced themselves from the REPs; the issue among the conservatives has been whether or not to close out all party contact or coalition discussions at the lower levels of the party with a decision from above.

The role of the SPD in the wake of REP successes has also been less than glorious, and reminds one that antifascism has frequently had stronger advocates than Social Democracy. Given a probable five-party constellation in future German elections (REPs, CDU/CSU, FDP, SPD, Greens) in which only the REPs are completely unacceptable coalition partners, the SPD is unquestionably being edged back into the political driver's seat, despite the fact that they have lost as many percentage points as they have gained in the recent reshuffling between the Right and Left fractions of the electorate. This results from the unacceptability of the REPs as coalition partners. The SPD's unmistakable first response was Schadenfreude over conservative problems.[38] The Greens held a party congress quickly after the Berlin and Frankfurt elections and passed a series of positions on the question of a multicultural society and refugee policies, typically somewhat contradictory, but which are the most liberal of any of the major German parties. Whether or not to use the state to repress the REPs was a common issue at first.[39]

There is, however, also a definite sense of the unpredictability of German politics, since the emergence of the radical Right has produced unease. A local-level coalition between the SPD and the NPD in the East Hessian city of Hanau is exemplary. There, Green opposition to a highway development led to a coalition breakdown. This, in the view of SPD activists there, "drove" the Social Democrats "into the arms of the NPD."[40] Meetings between Kohl and Kurt Waldheim, or between Lambsdorff and Haider, indeed the whole issue of a black-green coalition in Baden-Württemberg, is part of this unpredictability and the changing shape of German politics. Beyond this unpredictability, one sees a general adaptation of *all* of the parties to a reform of the immigration law designed, at least rhetorically, to address the concerns of the new Right voters. While Green "realists," SPD figures, and moderate conservatives have fixed on the formula to change the Basic Law on the issue of immigration in line with European unification,[41] conservatives such as the Baden-Württemberg CDU have advocated for several years an investigation of refugee status of incoming individuals directly at the border. Thus, an even more disturbing piece of the German past, namely the weakness of democratic parties in the fight against antidemocratic movements in Germany, must be identified along with the other continuities evident in the courts and the police. At the local level, the push has been made by CDU and CSU figures for coalitions with the REPs. Journalists in the *Frankfurter Allgemeine Zeitung* have argued that the CSU and the REPs are parties with policies "similar enough to mistake them."[42] The response by the ruling conservative-liberal coalition, such as the forced deportation of gypsies to Romania in September, 1992, reinforces the violent prejudices of those who have initiated the violence.

While the response of the news media has been quick and largely hostile (including, e.g., the normally conservative Second German Televison station), a most unsettling part of this German change of complexion comes from conservative but intellectually sophisticated newspapers like the *Frankfurter Allgemeine Zeitung*. This newspaper not only does not attack the REPs openly but also publishes strange articles on cults of leadership (such as paeans to the Japanese cult of the emperor by a former member of the Foreign Service who served in Japan in the thirties and forties) and cartoons depicting Germany as an overflowing Noah's Ark under the caption "The boat is full." The *Frankfurter Allgemeine Zeitung* is part of a sharply nationalist and conservative politics influenced by Carl Schmitt and his followers that sees the stronger state as a solution to problems great and small; this intellectual tendency includes intellectuals like the recently deceased Bernard Willms, the conservative protagonists in the "historians' debate," historian Helmut Diwald, and others who have ties to the radical Right. Indeed, these conservative tendencies merge into a vast panoply of rightist ideologies from sociobiology to the nouvelle droite (Benoist); and one finds various intellectually minded figures in the REPs as well, such as Rolf Schlierer, majority leader for the party in Baden-Württemberg.[43]

The New Right Electorate and Explanations
of Right-Radical Successes

An account of the electorate responsible for recent new Right successes, like the descriptive presentation above, suggests that a single-cause analysis of this new development is woefully insufficient. While the success of the new Right is obviously an aspect of the weakening integrative power of the big catchall parties,[44] this weakness is clearly a description rather than an explanation. This point is made unmistakably clear by the near total failure of political scientists focusing on party analysis to predict the rise of the REPs, while analyses focusing on discursive forms or structural social changes predicted it correctly or at least were caught much less off guard.[45] Equally, while political science failed completely to predict the rise of the REPs, it was also much too quick, along with many political commentators and ideologues inside the other political parties, to proclaim their decease after the splits and electoral losses during the period of German unification.[46] In my view, the recent successes can be clumped into several surface phenomena and two rather deeper, more structural kinds of problems in Germany.

Despite continuing economic and foreign-policy success on the part of the conservative-liberal governing coalition, an immediate cause can be seen in problems of legitimacy that have developed in the coalition in the last year, a period in which neither of the Left parties were able either to offer enticing alternative policies. Kohl is not regarded as a particularly strong or capable leader either in his own ranks or in the nation as a whole, and scandals or misfortune have plagued virtually every one of the conservative party organizations in the country. This long list begins with the scandal leading to the fall of the conservative Schleswig-Holstein government in 1987. The death of Franz-Joseph Strauss in Bavaria was followed by a series of setbacks for Kohl that continued until unification, and that arose again as rapidly as the bill for his free-market nationalist policies came due.[47] Kohl, the stalwart patriotic nationalist, received strong support during the period of unification, when his power and influence as the chancellor with control of state finances (along with the laws prohibiting the REPs and other new Right parties in the earlier period of the new federal states), led to electoral success in the East. But in the period following the unification, elections have been disillusioning, and Kohl's power has been weakening at the core. The capacity to draw absolute conservative majorities, long a given in such states as Bavaria and Baden-Württemberg where the REPs are strong, is now a piece of the Federal Republic's past. Increasing, voters are more "rational" and unaligned. Further, west Germans became annoyed about the costs of unification and the weak economy, as evident in the public-service strikes of May 1992. On the Right, opposition to the Maastricht and Schengen agreements and the development of a common European currency is has led to a so-called German mark nationalism, translating into REPs campaign slogans to the effect that they were the "German mark party."[48] Protest of unification was a big part of the European election successes for the REPs in June 1989 (8 percent nationally) and the state elections in Schleswig-Holstein and Baden-Württemberg in April 1992.

At a deeper level, two key explanations are probably most important in understanding the new Right as a structural development. First, one must look at the historical continuity of the German past in a *broad* sense. This is not merely the differing kind of brown continuity specific to West and East Germany respectively, but also the fact that the democracies of continental Europe, unlike the Anglo-Saxon ones, have not yet developed a capacity to deal with the increasingly multiethnicity of their states. And second, one sees the sharp reaction (in characteristic backlash form) by *specific* sectors of German society actually excluded or threatened with exclusion (by gender, race, professional, and geographically ascribed status) from participation in the "two-thirds society" model of economic growth that has been practiced by the conservative-liberal coalition that assumed governmental power in 1983.

While many commentators and German political scientists have emphasized that the REPs constitute a new phenomena that despite similarities ought not to be seen simply as a brown continuity, it is important not to lose sight of the continuity thesis. One must emphasize the disturbing opinions of the REP electorate. *Der Spiegel* polling from April 1989 found that 51 percent of REP followers have a positive or at least no negative opinion of Adolf Hitler. One hundred percent of their followers—a result never before attained in a *Der Spiegel* poll—are opposed to the electoral franchise for foreigners. The results in Bavaria—the intensive loss of 12.2 percent of the vote by the CSU, until then the strongest and most stable single catchall party in Europe—in the wake of Strauss's death seem to verify his claims that he had integrated the antidemocratic Right. One has images of him waving his mephistophelian magic wand from the CSU underworld. The most successful areas for the REPs in Bavaria were classical old NSDAP and NPD regions like Middle Franconia, where the Right-radical vote surpassed the 20 percent mark.[49]

If rural and small-town Bavaria, Baden-Württemberg, and Schleswig-

Holstein seem to emphasize noneconomic grounds for REP successes,[50] the 1989 West Berlin election rather supports a sectoral marginalization approach; and this circumstance is underscored by the successes of the REPs, NPD, and DVU in similar kinds of districts within most of the major German cities (Hamburg, Dortmund, Bremen, Northern Stuttgart, Lubeck, Frankfurt, and Munich). In Berlin, REP percentages were highest in old working-class neighborhoods like Wedding (9.9 percent), Neukoelln (9.6 percent), and Reinickendorf (8.5 percent); and these results mirror early developments in Bremerhaven or later satellite industrial settlements around Stuttgart.[51]

According to the polling group INFAS, the REPs did best in large apartment blocks and simple housing monstrosities built just after the war. They did poorest in areas characterized by "well-built, single family houses" and in "well-kept, old-style apartment" neighborhoods. Housing developments are not necessarily areas with an especially high percentage of foreigners, but rather petit bourgeois regions with high unemployment and few foreigners.[52] Such neighborhoods are characterized by high social anomie, broken down social milieus, overcrowded conditions, and absence of visible interest by the major parties—areas inside the city with a "declining social ecology."[53] Similar conditions are found in the huge apartment silos of the Walter-Gropius-City or in the outer urban regions of Frankfurt, such as Fechenheim, areas of NPD electoral success with otherwise firm SPD majorities. The REPs cashed in on the 1989 European elections in similar areas of Munich, drawing 22.2 percent in Feldmoching and 20.2 percent in Obergiesing. Vast, anonymous, grey apartment monoliths, onetime SPD regions like Neuekoelln or Wedding in Berlin, have similar profiles.

The 1992 elections in Schleswig-Holstein and Baden-Württemberg demonstrated trends similar to those seen in the European Parliament elections of 1989, as well as to recent successes of the National Front in the March 1992 local elections in France.[54] Here we see successes in Baden-Württemberg from Catholic rural areas in upper Swabia, but stronger support in the urban areas around Stuttgart (15–30 percent in places) or in industrial cities like Pforzheim. In Schleswig-Holstein, DNV success occurred in the rural areas, where it took votes from the CDU, but above all in depressed urban areas such as Lübeck and Kiel, where it received up to 12 percent of the vote and took it from the SPD. Indeed, whereas overall CDU votes remained the same between 1988 and 1992, the SPD lost nearly 8.6 percentage points, slightly more than the number of new Right voters for the DVU and the REPs. As the INFAS report of the elections emphasized, "The most important DVU reservoir was former SPD voters in large urban housing projects."[55]

In 1992 as in 1989, such developments refute hapless SPD hopes of using the new Right to come to power. In such areas the SPD loss came close to 7 percent, in great majority to the REPs, while the CSU's 11 percent loss went in part to the SPD and in large measure to the REPs. Serious migration of long-term SPD voters in Hamburg neighborhoods like Wilhelmsdorf or Ruhr areas like North Dortmund demonstrated this problem for the SPD even more seriously. A disturbing report by the Dortmund FORSA institute noted that, at 39 percent, former SPD voters constituted the single largest component in the 9.5 percent the REPs achieved in North Dortmund in 1989 in the European Parliament elections. Not a single one of the former SPD voters interviewed supported the planned introduction of the local franchise for foreigners; nor did a single one respond positively to the question of whether "politicians today care at all about what people like me think."[56] Here we see a general antagonism toward "foreigners" and resentment directed at the welfare state by those who feel disenfranchised among the voters, but not a strong ideological presence.[57]

Two other general factors need to be emphasized in explaining new Right successes, one of which is rather disturbing: namely, the large numbers of young men in the party, particularly first-time voters. According to Schönhuber, 70 percent of new members are under thirty years of age. 18.8 percent of all male first-time voters in Berlin voted REP, a result repeated country-wide in the European Parliament elections. In Berlin's elections, this meant that roughly one third of all REP voters were between the ages of 18 and 23. Right extreme parties in Germany, especially the REPs, have been dominated by young men—20 percent of those between 18 and 24 in Berlin and up to 10 percent in Frankfurt voting for the NPD, that is, more than double the votes received from other age groups.[58] Such youth are typically not highly educated and are from depressed inner city areas, the slums of big cities, such as Fechenheim in Frankfurt am Main, Moabit in Berlin, and the Ruhr cities. While this is a much broader, larger but also less visible collection than the small groups of neo-Nazi and skinhead gangs that tend to come from similar backgrounds, the overlap in social milieu between the REP voters and the neo-Nazis in the streets is significant: both come from areas characterized by pessimism, frustration, and hopelessness.[59] These statistics worry electoral analysts because such voters' political opinions and electoral behavior tend to be fixed during precisely these years. Such successes among young people—the dark side of the "no future" perspective—contrast sharply with the NPD results in West Germany at the end of the 1960s, which were characterized by backlash against the student movement by older generations who had lived in Germany before the Federal Republic was established. Further, the REPs are a male, macho phenomenon, indeed a "male party."[60] Two-thirds of all their voters are men.[61]

Such phenomena make it clear that the new Right-radical developments in the Federal Republic have many causes, and are drawing on many forms of social discontent, both real and imagined. The REP party itself is a mish-mash of elements, as Leggewie puts it, a party of "men without qualities" characteristic extreme Right groupings and traditional old NSDAP rural areas, traditional conservative Bavarian beer-hall milieus and small-city petit bourgeois not so much threatened by marginalization but set free to express stronger national conservative ideas, skinheads and the "football" crowds, younger sectors of society who feel their values no longer being expressed by the existing parties, large numbers of police officers (but also other civil servants, such fire fighters and above all professional soldiers)—all these are important ingredients. Kurt Biedendopf notably characterizes this development as a part of the "pluralization" of the German political landscape and notes another kind of sectoral marginalization parallel to that analyzed by observers of the new social movements. Not marginalized professional and university students, but those who are stuck at the lower end of the new, highly individualized, risk society support the REPs. The REP voters, he argues, come from the lower levels of society, those with smaller incomes and less education, training, or job qualifications, those who cannot "come to terms with the increasing complexity" of social life in the manner that the new educated middle classes can, and who receive their "political and social information exclusively from electronic media, and hence are in essence only passive information receivers."[62] If one explains the development of the new social movements and the Greens as the result of sectoral marginalization in the upper strata of the educational, wage, and power pyramids (e.g., marginalization of highly educated, failure of fit between university degrees and employment positions), the REPs draw their voters from the inverse end of this same pyramid.[63] Influential milieu analyses have indicated that the new middle-class areas enclose many potential voters with "alternative" life-styles and yuppie economic goals, milieus that are much broader than the actual number that votes for the Greens. Nothing has been more noticeable than that *all* of the west German parties (except the REPs) have been courting such a potential. On the other hand, the major parties have been indifferent to the concerns of neighborhoods like Neukoelln in West Berlin, Feldmoching in Munich, Bremerhaven, or North Dortmund. The REPs emerge in the vacuum left behind.

The emerging presence of women in West German political life can be seen—at least in "image" terms—within this framework of changing life-styles. Despite the enormous popularity of CDU Bundestag President Rita Süssmuth in the population as a whole, her call for a "soft revolution" of women brought confusion within the ranks of German conservativism.[64] Her attempt along with figures like Heiner Geissler to push the party to the Left and tap in on the new life-style voters from the educated middle classes may have backfired. The Springer press has attacked her call for "solidarity of all democrats" against the REPs, while defending them as a legitimate democratic party.[65]

Extreme Right Developments in the New Federal States

It is difficult to assess the role of the new federal states and the former socialist citizens in contributing to the potential power of the new Right. The GDR, in contrast to the old Federal Republic, did sponsor anti-Semitism. Organs of the state searched the offices of Jewish congregations and persecuted members as "antisocialist conspirators" and "Zionist agents."[66] Nonetheless, given the repression and official antifascism of the East German state, no true assessment of tendencies was possible until the Wall came down; and then the situation began to change rapidly.[67] One notes the rise of skinheads from the mid-eighties onward in the GDR.[68] The number and size of such groups, as well as the incidents they cause, has risen meteorically since then. Nazi and neo-Nazi groups formed a network, one with weak interregional contacts, but suprisingly tight local organizations; and some of the most violent, such as the "German Alternative," are among those recently prohibited by the Federal Government. Nazi groups were involved from early on in the breakdown of the GDR, and indigenous xenophobic and racist elements have been evident for some time, though the volume and intensity has risen recently. This involves not only residual anti-Semitism and intolerance of Poles, but also a virulent antipathy for the "guest workers" of the East from various poor Socialist countries like Vietnam, Ethiopia, and Angola, who were helping to pay their countries' foreign debt by working there.[69] In the new federal states we see the same kind of urban decay that serves as a breeding ground for REP and DVU voters in the old federal states: "rows and rows of concrete housing blocks like you see in the slums of East London, Peking, or Katowice."[70] Living in virtual isolation and on much lower wages than those of their neighbors, the foreign laborers have been given racist names. The Algerians are called "camel drivers" and the Southeast Asians "Fijis." Hoyerswerda is only the most noteworthy example of violent incidents. Local skinheads have attacked Polish workers on the borders (especially in Frankfurt an der Oder)[71] and beaten and murdered innocent foreigners. Because the rallies of skinheads have attacked the settlements of aslyum seekers, forcing them to depart, Hoyerswerda has become a "rally cry—a kind of Alamo for assorted xenophobes in Germany."[72]

We see here a development of more street-oriented, explicitly neo-Nazi developments in the new federal states and electoral forms of the radical Right in the old; but these developments tend to parallel one another. Both forms of extraelectoral and electoral radical right organizing have demonstrated potential in the East and in the West. While the most notorious attacks have occurred in the new federal states, the old states have accounted for some 75 percent of all incidents, roughly proportional to their population in comparison with the former GDR. In both East and West, the social composition of the rightist attackers is not reducible to any one factor, except that of youth and the role of youth culture. Recruitment comes from depressed areas, but not exclusively so, and the unemployed are, if anything, less, rather than more, involved in such attacks than those with regular employment.[73] It is difficult to say what will happen in the former GDR overall, but the formation of a great coalition in Berlin between Social Democrats and Conservatives is suggestive of an overall pattern, one emphasizing the formation of electoral initiatives in the West and movement energies in the East.[74] The great coalition itself is proving beneficial to the radical Right, and this development, among others, is forcing the ruling government to consider coalitions even with the Greens.

Foreigners, Immigrants, and the Federal Republic's Not-Yet-So-Republican Republic

A sociopolitical look at the rise of the REPs and the rest of the new Right in Germany underscores the fact they they are very likely a long-term and serious problem for the Federal Republic. But in a sense they are only the political expression of several deeper problems. First, there is the structural impermeability of the German state and the concomitant politicization of its overstressed police forces. Second, the conditions encouraging migration to Germany—inequality between North and South in a climate of increasing provincialism,[75] breakdown of the Eastern bloc, German dominance in Eastern Europe, and the requirements of German capital for more labor[76]—suggest fundamental sources of new Right discontent.[77] The fact that political refugees actually constitute only a small fraction of the "foreigners" in Germany and the disproportionate prominence of the political rhetoric of the Right means that the issue of Überfremdung, a "flood from the East," or a "multicultural" Germany will hardly die soon, even with acceptance of change in the Basic Law's right to asylum in line with European unification.[78] Similarly, in so far as unification provides little leeway in German economic policy (not unlike the issue of the national debt in the United States), the new Right's reaction to dismal economic and living conditions in the inner cities, scapegoating, is unlikely to end quickly.[79]

Finally, one can see yet a deeper problem: Germany still has an explicitly ethnoracial, and implicitly racist, constitutional order. A look at the REPs' main theme, the "foreigner question," underscores this more serious problem. On one level, conservative analyst Biedenkopf and the in-depth reporting of *Der Spiegel* tend to coincide. They agree that the number of foreigners living in the Federal Republic, above all in West Berlin, has risen dramatically since 1975, as has the number of refugees; and it is precisely the less successful members of German society most likely to be threatened or sense a "threat" through this increase.[80] The events surrounding the fall of the Berlin Wall and the breakdown of the Eastern bloc have only multiplied these numbers and problems.

Even Daniel Cohn-Bendit, recently named city administrator for "multicultural" affairs—a crucial demand of the Greens as a response to increasing radical Right influence in the country—has also emphasized, with the strong support of his party, that "nothing would be worse than generating a mistaken image of the good foreigners over against the bad Germans." Despite the fact that Cohn-Bendit has been pushing his somewhat sluggish party to take up the demand for *citizenship* for immigrants if they so choose, in his opinion a multicultural society is only achievable when one acknowledges one's own anxiety.[81] While focusing on "anxiety," Cohn-Bendit himself is still accepting a discursive distinction between *Germans* and *foreigners,* a discourse he shares with liberal as well as conservative opinion makers in Germany. Strikingly, the spectrum of German liberal opinion from the moderate conservative Biedenkopf through *Der Spiegel* and to the majority of figures in the Greens has failed to deal explicitly with the reality of Germany's racist constitutional definitions of citizenship or "structural racism."[82] The notion *German* distinguished from or operative in such notions as *foreigners, nonresident Germans, refugees,* or *guest workers,* remains de facto a racial distinction, and one that de jure anchors state-based institutional racism.[83] In this sense, Germany's constitution resembles that part of the Israeli constitution making Israel a religious state: its selective ethnic policy of aliyah. It is striking that this issue remains largely invisible to the most prominent liberal thinkers in the Federal Republic.[84] Liberalizing immigration and naturalization procedures so that ethnic minorities might become citizens and weakening the de facto racial identification of *German* and *Citizen of the Federal Republic* has not been an issue in the debate about a multicultural society and response to the new Right, until recent red-green discussion about making Germany a "country of immigration."[85] Despite supporting the most liberal immigration policies (the so-called universal right to remain), the Greens at first rejected the specifically nonracial proposal to give all children born in the Federal Republic immediate citizenship, as is the case in France or the Anglo-Saxon democracies. Germany's law is still based on the principle of *ius sanguinis* (citizenship acquired by descent) rather than *ius soli* (law of soil).[86] This latter, decisively republican, quality has been part of the definition and formation of political life as opposed to ethnic life since Kleisthenes's reforms in seventh-century Athens; and it is not surprising that this legal distinction marks a divide between those countries with successful bourgeois revolutions (England, America, France) and those without (German and the other Central European countries).[87] In the modern age, to use Arendt's expression, the distinction between *ius sanguinis* and *ius soli* has been exacerbated by the technological power of the state, making concern for statelessness crucial in recognizing the antidemocratic tendencies in modern twentieth-century states.[88]

This hits at core problems. While the Greens with large majorities pass unachievably radical (and therefore, in the opinion of many dissenting members, dishonest) resolutions on open borders, they are so unable to recognize the Arendtian distinction between nationalism and patriotism that they cannot really imagine why anyone would want to become a German citizen in the first place. But more seriously, their focus on the right to remain just *reinforces* the notion of the welfare-state parasite upon which Right-radical xenophobia thrives, namely on the idea that all our hard work and welfare benefits are going to fake refugees and not to our grandmas who rebuilt this country. Here it becomes clear that the patriotism of "our" economic miracle, which hides the thousands of hours of "foreign" labor involved with complaints about "mock asylants" soaking "our" already overstressed welfare state, is coming back to haunt the Federal Republic. "Asylum stop," the phrase of the CSU, and "right to remain," used by the Greens, do not focus on the hard problems of citizenship and statelessness. Rather, they bind a German tradition of importing foreign labor to a welfare-state discourse in which the central issue becomes a matter of technical policy, of opening or closing the foreigner tap a bit more or a bit less. Of course, the fact that "foreigners" and "guest workers" have substantially less access to the German welfare state and that their labor is extensively exploited to continue the German economic miracle falls completely by the side in rightist propaganda. But this is reinforced by a Left so unpatriotic that it cannot even propose the minimal constitutional reform—citizenship for those born in Germany.[89] Without such minimal reform, difficult given the tightrope upon which the SPD sits, there is no hope of even a minority of young Turks who have lived all of their lives in the Federal Republic feeling the slightest bit German, much less of there being a Turkish mayor in Germany. In this sense, a *Spiegel* article suggesting a Turkish chancellor is as irresponsible as Green open-border resolutions.

Not suprisingly, despite years of legal residence in the FRG, Turkish residents do not feel as though they have become or been accepted as Germans.[90] The contrast with the United States is notable and underscores the largely unperceived depth of the problem. Despite the efforts of Alan Simpson to introduce the reactionary and euphemistic legal ascription *guest worker,* even *illegal* residents begin to feel like "Americans" much more rapidly than *guest* workers feel German in Germany. A green card tends to open a path to citizenship for those who choose it. In the Federal Republic, liberalization is advanced not by naturalizing "foreigners" so that the state-controlled labor and population policies (which have an exceedingly gruesome tradition in Germany) can first become issues of "race," "ethnicity," and "integration," not to speak of "turkish is beautiful." Where one country celebrates the entrance of the one millionth "Guest worker" by publically giving the fellow a bouquet of flowers and a motor scooter (so he can "scoot" back home after he is finished making his Marks), the other makes the citizenship-ceremonies of long-term residents a mass ritual to be celebrated in football stadiums. Rather than abolishing the term *foreigner,* against sharp opposition, the most liberal Social Democratic ruled areas tried to introduce local electoral franchise for "foreigners."[91] In U.S. English, the only foreign things in everyday language are automobiles, and the only "aliens" outside of INS legalese are evil, bloodsucking extraterrestrials. *Illegals* are never regarded in such discourse as *foreigners,* and since they are *persons* according the Constitution, they are included in allocating voting districts. The Basic Law breaks up persons into Germans, nonresident Germans (Aussiedler), foreigners, and refugees. Racist policy using the state, as opposed to against the principles of the polity within civil society, is precisely the constitutional difference between the Federal Republic and the United States. It is the former sort that metamorphoses so rapidly into neofascist tendencies, while the latter, despite the intensive violence and difficulties of a multiethnic society, provides the legal parameters to give integration along with labor services. It is precisely at this level that the traditional causes for Germany's new Right radicalism bite deepest.

NOTES

1. In the present climate, advocating policies such as an economy of only "qualitative growth," "open borders" for an "immigration society," and increasing ownership by state and community are issues running "against the grain," to paraphase Walter Benjamin. For a discussion of "red-green" conception of government policy, see John D. Ely, "Red-Green Ecological Reconstruction in Germany: A Project on Hold," *Capitalism, Nature, Socialism* 2 (1991): 111–26.

2. See, e.g., Hajo Funke, "Kein Grund zur Verharmlosung—die 'Republikaner' sind eine Jungwählerpartei," *Die neue Gesellschaft/Frankfurter Hefte* 36 (1989): 312–20; Jorg Ültzhoffer, "The Chauvinism of Affluence: A Qualitative Study into Motives and Ideology of 'Republikaner' Voters" (Paper delivered at Annual Meeting of the American Political Science Association, San Francisco, September, 1990).

3. Tranferring the core/periphery metaphor from dependency theory into metropolitan areas was done by Joachim Hirsch in *Der Sicherheitsstaat* (Frankfurt am Main: Europäische, 1981); and he, along with Roland Roth, later identified it as a striking

feature of a new post-Fordist accumulation model arising from the breakdown of traditional Keynesian economic strategies, traditional class structures, and the big, integrative "people's parties." In the conservative climate of the 1980s, Hirsch and Josef Esser observed a continuation of "Model Germany" policies of social democracy: a split into a core of privileged corporative status groups (civil servants, higher white-collar workers, free professions, management and highly educated technicians, and skilled trades) on the one hand, and a growing periphery of poorly paid service jobs and generalized marginalization. See Hirsch and Esser, "Der CDU-Staat: Ein politisches Regulierungsmodell für den 'nachfordistischen' Kapitalismus," *Prokla* 36 (1984): 59–63; and Hirsch and Roth, *Das neue Gesicht des Kapitalismus* (Frankfurt: Europäische, 1986). In a climate of continuing economic difficulty, conservative government is maintained via an "authoritarian populism," borrowing the term from Stuart Hall's analysis of Thatcherism, which encourages the breakdown of traditional class groupings by reemphasizing nationalism and xenophobia.

4. Eike Hennig, *Die Republikaner im Schatten Deutschlands* (Frankfurt am Main: Suhrkamp, 1991): 108f., 112ff.

5. See, for example, Werner Perger's discussion of Jürgen Habermas's influence on Björn Engholm in "Voller Demut des Erfolges sicher," *Die Zeit,* 10 April 1992. On the issue of "civil society," see Helmut Dubiel et al., *Die demokratische Frage* (Frankfurt am Main: Suhrkamp, 1989).

6. See Jürgen Habermas, "Volkssoveränität als Verfahren," *Merkur* 43, no. 6 (1989), reprinted in *Faktizität und Geltung* (Frankfurt am Main: Suhrkamp, 1992): 600–631.

7. To make one comparison, the "Spiegel Affair," Franz-Joseph Strauss's invasion, as defense minister, of the offices of the liberal weekly probably constituted a greater threat to the democratic order. Yet its political flavor was more centered on Strauss and his authoritarian attitude to government rather than on "national identity," in the manner of the "historians' debate," or even Bitburg.

8. Andrei Markovits and Simon Reich, "*Modell Deutschland* and the New Europe," *Telos* 89 (1989): 57ff., 62ff.

9. But some features in the present raise causes for serious concern. For example, those depressed concrete housing projects in run-down industrial areas—Neukoelln and Wedding in Berlin, Feldmoching in Munich, Bremerhaven or northern Stuttgart— where the new Right has shown successes disturbingly resemble the rows and rows of faceless, decrepit, and neglected housing projects in the former GDR.

10. E.g., Gesine Schan, "Die Demokraktie wird brüchig," *Die Zeit,* 9 October 1992.

11. See Reinhard Kühnl et al., *Die NPD: Struktur, Ideologie, und Funktion einer neofaschistischen Partei* (Frankfurt am Main: Suhrkamp, 1969).

12. Bill Buford, "The Lads of the National Front," *New York Times Magazine,* 26 April 1992, 32ff. See also Buford, *Among the Thugs* (New York: Norton, 1992).

13. See the illuminating report on East German skinheads by Bernd Siegler, "Skinheads schüren Angst in Eberswalde," *Tageszeitung,* 23 April 1992.

14. Characteristically, one of these cofounders, onetime CSU Bundestag representative Franz Handlos, representing the Bavarian district of Deggendorf with up to 73.6 percent of the vote, left the CSU after Franz-Joseph Strauss delivered his "billion-

credits" to the German Democratic Republic. Claus Leggewie, author of the informative first book on the REPs, *Die Republikaner: Phantombild der neuen Rechten* (Berlin: Rotbuch, 1989), underscores as well the influence of key German radical Right intellectuals, such as *Criticon* founder Armin Mohler, as well as Professors Helmut Diwald (Erlangen, revisionist historian), Bernard Willms (Bochum, Hobbes scholar), Robert Hepp (Osnabrueck, "population sociologist"), Hans Joachim Arndt (Heidelberg, representative of anti-American "political science for the Germans"), and Wolfgang Seiffert (Kiel, onetime advisor to Erich Honecker). See 61ff. Prof. Karl Steinbuch, like Willms, writes for the party paper *Die Republikaner,* and Prof. Emil Schlee, state party chair in Schleswig-Holstein, organized meetings of the Stahlhelm in the late 1970s on themes such as "The forgotten fatherland." For information on Right intellectuals in the party circles, see Volksfront gegen Reacktion, eds., *Vorsicht Republikaner* (West Berlin, 1989). Nor ought this phenomenon be taken lightly. Guenther Willms, onetime lawyer and presently judge in the German Constitutional Court, is not only drifting in REP circles, he was also an early signatory to the "Heidelberg Manifesto" of the Schutzbund des deutschen Volkes (Federation for the Protection of the German People), a "manifesto" concerned with the "growing number of aliens (Fremder)" and expressing "collective concern over the future of our people." For information on Schönhuber's early activities, see Kurt Hirsch and Hans Sarkowicz, *Schönhuber: Der Politiker und seine Kreise* (Frankfurt am Main: Eichborn, 1989).

15. Franz Schönhuber, *Ich war dabei* (Munich: Langen Mueller, 1981). Subsequent citations in text.

16. The Berlin REP party headquarters was at the time in Spandau, site of the allied prison for convicted Nazi war criminals. The small signs that the REPs during press conferences place on the table next to the microphones are hung on little staffs like the old guild emblems adopted by the Nazis and so noticeable in Riefenstahl's film of the Nuremburg Nazi party congress. But along with coded signifiers there are more explicit evidence of brown in the hazel nut. Upon singing the National Anthem at the end of party meetings, despite leaving out the famous imperialist-tending verses, the "Heil Hitler" salute is raised by scattered but distinctly visible individuals in the audience.

17. His chief inner-party competition in the city, 25-year-old Carsten Pagels, a Young Turk from the youth organization of the Christian Democratic Union (CDU), edited the CDU Berlin youth magazine *Klartext* until he jumped ship just before being evicted from the party. In the inner-party wrangling following the 1989 elections, the grounds, among others, included an obituary honoring Wehrmacht Colonel Hans-Ulrich Rudel, the "eagle of the east front" and the "most successful fighter pilot of all times" against the "invading soviet hordes" (cited in Leggewie, *Republikaner,* 79). Pagels has since split and joined the recently founded German League for People (Volk) and Homeland (Heimat). He also writes for the important new radical Right monthly of the "conservative revolution," the *Junge Freiheit.* This newspaper has a claimed circulation of some 30,000; and it, along with figures like Pagels, are having success organizing right-wing students for the radical Right. See Holger Jenrich, "Die Rechte rüstet auf" and Sönke Braasch and Anton Maegerle, "Die 'Junge Freiheit' von Rechts: Intellektueller Rechtsextremismus," *Unicum,* November 1992, 9–13.

18. "Sympathisanten hinter den Gardinen," *Der Spiegel,* February 1989, 54ff.

19. "Im Wohlstandsgürtel um Stuttgart wuchs Schönhubers Ernte," *Frankfurter Rundschau,* 7 April 1992.

20. For discussion of the REPs program, see Hajo Funke, *"Republikaner": Rassimus, Judenfeindschaft, nationaler Grössenwahn* (Berlin: Action Sühnezeichen/Friedensdienst, 1989), 33–66; Manfred Kieserling, "Zur Psychologie der Republikaner," in Hennig, *Republikaner im Schatten Deutschlands,* 34–54.

21. Elements of the "third way" between capitalism and socialism appear, but it would be a mistake to overemphasize components at present. Ecology *as a social-political project* is consensus among all the parties in the Federal Republic, excepting the liberal Free Democrats. This is of course self-evident in the Greens ("ecological rebuilding of society"), but the SPD has for years partially, and recently almost fully, taken over precisely this vocabulary from the Greens in their "Progress 90" program; and the conservative CDU has as well replaced its call for a "social" market economy with "ecological." To be sure, one must not ignore the crucial Right-populist elements in the REPs.

Schönhuber was opposed to the (recently canceled) Nuclear Reprocessing Plant under construction in Wackersdorf, Bavaria. He is stridently anti-American ("Germany is now as before an occupied land"). He even supports the question of "rotating" parliamentary deputies, in the manner of the Greens when they introduced this issue. It is important to emphasize here, with respect to ecology that this is not a case of Schönhuber realizing the "brown essence" in a "green" appearance, as has been argued mistakenly on occasion, especially by English-speaking analysts. Rather this is a typical case of Right-radicals taking up specific historically leftist political items in rightist *populist* forms, which have a much broader consensus in the population than the leftist party (the Greens), which carries them systematically and programmatically. On the other hand, the anti-Americanism and anti-NATO attitude, which has, as Andrei Markovits emphasizes ("Anti-Americanism in the West Germany," *New German Critique* 34 [1985]: 10ff.), been a problematic feature of the German peace movement, may now be coming home to roost on its proper barn.

22. See especially Thomas Jahn and Peter Wehling, *Ökologie von rechts: Nationalismus und Umweltschutz bei der Neuen Rechten und den 'Republikanern'* (Frankfurt am Main: Campus, 1991). Note that "Foriegner Free Zone" was also used during the Nazi era. The "Citizen Initiative for Democracy and Identity" is a mix of REP figures and those from the neo-Nazi FAP or "Free German Labor Party." See ID-Archiv im ISSG, ed., *Drahtzieher im Braunen Netz* (Berlin: Editions ID-Archiv, 1992), 130.

One can also note this dynamic, with a greater focus on the academy, in the United States today. See Sigrid Müller and John D. Ely, "Multikulturelle Gesellschaft und die Neue Rechte in den USA," *Links* 3 (1992): 32–34.

23. For a good description of the black and brown views of German territoriality in Schönhuber's discourse, see Michael Schomers, *Deutschland ganz Rechts: Sieben Monate als Republikaner in BRD & DDR* (Cologne: Kiepenheuer & Witsch), 225ff.

24. Bernd Siegler, "'Republikaner' nur hinten raus," *Tageszeitung,* 2 March 1989.

25. The issue of "rotation" needs to be seen not just as a clever ploy, but in this context as well. Characteristically of Right-radical parties with one or two charismatic

figures and intellectual supporters in the background, but a large following of largely unsophisticated party members, local and regional REP figures have no particular role beyond introducing Schönhuber as a speaker. Indeed, there is much evidence to suggest that Schönhuber wants to keep independent thinkers out of positions threatening his hegemony. Rotation would serve his purpose in this respect. One can remain assured that he will not be "rotated."

26. Franz Schönhuber, *Die Türken* (Munich: Langen Müller, 1989), 54–70.

27. Other elements of moderation are evident as well. Despite the soldiering adventurism and the fact that all who do not recognize Germany in its 1937 boundaries are traitors, the open and strident militarism is not reappearing in Schönhuber's rhetoric. As well, the Right-radical political potential in the metaphorics of AIDs remains curiously untapped. But most importantly, the REPs, despite strong rightist-plebeian elements, do not use the word *movement,* do not strive to be a movement and a party, and underscore "law and order," support for the police, and strengthening the already existing executive elements of the German state.

28. Indeed, as mobilizations by the Left against the REPs and past mobilizations against attempted neo-Nazi demostrations have demonstrated, this would be a nearly suicidal political tactic. Attempts of this sort have been consistently dispersed by the Left; and the attempt of the radical and Autonomen Left to break up electorally oriented meetings of the REPs, defended by the police, only serves to underscore the "constitutional" and orderly character of the party, an element crucial to their successes. Hence, they are, importantly, an almost exclusively electorally oriented party. Strongly in contrast to the development of the Greens, for example, their massive growth comes as a result of electoral successes rather than movement mobilization on a large and long-term scale that functions as the precondition for electoral success. In this respect, Germany's electoral laws providing financial support by the state for electoral success has been an important factor. This exclusively electoral focus is a characteristic of Frey's DVU as well, whose financial state is much firmer, due to sales of the *Nationale Zeitung* and who knows what else. Frey poured some 18 million marks into the European Parliament elections of June 1989, a budget that was higher than that of the Free Democratic party (approximately 6 million) and the Greens (approximately 10 million) combined. Hence, despite the ubiquitious "brown" elements for those who "know the code," in Schönhuber's own words, the more traditional, national-conservative, law and order elements are at least as important in understanding the nature of the REPs and their recent successes.

29. As for example, Franz Neumann demonstrated in national socialism to the Weimar judicial institutions in his *Behemoth* (New York: Oxford University Press, 1942).

30. The same situation with Autonomen in Wackersdorf, Bavaria, helped the REPs in the state due to the huge confrontations around the Wackersdorf Nuclear Fuel Recycling Plant under construction; to a lesser extent this effect is characteristic in the Federal Republic as a whole.

31. Such individuals from largely rural backgrounds are not culturally prepared for the strange multiethnic, much more liberal and Left urban milieus in which they are most needed and most resented. This is a fabulous recipe for prejudicial views of

"foreigners" and "chaotics." More importantly, while they are expecting to be politically neutral defenders of society against criminals (a role as supported by German television "Krimi" series almost as much as U.S. television), they become frustrated with the highly politicized and unpopular nature of many tasks assigned to them.

32. Strikingly, the only actual "rightist" movementlike demos that have occurred in the Federal Republic in the context of the REPs recent successes were protest marches by the police. Despite their sympathy for a Right-radical party, one can sympathize with the situation in which the police have been placed. One poster at the police demonstration after the May First riots is worth a thousand analyses. It read: "Police = 'Bulls' = animals for slaughter? Is Article I of the Basic Law valid for us too?" See "Alle labern, keiner tut was," *Der Spiegel,* 25 June 1989, 36ff. *Bulls* is the equivalent in the West German Left for the word *pigs* used during the 1960s by the antiwar movement to describe to police. Article I of the Basic Law reads: "The dignity of humanity is inalienable. The duty of all state powers is to respect and protect it."

33. "NPD-Chef darf weiter richten," *Frankfurter Rundschau,* 31 November 1992. On the influence of Schmitt and his followers, see John D. Ely, " 'Similar Enough to Mistake Them': 'Black' and 'Brown' Versions of National Conservativism in Germany Today," (Paper delivered at the Annual Meeting of the American Political Science Association, September 1992).

34. Karl-Heinz Karisch, "Polizisten im Kampfanzügen stürmen Asylbewerberheim bei Dresden," *Frankfurter Rundschau,* 13 June 1992.

35. For discussion of Party responses to the REPs, see Manfred Kieserling, "Stellungnahmen der Parteien zu den Republikanern," in Hennig, *Republikaner im Schatten Deutschlands,* 58–65.

36. This involved taking up NPD campaign slogans word for word in CDU campaign advertisements, and using quotations from SPD candidate Volker Hauff and (Jewish) Green candidate Daniel Cohn-Bendit supporting more liberal asylum policies as evidence of the "misuse" of the constitutional right of asylum for political refugees. The most offensively anti-Semitic tone was produced by a headline in a boulevard-style CDU campaign newspaper: "Should Cohn-Bendit determine our homeland (Heimat)." The CDU claimed afterwards that they chose Hauff and Cohn-Bendit because they were the leading candidates of their respective parties. Cohn-Bendit, however, was not at the top of the Greens' list; in Frankfurt as elsewhere in the Federal Republic that position was held by a woman. Such tactics were not only initiated by the Frankfurt CDU but were also prominently defended by senior figures in the state and national party like the present minister-president of Hessia, Walter Wallmann.

The striking success of the neo-Nazi National Democratic party (NDP) in Hessen where the REPs did not campaign suggest that the NPD success was a kind of ersatz REP vote. With one exception, the NPD only succeeded in counties where the REPs did not post candidates; in those where both did so, the REPs were more successful. The European parliament elections in June verified this trend over virtually the entire Federal Republic. NDP success in Hessia was rather the result of a xenophobic conservative campaign than a hindrance to it. Winfred Kraus, chair of the Frankfurt NPD, complained on television after the 1989 local elections that the CDU "took up our political demands," and national first television channel (ARD) editorialized that such campaigning had put "wind in the sails of the NPD." Strikingly, *before* the results, only the Greens and the radical Left ran a campaign for racial tolerance and a "multicultural society"; the other parties, the unions, the media, and the churches were all silent on the theme.

37. For example, shortly after the 1989 Hessian results, the minister-president of neighboring Rhineland-Palatinate who replaced Bernard Vogel, Carl-Ludwig Wagner, publicly asserted that the REPs were as democratic as the Greens (implying their respectablity as possible coalition partners) only to be reprimanded by the cogoverning FDP, the chair of the state CDU, and Chancellor Kohl (who is from the Rhineland).

38. Oskar Lafontaine was really caught rather unpleasantly in debates with Heiner Geissler on election night shedding crocodile tears. He kept insisting that Geissler would not be able to keep the CDU from forming local coalitions with the REPs rather than raising the missing red flags in the popular front against an antidemocratic Right, tending to confirm his reputation as the SPD's number one opportunist. This muddy picture was strengthened by a SPD "strategy paper" from the SPD headquarters in Bonn published in the 14 July 1989 *Süddeutsche Zeitung*. The paper speculated on the possibility of the SPD becoming the strongest party in the FRG via the Right extremist parties; and hence the party ought to use the opportunity to become the strongest in the country. The paper was rapidly rejected as six months old and irrelevant by the SPD leadership, but the denials appeared weak since the "strategy paper" had indeed been an object of debate by the party executive.

39. The Greens in the government of Lower Saxony have also gotten into repeated problems with the SPD there over deportation proceedings ("Streit über kurdische Flüchtlinge," *Tageszeitung,* 14 January 1991); and realists like Daniel Cohn-Bendit and Joschka Fischer have made a big issue over liberal policies of immigration and refugee status, as in Fischer's spectacular early speech in the Bundestag quoting from Walter Benjamin and defending a Turkish refugee who committed suicide after hearing that his application for asylum had been rejected. Fischer blamed his death on the interior minister, Zimmerman. See Fischer, "Speech Before the German Bundestag," 8 September 1983, in *The German Greens: Paradox Between Movement and Party,* eds. Margit Mayer and John D. Ely (Philadelphia: Temple University Press, 1993).

Most Greens, like MP Eckhard Stratmann, supported an "intelligent nonviolent strategy of resistance" inside the realm of civil society without engaging in strong measures via the state. The SPD also opposed investigation by the Interior Ministry into the constitutional legality of the party; such proposals have been above all supported within the ranks of the CSU (Bavarian Interior Minister Eduard Stoiber); and such proposals seem to have been quenched by Schönhuber's confident statement that lots of his people can be found in the Office for the Protection of the German Constitution (Verfassungsschutz) as well. Proposals within the big parties (especially the Catholic Right of the CDU/CSU) to change the electoral laws—an important issue in view of the French government's approach to the National Front—were also rapidly rejected as suggesting bad historical precedents and being undemocratic.

40. Klaus-Peter Klingelschmitt, "Eine rot-braune Koalition in Osthessen," *Tageszeitung,* 10 April 1992.

41. Klaus-Peter Klingelschmitt, "Cohn-Bendit: 'Die CDU hat recht'" and Tissy

Bruns, "SPD wackelt beim Asyl-Grundrecht," *Tageszeitung,* 6 April 1992; interview with Wolfgang Schäubele, *Der Spiegel,* 17 April 1992, 25–30.

42. Roswin Finkenzeller, "Zum Verwechseln ähnlich," *Frankfurter Allgemeine Zeitung,* 30 July 1992.

43. He is influenced by Armin Mohler's right-wing journal, *Criticon.* See C. C. Malzahn, "Der adrette Rechtsradikale von nebenan," *Tageszeitung,* 8 April 1992. For a general overview of intellectual currents among radical and extreme rightists, see Thomas Assheuer and Hans Sarkowicz, *Rechtsradicale in Deutschland* (Munich: Beck, 1990), 110–80. See also Claus Leggewie, *Der Geist steht Rechts* (Berlin: Rotbuch, 1987).

44. See for example the *Frankfurter Rundschau*'s editorial "Dritte Kräfte," 7 April 1992.

45. Richard Stoess, for example, editor of the extensive "Party Handbook" for the Federal Republic, wrote in an article on "The Problem of Right-Wing Extremism in West Germany" (*West European Politics,* April 1988 [!]): "In the face of the enormous integrative power of the two bourgeoies parties . . . and their vitually hegemonic position within the bourgeois camp, the prospects for right-wing extremism in West Germany were and are very poor" (35). A similar comment can be made on Hans-Gerd Jaschke's *Die Republikaner: Profile einer Rechts-Aussen-Partei* (Bonn: J.H.W. Dietz, 1990). Based on a traditional analysis of party sociology, Jaschke observes the REPs "crisis" and predicts over several pages the imminent collapse of the party (74–80). While he later moderates his own analysis here (128), his final conclusion tends to blame the presense of a Gemeinschaft-oriented fundamentalism opposed to industrial society as the major problem, since such attitudes undermine the liberal-democrat state (128–31). That the characteristically *illiberal* elements of the German state—the courts and the police, the impermeable parties, the penchant for using the state to organize import and export of human labor as a commodity rather than presupposing the civic rights of those people who contribute to the economy (and the racist nature of German constitutional definitions of citizenship play an enormous role in this dynamic) goes largely unnoticed. Such traditional approaches focusing on the sociology of party organization and presupposing rather than focusing on the strength of German liberal-democracy constitute approaches much less successful at grasping the potential and danger of the REPs than those political scientists influenced by the regulation school (e.g., Hirsch and Esser, "Der CDU-Staat") or the innovative discourse-theory work of Jürgen Link. See for example Link's articles in the journal *KulturRevolution,* or Link, "Über den Anteil diskursiver Faktoren an neorassistischen Proliferationen," in *Rassismus und Migration in Europa,* eds. Institute für Migrations- und Rassimusforschung (Hamburg: Argument, 1992), 333–45.

46. See for example Dieter Roth, " 'Die Republikaner': The Rise and Fall of a Far Right Protest Party" (Paper delivered at the Annual Meeting of the American Political Science Association, Sept. 1990).

47. The death of Strauss was followed by the fall of conservative leader Bernhard Vogel in Rhineland-Palatinate, gambling scandals in Lower Saxony, the bugging scandal and other financial irregularities in West Berlin, "Libya-gate" (concerning the nerve-gas factory in the Rabta desert), and Jenninger's embarrassing speech on the

anniversary of "Crystal Night." Furthermore, unpopular policies carried out under the leadership of the CDU (such as labor minister Norbert Blüm's gouging the health system), or proposals for lengthening military service contributed as well. Finally, Gorbymania had a telling effect on the integrative power of conservative anticommunism. The *Frankfurter Allgemeine Zeitung* at that point recieved a case of the fidgets from polls showing that only 17 percent of the German population regard the Russians as a military threat. It is noteworthy that a virulent anticommunism is one of the key traditional fascist ideological components almost absent from Schönhuber's rhetoric, and it was as well before the breakdown of the Eastern bloc.

48. Bernd Siegler, "Rechte wollen Wende zu ganz Deutschland," *Tageszeitung,* 7 April 1992.

49. Quintessentially petit bourgeois hotel or restaurant owners in other areas of electoral success like the little Bavarian city of Rosenheim must be added in as well. Augsburg, despite being the major city in the FRG with the lowest unemployment rate (next to Munich and Stuttgart), drew a 19.6 percent REP vote. Here a more traditional continuity and the declining integrative power of the CSU seem to be playing a more crucial role than one of absolute marginalization or exclusion from the two-third's society. Nontheless, Augsburg is undergoing more specific kind of marginalization. From a city characterized historically by the textile industry and classical mechanical engineering, Augsburg is developing in a high-tech direction. The number employed in textiles, for example, has dropped from 25,600 to 7,300. Nonetheless, similar figures could be offered for a city like Munich; and there they are not transformed into REP voters. Weak university presence, the lack of a cosmoplitan and media-centered cultural wing of the new class, and the comparable intellectual backwardness of a city like Augsburg could be important factors. But such an example makes the simple assertion that REP election results are an alarm signal raised by the excluded lower third alone a woefully insufficient answer. Indeed, Bavaria itself, with its extraodinary REP percentages, is the most economically healthy state in a nation that itself is in generally good economic shape. This is also the case, for example, in Frankfurt am Main, as Hennig emphasizes, *Republikaner im Schatten Deutschlands,* 107ff.

50. Bascha Mika, " 'Kommen hierher und halten die Hand auf,' " *Tageszeitung,* 9 April 1992.

51. Karsten Plog, "Ein irrender Computer und die wichtige Rolle des Briefkastens," *Frankfurter Rundschau,* 7 April 1992; and C. C. Malzahn, "Die Angst vor Asylanten und sozialen Absteig," *Tageszeitung,* 9 April 1992.

52. INFAS-Report, *Politogramm Berlin 1989* (Bonn, 1989).

53. As Leggewie sharply observes, "Neukoelln is the most populated district of Berlin. 300,000 people live there, of which 45,000 are foreign and 17,000 are recieving social help. Neukoelln has the most dogs, the fewest cultural offerings, and the worst air in the state, especially when the wind comes 'from over there,' from the factories and incinerators in the East sector of the city." Leggewie, *Republikaner,* 20.

54. INFAS, "Strukturelle Veranderungen in politischen System: Stimmungstief für Regierungen wird andauern," *Frankfurter Rundschau,* 7 April 1992. The same was true in poor areas of Stuttgart as well in the 1992 Baden-Württemberg elections.

55. Ibid.

56. "Rechtstrend in SPD-Hochburg," *Frankfurter Rundschau,* 25 July 1989. Here the *cautiousness* in the SPD, which has in the meantime replaced apparent crocodile tears and the opinion that Schönhuber was merely a massive problem for the conservative voter block, is understandable. But what no one has observed is that the fissure between such ex-SPD voters and the "red-green" yuppie-affluence, "future" and "progress" orientation of the present SPD is much greater, and much more serious than that between long-term CSU voters in Bavaria who in the wake of Strauss's death are voting for someone who talks just the way they think, and have *always thought.* Though half of all of Schönhuber's votes come from the south of Germany, and according to present polls provide the basis for putting his party in the Bundestag in December 1990, he is not just a Bavarian problem, as these statistics emphasize. And his message reaches broader audiences as well; a one-time television journalist, he speaks a German unquestionably "higher" and less Bavarian than that of Strauss.

57. Mika, "'Kommen hierher.'"

58. Funke, "Kein Grund"; Leggewie, *Republikaner;* and Hennig, *Republikaner im Schatten Deutschlands,* 48–50.

59. See especially Hajo Funke, "Rechtsextreme Jugendliche," *Republikaner,* 26ff. See also Karlheinz Reif and Oskar Niedermayer, "Supporters of Extremist Right Parties in Western Europe: Social Structure and Political Orientations," (Paper delivered at Annual Meeting of the American Political Science Association, San Francisco, 1990).

60. See Jurgen Hofman-Gottig, "Die neue Recht: Die Mannerparteien," *Aus Politik und Zeitgeschichte,* B41–42 (1989): 21–31.

61. Of the 139 political positions in the party at the federal and state level, exactly 14 are held by women, mostly as "treasurers" or "deputy chairs." More importantly, the macho nature of party orientation is striking. An interview by *Frankfurter Rundschau* journalist Birgit Loff with one 63-year-old district representative for the REPs makes the point. In his neighborhood alone, argued the retired Paul Goehler, "some 300 to 400 husbands are regularly beaten by their wives." Goehler learned of this "brutal feminism" by reading the Springer Boulevard press; he brought headlines such as "A Million Women Beat Their Husbands" to his district meetings as grounds for his suggestion of setting up a "Men's House" as a refuge. West Berlin party chair, Andres, when confronted with such opinions, responded: "Men's Houses are to be found in Berlin's 5,300 bars. That's how I see it."

62. Kurt Biedenkopf, "Von 'Deutsch-Sein' und der Suche nach Überschaubarkeiten," *Frankfurter Rundschau,* 27 June 1989.

63. On sectoral marginaliation, see Hirsch and Roth, *Das neue Gesicht des Kapitalismus,* 186–91; Ulrich Beck, *Risikogesellschaft: Auf dem Weg in eine andere Moderne* (Frankfurt am Main: Suhrkamp, 1986), 205ff; Joachim Hirsch, *Kapitalismus ohne Alternative?* (Hamburg: VSA, 1990), 107–11.

64. See Volker Heins, "Die Aufhebung Rita Süssmuths," *Links* (February 1989): 2f.

65. To end the summer break in 1989, Chancellor Kohl fired the other central figure in the CDU who was striving for a "modernization" of the party from the left, Heiner Geissler, who was also REP fighter Number One in the ranks of the party. This raises

the serious question of how the CDU will manage discursively in a highly industrial-ized nation with a huge international market if it hacks off its entire "future" wing to save itself from Germany's new "republicanism." Again, super–Lear jet pilot Strauss managed to integrate such political elements not only in a distinctly liberal-democratic form, but also in a discourse of hyperindustrialization and world competitiveness. A striking characteristic of Schönhuber is that he spends more time talking about "rota-tion" and "ecological living room" than he does magnetic railways and satellite ven-tures.

66. Lutz Reuter, "Minorities in Germany After 1945," *Beitrage aus dem Fach-bereich Pädagogik der Universitaet der Bundeswehr* 2 (1990): 70f.

67. See for example Assheuer and Sarkowicz, *Rechtsradikale in Deutschland*, 95–110, which relies largely on East German government sources.

68. For a good general overview of the extreme right in the new federal states, see Bernd Siegler, *Auferstanden aus Ruinen: Rechtsextremismus in der DDR* (Berlin: Edition Tiamat, 1991). For a detailed description of recent neo-Nazi developments there, see Edition ID-Archiv, ed., *Drahtzieher in Braunen Netz*.

69. For a good description of this situation, see Ian Burana, "Outsiders," *New York Review of Books*, 9 April 1992, 18–20.

70. Ibid.

71. See Gisela Dachs, "Open or Closed Polish Borders Still Poses Problems," *German Tribune*, 21 April 1992 (originally *Die Zeit*, 12 April 1992).

72. Burana, "Outsiders." Hoyerswerda became a "people's festival" in which skinheads arriving from all over Germany became objects of sympathy for the local population (a kind of mirror image of Wackersdorf) because, as Burana quotes one pastor, "They like what these young people are saying about order, patriotism, and feeling good about our Heimat."

73. Steven Kinzer, "German Attacks Rise as Foreigners are Blamed for Economic Problems," *New York Times*, 2 November 1992.

74. Dieter Ruff, "Berlins Rechte im Wartestand," *Tageszeitung*, 14 April 1992.

75. See generally, Aristide R. Zollberg, "Die Zukunft der internationalen Migra-tionsbewegung," *Prokla* 21 (1992): 189–221; and Hans Arnold, "Süd-Nord-Migration und Nord-Süd-Konflikt," *Vierteljahresbericht* 127 (1992): 19–28. See also Samir Amin, *Eurocentrism* (New York: Monthly Review Press, 1989), 124ff.

76. German capital has made it clear that it will require new sources of labor. The institute for the German Economy in Cologne has seen a need for some 300,000 workers per annum in the FRG over the next twenty-five years (Herbert Wulfskuhl, "Verfahren nationale Debatte: Ein europaische Visms-, Asyl- und Einwanderungspoli-tik nach Maastricht. Ein Plädoyer für einen Übergang zur 'Normalität' der eu-ropäischen Integration," *Tageszeitung*, 14 April 1992). Other voices of capital offer a grimmer and more sensationalist view (e.g., Erich Reyhl, "Europe's States Before a Wave of Mass Migration," *German Tribune*, 28 April 1992, originally, *Handelsblatt*, 12 April 1992). Anticipations of upwards of five hundred thousand émigré Germans from Eastern countries are suggested as possible alternative strategies in some circles. Note, however, that these numbers dwarf those who actually become citizens annually (some fifteen to twenty thousand). Germany's rate of annual naturalization is mini-

scule as a percentage of the foreign population in comparison with the *ius soli*-based nations such as the U.S., Canada, or Britain. See William Rogers Brubaker, "Citizenship and Naturalization," *Migration and the Politics of Citizenship in Europe and North America,* ed. William Rogers Brubaker (Lanham, Md.: University Press of America, 1989), 118.

77. As Amin (*Eurocentrism,* 148) observes, "The North-South contradiction will inevitably become more and more explosive, thereby engendering, among other things, an intensifed aggressive racism in the countries of developed capitalism." Certainly the REPs tend to confirm this new North-South conflict in their arguments. In the words of Baden-Württemberg REP leader and lawyer Christian Käs, the flood of refuguees increases housing shortages, increases crime, and harms the environment. Hence, we have to make the borders tight, change the constitution, and kick the foreigner out—signals that would be heard "into the last negro village in Africa" (Bartholomäus Grill, "Signale ins Negerdorf," *Die Zeit,* 10 April 1992).

78. On political refugees, see Reuter, "Minorities," 106. See also Vera Gaserow, "Asyldiskussion: Mit Zahlen laßt sich trefflich Politik machen," *Tageszeitung,* 11 September 1991. On debates of constitutional change, see Wolfgang Schulth, "Asyl in der Zitadelle: Zum deutschen Umgang mit einem Menchenrecht," *Blätter für deutsche und internationale Politik,* no. 6 (1991).

79. In general, see Herbert Wulfskuhl, "Verfahren nationale Debatte." The Left has tended to criticize the new Schengen Agreement as the first step in a "fortress Europe" drawing a divide between North and South ("Schengener Vertrag verworfen," *Frankfurter Rundschau,* 27 April 1992), while the Right does not want to give up any facet of national sovereignty.

80. See "Im Jahr 2000 ein türkischer Kanzler," *Der Spiegel,* 7 Feburary 1989, 26–35. The *New York Times* observed more recently that Germany now attracts 60 percent of all asylum seekers coming to Western Europe. This amounted to more than two hundred and fifty thousand in 1991, costing the Government $2.5 billion to feed, clothe, and shelter them (Stephen Kinzer, "Last Straw? Refugees at Fest's Field," *New York Times,* 19 March 1992, sec. A).

81. Gerd Nowakowski, "Die Grünen auf der Suche nach der Multikultur," *Tageszeitung,* 17 June 1989.

82. On the structural racism inherent in such constitutional defintions, see Georg Auernheimer, "Ethnizität und Modernität," *Rassismus und Migration in Europa,* 124f.

83. In general, see Fritz Franz, "Das Prinzip der Abstammung im deutschen Staatsangehörigkeit," *Rassimus und Migration in Europa,* 327–46.

84. British welfare-state scholar Hillary Rose recently noted that the prominent leftist social scientists in central Europe who focus on welfare-state policies (Offe, Korpi, Himmelstrand) have never dealt with the problem of race or ethnic difference in their theories, a circumstance that would be unthinkable in Left welfare-state analysts in Britain or the United States.

85. For example, see Heiner Boehncke and Harald Wittich, eds., *Buntesdeutschland: Ansichten zu einer Multikulturellen Gesellschaft* (Reinbek: Rowohlt, 1991). The immigration initiative comes largely from the red-green state government in Lower Saxony (See "Schengener Vertrag verworfen"; and Willy Brandt's Paris speech on

Germany as a land of immigration, *Tageszeitung,* 27 January 1992). The Conservatives, since even before they took power in 1982, have blocked attempts to more rapidly grant citizenship to second generation immigrants (Brubaker, "Citizenship and Naturalization," 124)*;* and the commisioner for foreigner issues for the present government, Liselotte Funcke (FDP) has emphasized that in the period even before the rightist successes of 1992 the Federal Government had ignored her report of the worsening condition of foreign employees in the FRG (Ferdos Fordastan, interview with Liselotte Funcke, *Tageszeitung,* 6 May 1991).

86. In general on German law and immigration policy, see Kay Haibronner, "Citizenship and Nationhood in Germany," in Brubaker, *Migration.* 67ff.

87. Rogers Brubaker, "Introduction," in Brubaker, *Migration,* 7–10; Brubaker; Haibronner, "Citizenship," 75; and Zollberg, "Zukunft," 56.

88. See the selection of essays on "Flight, Deportation, Immigration" introduced with a passage from Arendt's *Origins of Totalitarianism* in *Die neue Gesellschaft/ Frankfurter Hefte* 38 (1991): 411ff.

89. This issue is, not surprisingly, one of those differentiating those nations which never had successsful bourgeois revolutions (southern, central, and eastern Europe) from those that did (France, England, and its ex-colonies, the United States). England, however, retreated from this more liberal position under the Thatcher government in 1983.

90. This repeats an old trauma between *Germans* and *Jews.* Citations by Schönhuber make it clear that he regards *German* and *Jew* as mutually exclusive categories, like the difference between *German* and *foreigner.* That the German/ foreigner difference is magnified by the existing legal racial distinctions between Germans resident in the FRG and those living outside the country—in Poland, the former USSR, etc.—is underscored by the illiberal opinions of conservatives such as Alfred Dregger, chair of the CDU/CSU Bundestag faction. Just as Israel is the "homeland for all persecuted and oppressed jews, so the Federal Republic is the homeland for all persecuted and oppressed Germans." One can only guess what Mr. Dregger has in mind concerning the possible "Germanness" of individuals of the Islamic religion and of Turkish descent who have grown up and lived their entire lives in the Federal Republic. Ubiquitious antifascist graffitti in the Federal Republic replacing "Turks Out" with "Nazis Out" suggests similar difficulties. Where ought one to send Germany's unwanted Nazis, to Uganda?

91. On the contitutional debates and ultimate failure of this initiative in the Federal Constitutional Court, see Götz Frank, "Auslanderwahlrecht und Rechtsstellung der Kommune," *Kritische Justiz* 32 (1990).

PART 6

Germany and Its External Environment

In the first essay, Andrei S. Markovits and Simon Reich argue that Germany is becoming a European hegemon. Yet German hegemony is likely to be benign, for a number of reasons. Drawing upon Gramsci's definition of ideological hegemony, they point to the growing German penetration of eastern European markets, the strong German role in helping to restructure these societies, and the popularity of the German model of capitalism, while also noting Germany's leading role in the EC.

Moishe Postone offers a more critical view of Germany's future politics, domestic and European. Postone finds troubling signs of political extremism in both the Right and the Left in Germany, and fears that German exceptionalism may not be dead.

Michael G. Huelshoff explores the impacts of German domestic politics on its EC policy. He argues that while neofunctionalist and intergovernmentalist integration theory purports to emphasize Germany in the EC, neither can account for key parts of the integration process, and neither can explicate German EC policy. He proposes a theory of regional integration that links domestic politics to intergovernmental bargaining and finds that the broad public consensus favoring European integration in Germany interacts with the domestic institutional order to reaffirm German commitment to integration in Europe. Germany, then, works as a counterweight to disintegrative forces in Europe today.

The remaining essay takes up the security dimension of German policy. James Sperling asserts that the Germans will remain committed to NATO at least for the near future, as a counter to nationalism and disintegration in eastern Europe. In the long run, the Germans are likely to prefer an independent western European defense entity, a reinforced WEU, and a significant strengthening of the CSCE, which incorporates both the United States and the Soviet Union. For the time being, fears of political and economic instability in Eastern Europe require Germany to maintain its special security relationship with the United States.

Should Europe Fear the Germans?

Andrei S. Markovits and Simon Reich

Nineteen eighty-nine can justifiably claim to be Germany's year. The unification of the two Germanys and the two Berlins meant the definite end of the two Europes, at least in their cold war dimension. But once the Western euphoria over the victory of capitalism over communism subsided, the crumbling of the Berlin Wall rekindled the latest stage in the long-running debate in Europe and the United States regarding the "German Question." In its current form it generates the issue of the new Germany's role in a changing European and global environment. Academic experts have responded to this question by offering opinions that fill the pages of Europe's and North America's papers. Their commentaries are divisible into two major categories: the majority optimistic, basically viewing Germany's unification as a boon to Germany, Europe, and global peace; and the minority pessimistic, worrying that a strong Germany will repeat the mistakes of its past. For understandable reasons, both voices have busily responded to the legacy of Auschwitz. The optimists have made it their mission to convince their audience (perhaps even themselves?) that all the ingredients that produced Auschwitz have been successfully extirpated by West Germany's exemplary democracy, commonly known as Modell Deutschland. The pessimists, in turn, worry that the Federal Republic's democratic institutions (*a*) are not really democratic (the Left's objections to a unified Germany), (*b*) are untested in a true crisis comparable to that of the depression of the early 1930s, and thus at best fair-weather institutions (the liberal apprehension), or (*c*) will ultimately prove irrelevant in a world ruled by power and renewed nationalism (the conservative fear).

In this chapter, we wish to address the issue of Germany's future role in Europe. We conform with neither the majority nor the minority view completely. Instead our formulation belongs to what we perceive to be a post-Auschwitz paradigm. We agree with the optimists that the Federal Republic's greatest achievement is its eradication of most factors that could potentially lead to yet another Auschwitz perpetrated by Germans. Where we part ways with the optimists is in their view of a democratic Germany with virtually no exercise of power in Europe and the world. Indeed, we will argue here that one of the factors that will make this new Germany particularly powerful (in a hegemonic sense) in a new multipolar world, where it constitutes a great power along with the United States, Japan, and Russia, is precisely the Federal Republic's democratic and commercialized nature. Contrary to the liberals' optimism and the conservatives' pessimism, we see democracy and power in a positive-sum relationship, particularly in increasingly complex (post)industrial societies. Successful democracies, such as Germany's, are powerful because of the consensual nature of their politics, which lends them legitimacy in the eyes of their regional partners, and the high productive and distributive efficiency of their markets. Indeed, the adage that deutschmarks might go much further than panzers in extending German power seems quite compelling. Concretely, we will examine German influence in western and eastern Europe to establish that it already approximates a hegemonic role in this theater. Furthermore, we claim that Germany will undoubtedly increase its power in the future as it extends its influence in the East—unimpeded by institutional constraints, assisted by its cultural legacies there, and encouraged to do so by its status as the model for eastern European states as they attempt to retrace Germany's steps successfully and accomplish the transition to efficient capitalism and stable liberal democracy.

In our article we therefore argue that Germany has become increasingly influential in Western Europe over the last decade, as the primary beneficiary from the present structure of trading relations within the European Community (EC) and the major contributor to sustaining those arrangements through the EC budget. We then suggest that this pattern will be replicated with greater rapidity and intensity in eastern Europe, where the Germans will have fewer institutional constraints with which to cope than in western Europe. The economic success enjoyed by Germany in the EC has provided it with the springboard for its future east European hegemony; once developed, the advantage it enjoys in the East will reciprocally help to cement its hegemony in western Europe. This emergent hegemony will not be the product of purposive, coercive behavior by the Germans themselves but of the voluntaristic behavior of Germany's partners, who associate the idea of trade with economic growth.

The New Germany, the New Europe

The Optimists' View. Arguments stressing the benign effect of German unification on European development reflect one of three critical elements. Although these arguments might involve more than one form, their intellectual content is preponderantly functional, institutional, or sociological. All of them focus on postwar history for supporting evidence.

The first argument extends of the functional approach used by integration theory, traditionally popular among scholars studying the development of the EC.[1] The argument focuses on the taming of German power and influence through its involvement in international organizations such as the EC and the North Atlantic Treaty Organization (NATO). There are at least two assumptions behind this approach. The first is that involvement in such institutions has bred a series of interdependent rather than dominant relationships between Germany and its partners that are likely to continue to promote friendship rather than friction. This same assumption lay behind the initial American promotion of Franco-German collaboration dating back to the early 1950s.[2] The product has been a Germany tamed by its international ties. Some, of course, have identified this strategy as part of America's postwar double containment policy against Germany and the Soviet Union.[3] Proponents of the functional approach suggest, in extending this logic, that just as a policy of military containment successfully restrained Soviet aggression, it will continue to limit any German imperialist designs and ambitions. The second assumption sees states as interested in absolute rather than relative gains; it is, therefore, important that Germany's trading arrangement with its partners are positive sum in effect, that is, that they are to the mutual benefit of both Germany and its partners.[4] In the context of this assumption, the hope is that the primary effect of Germany's involvement in organizations such as the EC will allow Germany's economic strength to act as a locomotive for broader European development as its foreign investment grows and it reciprocates in foreign trade. This point of view suggests that successful German development can only occur within the context of broad European growth.[5]

The second, institutional, argument supporting a benign image of the effects of German unification focuses on the postwar development of Germany's domestic political system. A centerpiece of this argument among certain American scholars, is that Bonn—in notable contrast to Weimar—"fragmented" the German state, which resulted in a similar taming of its capacities.[6] Advocates of this argument point to the acceptance of a system of federalism and democratic values as the new Germany assimilates the political structure of the old Federal Republic.[7] This essentially argues that the new Germany will merely be the institutional extension of the highly successful and well-adjusted Federal Republic. Advocates of this view therefore welcome the Anschluss-like character of the unification, which, so they believe, bodes well for the continuation of a democratic Germany in the domestic sphere and a tamed Germany in the international arena. Indeed, according to this approach, it is the democratic nature of domestic reforms that will continue to temper German foreign policy. Or differently put, the Federal Republic's success as a liberal democracy governing a prosperous economy has once and for all exorcised the demons of the German Sonder-weg. According to this logic, the new united Germany can—indeed should—be analytically divorced from the old authoritarian, predatory, Junker-dominated Germany of 1870–1945.[8] The institutional argument complements its functional counterpart in its positive view of the effects of German unification for the rest of Europe. The main difference between the two lies in which factors each chooses to stress: while the institutional concentrates on internal constraints to German dominance, the functional emphasizes external relations.

The third argument concentrates on a sociological explanation, emphasizing the evolution of Germany's elites. It rests on the premise of an evolutionary "knowledge through learning." It basically suggests that German economic, intellectual, and political elites have been acutely aware of their responsibility for Germany's terrible past and thus stand vigil, guarding against the reemergence of militarist, antiliberal, xenophobic, and cryptofascist tendencies in the new united Germany. Germans, so this argument goes, feel ambivalent about unification and retain a dire concern to avoid their past mistakes. In broad historical terms, the new German political and economic elites represent the postwar triumph of the bourgeoisie with its liberal and democratic values over the traditionally imperialist and aggressive ways of the feudal and aristocratic Junkers before 1945. These victorious bourgeois values stress a cosmopolitan culture within the context of a European economy in which Germany and its trading partners benefit by Germany's adherence to the advantages of free trade within an export oriented economy. As a result of this orientation, Germany's new and thoroughly commercialized economic elites recognize the country's sustained dependence on the willingness of foreigners to buy its goods. These elites therefore advocate policies that enhance free trade. The main representatives of this elite understand that such policies can only be implemented in an environment that adheres to the principles of reconciliation and mutual trust. Perhaps the Federal Republic's greatest asset in its secured democratization is the profound Westernization of its economic and business elite. This cosmopolitanization and bourgeoisification of West Germany's captains of industry represents perhaps one of the most fundamental differences between the Weimar and the Bonn republics. In the former, the business class as a whole adhered to a sense of hypernationalism, was profoundly authoritarian, detested the republic's democratic institutions, and tried to cow labor by destroying its independence. In marked contrast, the Bonn republic's business elites have been international in outlook and education, have accepted and supported the republic's democratic order, and have entered into intricate "corporatist" arrangements with labor as a fully accepted junior partner in what has widely been praised as Modell Deutschland. One of the its ultimate goals—to become world champions in global exports—was successfully attained for the first time in 1988 and then repeated in 1990.

The pessimists' view. The pessimists' anguish concerning prospective Germany hegemony, in view of Germany's unification and the vacuum in power and leadership created by American and Soviet withdrawals from Europe, takes two primary forms: one historical, the other cultural. In different ways, both stress evidence that predates 1945. The historical analysis emphasizes the notorious aspects of German development dating from unification to the national socialist period. It tends to decry the claims of traditional, conservative historians that German culpability for the outbreak of two world wars was limited and instead stresses the violent nature of the first German unification, the German bourgeoisie's unsuccessful quest for democratic authority, and the aggressive nature of Germany's foreign policy, all of which were necessary antecedents for the Holocaust itself.[9] Indeed, pessimists point to the recent attempts of conservative historians to "relativize" Germany's crimes through the Holocaust via the so-called historians' debate (Historikerstreit) as timely evidence for the continued presence of a certain aggressive German assertiveness that, if not an outright defense of German militarism, certainly represents an intellectual accommodation to it.[10]

Advocates of this historical approach see as unerring the truth that Germany's domestic problems have always been Europe's as well. In this view, the dominant way of compensating for Germany's internal conflicts has traditionally involved state policies designed to assist German economic and/or military expansion, whether those problems consist of labor or raw material shortages, or simply as a way of obfuscating German domestic turmoil by invoking a belligerent form of nationalism.[11] The discussions between politicians and bureaucrats sponsored by the former British government of Margaret Thatcher in 1989, and the subsequent "Chequers Pronouncement" after those discussions, reflected just such British concerns about the possibility of renewed German expansionism.[12] Advocates of such an approach would point to multiple problems that Germany faces in integrating the destitute East German population as one source of potential conflict. They would also note as evidence that one of Kohl's first acts when faced with the realistic prospect of unification was to generate a dispute about the legitimacy of Poland's postwar border with East Germany. Although Kohl recognized that the international uproar generated by his comments threatened to stall the unification negotiations and thus promptly withdrew his claims, critics noted that the Chancellor's motive was to attract support of right-wing members of the German electorate, many of whom were refugees from the former German territories and constituents of the Federal Republic's conservative bloc. This pattern of "spill-over"—whereby German domestic political conflict finds its expression in an expansionist foreign policy—furnishes an enduring characteristic of Germany emanating from Wilhelmine Germany's imperialist ideology of Weltpolitik. Weltpolitik propagated a nationalist belief that domestic security was contingent upon territorial expansion. It thereby quelled a series of potential social and class conflicts that otherwise might have erupted into civil strife. Revisionist historians in the late twentieth century contend that such domestic turmoil and the resulting nationalist ideology generated German policies that caused the outbreak of the First World War.[13]

A second, related pessimistic approach, which in many ways carries a greater mass appeal (although it has less supporting evidence), concentrates on culture. This approach is much more self-consciously voluntaristic and tends to reflect an angst—both within and outside Germany—about Germany's enhanced power and its new problems with the conjunction of reunification and global transformation. Such concerns have been expressed by German intellectuals, most notably Günter Grass, while foreigners have tended to dwell on the slightest sign of any of the recurrent German nationalist symbols, be they references to the weaknesses of Weimar or the joys of Wagner; to the German Volk or to its Vaterland.[14] Common to both German intellectuals and foreigners has been an unease with the prospect of the reappearance of tendencies for so long submerged and a concomitant fear that Germany's new democratic culture will ultimately prove illusory.

Like the historical approach, its cultural counterpart recognizes the ambivalence of Germany's pre-1945 and post-1945 experiences. However, this approach chooses to emphasize a concern that, freed of superpower constraints, the reunited Germany will relive old habits. The pessimists' greatest fear, in the early 1990s, is best reflected by Hermann Kantorowicz's comment, made in 1931, that "the new Germany's true foe is the old Germany."[15]

The debate between optimists and pessimists therefore really focuses on the degree of German centrality in the new European order, and its implications for its position in Europe and for global stability. Arguments on both sides stress structural, institutional, and cognitive attributes, disagreeing mainly on whether contemporary Germany's primary links are to the period that predates or postdates 1945. The optimists tend to reflect the institutionalist assumption that European integration is a positive-sum game in which the interests of Germany and its European partners are compatible. It was therefore no surprise to them to hear Helmut Kohl declare, at the first congress of the reunited Christian Democratic Union, that "for me German unity and European unity are two sides of the same coin . . . in truth we are

German patriots and convinced Europeans . . . Europe is our future, Germany our fatherland." The pessimistic view is best reflected in Margaret Thatcher's riposte that "it will be up to the rest of us to see that Germany does not dominate. Others of us have powerful voices."[16]

Germany's Hegemony in Western Europe

In this section we shall examine events since 1972 (when the last of the "big four" trading partners, Britain, joined the community) to assess two types of questions. The first type are structural and fiscal; how much Germany has benefited or lost, in both absolute and relative terms, in comparison to its major trading partners from the present system of EC trading relations, and how much Germany has proportionately contributed to the cost of maintaining that system through its contributions to, and receipts from, the EC budget. The answer to these questions may indicate the degree of Germany's economic influence in the EC. We seek to understand whether Germany's relationship with its west European trading partners is a positive-sum or a zero-sum arrangement, in order to assess whether the pessimists' fear about the foundation of German economic imperialism and the future course of European development is justified. The second type of question assesses how much influence the Germans have had in developing the policy agenda in Western Europe in this period.

German economic influence in the EC is dominant and growing as measured by intrastate trade flows such as the pattern and relative share of exports and resulting fiscal surpluses or deficits among EC members, tempting some to describe the EC as Germany's "co-prosperity sphere." The pattern dating from 1972 has been that Germany began the period with a much higher Gross Domestic Product (GDP) to export ratio than its major EC trading rivals—Italy, France, and Great Britain—and that Germany's global export penetration as a percentage of GDP grew from a fifth to a third of its economy in the 1970s and 1980s while the British, French, and Italian ratio expanded at a much slower rate (less than half as fast). Specifically within the EC, where free-trade arrangements dominate, while French and Italian exports to the EC as a percentage of their total exports stagnated or fell slightly despite the expansion of EC membership, and Britain's only grew from a miniscule to a small base as a result of initial EC entry, the percentage of German exports to the EC as a percentage of all exports grew by over 15 percent.[17] Germany's growth rate is all the more impressive when one bears in mind that these represented fairly mature markets for German exporters in this period.

In sum, when we assess Germany's pattern of EC export growth in the 1970s and 1980s against its major European rivals, its performance is extremely impressive. The Germans outsold their European rivals globally and regionally, in absolute and relative terms, at the start of the 1970s and at the end of the 1980s. Germany began the period by exporting more inside and outside the EC than any of its rivals. It increased this lead over the next two decades while augmenting its already substantial EC market penetration. As countries joined the EC they found themselves predominantly importing German goods as Germany consistently extended its regional export base. As a result, by as early as the mid-1980s, an unquestioned pattern of German domination of exports within the EC became evident.

As a result of this growing export penetration, the Federal Republic's market share was by far the largest at the start of the decade (25.6 percent compared to France's 16 percent in second place) and increased while its major rival fell (27.8 percent to France's 15.6 percent). Indeed, among potential challengers to German dominance, only Italy's market share grew (from 10.4 percent to 11.7 percent)—and that was at nearly half the German rate. Germany therefore strengthened its grip on exports with far and away the biggest percentage increase, starting from the already biggest percentage base.[18]

The distributive benefits were predictably lopsided. First, Germany consistently gained while its major trading rivals were heavy net losers, with Britain being the most adversely affected. Second, in examining the 1980s in particular, the relative surpluses and deficits became increasingly unequal over time. Both Germany's absolute profits and its relative advantage over its major partners, grew. The German balance of trade surplus surged in the second half of the 1980s while France's stagnated, Italy's got marginally worse, and Britain's went into a free-fall. Germany therefore proved to be the sole beneficiary among the major EC members as measured in terms of balance of trade surpluses.

So why did (and do) Germany's major trading partners in the EC willingly adhere to these arrangements when they so adversely affect these countries' balance of trade? There are two possible answers. Either they are recompensed through EC budget receipts or they mistakenly believe it is in their interest to sustain these arrangements.

Examining contributions to and receipts from the EC budget in the 1980s reveals three interesting things. The first is that the Germans were the overwhelming contributors to and reticent recipients from the EC budget in the 1980s. The second is that the indirect effects of EC programs partially mitigated the effects of their trade deficits for the French and the Italians. But when all is considered, the French and the Italians were significant net losers under the EC system in the 1980s. The third point is that Britain's claim that it did not benefit from EC membership in the mid-1980s is quite realistic in view of its net contributions to the EC budget and trade deficit with its EC partners. It was the largest trade loser, and the second largest budgetary contributor. While European officials consistently frowned upon Margaret Thatcher's manner and her insistence that Britain's budgetary contributions be renegotiated, these figures suggest that Thatcher's demands therefore appear quite legitimate.[19]

The Germans were therefore clearly the prime beneficiaries of the EC system in the 1980s and their dominance will probably continue to grow in the 1990s. In both absolute and relative terms, the present EC system enhances Germany's wealth and power vis-à-vis its major trading partners.

We stressed at the outset that complementing the growing magnitude of German economic influence was a growing capacity to set the policy agenda in the 1970s and 1980s. Historically, the Germans have not provided the political leadership for the EC that their economic domination of it behooves. For the Germans, initially, the EC served as yet another pragmatic vehicle for readmission to the community of nations in the shadow of Auschwitz. The Germans, however, had no vision of or desire for political leadership at the formation of the EC.

In stark contrast to the Germans' reticence, the French were very keen to assume the mantle of the EC's political leader from its very beginning. Fueled by visions of grandeur, the French believed that the EC provided them with the opportunity to achieve self-aggrandizing national and pan-European goals that were, if not openly challenging to the Americans, definitely perceived as being countervailing in nature. The French considered their leadership of the EC as a way of restoring their flagging continental prestige and autonomy by invigorating an independent, united Europe, and as the extension throughout Europe of the principles of French economic planning which would be facilitated by rehabilitating the idea of colonial (or in this case regional) preference discredited under the free-trade terms of the Bretton Woods Agreement.[20]

We are not suggesting that the Germans currently provide political leadership in its conventional sense. Nor that they are eager to be Europe's "moral leaders." Such a claim would rest on shaky grounds despite periodic attempts by Germans to assume leadership roles by taking the moral high ground—such as Willy Brandt's North-South efforts or the German peace movement's one-sided pacifism in the Gulf War, in which it contrasted the "bellicosity" of the Western Allies with its own morally superior opposition to violence.

Yet in important dimensions, Germany has in the meantime come to dominate the thinking of EC members. While French attempts to assert political leadership have lacked subtlety, often proved no more than symbolic in practice, and floundered mostly on the pragmatic considerations of France's trading partners, Germany's quiet influence in the EC has grown—

largely by virtue of its ideological leadership. Indeed the stabilization of democratic values within Germany and the country's sustained economic success have enhanced Germany's influence as a political and economic leader in the community over time. The German model of economic decentralization has won Europe's hearts and minds. The result has been a growth in Germany's influence in the EC accompanied by a concomitant decline in France's, a tendency most likely to become more pronounced in the future.

We are not suggesting that the Germans are now Europe's political leaders in a representative sense: nor are they the Continent's spokesmen. Though the Germans have never assumed an explicit role as representative leaders in the EC, they have in fact successfully buttressed their economic domination with their propagating of the originally Anglo-Saxon values of democracy and free trade. The Germans initially assimilated these values as a result of the reformist efforts of the postwar occupation. In fact the Germans needed to do remarkably little to convince the other West European states of their own reformation because the Allied boasts on that score proved sufficient. The ideological consensus of the view of contemporary Germany as democratic can be measured by the remarkable lack of European discussion about occasional antidemocratic state policies in Germany such as the Berufsverbot measures, which banned Communists from employment as civil servants, or the expulsion of foreign workers in the early 1970s in flagrant violation of the terms of their visas.[21] Such anomalies to democratic values were hardly noticed beyond a coterie of some vocal intellectuals and thus required little explanation in circles of policy-making and power.

Interestingly, however, while they have needed to do little beyond the Allied efforts to extend the principles of democracy in Europe, they have been active participants in establishing the universal free-trade system—first in Germany, then in Western Europe, and now in the East. Although the Americans favored free trade, this complemented the preferences of the Federal Republic's political and economic elites. One prime example concerns Ludwig Erhard, who, first as Economics Minister and then as chancellor, implemented the important initial policies that resulted in the development of a German economy run on free-trade principles. These policies emphasized currency reform and export-led growth. They have been commonly associated with Germany's early postwar "economic miracle" of high growth. As part of a rare domestic consensus among large advanced industrial states, German leaders of the Left and the Right (barring fringes on either end) have portrayed themselves as adherents of Erhard's unique policy mix of free trade and social welfare that was termed the "social market economy."

With the formation of the EC, these free-trade principles were integrated into the EC's structure at the insistence of the Germans and their American sponsors. Many EC members looked to Germany's combination of export-led growth and prudent fiscal conservatism as a suitable model for their own economic development. The image of Modell Deutschland was born in the minds of Germany's new trading partners and, crucially, in their belief that they, too, could take the same avenue as the Germans, by implementing free-trade policies, and achieve the same successful results. The countries of Eastern Europe are now following the same pattern and are using the same image of postwar German economic policy as a model for development as did the West Europeans before them. This belief of both the West and East European states ignores the possibility that Germany's benefits have been achieved at their expense and that these potential imitators could never match Germany's prosperity because that prosperity was built on an economic domination of these countries.

What some authors have claimed to be a process whereby the Federal Republic has extended its economic sphere of influence and authority is supported by two key examples: the discussions about economic monetary union (EMU) and those concerning the Lomé Convention in the 1970s. The EMU talks yielded reform proposals that threatened the appreciation of the deutsche mark and thus the export position of West German industry. These proposals were headed off by German efforts that resulted in a realignment of economic policies around West German priorities. The organizing principle of the Lomé Convention's predecessor, the popular Corea Plan, was to raise the price of basic agricultural and mining products in order to increase the revenue of Third World states. The implementation of such a plan would have had severe repercussions for an economy such as West Germany's, which is heavily reliant on cheap raw materials so that it can export competitively priced finished products. Here the Germans focused on the threat to the principles of free trade involved in such an agreement and constructed an alternative plan in the form of the Lomé Convention. Instead of threatening German competitiveness, as the Corea Plan did, the terms of the Lomé Convention benefited the Germans by stressing the importance of the total revenues of Third World states rather than price increases, enhancing the potential for growing resource supplies for the Germans while encouraging the dismantling of British and French systems of preferences with former colonies on the grounds that such systems were protectionist. This had two effects: it opened up hitherto exclusive British and French markets to German competition and encouraged the expansion of free trade because British and French goods would now have to compete in Europe in the absence of protected markets.[22]

Together the hegemony of democratic values in Western (and now most of Eastern) Europe coupled with the consensual characterization of the postwar FRG as democratic served German national interests because it contributed to a view of Germany as fragmented, pluralist, and thus benign. What is essential to our argument, however, is how the consensual belief in a democratic and benign Germany has complemented German economic interests by ensuring that German economic penetration has not been seen as part of an imperialist policy of an authoritarian state, as was the case in earlier epochs of Germany's relations with its European neighbors. But, as revealed in the prior discussion on West European trade, the effects of a system of interstate free trade among most members has proven to be deleterious to Germany's major West European partners. An explanation of an apparent anomaly is therefore needed. Why is it that liberal economic assumptions about the positive effects of free trade in the context of European integration remain unquestioned?

Germany's current image as politically stable and economically benign starkly contrasts with its earlier images. It has therefore obscured the effects of Germany's economic penetration of EC member states. Rather than worrying its European trading partners about their being adversely affected by Germany's extensive share of exports in the context of a free-trade zone, Germany has largely been admired by most Europeans and has been considered a model of development by them, easily defeating the French model as the only serious challenger. As always, assimilation is the sincerest form of flattery. The hegemony of the principle of unadulterated free trade among EC states has resulted in a series of attempts to copy the German example by the EC's individual members and by its federal organizational structure. The power of the ideological consensus about the virtues of free trade to which the Germans have contributed, partially by conscious efforts and partially by example, ensures that these actual and potential imitators remain blissfully unaware of the fact that the boundaries between German prosperity and undue influence remain uncomfortably narrow.

Germany's Hegemony in Eastern Europe

Germany's historical influence on Eastern Europe dates back to the early Middle Ages. Through much of the past centuries East European affairs centered on the often complicated and delicate navigation between the Scylla of German power in the West and the Charybdis of Russian and/or Ottoman power in the East.

Germany's unconditional surrender in 1945 and the subsequent Yalta world seemed to establish Russia via Soviet power as the sole political actor of any importance in that part of the world. But Germany was not to be dismissed so easily. In accordance with the Federal Republic's beneficent nature when compared to its Nazi predecessor, German influence towards Eastern Europe was to occur in the realms of economic cooperation and conflict reduction, instead of political bullying and military occupation. The two pillars of Germany's post–World War II influence in Eastern Europe have been Osthandel (pertaining to the economy and commerce) and Ostpolitik (its counterpart in politics and ideology).

As to Osthandel, one would find it extremely difficult to find *any* category of commerce and trade in which the Federal Republic has not consistently been the most important Western presence in Eastern Europe. Thus, for example, in 1989 West Germany's sales to all East European countries (excepting the Soviet Union) was nearly four times greater than Italy's, the runner-up, and still larger than those of Italy, the United States, and France combined. In the USSR, German sales exceeded those of its nearest rival, the United States, by nearly 50 percent.[23]

In every East European country, the Federal Republic has been far and away the most important Western trading partner in the case of both imports and exports. Perhaps more impressive than this dominance on the aggregate level is the fact that West Germany has been each of these countries' leading partner in virtually every conceivable category, ranging from cars, electronics, and chemical products to textiles, agricultural goods, and artwork.

German dominance, if anything, is even more pronounced on the micro level. Data on company investments and joint ventures in Eastern Europe show the Federal Republic's firms way ahead of the competition (mainly Austrian, Italian, and, to a much lesser extent, American). Be it such glamorous contacts as Volkswagen's purchase of the Skoda works in Czechoslovakia or the more than 300 joint ventures begun by German and Hungarian firms in Hungary in 1989, Osthandel's prowess in changing every facet of the East European economies can hardly be denied. Making matters even more pronounced is the fact that all these data pertain exclusively to West Germany, not taking into account the fact that the newly united Germany's position will in due course become even more formidable by virtue of inheriting the former German Democratic Republic's close "socialist" ties with Eastern Europe and the Soviet Union.[24]

Ostpolitik, developed by the Federal Republic's Social and Free Democrats under the intellectual leadership of Willy Brandt, was at the forefront of initially improving and subsequently institutionalizing East-West relations in the post-1945 world. It would be no exaggeration to view West Germany's Ostpolitik as the intellectual and structural precursor to détente. Compared to the Federal Republic's main competitors, Ostpolitik most certainly gave the Germans a running start in Eastern Europe for the post–cold war era.

By the time the annus mirabilis of 1989 changed Eastern Europe, it was hardly chance that the German model was the most cherished option for all these countries. Economically, East Europeans wanted to emulate the West German Wirtschaftswunder as the best agent of transition to a democratic order and, once established, as its most reliable guarantor. East Europeans have continued to hold the Federal Republic's currency reform of 1948 and Ludwig Erhard's market-propelled economy in high esteem.

In addition to the Free and Christian side of this Democratic ledger, the Social has also provided the German model with much legitimacy in many an East European's view. The social aspect of the Federal Republic's vaunted social market economy is mainly credited to a strong Social Democratic party and its ancillary world of trade unions. With most aspects of the postwar German order enjoying great respect in Eastern Europe, it should therefore come as no surprise that some countries have actively sought to emulate West German institutions in the establishment of their new polities. This ranges from the Hungarians' adoption of the West German electoral system to the Czechoslovaks' more than fleeting interest in the Federal Republic's constitution, the Basic Law.

Culture and language are among the most decisive transmitters of hegemonic rule. Especially concerning Eastern Europe, there can be no question that German culture and language provided a common bond and a lingua franca among the political class and cultural elite at least until 1945, perhaps even longer. Primarily a legacy of Habsburg and Hohenzollern domination, the role of German culture and language in Mitteleuropa far outlived its political originators as well as its Soviet repressors, only to emerge once again alive and well as one of the few genuinely transnational agents in this part of the world. Paralleling the Westernization and commercialization of the Federal Republic, the reemergence of German culture and language in post-1989 East-Central Europe denotes this region's attempt to become European, that is, Western, not, as was previously the case, the champion of German Bildung. In that sense, the study of German in contemporary East-Central Europe is meant to contribute to that region's Zivilisation, not its Kultur. German cultural hegemony in the region will assume a commercialized and capitalist character. Differently put, East Europeans are now learning German in order to converse with Siemens and Volkswagen executives, not to read the plays of Goethe or the poetry of Schiller.

Of the 16 million people currently studying German in primary, secondary, and postsecondary institutions worldwide, 12 million are in East-Central Europe and the Soviet Union. In terms of an intra-European breakdown, the presence of German in Eastern Europe far exceeds that in the continent's western and southern parts. Of the circa 140,000 German-language teachers in all of Europe in 1990, nearly 90,000 were in Eastern Europe, whereas there were only 38,000 in the West and not quite 10,000 in the South.[25]

In every East European country, be it Bulgaria or Poland, Hungary or Czechoslovakia, German is still the predominant second language. While English continues to gain everywhere and has in certain cases, such as Romania and Hungary for example, caught up with German as the premier foreign language, German's future has undoubtedly been substantially solidified in this part of the world as a direct consequence of the events of 1989. Add to this the still considerable presence of various German-speaking Volks-deutsche in this region and one has all the necessary prerequisites for the successful institutionalization of a cultural hegemony.

With the abolishing of Russian as a compulsory subject in Poland, Czechoslovakia, Romania, and Hungary, the unification of Germany, and the reassertion of identity on the part of a small though significant German population in East-Central Europe and the Soviet Union, there can be no doubt that German culture and language will experience a major proliferation in the coming years. Moreover, German language and culture will not be associated either with the dreaded Nazis or with the barely more popular East German Stalinists who basically monopolized everything German in Eastern Europe and the Soviet Union until 1989. German will become a greater necessity but will also enjoy a comparable growth in legitimacy. "Will we all have to learn German?" asked an article in the *Financial Times* of 10 March 1990.[26] Answering its own question, the piece suggested that though this might not yet be obligatory, it most certainly would prove helpful in the near future. There can be no doubt about this as far as East-Central Europe and the Soviet Union are concerned.

Conclusion

Should Europe fear the Germans? Our analysis suggests that it most certainly should not the way it once did. A new stage of the German Question has emerged. We do not believe that one can simply respond in the way offered by optimists or pessimists. Rather than being plagued by the traditional banes of Sonderweg and Zwischenkultur, authoritarianism and national chauvin-ism, today's German Question is much more subtle, nuanced, and part of the peaceful interaction among liberal democracies. None of Germany's neigh-bors, nor the great powers, worry about the prospect of German domina-tion—that is, Germany's purposive control of Europe through force of arms. We believe that the Germans share this view; they are not intent on military domination of any other country. In that sense, the allied attempts to reedu-cate the Germans so as to imbue them with a powerful propensity towards pacifism has proved to be successful on an historic scale. Indeed, in an ironic confirmation of the dialectic at work, it has been precisely the success of this comprehensive reeducation that in part made the Germans as a society so resistant to commit any of their own military forces to the allied cause in the Gulf War. The other part of this reluctance had, of course, a much seamier side: the Germans had developed a comfortable complacency as the unquestioned new hegemon in Europe that they were not about to jeopardize by becoming involved in dubious adventures in the volatile Middle East.

We do not claim in this article that the Germans are necessarily intent on achieving economic hegemony, although we do not completely discount that possibility. Yet the dynamics of the present transitionary process suggest that such an economic hegemony might well be the eventual outcome. Given the history of Germany's foreign policy during this century, one would expect Germany's neighbors to adopt a guarded approach in their dealings with the Germans. Yet our data suggest that these very countries are busily immersing themselves in a web of relations from which only the Germans are certain to emerge as beneficiaries. At the moment, the Germans benefit overwhelmingly from the present structure of EC trading relations on an absolute and relative basis. Critics might suggest that British, Italian, or French trading deficits in the EC may be offset by exports external to the market. But if these countries were not members of the EC, they could still trade with the Germans and thus be more select in taking advantage of the benefits of trade without incurring the currently lopsided deficits.

What the Germans have done in Western Europe, they now are poised do with greater intensity in Eastern Europe because here the fragmented economies and fragile polities have fewer rigorous institutional constructs, and therefore fewer impediments to external penetration. The Germans' long-term achievement in Western Europe therefore appears likely to be replicated in the East in a more comprehensive and speedier manner in the forthcoming decade.

Why is it that Germany's EC partners have allowed this to happen and that the Eastern European countries are similarly laying themselves open to vulnerability to a country historically so hostile to their interests? How can we explain this apparent anomaly? Why is it that the Europeans in East and West have been able to overcome their greatest fear and embroil themselves in a web of relations that threaten them with German hegemony? Our argument in this chapter suggests that, beyond purely structural analysis, integrating ideas into analysis is essential for a proper understanding of the dynamics of Germany's hegemony. What is apparent here is the significance of the voluntaristic behavior of these countries in entering into agreements with the Germans while ignoring the welter of evidence that questions the appropriateness of their behavior.

Europeans east and west of Germany believe that intensive contact with the Germans will enhance the welfare of their economies despite a lack of supporting evidence. In the East, indeed, this belief also pertains to the realm of politics, where most countries have used some of the Federal Republic's democratic institutions and arrangements as models in their transition to a liberal democratic order. The west Europeans see the German economy as the locomotive for their own growth while, paradoxically, believing that the EC's institutions will constrain German development and power. The east Europeans believe that proximity to the Germans is like "kissing Ireland's Blarney stone," that is, that its mystical healing powers are best achieved by close contact. For the east Europeans, to replicate Germany's historic transition to liberal democracy and prosperous capitalism is best achieved by returning to the original source—for both advice and investment.

This belief in the centrality of Germany's involvement—and indeed Germany's prosperity—to the development of these European states, provides the Germans, de facto, with tremendous influence whether they want it or not. The borderline between simple influence and hegemony is (at least potentially) crossed when one marries the authority and credibility that the Germans possess by virtue of Modell Deutschland to the large size and scope of their economy relative to the rest of Europe. A well-respected model is just that when it has a small and/or insulated economy. Conversely, it is a hegemon when it has a large, competitive, export-based economy. Thus, the ever-present wish on the part of many German liberals and leftists to see the Federal Republic merely as a larger Switzerland or Austria bespeaks either an incredible naiveté or a cynicism bordering on the irresponsible.

In the debate between the optimists and the pessimists concerning the contours of Germany's influence in Europe, it would appear that the latter's fears, though justified, are misplaced. German power will expand inadvertently rather than willfully, economically rather than militarily. National aggrandizement is not part of the German agenda but will be a necessary byproduct of Germany's hegemonic position in Europe. The present tendency towards an increasing regionalization of the world's economy will only exacerbate Germany's hegemonic tendency.[27]

Understanding the dynamics of Germany's trading relations with the rest of Europe is contingent on integrating the role of ideas into any analysis. It is the periodic embracing or rejection of the political and economic principles upon which Germany rests that determine Europe's relationship to that country. Hegemony requires the export of goods and ideas. Structure and ideology must therefore be integrated and their mutual importance recognized in any analysis of hegemony. In Germany's case, it is the export of ideas in the context of a changing structure that will give its cosmopolitan society the capacity to flourish in the new Europe.

NOTES

1. The classic books in this genre include Ernst Haas, *The Uniting of Europe: Political, Social, and Economic Forces, 1950–1957* (Stanford: Stanford University

Press, 1958); and Leon Lindberg and Stuart A. Scheingold, *Europe's Would Be Polity: Patterns of Change in the European Community* (Englewood Cliffs, N.J.: Prentice Hall, 1970).

2. Robert Gilpin, *U.S. Power and the Multinational Corporation: The Political Economy of Foreign Direct Investment* (New York: Basic Books, 1975), 107.

3. Wolfram Hanrieder, *Germany, America, Europe: Forty Years of German Foreign Policy* (New Haven: Yale University Press, 1989), 5–7.

4. For a critical discussion of the implications of assuming states are interested in absolute rather than relative gains see Joseph Grieco, *Cooperation among Nations* (Ithaca: Cornell University Press, 1990), 10.

5. See Helmut Kohl, "The Voice of Harmony That Stills National Rivalry," *Financial Times,* 29 October 1990, 2.

6. Peter J. Katzenstein, *Policy and Politics in West Germany: The Growth of a Semi-Sovereign State* (Philadelphia: Temple University Press, 1987).

7. See, for example, Josef Joffe's article "Reunification II: This Time, No Hobnail Boots," *New York Times,* 30 September 1990.

8. For two exceptions see Ralf Dahrendorf, *Society and Democracy in Germany* (New York: Norton, 1979) and Simon Reich, *The Fruits of Fascism : Postwar Prosperity in Historical Perspective* (Ithaca, Cornell University Press, 1990).

9. The originator of this approach was Eckhart Kehr, whose contribution is analyzed by Richard J. Evans in "Introduction: Wilhelm II's Germany and the Historians," in *Society and Politics in Wilhelmine Germany,* ed. Richard J. Evans (New York: Barnes and Noble, 1978), 13. Other notable proponents of such radical interpretations include Fritz Fischer, *Germany's Aims in the First World War* (New York: Norton, 1967) and *The War of Illusions* (New York: Norton, 1975); John A. Moses, *The Politics of Illusion: The Fischer Controversy in German Historiography* (New York: Barnes and Nobel, 1975); and Hans-Ulrich Wehler, *The German Empire 1871–1918* (Dover, N.H.: Berg, 1985).

10. For a brief summary of this debate see Charles Maier, *The Unmasterable Past: History, Holocaust, and the German National Identity* (Cambridge: Harvard University Press, 1988), 1–2. For a summary of this conservative intellectual tradition and the debates it engendered see Reich, *The Fruits of Fascism,* 6–19.

11. As an example of German economic imperialism designed to address its raw materials policy see Albert Hirschman, *National Power and the Structure of Foreign Trade* (Berkeley and Los Angeles: University of California Press, 1945) on Nazi German treatment of the Balkan states in the 1930s; as applied to labor see Edward Homze, *Foreign Labor in Nazi Germany* (Princeton: Princeton University Press, 1967); and for a more general argument suggesting that German militarism was a product of a disjointed social structure see Alexander Gerschenkron, *Bread and Democracy in Germany* (Berkeley and Los Angeles: University of California Press, 1943).

12. The original attitude of the participants of the Chequers conference was expressed in "Be nice to the Germans" in *New York Times,* 20 July 1990: for a critique of the "Chequers" view on the Germans, see David Childs and Robert Gerald Living-

ston, "Germany: A Joint Statement," *Politics and Society in Germany, Austria, and Switzerland* 3 (1990): 95–97.

13. The initial, and most famous proponent of this view is Fritz Fischer, *Germany's Aims.* Wehler in *German Empire* makes a similar argument.

14. This issue is discussed by Richard Gott, in an article entitled "State of Anxiety," *Manchester Guardian Weekly,* 7 October 1990, 1, 8.

15. Hermann Kantorowicz, *The Spirit of British Policy and the Myth of the Encirclement of Germany* (Cambridge: Cambridge University Press, 1931).

16. "Kohl pledges Global Role for Germany," *Manchester Guardian Weekly,* 7 October 1990, 1.

17. For example, Germany expanded its percentage of exports from 20.9 to 32.4 percent between 1972 and 1985; France went from 16.7 to 23.9 percent and Italy from 17.7 to 22.8 percent. So the French and Italian rate of expansion was about half the German rate. Britain expanded from 21.8 to 29.1 percent, so it grew approximately two-thirds of Germany's rate. All figures come from *OECD National Accounts: Main Aggregates,* vol. 1, 1960–88 (Paris: O.E.C.D., 1990).

18. Ibid.

19. See Brian Ardy, "The National Incidence of the European Community Budget," *Journal of Common Market Studies* 26 (1988): 408, 410, 413, 415.

20. See Louis Armand and Michel Drancourt, *Le Pari Europeen* (Paris: Fayard, 1968); Gilpin, *U.S. Power,* 240; and Fred Block, *The Origins of International Economic Disorder* (Berkeley and Los Angeles: University of California Press, 1977), 57–60, 68.

21. Gerard Braunthal, *Political Loyalty and Public Service in West Germany: The 1972 Decree against Radicals and Its Consequences* (Amherst: University of Massachusetts Press, 1990).

22. See Carl Lankowski, "*Modell Deutschland* and the International Regionalization of the West German States in the 1970s," in *The Political Economy of West Germany: Modell Deutschland,* ed. Andrei Markovits (New York: Praeger 1982), 93.

23. *Business Eastern Europe,* 3 September 1990, 291 and 23 April 1990, 139.

24. *Business Eastern Europe,* 4 June 1990, 188, 10 April 1990, 116, 117, and 25 June 1990, 212.

25. See German Foreign Ministry, "Förderung der deutschen Sprache in Mittel-Südost- und Osteuropa" (1990, Photocopy); Foreign Ministry, "Deutschschüler in Europa 1982/3–1990" (1990, Photocopy); Foreign Ministry, "Verbreitung und Bedeutung der deutschen Sprache in Osteuropa" (1988, Photocopy); and Foreign Ministry, "Deutsche Sprache und Deutsche Minderheit" (1990, Photocopy).

26. "Will we all have to learn German?" *Financial Times,* 10 March 1990.

27. Thus, even though today's Germany might very well be "peaceable, fearful, green," and "favor a low profile in world affairs," the objective fact is that Germany is in the process of becoming a hegemonic power in Europe and—quite likely—beyond. See "Today's Germans: Peaceable, Fearful—and Green," *Financial Times,* 4 January 1991, 2; and "Germans Reject Wider International Role," *Financial Times,* 4 January 1991, 16.

Germany's Future and Its Unmastered Past

Moishe Postone

The global changes of the recent past have raised the issue of history in two ways. On the one hand, they have raised the "German Question" again. On the other hand, they have placed the problem of historical dynamics, of global transformations, back at the center of political analysis and discourse. These two sets of issues are interrelated.

It is generally recognized that recent events such as the opening of the Berlin Wall (9 November 1989) and the unification of Germany (3 October 1990), the Gulf War (August 1990–February 1991), and the collapse and final dissolution of the Soviet Union (December 1991), have marked the end of an historical era. The period that has come to an end can be considered on a number of different levels.

The past five years can be seen as marking the end of the "Ice Age," of the twenty-year period of political stagnation, in which history was apparently frozen. This stagnation resulted from the successful resistance to fundamental systemic change in East and West following the upheavals of the late 1970s. History now has reemerged manifestly. With the reemergence of history, the cold war has come to a final end—that is, the bipolar postwar world, structured by the confrontation of the United States and the USSR, and materially inscribed in the division of Germany. The United States has emerged victorious in the superpower struggle with the Soviet Union. However, the fifteen years before the collapse of the Soviet Union also witnessed the relative decline of both superpowers vis-à-vis new centers of economic power—Western Europe, centered on Germany, and Japan. The unification of Germany and the Gulf War were rooted in this changing configuration of global power. The end of the postwar period can, then, on one level, be seen as a partial reversal of the outcome of World War II. Germany has reemerged on the stage of world politics as a power.

What has also come to an end (at least in the industrialized world) is

291

Communism, Marxism-Leninism. In that sense, what has also come to an end is a larger historical era, one beginning with World War I.

These major historical developments can be understood within the framework of another, larger epochal change. The twentieth century has seen the rise, the stabilization (after 1945), and the subsequent decline (after 1973) of a global phase of capitalist development, a phase frequently referred to as state-interventionist or, more recently, Fordist capitalism. In this regard, the dramatic events of the past three years can be interpreted as marking the final end of the period characterized by the "primacy of the political" over the economic sphere. The attempt to master the historical dynamic character-istic of capitalism by means of will, as embodied in the apparatuses of the Keynesian state in the West, and the Stalinist party-state in the East, has apparently failed. (An adequate account would require analyzing the nature of the "history" that apparently has resisted such acts of will, but such an account would exceed the bounds of this chapter.)

We find ourselves, then, in a period of flux, of transition, one character-ized by the decline of bipolarity and the reemergence of capitalist great-power competition. This transition is part of a larger structural transforma-tion, entailing the internationalization of financial markets, production, and labor markets, with social, cultural, political, and economic consequences as far-reaching as the earlier transformation from liberal, market-centered capitalism, to state-interventionist, organized capitalism.

The transitional nature of our period has posed serious challenges for oppositional politics. On the one hand, the politics of identity and nature characteristic of many new social movements were informed by the period of historical stagnation in which they were formulated. Such politics have been ill-prepared to respond the reappearance of history. On the other hand, the events of the recent past have also marked the end of a period in which an oppositional standpoint could be grounded in a spatial opposition between existing countries and/or "systems" rather than in historical terms. Such a standpoint was essentially inversely nationalist—whether its locus was the Soviet Union or the Third World. That is, the eruptions of the immediate past have called into question patterns of oppositional discourse that emerged after 1917 as well as newer patterns that were formulated during the 1970s and 1980s.

The general transition we find ourselves in involves a number of rever-sals (e.g., the weakening of the national state) and the resurgence of forms that had been considered historically surpassed (such as the primacy of the market and nationalism). It thereby has called into question any linear con-ceptions of historical development.

This reemergence of the past has a doubled meaning in the case of Germany. As a result of the resurgence of Germany's power, that country is, once again, about to become hegemonic in central and eastern Europe, if by very different means than in the past. This will have great effects on Europe as a whole, and, indeed, on the world. The possible meaning and consequences of Germany's rise to power is, however, inseparable from the Nazi past. The reemergence of the past has this additional meaning in the case of Germany. The end of the postwar period has also been marked by the resurgence of elements of the German past that, a decade ago, many thought had been left behind. The opening of the Berlin Wall on 9 November 1989 dramatically marked the end of the postwar era on both levels—it marked the beginning of a new era, and the reemergence of the past, however refracted its form. That the symbolic unification of the two Germany's was enacted on the anniversary of the Nazi pogrom of 1938 ("Kristallnacht") made manifest, once again, the problematic relation of past and present in Germany.

This relation is at the heart of the analysis of German predominance in Europe outlined by Andrei Markovits and Simon Reich.[1] Arguing that an irreversible historical break occurred in Germany after 1945, Markovits and Reich present a structural argument regarding the political nature of Germany today and its relation to the rest of Europe. They claim that Germany has become fundamentally democratic, that the present global situation is one characterized by the competition of liberal democracies, and that German predominance in Europe will, therefore, have the form of hegemony, rather than direct domination. Their position implicitly maintains that, in spite of recent negative political developments, such as the surge of neo-Nazi activity and xenophobia, Germany is a successful and stable liberal-democratic polity and is not about to change its peaceful economic policies.

I find much of their argument very well taken. Nevertheless, their attempt to inscribe the liberal-democratic character of Germany in an irreversible structural break is, at points, problematic. For example, Markovits and Reich point to postwar Germany's championing of free trade as indicative of its liberal democratic character. However, the necessary relation they posit between free trade and liberal democratic values is not self-evident. Free-trade policies are not always associated with democracy, but are related to a range of factors, as the differences between British trade policies in the nineteenth century and in the interwar period indicate.

A second structural argument they offer seems to depend on the sort of "modernization" thesis (e.g., Gerschenkron's), widespread in the United States in the immediate postwar period, that attributed the imperialist policies of Germany between 1870 and 1945 to the power of prebourgeois social strata. This thesis is questionable, as an analysis of the pan-German movement or of the Naval League, for example, would indicate. And indeed, Markovits and Reich themselves point to the hypernationalist character of the

German bourgeois class before 1945. In so doing, however, they suggest that future German policies will depend more on the political culture of German elites—or, more generally, on the character of political culture in Germany—than on the absence of prebourgeois strata. Political cultures, however, change and, in this regard, some political and cultural developments of the past decade do indeed give cause for concern. There may be little danger of a resurgence of fascism in Germany; nevertheless, it is by no means certain that German political culture has become irreversibly liberal and democratic.

While Markovits and Reich do, then, provide an accurate description of the current relation of Germany to the rest of Europe, and plausibly argue that an important break with the past has occurred, their structural account does not convincingly show that German policies will necessarily continue to be formulated along consensual, peaceful, democratic lines.

The problematic of German power today requires structural approaches on two different levels. It requires an analysis of the global conditions conducive to peaceful expansion and those that promote the creation of closed spheres (which could lead to political and even military competition among the new powers). Such an analysis would not identify peaceful expansion with bourgeois predominance and liberal capitalism in an essentializing manner. On another level, the problematic of German power also requires an approach to the relation of past and present in Germany that could do justice to recent negative political-cultural events as well as to the positive dimensions of postwar German historical development that Markovits and Reich have described. Such an account would neither consider the relation between the past and the present in Germany to be unbroken, nor posit an absolute break between them. I shall briefly outline an approach to this latter sort of account.

The problem of Germany's relation to its past should not be posed first and foremost in an empiricist fashion, namely whether German history can repeat itself. Nor should it be conceptualized too pedagogically and immediately in terms of the "lessons" that can be learned from the past. Rather, the core of the problem has been the degree to which the past has continued to inform the present—even "behind the backs" of the social actors.

A number of recent events and developments suggest that historical reality has existed on two levels in Germany since the war. Very important changes have indeed taken place in the political culture of West Germany since 1945, especially in the late 1960s. Nevertheless, another historical and psychic level, one related to the Nazi past, has continued to exist.[2] This was shown, for example, by the intense and widespread public discussions in Germany elicited by the American television film "Holocaust" in 1979.[3]

Those discussions illuminated retrospectively the nature and extent of post-war denial and revealed now much had been repressed psychically, even after 1968–69. They rendered apparent that historical reality had been bifurcated since the war, and that much of postwar life in Germany had been driven by a flight from history.

For some, this reemergence of history led to renewed attempts to work through that past. For many, however, it led to a kind of reaction. This reaction went hand in hand with a conscious conservative campaign during the past decade to reverse many political-cultural developments that had occurred in the Federal Republic after 1968–69, and to do so by establishing a greater degree of continuity with elements of the German past that had since been discredited. This campaign included such well-known events as the Kohl-Reagan visit to the military cemetery at Bitburg,[4] the Historikerstreit ("historians' controversy") of 1986,[5] as well as the more recent assault on postwar German literature initiated in the form of critiques of Christa Wolf.[6]

At first glance, this campaign does not seem to require a deeper analysis. It appears perfectly straightforward—an attempt by the Right to regain cultural and political hegemony by affirming continuity with the past. Nevertheless, aspects of that conservative campaign suggest that, behind its apparently straightforward character, a level of historical repression continued to operate.

I am referring to the degree to which the new conservatives presented Germany and the Germans during the Third Reich as having been a victim, or a potential one. One example is the law passed in the mid-1980s by the Bundestag implicitly equating the Holocaust and the expulsions of the Germans from the East in 1944–45. This motif of Germany as victim was central to the Historikerstreit. It was expressed most clearly by Ernst Nolte when he argued in the *Frankfurter Allgemeine Zeitung* in 1986 that the Holocaust was essentially defensive. Hitler's "asiatic deed" was impelled by the fear that the Soviets were planning such a "deed" against the Germans.[7] Similarly, Günther Gillessen argued in the same newspaper that the invasion by Nazi Germany of the Soviet Union in 1941 was undertaken in order to prevent an imminent Soviet invasion of Germany.[8] A variation of this theme of victimization was promoted by the official ideology of the GDR, which presented itself as representing the real victims of Nazism.

The identification of Germans and Germany as victim entails a process of reversal. It is not surprising, therefore, that it has been coupled with resentment directed against the Jews. During the controversy surrounding Bitburg, for example, articles appeared in the conservative German press emphasizing Jewish power in the United States, and suggesting that the negative reactions abroad to the Bitburg visit were generated and manipulated by Jews.

It seems plausible that such a reversal is rooted in repressed feelings of guilt, which elicits anger against those responsible—the Jews. As one commentator has put it, "Die Deutschen werden den Juden Auschwitz nie verzeihen" ("The Germans will never forgive the Jews for Auschwitz"). Such repression results in reversal that tends to reintroduce anti-Semitic images of Jewish power and destructive intentions.

While this reversal, coupled with the related theme of German victimization, does not necessarily mean that, on an empirical level, Germany is about to repeat its past, it does raise questions regarding the future development of the political culture of Germany. This is particularly the case because the German Left as well as Left-liberals, who potentially could constitute an oppositional force to the resurgence of German national power, have become, at best, very ineffectual in this regard. This already began to be evident at the time of the Bitburg visit, as well as during the Historikerstreit.

Why has this been the case? I would like to briefly touch upon one dimension of this complex problem—the extent to which the extraparliamentary Left of the late 1960s and its successors became caught in the toils of the very past they rejected.

The Left in postwar Germany has, of course, centrally defined itself in opposition to fascism. Nevertheless, I would argue that processes of repression and acting out have also characterized the Left, that these processes have had a distorting effect on oppositional politics, and that they have hindered the development of more effective opposition within the new Germany.

In the first place, without elaborating the historical course of left-wing analyses of national socialism in postwar Germany, I think it is fair to assert that the treatments of national socialism dominant in the Left blurred the specificity of national socialism. Such theories tended to identify Nazism with capitalism in an unmediated way (or, more recently, conflate it with patriarchy), and treat anti-Semitism as a peripheral aspect of national socialism. Such theories were not confined to Germany. Their general adoption there, however, was overdetermined. Theory served to block, rather than facilitate, a deeper understanding of the specificity of Nazism, anti-Semitism, and the Holocaust.

This process may have been due, in part, to the enormous difficulties on the part of the members of the postwar generation to deal with their parents both as their parents and as members of a nazified society. Whatever its complex grounds, this avoidance of the specificity of the Nazi past went hand in hand with a strong desire on the part of the German New Left for identification with historical victims. That such a process took place can most clearly be seen in the attitudes of the German New Left toward Israel.

As is well known, the New Left in much of the West became anti-Zionist after the 1967 war. Nevertheless, that switch was generally more radical in Germany. No Western Left was as philo-Semitic and pro-Zionist prior to 1967; probably none subsequently identified with the Palestinian cause as strongly. Israel's victory in the war of 1967 gave rise to a process of psychological inversion: the Jews, no longer victims, but victors, became identified with the Nazi past, and the Palestinians became identified as the "Jews." What was termed anti-Zionism went far beyond the bounds of a political and social critique of Israel. Indeed, the very word *Zionism* became as negatively informed as *nazism*.

In a sense, the Germans acted out their own past on the projected stage of the Middle East. The form of anti-Zionism that became very strong after 1967 can, retrospectively, be understood as serving two functions at the same time. On the one hand, because of the identification of Zionism and nazism, the struggle against the former could become the expression of the struggle against the latter, the Nazi past. On the other hand, the image of Zionism that became widespread was one that recapitulated anti-Semitic images. Zionism was not simply criticized as a bad, or objectionable, political program, but as a worldwide, very powerful, and deeply evil conspiracy.

This "doubled" function of anti-Zionism allowed anti-Semitic images to be transported into left-wing consciousness. It thereby—paradoxically—implicitly and unconsciously helped prepare the ground for a sort of reconciliation with the nation. That is, the antifascism that defined the Left and divided it from the Right, became, through the convoluted mediation of a particular form of anti-Zionism, conflated emotionally with the anti-Semitic ideology that once had united (nazified) Germany.

I have suggested that a sign of historical repression, and of the consequent working of the past on the present, has been the need on the part of many in Germany to identify themselves historically as victims—whether directly, as has been the case of the new conservatives, or indirectly as has been the case of the Left, who identify themselves with the victims of nazism, in however convoluted a form.

These two strands implicitly began to converge in the sort of virulent anti-Zionism that equated Jews with Nazis, and identified itself with the victims of Zionism. They have come much closer together recently, in popular reactions to the Gulf War. Many people in the peace movement not only were opposed to the war (a political position I sympathize with), but emotionally identified the bombing of Baghdad with that of Hamburg and Dresden during World War II, and expressed personal, immediate fear of the bombing. These reactions, I would argue, signified that left-wing identification with the victims had finally converged with the new conservative tendency to identify the Germans as victims.

This, however, placed the peace movement very close to the bounds of a newly reimagined national community. I have suggested that the anti-Zionism common within the Western New Left acquired an overdetermined significance in Germany and, behind the backs of the social actors, generated a new version of precisely the ideology against which the postwar German Left had organized itself. Similarly, the anti-Americanism of the New Left, first articulated during the Vietnam War, has come to acquire a different significance. On the one hand, it has begun to express the anticommercialism of romantic anticapitalism, like that directed against England in the past.[9] On the other hand, it has come to allow for the expression of anger against the Western allies for the bombing attacks that, unlike anti-Soviet anger, had been repressed in West Germany. Its significance has thereby been fundamentally transformed from what it had been two decades ago. The point is not, of course, that any critique of Zionism or the United States is objectionable. The full meaning and historical significance of any critical political position is a function of the determinate nature of the critique, as well as of its context.

Already in the 1980s, the peace movement concerned itself exclusively with American power, as if West Germany were a weak, colonized land, instead of (in nonnuclear terms) the second military power in the West. This repeated during the Gulf War. The peace movement has begun to be one of the harbingers of new German national feeling—one that sharply distinguishes itself from the West. This, in turn, creates the possibility of a bridge to neoconservative culture critics and aesthetes who argue that German culture since 1945 has been a truncated and colonized one, and who call for a recovery of Germanness, and of the idea of the nation.

This nationalist reaction seems to have been reinforced by another reversal. The idea that the division of Germany was a punishment for having lost the war was quite widespread before 1989. For many, therefore, the unification of Germany signified a sort of vindication.

As a result of what I have described, oppositional groups are not well positioned to contest possible negative expressions of growing German power. I am suggesting, in other words, that the apparent absence of an effective locus of such opposition within Germany can be understood, in part, as one of the consequences of an unmastered past.

The notion of a two-level relation of the German present to the past, one manifest, the other latent, constituted by processes of historical denial and repression, does not imply that Germany necessarily will develop in a particular direction. It does, however, suggest that the future of Germany, the most powerful country in Europe, will be influenced by the extent to which the past will be mastered, or will continue subterraneously to inform the present.

NOTES

1. See their essay, "Should Europe Fear the Germans?" in this volume.

2. See Dan Diner, "Negative Symbiose: Deutsche und Juden nach Auschwitz," *Babylon: Beiträge zur jüdischen Gegenwart* 1 (October 1986): 9–20. See also Alexander Mitscherlich and Margarete Mitscherlich, *The Inability to Mourn: Principles of Collective Behavior*, trans. Beverly R. Placzek (New York: Grove Press, 1975).

3. For discussions of the reception of the film *Holocaust* in the Federal Republic of Germany and the more general problems of the Holocaust and anti-Semitism, see *New German Critique* 19 (1980); 20 (1980); 21 (1980). Many of those articles were subsequently published in Anson Rabinbach and Jack Zipes, eds., *Germans and Jews since the Holocaust* (New York: Holmes and Meier, 1986).

4. See Geoffrey Hartman, ed., *Bitburg in Moral and Political Perspective* (Bloomington: Indiana University Press, 1986); and M. Postone, "Bitburg: May 5, 1985 and After," *Radical America* 19 (1985): 10–17.

5. Many of the relevant documents of the *Historikerstreit* have been published in one volume, Ernst Reinhard Piper et al., eds., *"Historikerstreit"* (Munich: R. Piper, 1987). See also Charles S. Maier, *The Unmasterable Past: History, Holocaust, and German National Identity* (Cambridge: Harvard University Press, 1988); and Wolfgang Marienfeld, *Der Historikerstreit* (Hannover: Niedesächsische Landeszentrale für Politische Bildung, 1987). For the broader debate about whether national socialism can be historicized, see Dan Diner, ed., *Ist der Nationalsozialismus Geschichte? Zur Historisierung und zum Historikerstreit* (Frankfurt am Main: Fischer Taschenbuch, 1987).

6. See Andreas Huyssen, "After the Wall: The Failure of German Intellectuals," *New German Critique* 52 (1991): 109–43.

7. Ernst Nolte, "Vergangenheit, die nicht vergehen will," *Frankfurter Allgemeine Zeitung*, 6 June 1986.

8. *Frankfurter Allgemeine Zeitung*, 20 August 1986.

9. This argument has also been made by Dan Diner in *Der Krieg der Erinnerungen und die Ordnung der Welt* (Berlin: Rotbuch, 1991).

Germany and European Integration: Understanding the Relationship

Michael G. Huelshoff

It is now commonplace to note that the revolutions of 1989–91 fundamentally changed the international system. The forces unleashed in mid-decade reached heights first in the collapse of Soviet orthodoxy in Eastern Europe in 1989, which facilitated the unification of the Germanys in 1990 and renewed fears of political fragmentation in Eastern Europe. The second peak was reached in the fall and winter of 1991 with the collapse of the Soviet Union. German unification and the end of the Soviet Union have pushed Germany again into the political and economic center of Europe and encouraged German leadership in the post–cold war era. This newfound German leadership takes place in a set of political and economic conditions that has no precedent in modern European history. Not only is Germany busy unifying and rebuilding its influence in eastern Europe at a time when divisive nationalisms are growing in the region, but also Germany is a (if not the) key actor in the European Community (EC) and its programs to complete the internal market, realize monetary union, democratize EC institutions, and expand cooperation on social and foreign policy.

In all instances, Germany has had an important voice in developing new EC initiatives, a voice enhanced by unification and the end of the cold war. For example, the German decision to recognize Croatia and Slovenia, which led the EC to follow suit, has been interpreted as a preliminary sign of Germany's newfound assertiveness in European politics.[1] German leadership was notably evident in the agreement to move toward monetary union at the Maastricht summit in December 1991, and the Germans are taking an active role in the political conflict over its ratification. German leadership is multifaceted, and it is imperative that we understand Germany's relationship with the EC and European integration.

In this chapter, I explore the theory of regional integration to understand German EC policy. There are two standard approaches to regional integra-

301

tion, neofunctionalism and intergovernmentalism, and neither provides a comprehensive framework for understanding Germany and the EC. I will use parts of both theories to inform a model of regional integration that begins with the assumption that a state's domestic and foreign policies are intertwined. This model relies upon analysis of interests, ideology, and institutions to explore the domestic component of regional cooperation. The model's international side relies upon reformulations of neofunctionalism and intergovernmentalism, which emphasize group and elite politics in interstate negotiations. This discussion will be shaped around analysis of the German polity, although the model can in principle be applied elsewhere. The essay concludes with a short case study of EC social policy making which demonstrates the usefulness of the model.

Neofunctional and Intergovernmental Integration Theory

The dominant school of integration theory, neofunctionalism, argued that the process of integration itself generates more cooperation and integration.[2] Spillover, or the linking of functionally specific tasks, occurred when "imbalances created by the functional interdependence or inherent linkages of tasks . . . press political actors to redefine their goals."[3] The transformation of elite and group allegiances from the nation-state to the region encouraged spillover, as did regional institutions.[4] As the implications of the 1965–66 French boycott of the EC became increasingly clear to scholars, some sought to balance spillover with other concepts within a decidedly neofunctionalist framework, to argue that spillover had not led to the creation of the Common Market, or that only limited forms of spillover were present in the EC.[5] Haas argued that actors' motives, perceptions, and objectives had changed, undermining the incrementalist logic of spillover, and that external influences, mostly ignored by the theory, had grown. The institutions that were to result from integration were not strong enough to cope with these changes.[6]

The 1992 project has renewed academic interest in neofunctionalism.[7] Yet as neofunctionalism failed to offer an empirically-based explanation for events in Europe during the 1960s and 1970s, and it remains unhelpful. First, neofunctionalism must be stretched to explain the failures to cooperate in the EC (if offering an account for the successes), and more significantly it can not explain the plethora of outcomes in the EC that fall between success and failure.[8] Second, by emphasizing the role of the Commission, neofunctional explanations point to the EC's formal policy-initiation process without capturing its politics, and the nation-state's continued domination of decision-making.[9] Despite the oft-noted growth in the Commission's influence under the leadership of Jacques Delors, neofunctionalism is incapable of balancing the policy-initiating powers of the Commission with the continued role of nation-states as gate-keepers, both in the Council of Ministers and the European Council.[10] Third, neofunctionalism underemphasizes the bargaining among members that results in tradeoffs among their interests, nor does neofunctionalism explain the full breadth of members' domestic politics, which shapes their positions in EC bargaining. Neofunctionalism therefore cannot help us to understand the ways domestic German politics affects its EC policy.[11] Despite these weaknesses, neofunctionalism's emphasis upon groups and elites—if inappropriately seen as easily transferring their allegiances from national capitals to Brussels—reminds us that the state cannot be viewed as a unitary actor in EC politics.[12]

A realist critique was leveled at neofunctionalism almost as soon as it came to dominate integration studies.[13] Intergovernmentalism, the second common theory of regional integration, rests upon the assumptions of realist international relations theory, including international anarchy, the central role of states as actors which derive their interests from the structure of the international system, the indivisibility of national interests, and a hierarchy of issues captured by the terms "high" and "low" politics.[14] The primary empirical focus in intergovernmentalism is upon coalition-building in the EC. Relations between France and Germany have received the most attention.[15] German money to modernize French agriculture, in exchange for German access to French manufactures markets, was a cornerstone of the Treaties of Rome in 1957. Beginning with at least the Schmidt-Giscard governments, the French and Germans coordinated bilateral and EC policy. Finally, intergovernmentalism's assumptions of states as unitary and gate-keeping actors in the EC led to reconsideration of the goal of the EC, moving the debate away from political union to loose cooperation.[16] Some scholars have used intergovernmentalism to understand the 1987 Single European Act (SEA).[17]

Intergovernmentalism reminds us of the role of national governments as gate-keepers in the EC, but the approach has experienced difficulty systematically explicating the components of national interest, or in other words the domestic politics of EC policy-making in member states. Additionally, the assumed centrality of states as actors in international politics was heavily attacked by the interdependence school.[18] The neoliberal institutionalists, the successors to interdependence, critique of realism in ways that are relevant to intergovernmentalism. Realism assumes that the international system is anarchic, and that states must ultimately protect themselves. This infers a relative gains motivation for states in international bargaining, or that states pursue foreign policies that are designed to enhance their interests and capabilities more than they enhance the interests and capabilities of others.[19] The relative gains assumption leads to the observation that international cooperation, including regional integration, is rare.

Neoliberal institutionalists have countered with two related arguments. First, they contend that repeated or structured interaction leads states to learn to cooperate, overcoming international anarchy.[20] Second, the neoliberals have asserted that states are often motivated by absolute gains, or the pursuit of foreign policies that benefit themselves with little reference to the benefits of others. They have argued that the relative gains motivation holds only under very specific conditions, many of which do not apply to the EC.[21] Thus, the prospects for regional integration are much better than the realists assume.

In sum, neofunctionalism emphasizes elites, groups, and group politics, but it must be shorn of the determinism which leads it to de-emphasize the state as a venue of decision-making. Intergovernmentalism reinforces the state as the prime actor in regional integration, but is unable to systematically analyze the domestic sources of the motivations of states in regional integration, and pessimistically predicts little regional integration. These predictions are out of synch with developments in the EC over the past few years, and neither approach clarifies the impacts of German domestic politics on its relation to the EC. We need a model which can both organize domestic politics and link them to intergovernmental bargaining.

Domestic and Intergovernmental Politics in the EC

Linking domestic and international politics is an old theme in political science, but it remains an underdeveloped field. There have been several attempts to link domestic politics and intergovernmentalism in the regional integration literature, including Puchala's study of fiscal harmonization in the EC.[22] Yet Puchala assumes that the domestic political systems of members are uniformly pluralistic, limiting the descriptive and analytic power of the domestic side of Puchala's model. Bulmer applies a policy styles model to the study of German EC policy.[23] Policy styles, however, assumes that the significant elements of a state's domestic politics are unique, and it fails to suggest specific linkages between the domestic and international systems. As Putnam argues in "Diplomacy and Domestic Politics: The Logic of Two-Level Games," it is now commonplace to note that these linkages exist, but few have actually modeled them.[24] Additionally, the assumption that each state's domestic politics are invariate or unique ignores recent theorizing on the state and interest groups. For the remainder of this chapter, I will argue for a theory of regional integration that begins with Putnam's two-level game metaphor, but which expands upon the metaphor to take account of the domestic context of EC policy-making, organized around interests, ideology, and institutions. The argument is cast in terms of our understanding of German EC policy. Finally, I will demonstrate the usefulness of the model in a case study of the 1989 Social Charter. Putnam begins with a simple metaphor: decision-makers can be seen to be involved in two interlinked sets of negotiations or games. One negotiation takes place among nation-states, at the intergovernmental level. Yet Putnam notes that the agreements possible among states are highly constrained by what is acceptable to a range of domestic groups. In the other game, decision-makers are said to seek power via coalitions among domestic groups, which in turn attempt to protect and enhance their interests. In the international game, decision-makers are motivated to "satisfy domestic pressures, while minimizing the adverse consequences of foreign developments."[25] The domestic game, therefore, takes precedence over the international game.

Regional integration, from the viewpoint of this perspective, is the pursuit by decision-makers of domestic power via (when the opportunity arises) regional agreements which meet the demands of enough domestic groups to guarantee ratification and the political survival of the decision-maker. This conceptualization of integration has much in common with intergovernmentalism, but relaxes intergovernmentalism's assumption that states are unitary actors motivated by single national interests, and the assertion that states pursue relative gains. The possibility of agreement is, in Putnam's terms, limited by the overlap of what is acceptable to winning coalitions (large enough to guarantee ratification) in each of the twelve members of the EC. This area is called a "win-set." Larger win-sets mean more possibilities for agreement, but also less bargaining power. As Putnam explains, negotiators with small win-sets can present credible "take it or leave it" positions to their opposite numbers.

Putnam introduces a variety of variables which affect win-sets. I shall focus on two groups: domestic politics (including interests and ideology) and domestic institutions.

German Domestic Politics and European Integration

European integration, more so than other forms of international cooperation, occurs in a political context which places high value on cooperation. Yet what precisely has motivated states to cooperate in Europe, has clearly varied across states and over time. Charles de Gaulle, for example, envisioned a Europe led by France, or the EC as an extension of French foreign policy. François Mitterrand has certainly changed the means through which de Gaulle's goal is to be reached, and arguably changed the goal itself. The Benelux countries see the EC as a mechanism to maintain their influence with larger neighbors. Spain, Portugal, and Greece are largely motivated by development needs, and the British have been reluctant members since 1973.

As is true of each EC member, German interests in European integration reflect historical, political, and economic constraints and opportunities. Unlike many other members, though, the German constitution (Grundgesetz, or Basic Law) includes a clause requiring the state to pursue European integration. Postwar German leaders saw the European movement as one strategy to gain trust in Europe, and overcome the legacies of the expansionism and political extremism that marked much of German politics from unification in 1871 until 1945. Economic gains from European integration reinforced pursuit of political goals. German trade with EC countries grew rapidly after 1958, and continues to expand. Between 1984 and 1989, the share of German exports going to other EC states grew from 49.9 percent to 55 percent. The first four largest markets for German exports, and five of the largest six markets, were in EC states. 39.3 percent of German direct foreign investment in 1988 was directed to the EC, up from 32.3 percent in 1984. The next largest target for German investment was the US, with 26.9 percent of total German direct foreign investment in 1988.[26]

With these strong political and economic interests, it is not surprising that Germany supports further integration along free market lines. Yet German backing of free European markets is also predicated upon the success of postwar liberal economic philosophy in Germany, the "social market economy," and its antecedents.[27] Although there were continuities between prewar and postwar models in the German economy,[28] since the mid-1960s German coalition governments of both the center-Left and center-Right have often been unwilling to support ailing industries, designate national champions, or restructure industries to the degree that is common elsewhere in Europe.[29] Further, state intervention in markets is limited, often relies on self-regulation, and is cooperative rather than confrontational. The German resistance to overtly dirigiste tendencies in the EC is predicated in part on the German domestic experience.[30]

There is broad mass support for European integration in Germany, but it is tinged with a degree of ambivalence.[31] With the exception of the Greens and some right-wing groups, the political parties also back European integration. While some German business groups were skeptical of the EC at the signing of the Treaties of Rome in 1957, they changed their minds once the benefits of easier access to European markets were not seen to come at the expense of German trade interests outside Europe.[32] The 1992 program has re-invigorated German business' endorsement of integration, which had slowly waned during the 1970s. Business remains actively behind completion of the internal market, although its expectations are not particularly high partly because German firms are already competitive in many European markets.[33] Business leaders also identify problems with 1992, including the Commission's apparent inability to police subsidies, and likely sector adjustment problems.[34] Union attitudes are a little more complex, reflecting splits between the accommodationist and activist segments of the union move-ment.[35] Regardless, both groups are resigned to the inevitability of 1992, either more or less willingly depending upon their perception of their relation to capital and capitalism.[36]

In Germany, European integration has led to debate about German fed-eralism, and the powers of German political institutions.[37] The debate fo-cuses upon the apparent and potential loss of sovereignty and policy-making initiative to European institutions which suffer from an oft-noted democratic deficit. Additionally, German unification renewed discussion within both Germany and Europe over the proper German role in the EC. Germans themselves have complained that their political leaders do not exercise Ger-man influence to its fullest.[38] The likelihood of German unification in the winter of 1989–90 reaffirmed long-standing debates about Germany and Europe, and even temporarily forced a wedge between France and Germany, close EC allies. The German and EC recognition of Croatia and Slovenia, is a preliminary sign of Germany's new-found leadership.

In sum, there is a broad mass and elite coalition in Germany backing European integration. It is based upon both German interests and values, which disposes the German domestic debate toward cooperation in the EC, and results in German support for further integration. The German domestic debate also raises important concerns about the EC's commitment to free trade and markets, and democratic decision-making. The recent uneasiness in Germany over potential European monetary union and the loss of deutsche mark stability may, however, be an indication of the beginnings of a more critical debate about German participation in the EC. To date, however, the continued uncertainty about the future of the Maastricht treaty has limited this debate.

German Domestic Institutions and European Integration

Putnam's discussion of domestic institutions focuses primarily upon the poli-tics of ratifying agreements worked out in the international game. The extent to which domestic institutions affect starting points in international bargain-ing is minimized. Putnam does discuss the impact of preliminary consulta-tions to soften up constituents and improve bargaining power in international negotiations by politicizing issues, but cautions that such steps often fail "to project an implacable image abroad" and may generate "irreversible effects on constituents' attitudes" by stirring up the domestic political cauldron.[39]

Logically, preliminary consultations can have precisely the opposite effect: by lining up domestic support, the negotiator can present other nego-tiators with a domestic "united front," and in turn pressure domestic groups to accept the outcomes of international negotiations. What will distinguish cases where preliminary consultations weaken the bargainer's position from cases where preliminary consultations strengthen the bargainer's position, is the range of groups included in the consultations, the ability of negotiators to punish defection, and the ability of the state to resist domestic pressure. Putnam's cautions about involving domestic groups in preliminary consultations is most applicable to pluralist interest group orders, where decision-makers are more likely to be initially "captured" by relatively narrow domestic groups, avoid politicization in fear of divisive domestic debates, need to reach out to include other groups at ratification, and hence have few mechanisms to punish defectors.

The observations are not as applicable in corporatist domestic orders where preliminary consultations are structured to include diverse domestic interests, but also to defuse domestic dissension, and where the state and the peak associations can impose costs upon later defectors. While both corporatist and pluralist domestic orders have elements of both cooperation and conflict, conflicts occur generally less often, and are often less intense, in corporatism than in pluralism.

Corporatism is a controversial concept in political science. Germany is often characterized as falling toward (but not at) the cooperative end of a pluralist-corporatist continuum, in societal (mode of policy-making) rather than state (institutional structure) terms.[40] The regular "EC summits" in Germany which bring together major domestic groups to discuss EC policy are an example of German societal corporatism. The German win-set on most EC issues is likely to be large, because to satisfy these diverse groups, the policies the domestic agreements advocate must be broad. Their breadth, in turn, allows the state some room to bargain. The discussions among German interest groups about EC policy also tend to eliminate the more extreme and parochial positions of the groups, as they strive to find compromises among themselves. These domestic compromises encouraged by German corporatism are more likely to fall within the win-sets of other states if the extreme positions are eliminated, if the breadth of domestic agreement gives the German state some bargaining room, and if domestic groups push the state to play the intergovernmental game. Further, the costs of defection from domestic agreements are high, because the state in corporatism can punish defectors. Finally, as Putnam notes large win-sets translate into little bargaining power, offering another explanation for those who have noted the seeming ineffectiveness of the FRG in EC politics.[41]

The organization of the German federal government itself also encourages cooperative decision-making. The German state is often characterized as weak or semi-sovereign, for several reasons.[42] First, German policy-making is sectoralized, meaning that relatively independent federal ministries have close associations with relevant interest groups. Further, para-public institutions "merge public and private bureaucracies," leading to additional public input on policy administration and implementation.[43] German federalism, as well, guarantees a role for Länder (state) governments in the policy process, although many Länder often complain that EC decisions are taken over their heads. Finally, the prevalence of two-party coalitions broadens the diversity of input in policy-making, and it is also not uncommon for chancellors to seek informal agreement with opposition parties on particularly controversial issues. Yet by including such diverse opinions in decision-making, the federal government also enjoys a degree of influence over them. The groups become part of the collective decision, and can be excluded from future decision-making if the groups fail to support the agreement.

These observations are about process, and one should not assume that the Germans begin each policy debate with the goal of enhancing European integration. Regardless, the broad public support for regional integration in Germany, cooperative decision-making encouraged by a highly penetrated state, and the ability of interest groups and the state to punish defection, suggests the hypothesis that in most cases the German domestic game will result in a consensus favoring regional cooperation, although on terms consistent with German ideology and interests. In sum, the Germans are generally "good Europeans" in part because their values and interests run in that direction, and in part because the state encourages cooperative decision-making that reduces the likelihood of the "state capture" by narrow interests (more likely in pluralist domestic orders), and increases the number of mechanisms to punish defection.

Domestic-IR Interactions

Now we turn to the international game. Neofunctionalism's emphasis upon spillover, encouraged by elites, groups, and regional organizations, captures part of the international game. The importance of elites in encouraging or restricting cooperation has long been noted in the field, but the evidence suggests that most Euro-pressure groups have limited influence in EC politics. While most of these data are pre-SEA, they indicate that at best the Euro-groups help to politicize issues.[44] The nation-state remains the primary point of lobbying. Finally, while regional institutions also help to politicize issues (this has been one of Jacques Delors main contributions to European integration), the Councils remain the main focus of integration-expanding decision-making in the EC. In each instance, elite, group, and institutional, regional actors play important roles that nonetheless fall short of the predictions of neofunctionalism. Yet it is clear that a certain momentum has characterized the EC recently, and that these actors help to maintain a highly constrained version of spillover.

Additionally, intergovernmentalism, revised to consider absolute gains and multiple national interests, offers a useful description of inter-state bargaining in the EC. Putnam points to the potential tradeoffs among issues in international negotiations which can add groups to the winning coalition at home. He emphasizes the importance of side payments—realized in either the international or domestic game—in expanding win-sets, and the need to target these side payments at wavering groups at home or abroad.

Evidence of such tradeoffs abounds in the EC, especially in the European Council. Most recently, at Maastricht in December 1991, political influence over the conditions necessary to move to monetary union was linked with agreement to strengthen the veto powers of the European Parliament, the diversion of more funds to southern members, and action on social policy. The limited scope of most of the Commission's policy proposals reduces the range of similar tradeoffs and side-payments in the Council of Ministers. Yet exemptions have been used in much the same way, for example in temporary auto emissions exemptions for small (primarily French and Italian) automobiles.[45] The frequent use of side-payments and tradeoffs underscores the positive-sum, absolute gains dimension of EC politics. Seen from the perspective of two-level games, the frequent use of side-payments in the EC is understandable in ways that intergovernmental theories of regional integration capture only incompletely.

What is lacking at the intergovernmental level is a formal treatment of coalition building in the EC. Yet the secrecy of Council debates and votes suggests that it is problematic that we can apply coalition theory successfully, even with the growing frequency of qualified majority voting in the Council of Ministers. To move beyond this impasse, we must reconstruct states' bargaining positions by analyzing their domestic politics, including goals and preferences, and institutions of policy-making. The following case study demonstrates the domestic/international model developed here.

German Domestic Politics and EC Policy-Making: The 1989 Social Charter

To demonstrate the impact of German domestic politics on its EC policy-making, we examine the case of the EC's 1989 Social Charter. Social issues were originally neglected in the EC because there were great differences in social policy among states.[46] Social policy was expected by some of the signatories of the Treaties of Rome to be a prime candidate for spillover, although social issues and problems were not seen to be acute in 1958.[47] The stagflation and social conflict of the 1970s encouraged a Social Policy Action Programme in 1974, yet as was true of much EC policy-making during the decade, social policy-making was slow, and often resulted in vague regulations and recommendations which were unevenly implemented.[48] Significant for the Germans, proposals to strengthen corporatist-style tripartite consultation in Community decision-making failed, as did proposals to encourage European-level works councils. The EC's legislative record on social policy is small, and is positively minuscule compared to the huge volume of market-oriented EC regulations.

The 1985 proposals to complete the internal market reaffirmed the need for stronger social policy coordination among EC members, to avoid social dumping and deterioration of the existing divisions of labor and wealth in the EC.[49] The European Trade Union Confederation (ETUC), whose members include both EC and non-EC trade unions, lobbied for a social dimension in the original proposals to complete the internal market in 1985, while the Union of Industries of the European Community (UNICE) saw the inclusion of social issues in the SEA as secondary to completion of the internal market. German business associations expressed similar doubts about the likelihood of significant social dumping.[50]

Yet there were few social policy provisions in the SEA. This negligence fueled the debate about the EC's social deficit, including conflict over the political implications of a continuing social shortfall. The Commission proposed in 1988 to strengthen EC social policy via a European Social Charter.[51] The debate between the ETUC and UNICE focused upon, most prominantly, whether a Social Charter was or was not necessary, and if so whether or not it would be binding. Hence, neofunctional group politics helped to politicize the need for a social policy, but also revealed strong differences among the groups over what kind of policy was needed.

When the French took over the Council presidency in the second half of 1989, President Mitterrand indicated that completion of a Social Charter was at the top of his political agenda. It quickly became clear, though, that a binding Social Charter would not be possible by the end of the French tenure in the presidency. Rather than wait and build up support for a binding agreement, as the Germans were suggesting, President Mitterrand went ahead.[52] Official German reaction was muted, although privately the Germans were quite displeased with the French decision.[53] The French decision helped sharpen political conflict in Germany.

German support for EC social policy is based on compromises worked out among capital, labor, and the state. In Germany the ratification of the SEA in 1987 set off a sharp political debate over the EC's social deficit among German trade unionists, and between the unions and business.[54] From the point of view of the Federation of German Trade Unions (Deutscher Gewerkschaftsbund, DGB), completion of the internal market would be politically possible only when the social dimension of the EC was also developed.[55] German business, like their European counterparts, supported nonbinding minimum standards for EC social policy, but rejected DGB calls for qualitative equalization of social conditions in Europe.[56]

Encouraged by Bonn, the DGB and the Federation of German Employers' Associations (Bundesvereinigung der Deutsche Arbeitsgeberverbände, BDA) issued a joint statement on EC social policy and the Social Charter in July 1989.[57] Yet strong differences of opinion continued between the leaders of Germany industry and the unions. The federal government sought compromise between capital and labor. Chancellor Kohl called for the maintenance of differences in social standards if necessary, to avoid lowest-common-denominator solutions. During the second national conference over EC policy in Bonn in August 1989, Kohl pushed capital and labor to develop common positions on EC matters, especially the European-wide adoption of German-style codetermination.[58] He sided with the unions against business in support of binding minimum social standards in the Social Charter, but was criticized for failing to specifically support key union demands.[59] Thus, the German government, driven by the need to find domestic compromises between capital and labor, lobbied the French to try to complete a binding Social Charter.

Such an agreement was in German interests, as raising European social standards to the German level would have improved German competitiveness in European markets. While German business made it clear that it preferred a nonbinding Charter, it was clearly in a stronger competitive position than its major European allies if EC social standards were harmonized up. Further, harmonization at high levels was broadly consistent with the thrust of postwar German industrial relations, which had resulted in a high level of protection for German workers. Finally, an agreement on social policy would have been politically rewarding to the conservative Kohl government, which had weakened some German work laws since winning the 1983 election, and which was facing what looked at that time to be a difficult election in 1990.

The Charter of Fundamental Social Rights was approved by eleven EC members (excluding the United Kingdom) in December 1989.[60] The Charter was non-binding. The result pleased neither the ETUC, German unions, nor Chancellor Kohl, yet the Germans voted for the Charter. Chancellor Kohl was able to convince union leaders to accept a nonbinding charter because that was all that was politically possible at the time. Kohl exposed union leaders to the implications of their rejection of the nonbinding Charter—no Charter at all—and won their grudging acquiescence. This was possible— and even necessary—because the unions were included in policy-making. Symbolic progress toward a social Europe was judged to be better than no progress at all. When it became clear that a nonbinding Charter was likely, the Germans offered their plan to implement it even before the December 1989 vote, which followed the Commission's planned Action Programme.[61]

The German government's push to seek to implement the Charter, even before it was signed, is an example of the judicious use of domestic side-payments to guarantee ratification. Further, the German government supported inclusion of social policy in the Maastricht treaty, and won a curious agreement to apply qualified majority voting rules and use EC institutions to harmonize social policy among all EC members but the U.K.

In the Social Charter case, we see examples of all approaches to integration at work. Neofunctionalism and intergovernmentalism point out the roles of transnational interest groups, elites, and national interest in developing the Social Charter. Yet a full explanation can only be achieved by looking at domestic politics. Only then can we understand the German willingness to accept a nonbinding Charter. Additionally, we see domestic institutions (cooperative decision-making) and domestic goals (further integration) working together to push the Germans toward support for the 1989 Social Charter. By including unions and business into the decision-making, the state was forced to find a solution that was acceptable to both domestic groups—a non-binding Charter, but also a proposal for implementation and linkage to future negotiations—and acceptable to enough other EC members to move ahead.

Conclusion

I have argued here for a model of European integration which explicitly links domestic politics to intergovernmental bargaining, via the two-level game metaphor. This model helps us to understand integrative processes more fully than do its rivals, neofunctionalism and intergovernmentalism, by linking members' domestic interests, ideology, and institutions to their bargaining positions in the EC. Thus, this model accounts for the complexity of demands that states bring to intergovernmental bargaining, suggesting the relevance of interest (the German economic needs), ideology (the German need to win friends in Europe, support for free markets, and protection for workers), and structure (corporatism and cooperative decision-making) variables in determining these bargaining positions. Further, the model points to the positive-sum, absolute gains motivations of the states in EC negotiations.

Examining linkages between German domestic politics and intergovernmental bargaining in the EC suggests two observations about German EC politics. First, the broad mass and elite backing for European integration has to date pushed the German polity toward cooperation. That is, German domestic politics generally favors more over less European integration. Yet there is no guarantee that this distribution of values and interests is fixed. Second, the way German positions on EC issues are developed encourages inclusion of a broad range of opinions, which while eliminating extreme positions also requires the resulting bargaining position to be large. Decision-making processes may prove to be a partial brake on a German drift out of the EC. The German proclivity to be "good Europeans," therefore, results from German interests, values, institutions, and decision-making procedures. While these factors do not preclude renewed German independence in Europe, they do make such independence politically difficult, and should provide plenty of warning if united Germany begins to reconsider its constitutional ties to Europe.

NOTES

1. See, for example, Leslie H. Gelb, "Tomorrow's Germany," *New York Times,* 22 December 1991, sec. A; Stephen Kinzer, "Germany Jostles Post-Soviet Europe," *New York Times,* 27 December 1991, sec. A; M. Lind, "Recognize the Power of the New Germany," *New York Times,* 27 December 1991, sec. A; C. R. Whitney, "As Germany Flexes Its Muscles, The New Europe Goes Along," *New York Times,* 29 December 1991, sec. A; Stephen Kinzer, "Europe, Backing Germans, Accepts Yugoslav Breakup," *New York Times,* 16 January 1992, sec. A; and J. Tagliabue, "How to Be Europe's Big Power Without Awakening the Old Fears," *New York Times,* 2 February 1992, sec. A.

2. For representative early neofunctionalists, see Ernst B. Haas, "International Integration: The European and Universal Process," *International Organization* 15 (1961): 366–92, and *Beyond the Nation-State* (Stanford: Stanford University Press, 1964); Leon N. Lindberg, *The Political Dynamics of European Economic Integration* (Stanford: Stanford University Press, 1963), and "The European Community as a Political System," *Journal of Common Market Studies* 5 (1967): 344–87. For a recent discussion of spillover, see Wayne Sandholtz and John Zysman, "1992: Recasting the European Bargain," *World Politics* 42 (1989): 95–128.

3. Joseph S. Nye, "Comparing Common Markets: A Revised Neofunctional Model," in *Regional Integration: Theory and Research,* ed. Leon N. Lindberg and Stuart S. Scheingold (Cambridge: Harvard University Press, 1971), 200.

4. Ernst B. Haas, *The Uniting of Europe: Political, Economic, and Social Forces* (Stanford: Stanford University Press, 1958), see also the preface to the 1968 edition; Lindberg, *Political Dynamics;* and Leon N. Lindberg, "Integration as a Source of Stress on the European Community System," *International Organization* 20 (1966): 233–65. On regional institutions, see the review in Jeppe Tranholm-Mikkelsen, "Neo-Functionalism: Obstinate or Obsolete? A Reappraisal in the Light of the New Dynamism of the EC," *Millennium* 20 (1991): 1–22.

5. Joseph S. Nye, *Peace in Parts: Integration and Conflict in Regional Organization* (Boston: Little, Brown, 1971); Leon N. Lindberg and Stuart A. Scheingold, *Europe's Would-Be Polity* (Englewood Cliffs, N.J.: Prentice-Hall, 1970); and Stephen George, *Politics and Policy in the European Community,* (Oxford: Clarendon, 1985). George argued that functional spillover was common in the EC, but that spillover

caused by groups and elites (political) and regional institutions (cultivated) was not. Lodge and Pentland found that there is little evidence that groups and elites were reorienting themselves from the nation-state to the EC. See Juliet Lodge, "Loyalty and the EEC: The Limitations of the Functionalist Approach," *Political Studies* 26 (1978): 232–48; and Charles C. Pentland, *International Theory and European Integration* (London: Faber and Faber, 1973).

6. Ernst B. Haas, *The Obsolescence of Regional Integration Theory,* Research Series no. 25, Institute of International Studies, (Berkeley and Los Angeles: University of California Press, 1975). Much the same argument has been made by Roy Pryce and Wolfgang Wessels, "The Search for an Ever Closer Union: A Framework for Analysis," in *The Dynamics of European Union,* ed. Roy Pryce (London: Croom Helm, 1987). Others criticized neofunctionalism for its inflexibility, and for its dependence upon stable economic growth. See R. Kaiser, "Toward the Copernican Phase of Regional Integration Theory," *Journal of Common Market Studies* 10 (1972): 207–32; Leon Hurwitz, *The European Community and the Management of International Cooperation* (New York: Greenwood, 1987); and Juergen B. Donges, *What Is Wrong with the European Communities,* Institute of Economic Affairs Occasional Papers no. 59 (London, 1981). On the issue of stable growth, see George, *Politics and Policy.*

7. On monetary spillover, see Paul Taylor, "The New Dynamics of EC Integration in the 1980s," in *The European Community and the Challenge of the Future,* ed. Juliet Lodge (New York: St. Martin's, 1989), 3–25. On social policy spillover, see Juliet Lodge, "Social Europe: Fostering a People's Europe," in Lodge, *European Community,* 303–18; and Tranholm-Mikkelsen, "Neo-Functionalism." Keohane and Hoffmann argue that limited versions of spillover might again be found in the "relaunched" EC. See Robert O. Keohane and Stanley Hoffmann, "Institutional Change in Europe in the 1980s," in *The New European Community: Decisionmaking and Institutional Change,* ed. Robert O. Keohane and Stanley Hoffmann (Boulder, Colo.: Westview, 1991), 1–40.

8. Carole Webb, "Theoretical Perspectives and Problems," in *Politics and Policy-Making in the European Communities,* ed. Helen Wallace, William Wallace, and Carole Webb, 2d. ed. (London: John Wiley, 1983).

9. Keohane and Hoffmann, "Institutional Change."

10. For a discussion of the gatekeeping role of nation-states in the environmental field, see Michael G. Huelshoff and Thomas Pfeiffer, "Environmental Policy in the EC: Neo-Functionalist Sovereignty Transfer or Neo-Realist Gate-Keeping?" *International Journal* 47 (Winter 1991–92): 136–58.

11. In one of the original neofunctionalist formulations, Haas noted that the key political conditions for spillover included the division of Germany, and the recognition of this division in the minds of German elites. See Haas, *Uniting of Europe.* Yet the relevance of German division in EC politics had been on the decline for some time before unification in 1990, as the two German states learned to accomodate their division, and as the West Germans became increasingly unwilling and unable to financially underwrite the EC.

12. Evidence has been found, for example, demonstrating the significance of domestic groups and group politics in German EC policy. See Simon Bulmer and

William Patterson, *The Federal Republic of Germany and the European Community* (London: Allen and Unwin, 1987). Further evidence of the role of elites in the politics leading to the SEA is found by Sandholtz and Zysman, "1992."

13. Stanley Hoffmann, "Obstinate or Obsolete? The Fate of the Nation-State and the Case of Western Europe," *Daedalus* 95 (1966): 862–915. See also Paul Taylor, *The Limits of European Integration* (New York: Columbia University Press, 1983).

14. Webb, "Theoretical Perspectives and Problems," 22, 26–27.

15. Helen Wallace, "The Conduct of Bilateral Relationships by Governments," in *Partners and Rivals in Western Europe,* ed. R. Morgan and C. Bray (Aldershot: Gower, 1986); Haig Simonian, *The Privileged Partnership: Franco-German Relations in the European Community 1969–1984* (Oxford: Clarendon, 1985). Wallace has also speculated on the growing importance of the United Kingdom in coalition building. See Helen Wallace, "Negotiations and Coalition Formation in the European Community," *Government and Opposition* 20 (1985): 453–72.

16. Puchala, for example, proposed the notion of concordance systems of loose cooperation among states as an alternative to integration. See Donald J. Puchala, "Of Blind Men, Elephants, and International Integration," *Journal of Common Market Studies* 10 (1972): 267–84.

17. Moravcsik, "Negotiating the Single European Act," in Keohane and Hoffmann, *New European Community,* 41–84. Cameron finds evidence of both neofunctionalism and intergovernmentalism in the politics of the SEA. See David R. Cameron, "The 1992 Initiative: Causes and Consequences," in *Euro-Politics: Institutions and Policy-Making in the "New" European Community,* ed. Alberta M. Sbragia (Washington, D.C.: Brookings, 1992), 23–74.

18. See Robert O. Keohane and Joseph S. Nye, *Power and Interdependence: World Politics in Transition* (Boston: Little, Brown, 1977); Webb, "Theoretical Perspectives and Problems."

19. See Joseph M. Grieco, *Cooperation among Nations: Europe, America, and Non-Tariff Barriers to Trade* (Ithaca: Cornell University Press, 1990). See also Kenneth Waltz, *Theory of International Politics* (Reading, Mass: Addison-Wesley, 1979); Kenneth Waltz, "Reflections on *Theory of International Politics:* A Response to My Critics," in *Neorealism and Its Critics,* ed. Robert O. Keohane (New York: Columbia University Press, 1986); Robert Gilpin, "The Richness of the Tradition of Political Realism," in Keohane, *Neorealism and Its Critics;* and Robert Gilpin, *War and Change in World Politics* (Cambridge: Cambridge University Press, 1981).

20. For a full review of the neoliberal and neorealist positions, see Helen Milner, "International Theories of Cooperation among Nations: Strengths and Weaknesses," *World Politics* 44 (1992): 466–96.

21. Snidal has argued that relative gains applies only under conditions of tight bipolarity and is not relevant if states are motivated at least in part by absolute gains, if the initial interaction among states is not prisoner's dilemma, or if there are more than two actors in the system. See Duncan Snidal, "Relative Gains and the Pattern of International Cooperation," *American Political Science Review* 85 (1991): 701–26. Powell argues that relative gains apply only in cases where the costs of conflict are low. See Robert Powell, "Absolute and Relative Gains in International Relations

Theory," *American Political Science Review* 85 (1991): 1316.

22. Donald J. Puchala, *Fiscal Harmonization in the European Communities* (London: Frances Pinter, 1984).

23. Simon Bulmer, "Domestic Politics and European Community Policy-Making," *Journal of Common Market Studies* 21 (1983): 349–63. The policy-styles concept was introduced by Jeremy Richardson. See Jeremy Richardson, ed., *Policy Styles in Western Europe* (London: Allen and Unwin, 1982).

24. Robert D. Putnam, "Diplomacy and Domestic Politics: The Logic of Two-Level Games," *International Organization* 42 (1988): 427–60. Garrett analyzes the interaction of domestic and regional politics in a study of the SEA, but does not fully articulate a model. See Geoffrey Garrett, "International Cooperation and Institutional Choice: The European Community's Internal Market," *International Organization* 46 (1992): 533–60.

25. Putnam, "Diplomacy and Domestic Politics," 434.

26. Trade and investment data are from Statistisches Bundesamt, *Statistisches Jahrbuch 1990 fur die Bundesrepublik Deutschland* (Stuttgart: Metzler-Poeschel, 1990), various tables. Data for 1989 are estimates. Author's calculations.

27. For an early postwar analysis of the limited state role in the economy, see Hans-Joachim Arndt, *West Germany: Politics of Non-Planning* (Syracuse, N.Y.: Syracuse University Press, 1966). In the classic text *Modern Capitalism: The Changing Balance of Public and Private Power* (London: Oxford University Press, 1965), Andrew Shonfield also notes the significance of organized private interests in Germany, echoed in Peter Katzenstein's decentralized state-centralized society hypothesis. See Peter J. Katzenstein, *Policy and Politics in West Germany: The Growth of a Semi-Sovereign State* (Philadelphia: Temple University Press, 1987).

28. See Simon Reich, *The Fruits of Fascism: Postwar Prosperity in Historical Perspective* (Ithaca: Cornell University Press, 1990).

29. Katzenstein, *Policy and Politics,* 107.

30. Horst G. Krenzler, "Zwischen Protektionismus und Liberalismus: Europäischer Binnenmarkt und Drittlandsbeziehungen," *Europa Archiv* 42 (1988): 241–48.

31. U. Sundhaussen and I. F. Nicolson, "Attitudes to European Integration: The Cases of West Germany and Britain in 1979," *Australian Journal of Politics and History* 27 (1981): 197–209; Werner J. Fels and Helmut Wagner, "West Germany and European Integration: Economic and Political Interests and Policy Motivations," *Revue d'Integration europeene* 4 (1980): 59–81; Bulmer and Patterson, *Federal Republic.*

32. Bulmer and Patterson, *Federal Republic,* 94–97. See also Wolfram F. Hanrieder, *West German Foreign Policy 1949–1963* (Stanford: Stanford University Press, 1967).

33. Michael G. Huelshoff, "German Business and 1992," in *United Germany in Europe,* ed. Carl Lankowski (New York: St. Martin's and London: Macmillan, forthcoming 1993).

34. See M. Casperi, "The Aid Rules of the EEC Treaty and Their Application," in *Discretionary Powers of the Member States in the Field of Economic Policies and*

Their Limits under the EEC Treaty, ed. Jürgen Schwartz (Baden-Baden: Nomos, 1988), 37–52; "BDI zur Europapolitik: Vorrang für Marktwirtschaft," *Nachrichten für Außenpolitik,* 4 January 1988, 6; "Etwas Weniger Europaduselei, Bitte Schon!," *Wirtschaftswoche,* 29 January 1988, 22; "Abscheid vom Staatlichen Schutz," *Die Zeit,* 22 January 1988, 12; "Plädoyer für den gemeinsamen Binnenmarkt," *Süddeutsche Zeitung,* 20 April 1988, 5; "Battle of Brittan," *The Economist,* 10 June 1989, 34.

35. For a sample of union opinion on the 1992 program, see G. Siebert, ed., *Wenn der Binnenmarkt kommt . . . Neue Anforderungen an gewerkschaftliche Politik* (Frankfurt am Main: Nachrichten, 1989); G. Siebert, ed., *Europa 92: EG-Binnenmarkt und Gewerkschaften* (Frankfurt am Main: Nachrichten, 1989); Franz Steinkuhler, ed., *Europa '92: Industriestandort oder sozialer Lebensraum* (Hamburg: VSA, 1989); Ernst Breit, ed., *Für ein soziales Europa* (Cologne: Bund, 1989); Ernst Breit, ed., *Europäischer Binnenmarkt: Wirtschafts- oder Sozialraum* (Bonn: Europa Union, 1988).

36. See Andrei S. Markovits and Alexander Otto, "German Labor and the European Internal Market," *German Studies Review* 14 (1991): 103–21.

37. On federal institutions, see G. Jaspert, "Der Bundesrat und die europäische Integration," *Aus Politik und Zeitgeschichte* 27 (1982): 17–32; A. Bruck, "Europäische Integration und Entmachtung des Deutschen Bundestages: Ein Unterausschuss ist nicht genug," *Zeitschrift für Parlamentsfragen* 19 (1988): 220–24; Siegfried Magiera, "Die Rechtswirkungen von EG-Richtlinien im Konflikt zwischen Bundesfinanzhof und Europäischem Gerichtshof," *Die öffentliche Verwaltung* 38 (1985): 937–44; Peter Malanczuk, "European Affairs and the Länder (States) of the Federal Republic of Germany," *Common Market Law Review* 22 (1985): 237–72; E. Grabitz, "Die Rechtsetzungsbefugnis von Bund und Länder bei der Durchführung von Gemeinschaftsrecht," *Archiv des öffenlichen Rechts* 111 (1986): 1–33; Klaus Otto Nass, "'Nebenaußenpolitik' der Bundesländer," *Europa Archiv* 41 (1986): 619–28; Rudolf Hrbek, "Die deutschen Länder in der EG-Politik," *Aussenpolitik* 38 (1987): 120–32; Edmund Stoiber, "Auswirkungen der Entwicklung Europas zur Rechtsgemeinschaft auf die Länder der Bundesrepublik Deutschland," *Europa Archiv* 42 (1987): 543–52; M. Borchmann, "Bundesstaat und europäische Integration: Die Mitwirkung der Bundesländer an Entscheidungsprozessen der EG," *Archiv des öffentichen Rechts* 112 (1987): 586–622; R. Hellwig, "Die Rolle der Bundesländer in der Europa-Politik: Das Beispiel der Ratifizierung der Einheitlichen Europäischen Akte," *Europa Archiv* 42 (1987): 297–302; G. Oschatz and H. Risse, "Europäische Integration und deutscher Föderalismus," *Europa Archiv* 43 (1988): 9–16.

38. See Klaus Otto Nass, "Der 'Zahlmeister' als Schrittmacher?" *Europa Archiv* 10 (1976): 325–36; Fritz Franzmeyer, "Wirtschaftliche Dominanz als Integrationsproblem," *Europa-Archiv* 24 (1981): 737–45; Holm A. Leonhardt, "Die Bundesrepublik Deutschland in der EG; Der 'dumme August' der Integration?" *Frankfurter Hefte* 34 (1983): 3–16; Werner Ungerer, "Deutsche Interessen in und an der Europäischen Gemeinschaft," *Aussenpolitik* 37 (1986): 363–74; Lutz Stavenhagen, "Politische Prioritäten der deutschen EG-Präsidentschaft," *Aussenpolitik* 43 (1988): 14–24.

39. Putnam, "Diplomacy and Domestic Politics," 450.

40. The corporatism literature is vast, and I make no effort to review it here. For a recent debate on the concept, see Andrew Cox, "The Old and New Testaments of Corporatism: Is it a Political Form or a Method of Policy-Making," *Political Studies* 36 (1988) 294–308; and Alan Cawson, "In Defense of the New Testament: A Reply to Andrew Cox," *Political Studies* 36 (1988): 309–315. For measures of corporatism, see Kerry Schott, *Policy, Power, and Order: The Persistence of Economic Problems in Capitalist States* (New Haven: Yale University Press, 1984), 41–42. Phillippe C. Schmitter distinguishes between state and societal corporatism, see "Reflections on Where the Theory of Neo-corporatism Has Gone and Where the Praxis of Neo-Corporatism May Be Going," in *Patterns of Corporatist Policy Making,* ed. Phillipe C. Schmitter and Gerhard Lehmbruch (Beverly Hills, Calif.: Sage, 1982). While the formal, institutional mechanisms of corporatism do not exist in Germany, I argue that many policy issues are resolved by in a fashion that often approximates Schmitter's second use of the term, societal corporatism.

41. Simon Bulmer and William Patterson, "West Germany's Role in Europe: 'Man-Mountain' or 'Semi-Gulliver'?" *Journal of Common Market Studies* 28 (1989): 95–117.

42. I adopt here Katzenstein's characterization of German politics in *Policy and Politics.* Smith defines Germany as a state without a center. See Gordon Smith, "Structures of Government," in *Developments in West German Politics,* ed. Gordon Smith, William Patterson, and Peter Merkl (Durham: Duke University Press, 1989). For a dissenting view, see J. P. Nettl, "The State as a Conceptual Variable," *World Politics* 20 (1968): 559–92.

43. Katzenstein, *Policy and Politics,* 59.

44. A. Butt Philip, *Pressure Groups in the European Community* (London: UACES, 1985); H. Platzer, *Unternehmensverbände in der EG—ihre Nationale und Transnationale Organization und Politik* (Kehl am Rhein: N. P. Engel, 1984).

45. "EG-Umweltminister beschliessen niedrige Abgaswerte für Kleinwagen," *Frankfurter Allgemeine Zeitung,* 30 June 1988.

46. H. Mosley, "The Social Dimension of European Integration," *International Labour Review* 129 (1990): 149–50; Paul Venturini, *1992: The European Social Dimension* (Brussels: Commission of the European Communities, 1988), 15.

47. Venturini, *1992,* 16.

48. Mosley, "Social Dimension," 152–53.

49. Mosley, "Social Dimension" 160. See also Otto Mayer, "Zur Sozialen Dimension des Europäischen Binnenmarktes," in *Europäische Binnenmarkt: Perspektiven und Probleme,* ed. Otto Mayer, H. Scharrer, and H. Schmal (Hamburg: Verlag Weltarchiv, 1989), 355–56; and G. Muhr, "1992: The Social Aspects," *Labour and Society* 15 (1990): 5.

50. ETUC, "EC Commission's Programme and the Brussels European Council," ETUC Statement, 29–30 March 1985; "The EEC at the Crossroads," ETUC Statement to the European Council in Milan, 28–29 June 1985; ETUC Statement on the Internal Market, October 1985; ETUC, "Internal Market and the European Social Dimension," 12–13 December 1985; ETUC, "Delors Plan: Making a Success of the Single Act—A New Frontier for Europe," Statement of the Executive Committee of the ETUC,

23–24 April 1987; "Statement on the European Council Session," ETUC Executive Committee, December 1987; "Creating the European Social Dimension in the Internal Market: European Social Programme," Statement by the ETUC Executive Committee, 11–12 February 1988; Z. Tyszkiewicz, "European Social Policy—Striking the Right Balance," *European Affairs* 3 (1989): 70–75; Bundesvereinigung der Deutsche Arbeitsgeberverbände, *Stellungnahme zur Sozialen Dimension des EG-Binnenmarktes,* EuroInfo no. 4, 16 February 1989.

51. Jürgen Kohl, "The Social Dimension of the 1992 Project" (Paper delivered at the conference The Franco-German Partnership and the European Project, Northwestern University, 4–5 May 1991); Commission of the EC, "The Social Dimension of the Internal Market," Commission Communication, September 1988.

52. Author's interviews in Bonn, March and April 1991. A full explanation of the French decision to back a nonbinding charter is found in French domestic politics, and beyond the scope of this paper. Briefly, in France, the labor movement is split along sharp ideological lines and was in political decline in the 1980s as membership dropped and the French government passed laws to increase flexibility in the workforce. Hence, Mitterrand felt little pressure from French unions to push for a binding charter. Mitterrand's move to the right, though, is only part of the explanation. A nonbinding charter was certainly better for French prestige than no charter at all. The chair of the European Council rotates every six months, and each head of government feels pressure to show that its tenure was successful. Author's interviews in Brussels and Bonn, January 1990.

53. Author's interviews, Bonn, Spring 1991.

54. Breit, *Europäischer Binnenmarkt;* Breit, *Für ein soziales Europa:* Steinkuhler, *Europa '92;* Siebert, *Europa 92;* Siebert, *Wenn der Binnenmarkt Kommt.*

55. DGB, *Europas Wirtschaft 1992* (Düsseldorf: DGB, 1990).

56. W. Adamy, "Soziale Grundrechte in der Europäischen Gemeinschaft," *WSI Mitteilungen* 42 (1989): 554–55.

57. Ernst Breit and K. Murmann, "Gemeinsame Erklärung von DGB und BDA," in Bundesministerium für Arbeit und Sozialordung, *Der EG-Binnenmarkt und die Sozialpolitik* (Bonn: BAS, 1989), 46.

58. "Deutscher Sozialstandard für die EG Abgelehnt," *Süddeutsche Zeitung,* 31 August 1989.

59. "Kohl Backs Unions on EC Social Charter," *Financial Times,* 1 September 1989, 2.

60. Council of the EC, Community Charter of Basic Social Rights of Workers. 10928/89, SOC 467, 19 December 1989. Margaret Thatcher had opposed any charter, binding or not, from the beginning of the debate. See "Britain Warns of Harmful Risk in EC Social Charter," *Financial Times,* 8 September 1989, 3; "Government Unlikely to Approve EC Charter," *Financial Times,* 29 September 1989, 2; "Eggar Faults Social Rights 'Restrictions,'" *Financial Times,* 7 October 1989, 3.

61. Bundesministerium für Arbeit und Sozialordnung, "Vorschläge der Bundesregierung für Soziale Mindeststandards," *Die EG-Binnenmarkt und die Sozialpolitik,* Vol. 2 (Bonn: BAS, 1990) 7–8; Commission of the EC, "Action Programme for the Implementation of the EC Social Charter," COM (89) 568, 29 November 1989.

German Security Policy and the Future European Security Order

James Sperling

The long European peace after the Second World War was the product of political-military bipolarity, the nuclear stalemate between the Soviet Union and the United States, and the division of Germany. German foreign and security policies were constrained by the triple imperative of acquiescing to American superiority in Europe without shattering its fragile political-security partnership with France, of suffering French pretentions to European leadership without jeopardizing the American protectorate or foreclosing the prospect of Franco-German codetermination, and of acknowledging Soviet interests in Europe without foregoing the objective of German unification. Today, the postwar bonds on German policy are dissolving; the threat of war between the major European states has receded into the background; political-military bipolarity has evaporated as has the ideological hostility that helped sustain it; Germany is unified and fully sovereign; and France, the United States, and Russia acknowledge Germany's leadership role in Europe and seek its partnership.

Whither German security policy? The unified Germany's geographical position at the center of Europe, status as an economic superpower, and latent military power make this a particularly compelling question. German history makes it a chilling question for many: during the period 1871 to 1945, Germany pursued a *Weltpolitik* designed to challenge the privileged position of the Anglo-Saxon maritime powers outside the limited compass of Europe, anticipated a *Mitteleuropa* under German hegemony as the material basis both for that challenge and its bid for European hegemony, and conducted its European diplomacy in the idioms of preferential trade arrangements, war, and territorial annexation.[1] The disastrous bid for German hegemony in Europe between 1871 and 1945 has provided the deep background for any responsible analysis of postwar German security policy; 1945 was not "year zero" for the European state system. Mindful of the past, the chapter will address a number of important questions about post-postwar German security policy: How are German security interests defined in the post-postwar world? What are the elements of continuity and change in German security policy? What institutions and institutional configurations do the Germans favor for the construction of a European security order? What are the elements of the German architecture for the future European security order? In the conclusion, I consider the implications of the changed international environment for Germany's future relations with the United States, the former Soviet Union, and its partner states in the European Community.

The Redefinition of German Security

The turbulence of alliance relations and the uncertainties of the East-West conflict between 1949 and 1989 now appear, in retrospect, to be a long period of continuity, certainty, and stability. The content and direction of German security policy was narrowly circumscribed by the Federal Republic's membership in NATO and dependence upon the United States and defined by the need to contain Soviet power in Europe. But the changes that have taken place in the European state system, particularly the unseemly and hasty Soviet retreat from empire and consequent internal disintegration, the prospect of an unwelcomed American retreat from *its* empire, driven by frustration with European demands compounded by severe domestic disabilities, and the process of western European political and economic integration have pushed into the background the traditional security concern over Germany's territorial integrity. The question has arisen, from whom and for what reason should the Germans prepare to defend themselves militarily?

At the same time, the Germans have refined and broadened their concept of security to conform with the pressures generated by, and to exploit the opportunities offered by, the evolution of the European state system. Today, German security is threatened not by an invasion of the Soviet army, but by ethnic implosions in eastern, central, and southern Europe and the former Soviet Union that could draw the Germans into civil wars as mediators or as protectors of a threatened German minority; by the inability of Germany to control its borders in the event of mass migrations from eastern and southern Europe driven by political chaos (particularly in the former Soviet Union) or economic deprivation; by the proliferation of terrorist groups operating in Germany, both indigenous and foreign; and by threats to German economic security, defined not only in the traditional terms of access to foreign markets or of assured supply to raw materials, but in terms of protecting the German social market economy, the German preference for price stability and fiscal rectitude, and the German environment.

This broadened and evolving redefinition of German security interests also reflects a redefinition of the German state; the Germans have seized upon the idea that Germany must play the role of a "civilian" power in Europe, since the role of a great or middle power defined militarily has been proscribed by history, conscience, treaty, and self-interest.[2] The Germans are unwilling (and unable) to contribute to the military requirements of global stability; it is acceded that these tasks are best left to the United States, France, and the United Kingdom.[3] Nonetheless, the German role in the future European order, although militarily circumscribed, is expansively defined economically, technologically, environmentally, and politically. Germany desires full participation in the political and economic reconstruction of eastern Europe, in the creation of European political and economic union, in the restoration of the European environment, and in the construction of a functioning security structure encompassing the whole of Europe and based on the twin principles of democracy and the market economy. Germany remains satisfied to contribute to the economic requirements of security and to accelerate the demilitarization of interstate relations, particularly in Europe—a development that plays to Germany's economic capacity and not coincidentally enhances German influence in the reconstruction and recasting of the European order.

German Security Policy and the Evolution of the European State System, 1949–92

In the postwar period, German foreign policy was framed and constrained by the American policy of double containment: the containment of the Soviet Union and the containment of Germany.[4] The containment of Germany gained its legitimacy for both the Germans and the other Europeans (western and eastern) from the series of German-initiated wars beginning in 1871 and ending in 1945; and the containment of the Soviet Union gained its legitimacy from the bipolar structure of power that emerged at the end of the Second World War. The American policy of double containment was aided and abetted by what can be called Germany's self-conscious policy of self-containment,[5] a policy that began with the creation of the Federal Republic in 1949, when the Germans agreed to the allied reservation of special rights in the Federal Republic, that was promised by the Grundgesetz (the fledgling Federal Republic dedicated itself to the political unification of Europe), and that was concretized with the German transferral of sovereignty to various multilateral and supranational institutions (e.g., the miscarried European Defence Community, NATO, the European Coal and Steel Community, and the European Economic Community). The process and practice of transferring sovereignty to multinational and supranational institutions was not limited to the Germans among the nations of the West, but unlike those nations, the

Germans felt compelled in the early part of their postwar history to prevent the spectre of a revanchist or revisionist Germany from arising—a development that could only serve to complicate and debilitate West German foreign policy, particularly with respect to the objective of unification. Consequently, the Germans conflated their national interest with the stated objectives of the security and economic institutions of the European and Atlantic communities; German policymakers have systematically translated German interests into the interests of the many over the course of the postwar period. For example, West Germans defined their economic interests in the language of European integration and the European Community; German political interests were framed in the language of a pan-European security order and the political unification of Europe (and Germany); and German security interests were expressed in terms reflecting the declaratory policies of NATO, particularly the Harmel Doctrine. This pattern continues today, albeit there has been a remarkable shift in German self-confidence and sense of importance.

The passing of the postwar order has created an ambiguous and confounding international system.[6] The Germans (and everyone else) are faced with an acknowledged and well-known, but potentially introspective superpower (the United States), a politically fragmented and crippled military superpower (the former Soviet Union), and within the Atlantic context two poles of economic power (the United States and a European Community anchored by Germany) that hover in equal measure around the pole of discord and the pole of collaboration. The dissolution of the Warsaw Pact-CMEA system underpinning Soviet power in Europe has left the Untied States without an adversary and Germany without a credible military or political threat to its territory or polity. As a consequence of these developments, the American policy of double containment has become irrelevant and inappropriate. It is irrelevant because the first object of American containment, the expansion of Soviet power in western Europe, no longer presents a credible security risk to the United States or its European allies. It is inappropriate because the American strategy for the "new world order" relies heavily upon the successful drafting of Germany as a partner in leadership. Thus, the American interest lay in effecting the positive objective of integrating Germany into the post-postwar order and preparing Germany to assume the responsibilities of a major power, rather than the negative objective of containing Germany and preventing the exercise of German power.

The Kohl-Genscher government greeted and embraced the Bush administration's stated preference for Germany and America to act as partners in leadership in the Atlantic alliance.[7] But the American strategy of creating a durable political axis linking Bonn and Washington has been tested and strained by several developments in the last two years: the German-Soviet

Stavropol agreement was reached without prior consultation with the United States, limited the Bundeswehr to 370,000 men, and proscribed NATO troops from the territory of the former German Democratic Republic (GDR); German hesitancy to undertake an obligation to defend Turkey during the Gulf War raised troublesome questions about the depth of Germany's commitment to its NATO partner states; Germany's conspicuous role as Zahlmeister during the Gulf War transformed Britons and Americans into latter-day condottiere;[8] Germany, in opposition to the United States, supported President Gorbachev's request to attend the July 1991 Group of Seven summit and pushed for full Soviet membership in the IMF and IRBD;[9] and most recently, Germany recognized the independence of Slovenia and Croatia despite the severe reservations of the major western European powers and the active opposition of the United States.

The unraveling of the Soviet empire in eastern Europe and of the Soviet Union itself requires, from the German perspective, the integration of the former members of the Warsaw Pact, particularly Hungary, the Czech and Slovak Federal Republic, and Poland—nations sharing a common border with a unified Germany—into the western political, economic, and security systems. The political objectives of German foreign policy have not been fundamentally changed by the transformation of the European security order: Germany's foreign policy objectives remain the political and economic unification of Europe and the creation of a pan-European security system that preserves the indivisibility of German and American security.[10] Nor has the method of achieving those objectives changed: the Germans continue to prefer to work within multilateral and (increasingly) supranational or (con)federal frameworks. What has changed, however, is the content of those objectives, the actors involved, and the relative power of the unified Germany in the process.

The German security strategy in the evolving European state system is a strategy of integration rather than independence for exactly the same reasons offered by Adenauer and those in power since that time: it is a German responsibility to insure that "power politics" never again be the source of a European war; in the absence of integrative and confederal institutions constraining and managing German power, Germany's neighbors would be unsettled by German power and suspect its exercise; and only a pan-European solution combined with an integrative framework will secure the peace by laying to rest the German Problem once and for all. Unstated reasons for preferring integrative institutions include the real leverage gained by the Germans over their partner states in such settings: the Germans can make arguments framed in the pacific and nonthreatening language of European economic prosperity or of European security rather than in the ominous and tainted language of German economic or security interests. German history and the acute awareness of that history by Germans and Germany's neighbors will insure that Germany continues to tread the path followed for over forty years—as Theo Sommer has noted, "normality" in German foreign policy must be defined differently from British, French, or American foreign policy in terms of content, conception, and execution.[11]

An important nonmilitary component of the German security strategy is the deepening and widening of the European Community: the Germans hope to contain the economic and political disintegration of eastern Europe by providing a home port for the nations of north central Europe and a stabilizing magnet for the remainder of the Soviet empire (including the former republics of the Soviet Union as well as the untested and unformed Commonwealth of Independent States). Embedding Germany in the European Community will also reassure Germany's neighbors of German intentions and place limitations on Germany's freedom of action, two outcomes that lower the risk of cooperation with and of coercion by Germany. But this dependence upon the EC is contingent upon the continued viability of NATO and the American connection. The American connection reinsures the Germans against untoward events in eastern Europe that the EC or a "civilian" power is presently ill-equipped to deal with—for example, mediating a civil war or stabilizing a disintegrating neighbor state—and reassures Germany's neighbors that the United States is available to countervail the German exercise of power, a reassurance that paradoxically allows the Germans to press forward with a foreign policy agenda tailored to German interests and preferences in Europe.

The post-postwar German security strategy, expressed as it is in the idiom of European political and economic union, depends upon the continued demilitarization of the European state system. The demilitarization of international relations—what Foreign Minister Genscher has called the "Helvetiaization" of politics in Europe—reduces American leverage over the Germans on monetary and trade issues, because it devalues the American extended nuclear deterrent, the source of American influence in Europe and leverage over the Germans; and it enhances German influence with the former Soviet Union, its European neighbors and the United States, because it plays to the source of German power, Germany's economic capacity. But without European union, German foreign policy would not be free from the suspicion and fear of German hegemony or the unwelcomed imposition of German preferences on its weaker European neighbors.[12] And if the progressive demilitarization of the European state system is slowed or reversed, Germany will face a comparative disadvantage in its dealings not only with the Americans, but with the French and British: the Germans may find themselves once again trading economic concessions in exchange for an American (French or British) security guarantee of questionable value.

The Institutions of European Security:
The German Perspective

The redefinition of Germany security and the changed (and changing) European state system have shaped and reshaped the role and promise of the existing institutions of European security. Germany, the key continental European partner of the United States in NATO, now faces a choice in the procurement of its security: whereas NATO had the character of an automatic alliance over the course of the postwar period—the Germans had little choice but to support NATO in exchange for an extended American deterrent—the collapse of the Warsaw Pact and the absence of a countervailing order in the eastern portion of the European continent has had the unsettling effect of providing Germany with choice.[13] While it remains true that NATO remains the essential institutional guarantor of security and stability in Europe and for Germany, it faces a longer-term challenge from the Conference on Security and Cooperation in Europe (CSCE), the European Community (EC), and the Western European Union (WEU).

The German security strategy envisions specific roles for NATO, the CSCE, the EC, and the WEU, but that strategy remains contingent upon the evolution of the European state system and the evolving redefinition of German interests, both of which will be influenced by the path taken by the erstwhile republics of the former Soviet Union, and by the unfolding relationships among the major European powers and between Europe and America in the post-postwar world.

NATO: From Military Alliance to Transatlantic Security Bridge?

NATO, and the extended American nuclear deterrent, guaranteed German security in the postwar period, supported the German effort to achieve West European political and economic integration, and was considered essential to the eventual unification of the two Germanys. Prior to unification, the German adherence to NATO derived from the structure of power in the international system and the geostrategic position of Germany in Europe. It was not surprising, therefore, to find Chancellor Kohl stating in 1988 that "the Western alliance is a part of our Staatsraison" or that NATO is "the cornerstone of [German] security policy."[14] The Germans reassured the Americans that the they did not want to replace NATO with an autonomous European security structure; embraced the strategy of flexible response; rejected the option of a denuclearized Europe; and dismissed the possibility of a third zero in the area of land-based nuclear systems under 500 kilometers.[15]

The fundamental changes that transformed the European state system between 1988 and 1991 altered the German position on the prospect of the denuclearization of Europe and the viability of flexible response. By the summer of 1990, Defense Minister Stoltenberg began the slow reversal of German policy: although the Germans did not advocate the denuclearization of Europe, the Germans greeted with enthusiasm the American decision neither to deploy a follow-on to the Lance short-range nuclear missile nor to modernize nuclear artillery. The German preference on nuclear matters revealed a preference for a new form of singularization: the deployment of nuclear weapons at sea (or in the United Kingdom or France) would leave the Germans defended, but at the same time relieve them of the political costs or military risks attending the stationing of nuclear weapons on German soil. Moreover, Stoltenberg advocated a lessened dependence upon nuclear deterrence in favor of a system that provided mutual security and stability to the European area.[16] In his policy declaration of January 1991, Chancellor Kohl urged the United States and the Soviet Union to begin negotiations to remove from Europe land-based short-range nuclear weapons as well as nuclear artillery; and greeted as a timely response to the changed political status quo in Europe the NATO decision to refashion the concept of forward defense and to relegate nuclear weapons to weapons of "last resort." By February 1991, Foreign Minister Genscher stated unequivocally that a continuation of the disarmament process in Europe was essential and that "short-range nuclear weapons and nuclear artillery must disappear from Europe."[17] The alliance conformed with Foreign Minister Genscher's exhortation by the time of the November 1991 Rome NATO summit, when the allies agreed to reduce the number of substrategic nuclear weapons by 80 percent.[18] But the Rome Declaration only ratified President Bush's decision in late September 1991 to eliminate all American land- and sea-based short-range nuclear weapons, including nuclear artillery, stationed in Europe.[19]

The German-American security tie within NATO has been and remains essential for German security and European stability.[20] But the sources of cohesion in the alliance have undergone a subtle, but significant change: NATO member states, to be sure, share common security interests, but the Germans argue that glue that holds the alliance together are the values common to them.[21] For the Germans, the American role in Europe has evolved into the explicit role of night watchman.[22] The necessity of NATO for the success of the EC or the CSCE in the security field has forced the Germans to argue against the proposition that NATO, the EC, and the CSCE have conflicting purposes or conflicting logics; hence the slogan "Sowhol-Als auch" (this as well as that) and the emphatic rejection of "Entweder-Oder" (either this or that).[23] The Germans desire to have it three ways—NATO and the American security guarantee, the European Community and a single European security identity, and the CSCE and a pan-European security order.

But this position has not left them shy about giving pride of place to NATO and accentuating the continued need for the presence of American troops in Europe.[24]

NATO remains attractive to the Germans because it provides them with a number of external economies: first, the stability afforded by the alliance "reach[es] beyond the immediate circle of its member states" and contributes to the stability of the reforming nations of eastern and central Europe;[25] second, NATO serves as a hedge against neoisolationism in the United States;[26] and finally, as Defense Minister Stoltenberg noted, NATO is "the single functioning security structure in Europe" and serves as a yardstick against "fair-weather security structures" that are pretenders to NATO's role.[27] Within the German government there is general agreement that NATO, as the sole functioning security structure in Europe, is necessary for the foreseeable future. It is also clear that the Germans believe that without NATO, the CSCE and probably European political union would be nonstarters.[28] This position answers in the affirmative the question, Is NATO a key element of the German security strategy? But it also raises a number of other significant questions: Is NATO important simply because it is the only realistic alternative facing the Germans? Is NATO important because it remains part and parcel of a unified Germany's Staatsraison? Is NATO important because it is the foundation upon which a collective security system spanning the Atlantic to the Urals can be safely constructed? Or has NATO merely become, in the words of Foreign Minister Genscher, "a transatlantic security bridge for the whole of Europe, for the democracies of eastern and western Europe."[29] The answer to these questions turns upon the expectations that the Germans have for the CSCE, the EC, and the WEU in the future European security order.

CSCE: The Security Institution of the Future?

The CSCE will serve two specific functions for the Germans in the future European order: it promises the institutionalization of a pan-European peace order based upon the principle of collective security; and it offers an additional mechanism for overcoming the "prosperity barrier" (Wohlstandsgrenze) between the nations of western and eastern Europe with the establishment of a free-market regime throughout Europe.

The Germans agree with former President Gorbachev that the security concerns of Germany's neighbors can only be resolved in a "common European house," although the intellectual lineage of "a common European house" is traced not to President Gorbachev, but to Chancellor Adenauer and the former Finance and Defense Minister Franz-Josef Strauss.[30] Despite the Germanic pedigree of the CSCE, the German government's attitude towards the CSCE remains somewhat ambivalent. In repeated policy statements, Chancellor Kohl first expresses German dependence upon NATO for German security, then discusses the prospects for a European security identity that would serve as the second pillar of the Atlantic security system, and only then mentions the CSCE, normally highlighting the institution's future promise as the framework for a pan-European peace order. But even then, Chancellor Kohl (and Foreign Minister Genscher) carefully note that any European security arrangement dominated by the CSCE cannot exclude the two North American powers.[31] Nonetheless, the CSCE frames Germany's security (and economic) aspirations in eastern and central Europe.[32]

At this stage of the evolution of the European state system, the Kohl-Genscher government views the CSCE process as supplementary to NATO in the following sense: NATO provides insurance against any military threat to the territorial integrity of Germany, while the CSCE makes a positive contribution to European security by integrating the former Warsaw Pact member states, including the former Soviet Union, into the western economic and political orbit. Yet, the Germans remain dependent upon the United States: the success of the CSCE requires a continuing American imprimatur to lend it legitimacy and effectiveness.[33]

The Germans argue that economic envy (Wirtschaftsneid) on the part of the immiserated nations of Europe, rather than the exercise or exploitation of Germany's economic power (Wirtschaftsmacht) is an important and very real threat to the stability of Europe, and consequently to the German polity and economy.[34] Although the EC plays the dominant role in securing the economic dimension of German security, the CSCE provides an important mechanism for constructing a stable and prosperous European economic space. The Germans proposed and hosted the 1990 CSCE Bonn conference on economic cooperation in Europe.[35] The Bonn CSCE document obligated the nonmarket economies of Europe to institute price reform, to implement policies that would lead to currency convertibility, and to adopt the principles of the market economy. The Germans believe that the Bonn CSCE document on economic cooperation provides a stable framework for the creation of a single, integrated European economic space spanning the Atlantic to the Urals; that in effect it establishes a European economic regime favoring the principles of the market economy.[36] The emphasis on the economic aspect of the relations amongst the nations of Europe reflects the German redefinition of security, and it has the practical consequence of altering the calculus of power in the European area: it shifts attention away from the military potential of a state to its productive capability and rate of technological innovation, a development that would further strengthen German diplomacy at the expense of France and Britain. Moreover, the German government views pan-European economic cooperation as an essential aspect of the

CSCE process because the basis for social stability, and therefore for national security, is economic welfare. For the Germans, security cooperation is contingent upon economic cooperation, an assumption that goes a long way to explain German enthusiasm for European economic and monetary union as well as the Bonn CSCE document.[37]

The CSCE plays an important function for the Germans that NATO cannot play and the EC is unlikely to play, now or in the future: CSCE provides an institutional mechanism for integrating the former republics of the Soviet Union into a pan-European security and economic space without necessarily compromising or threatening the geopolitical and military logic of NATO or undermining the progress towards European political union within the framework of the EC. The meaning and importance of the CSCE for the Germans may be located as well in Foreign Minister Genscher's assertion in early 1991 that "the German-Soviet relationship possesses a central importance for the stability of Europe."[38] The fragmentation of the former Soviet Union and the uncertain future of the Commonwealth of Independent States makes it uncertain whether Germany will have a lone partner or a number of partners in the place of the Soviet Union. But if the Commonwealth of Independent States survives (or is replaced by a loose confederation of states conducting a common foreign policy), then only the CSCE provides a ready-made mechanism for ordering that relationship within a multilateral framework. The CSCE also unburdens Russo-German cooperation by diminishing the spectre of a second Rapallo, because the relationship between a Russian-dominated Commonwealth of Independent States and Germany will be conducted within and sanctioned by an established multilateral framework.[39]

The European Community: Second Pillar
or Independent Power?

The political unification of Europe, a foreign policy objective mandated by the Grundgesetz was intended initially as a method of burying European animosities built up after seven decades of intermittent war; and as a method of eradicating its source, Franco-German competition for European hegemony. For the Germans it also served the larger political purpose of reintegrating Germany into the society of Western states after the Second World War; and it eventually became the idiom in which German interests, particularly in the economic sphere, were expressed and identified. Today leading German politicians describe the European Community as "the stability anchor of Europe," as "the stable anchor in a stormy sea," and as "the cornerstone of European stability and an essential component of the future European political structure." The Germans claim that since the EC is the only "area of stability" (Stabilitätsraum) in Europe, it demonstrates that stability on the European continent need not reflect or depend upon military power.[40] The combination of historical escape, tactical necessity, and strategic realism has left a legacy of a genuine German dedication to European political and economic integration, albeit on German terms.

The EC plays a triple role in the German security strategy for Europe: first, the progress towards political union and economic and monetary union provides a magnet for the reforming states of central and eastern Europe that will contribute to the erasure of the Wohlstandsgrenze between capitalist and protocapitalist Europe; second, the inevitable trend towards the creation of a common security and foreign policy will enable "Europe" to function as a second pillar within NATO and assume responsibilities commensurate with Europe's economic and military power; and third, the political unification of Europe will create the framework for common immigration, asylum, and terrorism laws that will protect the German domestic order.[41] Moreover, the European Community (along with NATO and the CSCE) assures Germany's neighbors and partners that Germany is cognizant of and will respect the "security needs and the feelings of all Europeans, understandably and above all our neighbors;" and German enthusiasm for the EC demonstrates, at least from the German perspective, that Germany has renounced, once and for all, the "national unilateralism and the Sonderweg" that has shaped modern European history.[42]

In the discussions leading to the Maastricht summit in December 1991, particularly within the intergovernmental conference drafting the EC treaty on European political union, the Germans insisted that political union requires the coordination and convergence of the security and foreign policies of the member states of the European Community. Moreover, the Germans view the process of European political union and the absorption of the WEU by the EC as a major contribution to the stabilization of Europe and the creation of an effective second pillar in the Atlantic Alliance. The benefits of a European security identity flow from the "enormous economic, social, and ecological problems facing the world" that NATO is ill-equipped to deal with.[43] Thus, the German dependence upon NATO—as reinsurance against the unraveling of the reform process in eastern Europe and the former Soviet Union and as the nexus for the coordination of policy on a broad array of issues ranging from security to the environment to debt relief—has not precluded a European option for Germany, an option seen as complementary to rather than competitive with continued German membership in NATO or partnership with the United States.[44]

The European Community also holds the key to a critical problem facing the Germans and western Europe at large, namely, the prospect of mass migrations from the pauperized nations of eastern Europe and the impoverished regions of the Third World, particularly the nations of the Balkans and Mediterranean basin.[45] The concurrent freeing of travel in eastern Europe and the collapse of those nations' economies have left open the possibility of mass migrations that pose "a special risk factor to western Europe."[46] It poses an especial risk to the Germans given the present financial burden of reconstructing the eastern portion of the country, the unpleasant fact that Germany is the preferred destination of economic refugees from eastern Europe for cultural as well as financial reasons, and the liberal provisions of Articles 16 (which guarantees the right to political asylum) and 116 (which provides a citizenship guarantee to ethnic Germans living in eastern Europe).[47] The large number of foreign residents in Germany, now accounting for almost 8 percent of the German population, and the economic dislocations associated with German unification have increased the attractiveness of the extreme right Republikaner party and the incidence of violence against non-Germans in both eastern and western Germany. The legacy of national socialist Germany has made it virtually impossible for any of the mainstream political parties in Germany to advocate a national solution to the immigration problem by repealing or significantly amending Articles 16 and 116 of the constitution; the SPD and FDP are dead set against any change in the Grundgesetz, and the CDU/CSU's hesitation is located in the uncertain external ramifications of such an action. The Kohl-Genscher government has adopted the position that there should be no immigration to Germany from nations outside of the EC; and the justification for this policy is located in the traditional (and largely fictional) homogeneity of European nation-states.[48] But the Germans do desire a mechanism for stanching the flow of economic refugees that are placing a strain on the already strained German economy and polity. The Germans actively seek the cover of a common European immigration policy that will override the provisions of Grundgesetz and prevent economic refugees from finding a safe haven in the Federal Republic.

The fear of economic refugees and non-German immigrants is reinforced by two other concerns: the proliferation of terrorist groups in Germany and the continuation of eastern European civil wars on German soil.[49] The *Verfassungsschutzbericht 1988,* for example, listed 101,000 foreigners involved in 112 extremist groups; and Germany is now the home of Croatian extremists, some of whom have left Germany to fight against Serbia in the civil war and some of whom were arrested for smuggling weapons to Croatian forces.[50] The prospect of the Yugoslavian civil war being continued by terrorist means from or on German soil remains hypothetical, but the prospects for continued political turmoil in eastern and southern Europe remain good, as do the prospects of future conflicts being played out in the Federal Republic by the large number of recent immigrants and asylum seekers. The Germans recognize that the problem of asylum and mass migration cannot be solved within the national context and requires a solution at the Community level; and the Germans believe that the inability to control their national borders poses perhaps the most immediate and real threat to the stability of their economy and polity.[51]

Western European Union: Atlanticism Reaffirmed or Gaullism Reestablished?

The relationship between the European Community and the Western European Union did not gain momentum until 1990, but the contemporary "prehistory" of the WEU is instructive.[52] When French Prime Minister Chirac suggested the revitalization of the WEU and the creation of a European security identity in December 1986, the European member-states responded in October 1987 with a "Platform on European Security Interests." This platform drew in varying degrees on the Atlanticist, Gaullist, and Europeanist catechisms. American and European security was indivisible and the Alliance required a credible European pillar. But at the same time, the protection of European interests in the Atlantic area required the creation of a European security identity independent of the United States. Moreover, the Europeans agreed that "the construction of an integrated Europe will remain incomplete as long as it does not include security and defense"; and the revitalization of the WEU was linked to the process of European political union.[53]

Two ambiguities arose from the envisaged role of the WEU. First, would it become the second pillar of the Atlantic Alliance or the security and defense policy arm of the European Community? And second, would it promise intensified security cooperation or conflict between the United States and Europe not only on security issues that were "out of area," but on security issues within the purview of NATO as well? In 1990, French President Mitterrand and Chancellor Kohl agreed that both NATO *and* the WEU were essential to the continued stability and cooperation in Europe; and that both institutions occupied the same "security area" and needed to intensify their cooperation. President Mitterrand and Chancellor Kohl later proposed that the EC intergovernmental conference on political union consider how the WEU could be strengthened and how it could become merged with the European Community.[54] Their purpose was twofold: it could serve as a transitional institution prior to the creation of a federal Europe and would thus enable the Europeans to jump-start their security cooperation by grafting an existing institution onto the EC; and it would enable France and Germany to cooperate on security policy without forcing France to relinquish an ever-ephemeral (and pointless) security independence and without forcing the Germans to make (an increasingly irrelevant) choice between the United

States and France, between NATO and Europe. The importance vested in the WEU reflects the German calculation that European political union has made the concept (and practice) of national military autonomy outmoded.[55]

The June 1991 Viaden communiqué of the WEU did not clarify the ultimate shape of the institutional linkages between the WEU, the EC, and NATO; in fact the WEU ministers settled to have it both ways: the communiqué described the WEU as an important component of the process of European union; as the basis for expanding defense cooperation between the member states of the WEU and the EC; and as the institutional vehicle for strengthening the European pillar of the Atlantic Alliance.[56] This policy position was common to the communiqués issued by the European Council at the June 1991 Luxembourg Meeting and the NATO Council at the June 1991 Copenhagen meeting, and it was even included in the Franco-German-Polish Weimar declaration.[57]

The German policy position shifted firmly in favor of subordinating the WEU to the EC beginning in July 1991.[58] By October 1991, the institutional relationship between the WEU, NATO, and the EC became a highly charged affair when France and Germany responded to the Anglo-Italian proposal that the WEU remain subordinated to NATO, represent Europe out of area, and exist independently of the EC. The Franco-German counterproposal suggested that the WEU serve as the basis of a European security identity within as well as outside of Europe and that it be subordinated to the EC for security issues within Europe as well as out of area. The Franco-German proposal called for closer institutional cooperation between the EC and the WEU at all levels, for closer coordination between WEU member states in order to reach common positions within NATO, for moving the WEU general secretariat from London to Brussels, and for expanding relations with the other nations of Europe in conformity with the Copenhagen and Vianden communiqués.[59]

At the Maastricht summit, the Europeans agreed to the Franco-German position in substance, but employed language allowing the British to claim that the WEU will remain subordinated to NATO. The EC draft treaty on political union commits the member states to "the eventual framing of a common defense policy, which might in time lead to a common defense" and identified the WEU as an "integral part of the development of the European Union." The draft treaty also provided that the WEU could be requested to "elaborate and implement decisions and actions of the Union which have defense implications."[60] Although language in the treaty provided that the evolution of this relationship between the WEU and the EC be compatible with NATO, it is also clear that the Franco-German design for a separate security identity won the day.[61] What remains uncertain, however, is the future relationship of the WEU and the EC to NATO; and that in turn raises a question about the future relationship between Germany and the United States.

Future European Security Order: The German Architecture

The Germans increasingly view NATO as a short- to medium-term vehicle for addressing the symptoms of security dilemma facing the Europeans and Germans and for reinsuring Germany against the failure of the CSCE, the institution viewed as best suited to the task of resolving the conflicting demands of Germany's security interests. The Germans view the EC as the economic and political magnet for north central and nordic Europe, as the "stability anchor" for all of Europe, as the core of a future European (con)federation, and as the vehicle for ensuring Germany's economic security. The Germans consider the WEU the most promising European security institution, because it will allow a uniting Europe to forge a single foreign and defense policy without requiring the Europeans to jettison NATO prematurely.[62] The fortunes of the WEU, however, are dependent upon the process of European political unification.

The institutional solution to Germany's security dilemma—retaining the American extended deterrent, building an independent Europe, and creating an inclusive pan-European security system—can not be found in a simple choice between NATO, CSCE, the EC, or WEU. The Germans in fact reject the notion that a choice must be made. For the Germans all four security institutions are compatible and mutually reinforcing. Each serves specific and interrelated tasks for the Germans. NATO reinsures against the unraveling of the post-postwar order as the Germans (and other Europeans) construct a (con)federal Europe and a European security identity. The CSCE is inclusive (both the United States and the former Soviet Union are members), provides a framework for the continued demilitarization of European foreign affairs with accelerated arms control and disarmament, and furnishes Europe with embryonic regimes that lend support to the embrace of the market economy and democracy in eastern Europe and the republics of the former Soviet Union. And the EC and the WEU provide the Germans with a mechanism for ensuring a German voice in the evolution of the European order, for providing the Germans with the consummation of the constitutionally dictated objective of European unification, for creating a European security identity capable of contesting American pretensions in Europe, and for constructing a political entity capable of withstanding pressures from a renascent Russia. Despite the seeming compatibility of these institutions, the logic of the German security strategy leads inexorably to the conclusion that the CSCE and the EC will inevitably become the preferred institutions of European security.

Yet paradoxically NATO remains the key institution in the German strategy: NATO is considered essential to the creation of a European political and security identity; NATO is considered the only credible guarantor of European (and German) security; NATO serves as insurance against the misfiring of the political and economic liberalization in eastern Europe or the political disintegration of the former Soviet Union into any number of disparate republics; and only NATO can support the transition to a CSCE-dominated, pan-European security system by providing a stable international environment.

The Germans refuse to make an unambiguous choice between these institutions, partly because there is no compelling reason to make such a choice at this juncture and partly because these institutions are in fact complementary rather than competitive, at least for now. The German preoccupation with the institutional character of the post-postwar order and the mutual dependence of these institutions reflect, no doubt, two lessons of history: first, peace and stability in Europe are only possible if Germany is closely tied to its neighbors in a manner that benefits each reciprocally; and second, NATO provided Germany and the other European democracies with the longest period of peace in contemporary history.[63]

Conclusion

The collapse of the postwar security order has created a security vacuum in Europe. The fluidity of the current European state system stands in stark contrast to the constancy and predictability of the postwar order. The Germans seek the creation of a European security order congenial to the instruments, concerns, and calculations of power and interest of a civilian power. It is questionable whether the final contours of the post-postwar European security system will conform to the cooperative security system anticipated by the Germans. A cooperative European security order would require, at a minimum, the continued and permanent demilitarization of European affairs, an economic, social, and environmental definition of security by the major players of the European system, and the acknowledgment and internalization by national elites of the linkage between economic stabilty and political security. Put simply, the contours of the European state system will depend upon the ability of the Germans, Americans, and other Europeans to overcome the ingrained habits of the postwar order, and upon the acceptance of the German definition of security and the success of the German strategy for demilitarizing the political space occupied by Europe. These conditions require the transformation of the European state system—from a system driven by the competitive logic of power and Staatsraison to a system ordered by the cooperative logic of economics and transnationality. Moreover, it requires that the dynamics of a bipolar economic system differ fundamentally from those of a bipolar political-military system.[64]

The German security strategy has three primary elements: self-containment of German power in order that Germany may use its power to influence its European neighbors to effect German policy objectives; the creation of an independent Europe capable of negotiating on an equal basis with the United States on economic issues; and the continued demilitarization of Europe that depends upon the sustained growth of democracy and the free market in the former member states of the Warsaw Pact. The primary instruments of that strategy are the CSCE, EC, and WEU. NATO, the instrument of American influence in Europe, is ill-equipped to cope with the real security threats facing the Federal Republic, economic collapse in eastern Europe and mass migrations to Germany. But paradoxically, NATO remains an essential component of the German security stratgy and still best protects Germany's security interests.

The German-American relationship remains the most important for Germany. And in the short term, there is no manifest conflict of interest between the United States and the Federal Republic on the institutional configuration of the present European security order. The United States favors the continued dominance of NATO and the corresponding influence that NATO extends for the United States. Although the United States casts an increasingly wary and jaundiced eye at the ultimate purposes and implications of the European Community and the WEU, the success and strengthening of both are important if there is to be a second pillar of the Alliance. The CSCE is not central to the American security calculus; its importance has been diminished by the collapse of the Soviet empire. For the Germans, these institutions are interdependent and reinforcing; each services a different aspect of German security policy. NATO ensures Germany's military security and provides a fail-safe environment where Germany can pursue its economic and political objectives in Europe. The EC ensures Germany's economic security and welfare, provides an important mechanism whereby German can effectively wield its influence, and contributes to the development of a credible second pillar within NATO, as does the institutional elaboration of the WEU. The CSCE has established, particularly with the Charter of Paris, a political regime establishing democracy as the political norm and an economic regime establishing capitalism as the economic norm. It is incontrovertible that German policy depends upon NATO as reinsurance against the failure of the others.

The institutional configurations and institutions favored by the United States and the Federal Republic reveal an intractable and substrated source of discord in German-American relations. For the Germans, NATO is but an instrument for achieving the larger (and longer-term) objectives of pan-

European security and economic cooperation and provides the Germans with some insurance against unforeseen developments in eastern and southern Europe. The Americans are content to preserve NATO, draft Germany as their partner in leadership within the alliance, and prolong American influence over German foreign policy. As the Germans grow more comfortable with the exercise of power, as the process of European union enables the Germans to exercise their power through and in the name of European institutions, and as eastern and western Europe grow closer together economically and politically, the time will come when NATO—and the American security connection—will have outlived its usefulness for the Federal Republic.

The prospects for a German-American partnership framed by NATO is contingent upon the political evolution of the former Soviet Union and the European state system. Instability and the fear of instability in Europe, rather than the American nuclear deterrent, sustain German dependence upon the United States. The prospects for the German security strategy is contingent upon the evolution of the European state system. If the European state system continues upon a trajectory of political union and demilitarization, the CSCE and the EC-WEU will provide the institutional framework for the security needs of a civilian power. It remains to be seen, however, if the world remains an uncivil place.

NOTES

1. For more background on the historical context of German foreign policy, see Ludwig Dehio, *Germany and World Politics in the Twentieth Century* (New York: Knopf, 1959); V. R. Berghahn, *Modern Germany: Society, Economy, and Politics in the Twentieth Century* (Cambridge: Cambridge University Press, 1982); Fritz Fischer, *Krieg der Illusionen* (Düsseldorf: Droste, 1969) and "German War Aims 1914–1918 and German Policy Before the War," in *War Aims and Strategic Policy in the Great War 1914–1918*, ed. Barry Hunt and Adrian Preston (London: Croom Helm, 1977): 105–23; and George Liska, *Quest for Equilbirium: America and the Balance of Power on Land and Sea* (Baltimore: Johns Hopkins University Press, 1977).

2. For a discussion of the redefinition of state and nation in Germany, see Ole Waever, "Three Competing Europes: German, French, and Russian," *International Affairs* 66 (1990): 477–94. On Germany as a civilian power, see Theo Sommer, "Die Deutschen an die Front?" *Die Zeit*, 29 March 1991, 3; Hanns W. Maull, "Germany and Japan: The New Civilian Powers," *Foreign Affairs* 65 (1990–91): 92–93; and Stephen Szabo, *The Changing Politics of Germany Security* (New York: St. Martin's, 1990). John Mearsheimer, "Back to the Future: Instability in Europe after the Cold War," *International Security* 15 (1990): 5–56, and David Garnham, "Extending Deterrence with German Nuclear Weapons," *International Security* 10 (1985):

96–110, advocate the acquisition of nuclear weapons by Germany. I agree with Thomas Kielinger that Germany is an unlikely candidate for nuclear proliferation because "for the German people this is a matter of holy writ as they have once and for all renounced production or possession of nuclear weapons. Any office holder attempting even to mention a change in this policy would be committing suicide." Thomas Kielinger, "Waking Up in the New Europe—With a Headache," *International Affairs* 66 (1990): 261.

3. It appears that the Grundgesetz does not prohibit the Bundeswehr from participating in UN peacekeeping missions; rather the Germans have made a conscious political decision not to participate. See Peter Bardehle, "'Blue Helmets' from Germany? Opportunities and Limits of UN Peacekeeping," *Aussenpolitik* 4 (1989): 381ff.; and Christoph Bertram, "Wo nicht hin mit der Bundeswehr?," *Die Zeit,* 7 June 1991, 1.

4. This theme is a dominant one in Wolfram F. Hanrieder, *Germany, America, Europe: Forty Years of German Foreign Policy* (New Haven: Yale University Press, 1989).

5. See for example the comments of Bundesminister für besondere Aufgaben Rudolf Seiters, "Perspektiven der Deutschlandpolitik im geeinten Europa," 30 November 1990, *Bulletin des Presse- und Informationsamt der Bundesregierung* (hereafter *Bulletin*), no. 141, 5 December 1990, 1485.

6. See Pierre Hassner, "Europe beyond Partition and Unity: Disintegration or Reconstitution?," *International Affairs* 66 (1990): 461–77; John Lewis Gaddis, "Toward the Post-Cold War World," *Foreign Affairs* 70 (1991): 102–22; Earl C. Ravenal, "The Case for Adjustment," *Foreign Policy* 81 (1990–91): 3–19; Jack Synder, "Averting Anarchy in the New Europe," *International Security* 14 (1990): 5–41; John J. Mearsheimer, "Back to the Future"; and Stephen van Evera, "Primed for Peace: Europe After the Cold War," *International Security* 15 (1990–91): 7–57.

7. For example, see the remarks of Chancellor Helmut Kohl, "Tanner Lecture an der Universität Kalifornien in Berkeley," 13 September 1991, *Bulletin* no. 102, 20 September 1991, 811; and of Foreign Minister Hans-Dietrich Genscher, "Europäisch-japanische Zusammenarbeit im Aufbau einer neuen Welt," 13 September 1991, *Bulletin* no. 101, 19 September 1991, 801.

8. For other assessments of the German role during the Gulf war, see Ronald D. Asmus, "Fragen unter Freunden: Der Golfkonflikt hat zu einer schweren Betrauenskrise zwischen Bonn und Washington geführt," *Die Zeit,* 22 February 1991, 4; David Hamilton and James Clad, "Germany, Japan, and the False Glare of War," *Washington Quarterly* (1991): 39–49; Uwe Nerlich, "Deutsche Sicherheitspolitik und Konflikte ausserhalb des NATO-Gebiets," *Europa Archiv* 46 (1991): 303–10.

9. See Wilfred Herz, "Zahlmeister sucht Freunde: Die Deutschen wollen die Hilfen für die Sowjetunion nicht allein finanzieren," *Die Zeit,* 7 June 1991, 3; Dieter Buhl, "Die sieben sind keine Samariter: Aber der Londoner Weltwirtschaftsgipfel muss Gorbatschow entgegenkommen," *Die Zeit,* 19 July 1991, 1; and Thomas Hanke, "Kurzsichtige Egoisten," *Die Zeit,* 9 August 1991, 12.

10. Kohl, "Tanner Lecture," 812.

11. See Sommer, "Die Deutschen an die Front."

12. On the issue of German hegemony, see Andrei Markovits and Simon Reich, "The New Face of Germany: Gramsci, Hegemony, and Europe" (Paper delivered at the Annual Meeting of the American Political Science Association, Washington, D.C., 1991). A more modest assessment of German power is found in Simon Bulmer and William Patterson, "West Germany's Role in Europe: 'Man-Mountain' or 'Semi-Gulliver'?" *Journal of Common Market Studies* 28 (1989): 95–118.

13. For an extended discussion of NATO as a "fated community" (*Schicksalsgemeinschaft*), see Emil J. Kirchner and James Sperling, "The Future Germany and the Future of NATO," *German Politics* 1 (April 1992): 50–77.

14. Chancellor Helmut Kohl, "Die Streitkräfte als wichtigstes Instrument der Sicherheitspolitik," 13 December 1988, *Bulletin* no. 175, 16 December 1988, 1550–51.

15. This rejection was qualified by the statement that the structure of the alliance's nuclear weapons depended "upon the changes in the political situation and the military threat, of the results of arms control and disarmament negotiations, and of technological developments." Kohl, "Die Streitkräfte," 1552. See similar statements in Helmut Kohl, "Regierungserklärung des Bundeskanzlers vor dem Deutschen Bundestag: Arbeitsprogramm der Bundesregierung–Perspektiven für die neunziger Jahre," 27 April 1989, *Bulletin* no. 40, 28 April 1989, 370. It is also the case that there was considerable divergence within the CDU/CSU, between coalition partners, and between government and opposition on the SNF issue. I am indebted to Christoph Bluth on this last point.

16. Defence Minister Gerhard Stoltenberg, "Künftige Perspektiven deutscher Sicherheitspolitik," 13 June 1990, *Bulletin* no. 76, 14 June 1990, 654.

17. Compare these statements with those made by Chancellor Kohl in his 1989 Regierungserklärung, where he acknowledged the need for land-based, short-range nuclear weapons and nuclear artillery to sustain the strategy of deterrence. Kohl in fact stated that there was "no alternative to [nuclear] deterrence" to prevent the outbreak of war. Kohl, "Regierungserklärung," 1989, 370. Hans-Dietrich Genscher, "Eine Vision für das ganze Europa," 3 February 1991, *Bulletin* no. 14, 6 February 1991, 92.

18. "NATO-Gipfelkonferenz in Rom: Erklärung von Rom über Frieden und Zusammenarbeit," 8 November 1991, *Bulletin* no. 128, 13 November 1991, 1034.

19. "Remarks by President Bush on Reducing US and Soviet Nuclear Weapons," *New York Times*, 28 September 1991, sec. A. The President announced that the United States would retain only "an effective air-delivered capability in Europe"; a capability viewed as "essential to NATO's security." The American decision to eliminate ground- and sea-based tactical nuclear weapons from the European theatre was reciprocated by President Gorbachev in early October. *New York Times*, 6 October 1991, sec. A.

20. On this issue there is little disagreement. See Michael Broer and Ole Diehl, "Die Sicherheit der neuen Demokratien in Europa und die NATO," *Europa Archiv* 46 (1991): 372–76; Joseph Joffe, "The Security Implications of a United Germany: Paper I," *Adelphi Paper* no. 257 (1990–91): 84–91; Robert D. Blackwill, "The Security Implications of a United Germany: Paper II," *Adelphi Paper* no. 257 (1990–91): 92–95; Gerhard Wettig, "German Unification and European Security," *Aussenpolitik*

42 (1991): 13–19; Rupert Scholz, "Deutsche Frage und europäische Sicherheit. Sicherheitspolitik in einem sich einigenden Deutschland und Europa," *Europa Archiv* 45 (1990): 239–46; Michael Howard, "The Remaking of Europe," *Survival* 22 (1990): 99–106; and Stanley Hoffmann, "The Case for Leadership," *Foreign Policy* 81 (1990–91): 20–38. Contrary views are found in Earl C. Ravenal, "The Case for Adjustment," *Foreign Policy* 81 (1990–91): 3–19; and Christopher Layne, "Superpower Disengagement," *Foreign Policy* 77 (1989–90): 17–40. A sceptical view of NATO's future, relevant although written before the collapse of the postwar order, is found in David P. Calleo, "NATO's Middle Course," *Foreign Policy* 69 (1987–88): 135–47.

21. Chancellor Kohl, for example, stated that "NATO must always be understood as a community of values . . . and this means that we neither can nor desire the replacement of NATO." See his remarks in "Die Rolle Deutschlands in Europa," 13 March 1991, *Bulletin* no. 33, 22 March 1991, 244. See also, Helmut Kohl, "Aufgaben deutscher Politik in den neunziger Jahren," 20 May 1991, *Bulletin* no. 56, 22 May 1991, 443.

22. In Chancellor Kohl's estimation, the American role and responsibility "in and for Europe remains of critical meaning for the peace and security of our continent and above all for the unified Germany in the middle of that continent." Helmut Kohl, "Regierungserklärung des Bundeskanzlers vor dem Deutschen Bundestag: Unsere Verantwortung für die Freiheit," 30 January 1991, *Bulletin* no. 11, 31 January 1991, 73–4.

23. See Kohl, "Rolle Deutschlands," 245; and "Aufgaben deutscher Politik," 441. This formula is endorsed by Jiri Dienstbier, foreign minister of the Czech and Slovak Federal Republic, in "Central Europe's Security," *Foreign Policy* 83 (1991): 125–27.

24. Chancellor Kohl, "Verantwortung für das Zusammenwachsen Deutschlands und Europas," 6 June 1991, *Bulletin* no. 64, 7 June 1991, 513. See also, Minister of Finance Theodor Waigel, "Haushaltsgesetz vor dem Deutschen Bundestag," 3 September 1991, *Bulletin* no. 93, 4 September 1991, 747. Waigel, in response to SPD criticism that he ignored the CSCE, argues that NATO and the CSCE are not in opposition to one another and that "both are necessary instruments for peace in Europe and the world."

25. Chancellor Kohl, "Erstes Treffen des Rates der Aussenminister der Teilnehmerstaaten der KSZE," 19 June 1991, *Bulletin* no. 72, 22 June 1991, 579. This position reflected the outcome of the Cophenhagen NATO Summit on 6 June 1991 where the allies made an effort to reassure the nations of the former Warsaw Pact with language that stopped short of offering a unilateral security guarantee. *New York Times,* 7 June 1991, sec. A.

26. Genscher, "Eine Vision," 92.

27. Defense Minister Gerhard Stoltenberg, "Zukunftsaufgaben der Bundeswehr im vereinten Deutschland," 13 March 1991, *Bulletin* no. 29, 15 March 1991, 215. See also, Stoltenberg, "Der Selbstverständnis des Soldaten in der Bundeswehr von morgen," 17 June 1991, *Bulletin* no. 70, 19 June 1991, 566.

28. Defense Minister Gerhard Stoltenberg, "Deutsche Einheit und europäische Sicherheit," 1 May 1990, *Bulletin* no. 52, 5 May 1990, 406.

29. Genscher, "Eine Vision," 92.

30. On the attribution to Adenauer, see Gerhard Stoltenberg, "Erklärung der Bundesregierung: Die Bundeswehr in den neunziger Jahren," 7 December 1989, *Bulletin* no. 140, 8 December 1989, 1189 and "Sicherheits Fragen eines künftigen geeinten Deutschland," 19 February 1990, *Bulletin* no. 28, 21 February 1990, 218; and on the attribution to Strauss, see Chancellor Kohl, "40 Jahre Soziale Marktwirtschaft in der Bundesrepublik Deutschland," 25 October 1989, *Bulletin* no. 115, 30 October 1989, 988.

31. See Kohl, "Regierungserklärung," 1991, 72–5; and "Verantwortung," 513. See also Hans-Dietrich Genscher, "Rede des Bundesaussenministers vor den Vereinten Nationen," 25 September 1991, *Bulletin* no. 104, 26 September 1991, 825. For an analysis of Genscher's foreign policy strategy, see Emil J. Kirchner, "Genscher and What Lies Behind 'Genscherism'," *West European Politics* 13 (April 1990): 159–77.

32. The German-Polish Treaty of June 1991, for example, is littered with references to the various CSCE meetings and documents; and article three of the treaty commits the contracting parties to "seek peace through the elaboration of cooperative structures of security for the whole of Europe [including the full implementation of] the Helsinki Final Accords, the Charter of Paris [as well as other documents relating to the CSCE process]." "Vertrag zwischen der Bundesrepublik Deutschland und der Republik Polen über gute Nachbarschaft und freundschaftliche Zusammenarbeit," 18 June 1991, *Bulletin* no. 68, 18 June 1991, 542. More generally, the Germans consider the CSCE to be "the stability framework for the enlarged Europe" and "the bracket for the emerging pan-European order in all spheres"; and the Paris Charter is viewed as the quasi-constitutional framework for a pan-European system ordered by the principles of democracy, human rights, and the market economy. See Genscher, "Eine Vision," 92–3; and "The Future of Europe," 12 July 1991, *Statements and Speeches* 14 (1991): 3–4.

33. Helmut Kohl, "Deutsche-amerikanischer Beitrag zur Stabilität und Sicherheit," 21 May 1991, *Bulletin* no. 58, 28 May 1991, 458. This argument is also made by Stanley Sloan, "NATO's Future in a New Europe: An American Perspective," *International Affairs* 66 (1990): 504ff.

34. Kohl, "Rolle Deutschlands," 245.

35. For an analysis of the Bonn conference, see Hans-Christian Reichel, "Die Bonner Wirtschaftskonferenz und die Zukunft der KSZE," *Europa Archiv* 45 (1990): 461–70; and Task Force on German Unification, *The United States and United Germany* (Washington, D.C.: Atlantic Council of the United States, 1990): 22.

36. See "KSZE-Konferenz über wirtschaftliche Zusammenarbeit in Europa. Dokument der Bonner Konferenz," 11 April 1990, *Bulletin* no. 46, 19 April 1990, 357–62. The role of economic cooperation in the creation of a pan-European security system were acknowledged in the Paris Charter of the CSCE. See "Charta von Paris für ein neues Europa. Erklärung des Pariser KSZE-Treffens der Staats- und Regierungschefs," 24 November 1990, *Bulletin* no. 137, 24 November 1990, 1412–13; Economics Minister Helmut Haussmann, "Neue Chancen und Impulse der West-Ost-Zusammenarbeit," 31 January 1990, *Bulletin* no. 20, 2 February 1990, 162; "Rede des Bundesministers des Auswärtigen der Bundesrepublik Deutschland, Hans-Dietrich

Genscher, auf der Konferenz über wirtschaftliche Zusammenarbeit in Europa im Rahmen der KSZE in Bonn am 11. April 1990," *Europa Archiv* 45 (1990): D218–24.

37. Helmut Kohl, "Ein geeintes Deutschland als Gewinn für Stabilität und Sicherheit in Europa," 25 May 1990, *Bulletin* no. 68, 29 May 1990, 587. See also Kohl, "Regierungserklärung," 1991, 30 January 1991, *Bulletin* no. 11, 31 January 1991, 63; President Richard von Weizsäcker, "Ansprache des Bundespräsidenten," 9 April 1990, *Bulletin* no. 46, 19 April 1990, 362–63. Similar sentiments were expressed by Helmut Haussmann, "Abschlusserklärung des Bundeswirtschaftsminister," 9 April 1990, *Bulletin* no. 46, 19 April 1990, 363; Hans-Dietrich Genscher, "Rede des Bundesaussenministers," 11 April 1990, *Bulletin* no. 46, 19 April 1990, 365; and Stoltenberg, "Deutsche Einheit," 408; Helmut Kohl, "KSZE-Wirtschaftskonferenz in Bonn," 19 March 1990, *Bulletin* no. 37, 20 March 1990, 287; "Geeintes Deutschland," 589.

38. Genscher, "Eine Vision," 93.

39. Less relaxed appraisals of the new German-Russian relationship can be found in W. R. Smyser, "USSR-Germany: A Link Restored," *Foreign Policy* 84 (1991): 125–41; and Marian Leighton and Robert Rudney, "Non-Offensive Defense: Toward a Soviet-German Security Partnership?," *Orbis* 35 (1991): 377–94.

40. Kohl, "Regierungserklärung" 1991, 72; Genscher, "Eine Vision," 91; Stoltenberg, "Selbstverständnis des Soldaten," 566; Kohl, "Erstes Treffen," 578.

41. Hans-Dietrich Genscher, "Bewertung des Ratsvorsitzenden," 20 June 1991, *Bulletin* no. 72, 22 June 1991, 584; "Deutschland, Frankreich und Polen in der Verantwortung für Europas Zukunft. Gemeinsame Erklärung der Aussenminister von Deutschland, Frankreich und Polen in Weimar," 29 August 1991, *Bulletin* no. 92, 3 September 1991, 735. The German position was embraced by the Community. The Luxembourg European Council Meeting communique of June 1991 stated that "the European Council considers the creation of a European economic space to be an essential element of the future architecture of Europe." See "Europäischer Rat in Luxembourg," 29 June 1991, *Bulletin* no. 78, 9 July 1991, 625. On Europe and NATO, see Stoltenberg, "Künftige Perspektiven," 655. On unification and German domestic order, see Kohl, "Regierungserklärung" 1991, 72.

42. Gerhard Stoltenberg and Hans-Dietrich Genscher, "Sicherheitspolitische Fragen eines künftigen geeinten Deutschland," 19 February 1990, *Bulletin* no. 28, 21 February 1990, 218.

43. See the comments of Stoltenberg, "Selbstverständnis des Soldaten," 566. Finance Minister Waigel has stated the need for European union in starker terms: "The world needs a single Europe as an world economic and world political stability factor." Waigel, "Haushaltsgesetz 1992," 747.

44. Kohl, "Verantwortung," 513.

45. Chancellor Kohl was unable to press the German claim that the EC should become primarily responsible for asylum and immigration policy at the EC Maastricht summit. The Maastricht participants did to consider moving asylum policy to the EC at the 1993 summit. *Economist,* 14 December 1991, 54.

46. Interior Minister Wolfgang Schäuble, "Vorschläge und Bemühungen zur Lösung der Asylproblematik," 7 August 1991, *Bulletin* no. 85, 9 August 1991, 689.

For an overview of the problem of migration, see Francois Heisbourg, "Population Movements in post-Cold War Europe," *Survival* 33 (1991): 31–44.

47. Sixty percent of those seeking political asylum in the EC choose Germany. Moreover, the number of those seeking asylum has risen dramatically: in 1978, 33,000 individuals sought asylum in Germany; in 1990, 193,063 individuals sought asylum in Germany. And close to 70 percent of today's asylum seekers come from eastern and southeastern Europe. The number of *Aussiedler* (ethnic Germans immigrating to Germany) rose from 54,887 in 1979 to 397,073 in 1990. Moreover, the number of foreign residents in Germany rose from 1.2 percent of the German population in 1961 to 7.2 percent of the population in 1991. German Press and Information Office, "Focus On . . . Foreigners in Germany" (mimeo, November 1991), 3 and tables 1 and 2.

48. German Information Center, "Focus On . . . Foreigners," 2.

49. See Peter J. Katzenstein, "Coping with Terrorism: Norms and Internal Security in Germany and Japan" (Paper delivered at the Annual Meeting of the American Political Science Association, Washington, D. C., 1991); and *West Germany's Internal Security Policy: State and Violence in the 1970s and 1980s,* Center for International Studies, Western Societies Program, Occasional Paper no. 28 (Ithaca: Cornell University, 1990).

50. Wolfgang Schäuble, "Innere Sicherheit und Stabilität der rechtsstaatlichen Demokratie: Erklärung des Bundesministers des Innern zum Verfassungsschutzbericht 1988," 4 July 1989, *Bulletin* no. 73, 8 July 1989, 640; *New York Times,* 16 December 1991, sec. A.

51. Chancellor Helmut Kohl, "Erklärung der Bundesregierung," 6 November 1991, *Bulletin* no. 124, 7 November 1991, 987. These concerns are not unique to the Germans; the French and British are equally concerned about immigration and border control. The difference, however, is found in Germany's geography and historical experience which constrain Germany in ways that France and Britain are not constrained.

52. For a historical overview of the WEU, see Alfred Cahan, *The Western European Union and NATO: Building a European Defence Identity within the Context of Atlantic Solidarity* (London: Brassey's, 1989). On the future roles of the WEU, see Guenther van Well, "Zur Europa-Politik eines vereinigten Deutschland," *Europa Archiv* 45 (1990): 35.

53. Western European Union, *Platform on European Security Interests* (The Hague, 27 October 1987, Mimeographed).

54. "Gemeinsame Erklärung anlässlich der 56. deutsche-französischen Konsultationen am 17. und 18. September 1990 in München," 18 September 1990, *Bulletin* no. 111, 19 September 1990, 1170; Kohl, "Regierungserklärung," 73. The logic of the Franco-German position is presented in Jacques Delors, "European Integration and Security," *Survival* 33 (1991): 99–110.

55. Stoltenberg, "Das Selbstverständnis," 566.

56. "Kommuniqué des Ministerrates der Westeuropäischen Union," 27 June 1991, *Bulletin* no.77, 5 July 1991, 621.

57. "Europäischer Rat in Luxembourg," 625; and "Kommuniqué der Ministert-

agung des Nordatlantikrats," 7 June 1991, *Bulletin* no. 66, 11 June 1991, 527; "Deutschland, Frankreich und Polen in der Verantwortung für Europas Zukunft," 29 August 1991, *Bulletin* no. 92, 3 September 1991, 734; and "Kommunique des Ministerrates der Westeuropäischen Union," 621.

58. Hans-Dietrich Genscher, speech before the WEU, 8 July 1991, *Statements and Speeches* 14 (1991): 1.

59. The French and Germans also proposed an expansion of the Franco-German brigade from 5,000 to over 30,000 troops. *New York Times,* 17 October 1991, sec. A. For a detailed statement of the Franco-German proposal, see "Botschaft zur gemeinsamen europäischen Aussen- und Sicherheitspolitik," 14 October 1991, *Bulletin* no. 117, 18 October 1991, 929–31. For American objections to the proposal, see Jenonne Walker, "Keeping American in Europe," *Foreign Policy* 83 (1991): 141; and for Italian objections, see Marta Dass, "The Future of Europe: The View from Rome," *International Affairs* 66 (1990): 302–3.

60. *Economist,* 14 December 1991, 52. For a post-Maastricht statement on the WEU and the EC, see Chancellor Helmut Kohl, "Erklärung der Bundesregierung," 986.

61. Nonetheless, German public support for an independent European army remains lukewarm at best. A public opinion survey conducted by the Socialwissenschaftliches Institut der Bundeswehr found that 66 percent of the respondents believed that any European army should remain within the NATO framework and only 22 percent believed that it should operate outside it. Poll cited in Hans-Joachim Veen, "Die Westbindung der Deutschen in einer Phase der Neuorientierung," *Europa Archiv* 46 (1991): 35.

62. It is also the case that the WEU allows the Europeans to sidestep the immediate problems associated with Irish (and Austrian and Swedish) neutrality and the longer-term problems associated with the EC membership of former member states of the Warsaw Pact, particularly Poland, Hungary, and the Czech and Slovak Federal Republic.

63. Helmut Kohl, "Geeintes Deutschland," 586; Seiters, "Perspektiven"; Helmut Kohl, "Besuch des Bundeskanzlers in den Vereinigten Staaten von Amerika," 5 June 1990, *Bulletin* no. 74, 13 June 1990, 638.

64. Economic tripolarity—a German-dominated Europe, North America, and a renascent Russia—would enhance the prospects for cooperation in the Euro-Atlantic area and cannot be discounted. The eventuality of economic tripolarity in the Euro-Atlantic area was argued as early as 1949 by Andreas Predöhl in *Aussenwirtschaft: Weltwirtschaft, Handelspolitik, und Währungspolitik* (Göttingen: Vandenhoeck & Ruprecht, 1949): 118ff. For formal demonstrations that cooperation is more likely in a tripolar rather than bipolar structure of power, see Duncan Snidal, "Relative Gains and the Pattern of International Cooperation," *American Political Science Review* 85 (1991): 716–19 and "International Cooperation Among Relative Gains Maximizers," *International Studies Quarterly* 35 (1991): 387–402. For a contrary analysis, see Joanne Gowa, "Bipolarity, Multipolarity, and Free Trade," *American Political Science Review* 83 (1989): 1245–56.

PART 7

Conclusion

Continuity, Change, and the Study of Germany in the New Europe

Simon Reich

Germany and the Germans constantly defy our most emphatic expectations. Stereotypes begrudgingly concede our envy of the Germans' capacity to get things done efficiently and effectively. Similarly, political scientists as well as historians often attribute a predictability to developments both within Germany and in terms of Germany's relationship with the rest of Europe and the world that, we believe, is inconsistent with an accurate interpretation of history. Indeed, it is the institutionalization of concepts like Die Wende, Der Sonderweg, and the "German Question" that lends the unpredictable a semblance of the expected. To depart from the formulation that the only thing predictable about Germany is its unpredictability would require us to reassess fundamentals in our thinking about Germany. There seems at times to be an intellectual sleight of hand about the whole exercise. The most egregious offenders in the acceptance of this fallacy have been scholars in the area of international relations and, to a lesser extent, those in comparative politics. Although it might be claimed that those studying security policy have erred to a greater degree than students of political economy, both have had their basic assumptions and expectations about Germany confounded by developments in the last three years. Yet these scholars have often simply ignored the fact that history has rendered political science's most "incontrovertible" theories irrelevant. This pertains particularly to structural theories. Scholars subscribing to these theories have generally toiled afresh in the new context, apparently unreflective of the bankruptcy of some of their most profound formulations.

This concluding chapter begins with a recognition of these facts and attempts to establish the reason political scientists have failed so miserably. Why did students of international relations, in particular, prove to be so mistaken in their expectations about the course of events in Germany in the late 1980s? In broader terms, why did they attribute a continuity and coherence to German development that contradicts historical reality, thus assuming continuity when even a cursory study would lead us to expect otherwise? Why is it that they treat the truly exceptional as if it were routine when these scholars discuss it in relation to Germany? After all, it is Germany as a country among advanced industrial states whose development uniquely defies the neat, conventional patterns of modernization and the attribution of grand, sweeping causal patterns.

We will attempt to address these questions by arguing that Germany may represent the most exaggerated example among advanced industrial states of the scholarly propensity to emphasize purely structural factors in the study of external relations. We suggest that this tendency has cost our capacity to understand, interpret, and, above all, explain developments there. While Germany's geographic, economic, and military centrality to a degree justifies such an approach in political science, much of the explanation for this tendency lies in the intellectual roots of structuralism and the emphasis placed on structure by German historians. In this chapter we will examine the role of structural analysis in the study of Germany and suggest why it might have led to our being blindsided by recent events. We will then suggest that the contributions in this volume offer a series of agendas for the future study of Germany that, while not ignoring the role of structure, focus more on the importance of process and ideas, thus providing a basis for a series of research projects that offer an understanding of past, present, and future developments in Germany.

What Is Structure?

Although many political scientists use the term *structure,* lack of a conventional definition has made it an amorphous concept open to varied usage. In simple terms, many who talk about structural theory (particularly in the realm of international relations) refer to types of structural theories such as neorealism, neoliberalism and world systems analysis rather than defining structuralism itself. Robert Gilpin, an advocate of structural theory, is an exception in providing a definition of structure proper:

> By "structure," I mean simply "the parts of an economic whole which, over a period of time, appear relatively stable alongside the others." These structures provide constraints and opportunities within which actors attempt to achieve their objectives. A major goal of states and powerful organizations is to change the structures themselves. These structures include social institutions, the distribution of property rights, the division of labor and location of economic activities, the organiza-

tion of particular markets, and the norms or regimes governing economic affairs.[1]

The purpose of structural theory, according to Kenneth Waltz, is to explain continuity, not change, defining the parameters of behavior and recurrent themes across time and space.[2] Germany therefore seems a most unlikely object for the application of structural theory, given the vagaries of its unique historical pattern of development. Yet, paradoxically, structural explanations have predominated among students of German external relations, be they those offered by historians or political scientists. Perhaps part of the answer lies in the philosophical and social scientific foundations of German intellectual thinking itself. Furthermore, such predilections towards structuralist formulations in an analysis of Germany are firmly rooted in the discipline of history (which, prima facie, should be among the most hesitant to employ structural analysis) and that of political science. In fact the two disciplines in this case are, in certain respects, symbiotically related, with formulations first developed by German historians providing many of the central foundations to realism, the dominant postwar paradigm of international relations, and to state theory, recently in vogue in the field of comparative politics.

Emanuel Adler has been among the most vocal critics of the structural approach. An emphasis on structural analysis, he suggests, encourages the development of static and mechanistic theories aimed at explaining stability, efficiency, and hierarchy—thus continuity rather than change. Adler suggests that structuralism, given its deductive character, has a propensity to develop theories that emphasize the view that causality is linear. He recoils against this determinism and prefers to stress the importance of voluntarism, the decision-making process and the synthesis of knowledge over time.[3]

Noting Adler's criticisms, we begin by examining the intellectual roots of structuralism among German historians, from whom political scientists have so heavily borrowed. We will then discuss the application of many of these assumptions to political science's study of Germany and conclude with a discussion of the fundamental questions concerning the new Germany, and how political scientists might most profitably study them.

Structure and the Study of German History

As already suggested, German historians have traditionally employed structural theories that encompass great historical sweeps in an effort to instill a degree of coherence to the study of German history. Nineteenth-century formulations themselves emphasized the preeminence of the autonomous, deified state as the synthesis of Macht and Geist (power and spirit). Conservatives, notably Max Lenz, Erich Marcks, and Felix Rachfahl, fused principles derived from Wilhelm Friedrich Hegel and Leopold von Ranke to develop a perspective consistent with the contemporary realist approach familiar to political scientists. Ranke's primary assumptions were that the state represented the divine expression of the political spirit of its populace and that its foremost purpose was to survive in an amoral, anarchic international environment. Lacking any mechanism to impose international law, states were obliged to maximize their power, with war being the natural outcome of the struggle between states in a divine process. States therefore had to emphasize the "primacy of foreign policy" in order to ensure survival; the result would be reduced international conflict.[4] Consistent with these neo-Rankean assumptions, the parochial late-nineteenth- and early-twentieth-century ideology of Weltpolitik justified German expansion as a means of securing national survival through its establishment among the "Great Powers." The Germans could thus use deterrence to "command the peace."[5] In application, the neo-Rankean method therefore rejected explaining the outbreak of war as a consequence of the nature of Germany's internal social structure. Like contemporary realism, neo-Rankeanism assumed that the state was monolithic, with decisions made by elites personified in the chancellor. Unlike contemporary realism, according to critics of neo-Rankeanism, however, this approach was more or less consciously ideological, did distinguish between states rather than treating them as equals (by discriminating between Germany and everyone else), and was prescriptive in intent.[6] The neo-Rankean objective was to legitimate a perspective that recommended maximizing German power through the development of an aggressive foreign policy. Security lay in foreign expansion,[7] specifically the defeat of France, the foundation of a Central European federation under German leadership, and the development of Germany as a world power through the acquisition of new colonies. Neo-Rankeanism thus vindicated expansionist Wilhelmine foreign policies in the prewar period and subsequently defused accusations of German culpability for the outbreak of war in 1914.[8] Like other states, according to Gerhard Ritter and Golo Mann, Germany had simply pursued foreign policies consistent with its national interest. Miscalculation and conflicting interests combined to spark a war, while a lack of communication and the failure of leadership explained Germany's defeat.[9]

Eckhart Kehr was the first historian to "turn this thesis of the so-called 'primacy of foreign policy' (Primat der Aussenpolitik) on its head and argue instead for the 'primacy of internal policy' (Primat der Innenpolitik) in determining matters of peace and war" in the 1920s.[10] But it was Fritz Fischer four decades later, in his landmark work *Griff nach der Weltmacht* (subsequently translated as *Germany's Aims in the First World War*), who mounted the greater challenge to the traditional conservatives. While opposing the traditional conservatives on the issue of German culpability, Fischer nonetheless also adopted a structural analysis—specifying a relatively rigid causal linkage between the internal structure of the Bismarckian and Wilhelmine states, on the one hand, and both the outbreak of World War I and, more indirectly, the Nazi attainment of power, on the other.[11]

Fischer's heretical declaration of German guilt was founded on the claim that German intellectuals, as representatives of the interests of the conservative elite that dominated the state, prepared a climate conducive to the development of an aggressive form of nationalism, increasing the probability of war.[12] Domestic elites promulgated principles consistent with militaristic and nationalistic values because they considered foreign expansion to be a way of defusing internal tensions; the German leadership's goal was to annex much of Europe and dominate the rest of it, in a scheme conceived well before the outbreak of war.[13] John A. Moses summarizes Fischer's position with the comment that "the war of 1914–1918 was therefore not the result of some tragic diplomatic error but a conscious, if nervous calculation by a power-deluded state which believed that her hour of destiny in world history had arrived."[14]

Fischer's analysis prompted the historical debate that became known as the "Fischer controversy," in which conservatives such as Ritter and Mann conceded that German policies might have acted as the immediate catalyst for World War I but retained their neo-Rankean assumptions in claiming that Germany's actions had constituted preemptive defensive measures in the face of an imminent Allied attack.[15] Both sides recognized that the implications of Fischer's claims went well beyond the issue of German war culpability. By attacking many of the cherished values and institutions of the Wilhelmine period, Fischer implied that Germany's nationalist, imperialist, anti-Semitic and Prussian statist traditions provided the antecedent conditions for Hitler's subsequent emergence.[16] This was therefore not only a claim about the causes of the war but a sweeping structural and historical analysis of German state and society that causally linked discrete periods of German history, the advent of the Third Reich, by implication, being explained by the structure of the Second Reich.[17] The combination of the historical and structural approaches has come to be known as *historicist.*

Fischer inspired the emergence of an alternative, antistatist orthodoxy based on an analysis of social forces in which the state was treated as an instrument of the dominant elites. Yet much of that too had a structuralist formulation. One of its most notable representatives was Hans-Ulrich Wehler, whose analysis of the German Empire owed much to Fischer, despite Wehler's criticism of Fischer.[18]

Wehler's interest-based, class analysis suggested that the internal structure of the German state was one dominated by the vested interests of elites, whose policies were legitimated by a manipulative ideology.[19] This new approach focused on the governing coalition of "iron and rye"—the economic influence of the leaders of heavy industry coupled with the political dominance of the Prussian Junker class, the agrarian, feudal elite who owned the large estates located east of the Elbe and dominated the ranks of the German bureaucracy, the officer corps of the armed forces, and the Prussian Diet (legislature).[20]

According to Wehler the Prussian conquest that generated Germany's unification largely explains Prussia's domination of Germany's political institutions, in the context of what Wehler identified as "pseudo-constitutional semi-absolutism," manifest in the constitutional authority of the Prussian king as German Kaiser, the Prime Minister of Prussia as Chancellor of the Reich, and the three-tiered electoral system for the legislature that favored Prussian voters.[21] Volker Berghahn succinctly captures the spirit of Fischer's and Wehler's conception of the social, geographic, and economic distribution of political power in Bismarckian and Wilhelmine Germany with the statement that "Prussia and the German Empire as a whole was, in effect, ruled by an elite, led by the crown and a "strategic clique," whose social and economic power base was the German countryside."[22] As Geoff Eley, perhaps caricaturing both Fischer's and Wehler's analyses, stated, "The continuity of German imperialist ambition across the two world wars was seen to reflect a more basic continuity of dominant socio-economic interests at home."[23]

The new orthodoxy suggested, according to Richard Evans, that the successful aim of the Junker strategy was to divert emancipatory and reformist impulses among the masses into an enthusiasm for foreign conquest, empire, and generally greater international prestige.[24] Wehler suggests that "the intentions behind Germany's overseas expansion, and the function it performed, served the interests of a 'social imperialism.' This amounted to a defensive strategy which aimed at the social goal of a preserving traditional structures; a conservative 'taming' policy which sought to divert abroad reform attempts which found their expression in liberal and socialist emancipatory forces. These conservatives thus hoped to preserve the inherited pre-industrial social and political structures of the Greater Prussian Empire, while defending the industrial and educated middle classes against the rising proletariat."[25]

This newer literature consciously rejected the view that the state constituted an autonomous entity, in favor of an analysis of the instrumental manipulation of the state by society's dominant forces. It put more emphasis on political relationships among the dominant classes as opposed to the continuity of the state bureaucracy.

Yet both the new and traditional orthodoxies retained some crucial features. The former approach maintained the view that the German decision-making elite was monolithic—even if that elite, the Junkers, was analyzed as a social class rather than as a bureaucratic hierarchy. Both sides, moreover, agreed about the authoritarian character of the state (although they differed about whether these features were desirable). Finally, fundamental to both was an emphasis on structure rather than process, allowing both to retain a macrohistorical element.

Certainly, these two opposing perspectives were not the only alternatives. A third, subsequent wave of literature emerged that challenged the structural perspective common to both of the previous two waves.[26] Possibly the best example of this type is to be found in the work of Geoff Eley, who, for example, concluded that there is an unmistakable commitment by Fischer and Wehler to the notion of structural continuity in Germany's historical development in linking Bismarck to Hitler. Eley criticized this form of argument for its willingness effectively to redefine the problem of fascism into a more general problem of political backwardness.[27] Furthermore, Wehler's and Fischer's depiction of the peasantry as manipulated was specifically contradicted by Eley's own empirical findings, while Eley also had difficulties recognizing the continuities their work claimed existed over a six-decade period. In general terms, Eley criticized members of the first two waves of German historians because they chose to study structure rather than process, valued parsimony and generality over accuracy, and emphasized thematic unity rather than interpretative caution. The result, Eley claimed, was a static analysis that oversimplified reality, missing the historical processes of "decomposition and regroupment" dating from the 1860s until the late 1920s.[28] The implication of Eley's critique was that by retaining elements of both structure and process in an analysis one might lay the foundations for understanding both aspects of continuity and change. James McAdams's contribution to this volume on the changing nature of inter-German cooperation in the 1980s in the context of an evolving domestic and international environment provides an interesting example along these lines.

But political scientists studying Germany have often ignored Eley's suggestion, overstating the role of structure to the exclusion of other pertinent factors. In the section that follows we shall demonstrate where, how, and to what degree structuralism has influenced the thinking of political scientists.

Political Science and Structure in the Study of Germany

Although this "third wave" of historical analysis—led by scholars like Eley—provided a viable and lively alternative approach, structuralism remained popular among German historians. It also imperiously influenced the development of political science on both sides of the Atlantic, as refugees, fleeing the Holocaust in Europe, developed new structural analyses largely neglected in American political science to that point. Most pointedly, the assumptions of neo-Rankean and, to an extent, Weberian social theory, did much to reify the state, which had always been treated as pluralistic and fragmented by Americans. This influence was evident initially among those comparativists writing about Germany as well as among scholars working in the field of international relations, who adapted structural assumptions and analyses in order to generate new "grand theories," the most notable example being Hans Morgenthau in his seminal book *Politics among Nations*.[29]

Indeed, the concepts of Die Wende (literally "the big change"), Der Sonderweg (which emphasized the uniqueness of German development in comparison to the supposed Western norm), and the evolving form of the German Question have, alone among advanced industrial states, made the whole notion of major change endemic to the study of Germany among political scientists. An interesting paradox has befuddled their studies of Germany. While on the one hand political scientists have come to expect the abnormal and unpredictable in their analysis of German development, they simultaneously—encouraged by historians—seek to find continuities in this development spanning from the Bismarckian period to its latest stage, the new, unified Federal Republic. Change, in this view, is subsumed under continuity.

The whole concept of the German Question has thus endured for over a century—an amorphous concept with security, economic, and political implications. Successive forms of this question have considered the causes of the unification of Germany in 1871, of World Wars I and II, the Nazi seizure of power, the advent of Auschwitz and the Holocaust, and the postwar "economic miracle."[30] To these will inevitably be added the new version considered in this volume by many of the authors—the causes and consequences of unification in the 1990s.

Rather than trying to tackle these macroquestions, many have sought to address subcomponents of one of them. One example is Peter Katzenstein, who recently asked how one "could account for the absence of large-scale policy change in the face of changes in the composition of government." His response, that Germany's contemporary semisovereign state, with its coalition governments, parapublic institutions, cooperative federalism, and circumscribed bureaucracy, has "tamed" the authoritarian traits of former incarnations of that state, begins to provide him with an answer to that question.[31] But the implications of Katzenstein's conclusion will not satisfy those whose fears about a renewed aggressive German foreign policy in the context of the power vacuum created by the implosion of the Soviet empire have been fueled by recent German policies towards Croatia and Slovenia.[32]

Others, however, have been more ambitious. Among this number are a group of non-Germans who have largely defined European history since 1870 as an attempt to contain the military, political, and economic expansion of Europe's most influential actor.[33] This project has thus set itself an elusive task—that of defining and implementing a series of strategies intended to constrain postwar German expansion. Be they de Gaulle's embracing tactics, Giulio Andreotti's strategies of weakening German prowess through division and fragmentation, or the Morgenthau Plan for the pastoralization of Germany, postwar European politics and political thinking is replete with an array of schemes all in one way or another designed to bridle the dangers of German expansion.

Germans themselves, according to sociologist Ralf Dahrendorf, have been similarly interested in the issue of Germany's external relations: "German interest is not devoted to German society and domestic affairs but to the external power structure of world politics and its significance for Germany. German concerns are not social but national." Dahrendorf contends that "for Germans, their society is an unknown; and this in itself is a version of the German Question: Why do people in Germany have so little sense of the patterns, hopes and frustrations of their social world? Why do they devote so little energy to controlling their society, which, after all, concerns the individual much more immediately than the hotly debated abstractions of 'the past,' 'the future,' or 'the nation'?"[34]

A. J. P. Taylor indeed attempted to reconcile both the German and non-German formulations with the statement that "the 'German problem' has two distinct sides. How can the peoples of Europe be secured against repeated bouts of German aggression? And how can the German people discover a settled, peaceful form of political existence?"[35]

Postwar Variants of the German Question

Efforts directed towards the varying goals defined by successive formulations of the German question have achieved differing degrees of success since the 1870s. Dahrendorf notes that the options consist of killing the Germans, domesticating them, driving them away, or letting them tear each other apart.[36] All of these have been tried by Germany's European neighbors over the course of the last century with limited success. Yet three issue areas remain that have constituted the postwar agenda of the German questions among political scientists. These are the issues of European security, German economic prosperity, and the establishment of democracy in Germany. Work in each area reveals, in decreasing degrees respectively, a reliance on structural approaches.

European Security

This first dimension has been the most reliant on structural formulations, represented in the realist paradigm whose intellectual origins, according to its proponents, lie in the work of Thucydides and von Clausewitz, and among whom the most notable postwar proponents include the aforementioned Kenneth Waltz and John Gaddis.[37] As mentioned previously, this dominant realist security paradigm largely defined the German Question in one of two ways; how to constrain German military expansion, or in a more limited sense, the now-defunct issue of how to contain the prospects for reunification.[38] Historically, the security solution, in practical terms, successively involved subduing the Germans; first through a balance-of-power structure in the period before 1914, then by punishment in the form of sanctions in the interwar period, subsequently through war and division, and finally by cooptation through a series of transatlantic institutions in the context of a bipolar world in the postwar period.[39] In the recent wake of superpower decline, many have openly wondered whether the Germans will reassert themselves in the form of a nationalist and imperialist foreign policy—an issue discussed in Markovits and Reich's and in Sperling's contributions to this volume. But it was David Calleo who in the 1970s, with remarkable prescience, pointedly linked the issue of American decline to the question of whether Germans might revive the "nationalist option."[40]

Structural assumptions have been reflected in security debates about the centrality of the transatlantic alliance and, more particularly, the capacity of international institutions like NATO to sustain the stable bipolar order.[41] Correspondingly, it is perhaps in this realm that expectations have been most confounded by the events in Germany. The response to the latest Wende has been baffling at times. With a recognition that the terms of the security debate has changed, scholars have busily immersed themselves in debates about the respective roles and importance of the WEU, CSCE, NATO and any other acronym thought suitable without substantial reflection about the causes of such massive changes in the distribution of power. We suspect that this focus on the implications of the new content, rather than the cause of the new context, is best explained by the fact that to pursue the latter would challenge the fundamental belief of such structural theories, namely that the realities of international relations are more profoundly marked by continuities than great changes. It is easier to concentrate on the effects of the latest Wende than to focus on its cause—for fear that it will invoke a recognition that the emperors of security studies have lost their clothes.

German Economic Prosperity

This second dimension of the German Question has focused on German economic prowess. It has been far less unqualified in its reliance on purely structural formulations and has thus been less myopic in failing to recognize the changes of the late 1980s. One set of scholars have sought to explain the resilience of the German economy while others have had a more consciously normative agenda—trying alternatively to constrain Germany's economy or harness it as a locomotive of European development.

Those interested in the resilience of Germany's economy in the second half of the twentieth century have tended to focus on the work of Rudolf Hilferding and Alexander Gerschenkron, who both stressed, in differing ways, the importance of what Hilferding described as the German system of "organized capitalism" in explaining the pattern and success of German economic development.[42]

Certainly, historically, the political economy literature on Germany has been more nuanced than the literature in the security field, with a more profound emphasis on domestic development and historical detail than the security literature of scientific realism.[43] There is perhaps no better example of this integration of structure and history than that of Alexander Gerschenkron, whose work on Germany has now influenced two generations of political scientists, concerning not only the development of Germany but, more broadly, the dynamics of capitalism. His book, *Bread and Democracy in Germany,* offered an analysis in many ways consistent with that of Fischer and Wehler. He explicitly linked the philosophy, designs, and strategies of the Junkers to the downfall of the Weimar Republic and the rise of fascism. According to Gerschenkron, important elements of the fascist Weltanschauung—nationalism, political and economic autarchy, anti-Semitism, and a contempt for international obligations—could all be traced from the Junkers to the Nazis. Gerschenkron states that "the basic element of what was to become the Weltanschauung of nazism can be perceived distinctly in the policy of an agriculture politically and spiritually dominated by the aristocratic landowners in the eastern half of the German Reich." In ascribing cause, Gerschenkron added that "it is impossible to overestimate the momentous role which the economic and political interests of the Junkers played in the long process of disintegration of democracy leading to the untimely end of the Weimar Republic, and in the initiation of a system which, barely seven years later, destroyed the peace of the world and came close to destroying its freedom."[44]

This explanatory linkage across successive formulations of the German state—Bismarckian, Wilhelmine, Weimar, and Nazi—provided much of the foundation for Gerschenkron's subsequent major work, *Economic Backward-*

ness in Historical Perspective.[45] Here Gerschenkron emphasized the importance of "Germany as a latecomer" to the developmental process of advanced
industrial states in which the state played a more central role as an economic
locomotive in the late nineteenth century by virtue of the German need to
catch up with the then more advanced countries—most pointedly Britain.[46]
The timing of industrialization thus heavily influenced the structure of capital
in the twentieth century. Yet, it must be noted, Gerschenkron here went
beyond the purely structural formulation by integrating economic with political factors, and structure with process, thus providing an explanation of the
dynamics of modern capitalism. This approach therefore fundamentally differed from the more simplified structural formulations often found, for example, in security studies.

Subsequent work by two generations of political scientists have seized
upon this Gerschenkronian formulation, extending and applying it in understanding the dynamics of twentieth-century capitalism. Indeed, it has been
used, at least partially, to explain comparative rates of postwar prosperity
by emphasizing the "advantages of backwardness"—the reduced costs, and
the enhanced strategic innovative benefits, and the appropriateness of institutional structures for contemporary capitalism associated with late development.

Two notable examples of those acknowledging the integration of Gerschenkron's "advantages of backwardness" thesis into their own broader,
comparative work include Andrew Shonfield and, more recently, John Zysman. Both Shonfield's seminal *Modern Capitalism* and John Zysman's *Governments, Markets, and Growth* comparatively analyze the structure of postwar German industry and capital markets in terms of the timing of their
development—and, indirectly, attribute these characteristics to the success
of the German economy. Each, in their own way, stress structural continuities in explaining postwar German development.[47] Peter Hall also recently
adapted Gerschenkron's insights in developing an institutional analysis in
primary application to Britain and France (and secondarily to Germany) in
his excellent book, *Governing the Economy.*[48] Gerschenkron's emphasis on
the resolution and appropriateness of institutions dating from the nineteenth
century in explaining postwar German prosperity is reflected in Christopher
Allen's contribution to this volume, where he emphasizes the durability of
German economic structures—what Allen terms "framework regulations"—
as part of the architecture of what Hilferding described in the opening decades of the twentieth century as "organized capitalism."[49]

To be sure, while none of these significant scholarly contributions focuses primarily on Germany, Germany's centrality to European political
economy is demonstrated by the fact that all these works pay considerable
attention to Germany in their comparative approach. These contributions lack

the rigidity of the structural epistemology common to security studies. But they nevertheless retain an emphasis on institutional continuities dating from the nineteenth century that, it is suggested, define the parameters of German economic policy-making in the postwar period.

While a series of works, based on Gerschenkron's analysis, have stressed continuity in German development, rivals from varied perspectives have emphasized change as a striking feature. My own recent book sought to link the structure and prosperity of the postwar German economy in the formative decade of the Bonn Republic to innovations introduced during the fascist period. I thus argued for a more limited conception of continuity, spanning from the 1930s to the early 1960s, this period being fundamentally different from those both preceding and postdating it.[50] Other works have emphasized the discontinuities dating from 1945 in explaining the postwar development of German capitalism. These arguments have taken two forms. The first, offered by Peter Katzenstein, emphasizes the qualities of stability and consensus found in the Federal Republic, suggesting that the institutional reforms of a federal, democratic system have created an effectively functioning decentralized society. In a radically different argument, initially offered in general, deductive terms by Mancur Olson and then more specifically about Germany by Simon Bulmer, it is suggested that relatively high German growth rates in the early postwar period are to be explained by the then entrepreneurial character of both Germany's polity and economy—a product of the combined effect of fascism, war, and occupation in creating a tabula rasa.[51] These works, although very different in their approaches, all stress discontinuity between Germany's early- and late-twentieth-century polity, economy, and society.

The second element of the political economy literature is both more self-consciously structural and more closely affiliated to the security agenda that involves the containment of Germany. Much of this work recognizes that, in historical terms, when a British policy of direct competition with the Germans failed between 1880 and 1914, a policy of stymied development through the sanctions of war reparations policy was instituted in the interwar period, only to be succeeded by a post-1945 cooptation strategy by virtue of the formation of the EC.[52] The explicit design and purpose of the EC was to tie West Germany to the transatlantic bloc economically, politically, and militarily, while simultaneously addressing Anglo-French fears about German economic domination.[53] The evolving debate between neoliberals and neorealists in international relations now focuses on the issue of whether the present structure of international institutional arrangements will be enough to subdue German expansionist tendencies while simultaneously encouraging Germany to provide a public good by acting as a locomotive for European economic development. Unlike all the comparative political economy literature discussed in the preceding paragraphs, both the neorealist and neoliberal formulations are primarily structural, although, as one might expect, they arrive at rather different prognostications about Germany's future pattern of relations with its neighbors. Neither formulation thus emphasizes the significance of ideas or process—a view critiqued extensively by Markovits and myself in our recent work on Germany's development in the new European construct.[54]

Establishment of Democracy in Germany

The third dimension of the German Question studied by political scientists in relation to German external relations has sought to address the evolution of liberal democracy in Germany in the broader context of political stability. This work has been diligently prescriptive in intent, trying to ascertain the reasons for the downfall of Weimar as well as the scope and domain of democratic values in the postwar Federal Republic. The former issue, the onset of German fascism, was indeed in many ways the central issue in comparative politics in the 1950s, and although interest in that issue has somewhat waned in recent years, debate occasionally erupts with a passion— as David Abraham's controversial analysis demonstrates.[55]

The work on the postwar evolution of democracy can broadly be divided into two elements. The first has been largely institutional, asking macrolevel questions about the evolution of national constructs in which democratic principles can be fostered. Dating from the early work of Carl Friedrich and Zbigniew Brzezinski, scholars have sought to understand the causes of the collapse of Weimar—with a view to avoiding its repetition in Bonn.[56] While much of this work has been optimistic in suggesting that Germany has effectively integrated democratic values, not all has arrived at this conclusion—a pointed example being Gerard Braunthal's recent study of the treatment of political dissidents in the Bonn Republic.[57]

The second aspect of the work on the evolution of German democracy has diligently focused on the integration of democratic principles into the value structure of German individuals through the extensive use of public-opinion survey techniques. Such work, reflected effectively in this volume by the contribution of Manfred Kuechler, but also elsewhere by Samuel Barnes and Max Kaase, Russell Dalton, Elisabeth Noelle Neumann, and Thomas Risse-Kappen, diametrically contrasts with the structural approaches that predominate elsewhere, which is not surprising given the American origins of this social scientific method.[58] Equally predictably, these studies have had more limited objectives—providing limited indicators of the intrusion of nationalist, racist, antiliberal values rather than extensive overviews of the evolution of democratic and capitalist institutions.

There thus appears to be a pattern to these different formulations of the German Question. The security studies have often retained the purely structural formulations of the nineteenth-century historians; the political economy studies have often integrated structural assumptions with an appreciation of the role of process, history, and ideas; while the efforts to understand the role of liberal democracy have often rejected structural analysis in search of microlevel analyses, such as public-opinion surveys as exemplified by the Kuechler piece in this volume.[59] Of the three, security studies thus appear the least adept at confronting the new reality of the post–cold war world, facing the problem that structural analysis emphasizes the theme of continuity rather than change.[60] Evidence of structuralism's incapacity to confront a novel context is reflected in the analysis of John Mearsheimer, whose purely deductive, structural analysis arrived at the alarming conclusion (for students of European history) that nuclear proliferation should extend to Germany as a means of ensuring European peace.[61] Political economists and more traditional comparativists, employing what Kenneth Waltz derisively terms "reductionist" forms of analysis, seem to have a lot more utility in making the transition to understanding a world in flux.[62]

Continuity, Change, and the German Question: Forming a New Agenda

What is most amazing is the credulous way that both academics and policymakers have received German unification, given that any prediction of such as late as 1989 would probably, at best, have been considered as amusing by any audience. Once aberration and change becomes the norm, structural analysis retains credibility by claiming, in a contradictory manner, both that the world retains universal themes that transcend change and that change itself can be explained. Thus no one could either explain or predict the latest *Wende*, unification, yet political scientists have indulged in remarkably little self-criticism in view of that fact.

The thrust of this chapter is obviously a critique of an overreliance on structuralism, stressing instead the elements emphasized in the contributions to this volume—an appreciation of the role of ideas, process, and history in explaining both continuity and change in Germany. The contributions to this volume have tried to formulate an agenda based on that realization. The chapters by Hanhardt, McAdams, Lemke, and Riemer, for example, all demonstrate a keen awareness of the importance of process in policy debates, while that by, for example, Markovits and Reich weighs more heavily towards the importance of ideas. All of these nevertheless retain an understanding of the significance of structure and history in defining the parameters of public discourse and policy-making.

Ultimately the themes articulated in the introduction and emphasized in the individual chapters are thus echoed in this conclusion. We have collectively tried to offer a new agenda for the study of the new Germany, recognizing that our intent is to try and explain aspects of both continuity and change. While political scientists have succeeded in the latter, they have generally failed in the former. Structure, as Kenneth Waltz suggests, can capture life's continuities. It therefore appears least appropriate for primary use in the case of a country like Germany, whose experiences over the course of the last century have been the singularly most turbulent of any advanced industrial state. Certainly, invoke the role of structure where appropriate, but only as a part of an explanation—not *the* explanation itself. For political scientists this is the first lesson we should have derived in view of the events of 1989 and should be the last one forgotten.

NOTES

1. Robert Gilpin, *The Political Economy of International Relations* (Princeton: Princeton University Press, 1987), 81.

2. Kenneth Waltz, *Theory of International Politics* (Reading, Mass.: Addison-Wesley, 1979), 69.

3. Emanuel Adler, *The Power of Ideology: The Quest for Technological Autonomy in Argentina and Brazil* (Berkeley and Los Angeles: University of California Press, 1987), 1–3. Adler acknowledges his intellectual debt to the work of Ernst Haas in adopting this approach. See 43.

4. For a defense of the claim that hegemony was the primary objective see Fritz Fischer, *The War of Illusions* (New York: Norton, 1975), 30. For a defense of the alternative claim that Germany merely sought to become an equal partner among world powers see John A. Moses, *The Politics of Illusion: The Fischer Controversy in German Historiography* (New York: Barnes and Noble, 1975), 24.

5. Alexander Gerschenkron, *Economic Backwardness in Historical Perspective* (Cambridge, Mass.: Belknap Press, 1962), 23.

6. See, for examples, Moses, *Politics of Illusion,* xiii; Fritz Fischer, *Germany's Aims in the First World War* (New York: Norton, 1967), 8.

7. For a full discussion of the assumptions of Ranke and his successors, see Moses, *Politics of Illusion,* the foreword, preface and 1–29, especially 17.

8. Fischer, *Germany's Aims,* 34–35.

9. Moses, *The Politics of Illusion,* 31–41, 48.

10. Richard J. Evans, "Introduction: Wilhelm II's Germany and the Historians," in *Society and Politics in Wilhelmine Germany,* ed. Richard J. Evans (New York: Barnes and Noble, 1978), 13.

11. For example, see Fischer, *Germany's Aims,* 635–36; and subsequently his *War of Illusions,* vii–ix.

12. Fischer, *Germany's Aims,* 637–38.

13. Evans, "Introduction," 12.

14. Moses, *Politics of Illusion,* 47.

15. Fischer, *Germany's Aims,* 637; and Hans-Ulrich Wehler, *The German Empire 1871–1918* (Dover, N.H.: Berg, 1985), 192.

16. For example, see Fischer, *War of Illusions,* 14.

17. Perhaps the clearest statement of this position is made by Hans-Ulrich Wehler, *Das deutsche Kaiserreich 1871–1918,* translated as *The German Empire 1871–1918.* For his critical comments on Fischer, see 230–31. For an interesting summary and effective critique of Kehr's, Fischer's, and Wehler's work, see Wolfgang Mommsen, "Domestic Factors in German Foreign Policy before 1914," *Central European History* 6 (1973): 3–43.

18. Wehler, *German Empire,* 192–95.

19. Wehler, *German Empire,* 238–39.

20. While Wehler takes a more balanced approach when examining the influence of the forces of "organized capitalism" and the Junker class, Fischer places greater weight on the significance of the Junkers. See Wehler, *German Empire,* 42–45, and Fischer, *War of Illusions,* 13.

21. Evans, "Introduction," 16; and Wehler, *German Empire,* 52–55.

22. Volker Berghahn, *Germany and the Approach of War in 1914* (New York: St. Martin's, 1973), 9.

23. Geoff Eley, *From Unification to Nazism: Reinterpreting the German Past* (Boston: Allen and Unwin, 1986), 3.

24. Evans, "Introduction," 19.

25. Wehler, *German Empire,* 173.

26. For notable examples of historical work challenging this structural formulation, see Geoff Eley's *From Unification to Nazism* and his *Reshaping the German Right: Radical Nationalism and Political Change after Bismarck* (New Haven: Yale University Press, 1980). For a collection of interesting perspectives see also Evans (ed.), *Society and Politics.* Simon Reich, *The Fruits of Fascism: Postwar Prosperity in Historical Perspective* (Ithaca: Cornell University Press, 1990), attempts the same in the realm of political economy.

27. Eley, *From Unification to Nazism,* 4, 7–8, 11–13.

28. Eley, *Reshaping the German Right,* 11, 13.

29. Although the list of such contributors is long and distinguished, some of the more prominent representatives are Hans Morgenthau, *Politics among Nations: The Struggle for Power and Peace* (New York: Knopf, 1948); Karl Deutsch, for example his article coauthored with J. David Singer, "Multipolar Power Systems and International Stability," *World Politics* 16 (1964): 390–406; Dankwart Rustow, *A World of Nations: Problems of Political Modernization* (Washington, D.C.: Brookings, 1967); and Henry Kissinger, *A World Restored: Metternich, Castlereagh and the Problems of Peace, 1812–22* (Boston: Houghton Mifflin, 1957).

30. For a general discussion of definitions of the German question see Ralf Dahrendorf, *Society and Democracy in Germany* (New York: Norton, 1979), 3–16.

31. Peter Katzenstein, *Policy and Politics in West Germany: The Growth of a Semisovereign State* (Philadelphia: Temple University Press, 1987), 4, 350.

32. For an example of such new assertiveness, consider Germany's behavior towards its EC partners in its recognition of Croatia and Slovenia. See "Germany Flexes Its Muscles on Croatia's Behalf," *Independent,* 19 December 1991; "Kohl Hijacks Brussels Policy," *London Times,* 18 December 1991; and "Hurd Raises Spectre of Past Wars over Balkan Rivalries," *Independent,* 19 December 1991.

33. For example see David Calleo, *The German Problem Reconsidered: Germany and the World Order, 1870 to the Present* (Cambridge: Cambridge University Press, 1978). This reference to Germany as Europe's most influential actor is defined largely in terms of how Germany has dominated the agenda of other countries. I assume that the Soviet Union was not purely a European country, and that Germany's geographical centrality aided its influence.

34. Dahrendorf, *Society and Democracy,* 3, 4. For different interpretations of this question, see Gerhard Ritter, *The German Problem: Basic Questions of German Political Life, Past and Present* (Columbus: Ohio State University Press, 1965) and Wilhelm Röpke, *Die Deutsche Frage* (Erlenbach-Zürich: Rentsch, 1945).

35. A. J. P. Taylor, *The Course of German History* (London: Hamilton, 1945), 8f, Cf. Dahrendorf, *Society and Democracy,* 7.

36. Dahrendorf, *Society and Democracy,* 7.

37. Gaddis's analysis provides the historical base for the realist claim that the bipolar structure of the international system explains the absence of great or superpower war for a four-decade postwar period. See John Gaddis, *Strategies of Containment: A Critical Appraisal of Postwar American National Security Policy* (New York: Oxford University Press, 1982).

38. These points are repeatedly discussed at great length in Wolfram F. Hanrieder, *Germany, America, Europe: Forty Years of German Foreign Policy* (New Haven: Yale University Press, 1989). See, for example, 62.

39. Ibid., 5–7.

40. See Calleo, *German Problem Reconsidered,* 194–203.

41. See, as examples, Ludwig Dehio's *Germany and World Politics in the Twentieth Century* (New York: Knopf, 1959) and his *The Precarious Balance: Four Centuries of European Power Struggle* (New York: Knopf, 1962); Helga Haftendorn, *Security and Detente: Conflicting Priorities in German Foreign Policy* (New York: Praeger, 1985); Timothy P. Ireland, *Creating the Entangling Alliance: The Origins of the North Atlantic Treaty Organization* (London: Aldwych, 1981); Catherine McArdle Kelleher, "Nation-State and National Security in Postwar Western Europe," in *Evolving European Defense Policies,* ed. Catherine McArdle Kelleher and Gale A. Mattox (Lexington, Mass.: Lexington Books, 1987), 3–14.

42. Rudolf Hilferding, *Finance Capital: A Study of the Latest Phase of Capitalist Development* (London: Routledge and Kegan Paul, 1981).

43. For an example of the latter see John J. Mearsheimer, "Back to the Future: Instability in Europe After the Cold War," in *The Cold War and After: Prospects for Peace,* ed. Sean Lynn-Jones (Cambridge: MIT Press, 1991), 141–92.

44. Alexander Gerschenkron, *Bread and Democracy in Germany* (Berkeley and Los Angeles: University of California Press, 1943), 16–17, 53, 153.

45. See Gerschenkron, *Economic Backwardness.*

46. For a discussion of the "Germany as latecomer" thesis, see Peter Katzenstein, *Policy and Politics,* 10–15.

47. See Andrew Shonfield, *Modern Capitalism: The Changing Balance of Public and Private Power* (London: Oxford University Press, 1965), 240–41; John Zysman, *Governments, Markets, and Growth: Financial Systems and the Politics of Industrial Change* (Ithaca: Cornell University Press, 1983), 252–53, 259, 260, 262–63.

48. Peter Hall, *Governing the Economy: The Politics of State Intervention in Britain and France* (Cambridge, Mass.: Polity, 1986), 37.

49. See Christopher Allen's essay in this volume. See also Hilferding, *Finance Capital.*

50. Reich, *Fruits of Fascism.*

51. Peter Katzenstein, *Policy and Politics;* Mancur Olson, *The Rise and Decline of Nations: Stagflation and Social Rigidities* (New Haven: Yale University Press, 1982); Simon Bulmer, ed., *The Changing Agenda of West German Public Policy* (Aldershot, Hampshire: Dartmouth, 1989).

52. For a discussion of Anglo-German competition in the late nineteenth century, see W. Arthur Lewis, "The British Climacteric," *Growth and Fluctuations, 1870–1914* (London: Allen and Unwin, 1978), 112–34; Charles Kindleberger, "Germany's Overtaking of England, 1806–1914," *Economic Response: Comparative Studies in Trade, Finance and Growth* (Cambridge: Harvard University Press, 1978), 185–236; Andrew B. Tylecote, "German Ascent and British Decline, 1870–1980: The Role of Upper-Class Structure and Values," in *Ascent and Decline in the World System,* ed. Edward Friedman (Beverly Hills, Calif.: Sage, 1982), 41–68.

53. See Robert Gilpin, *U.S. Power and the Multinational Corporation: The Political Economy of Foreign Direct Investment* (New York: Basic Books, 1975), 107–9.

54. For an example of a neoliberal formulation, see Jeffrey Anderson and John Goodman, "German State Strategies and the Post–Cold War Settlement" (Paper delivered at the Annual Meeting of the American Political Science Association, Washington, D.C., 1991). See Andrei S. Markovits and Simon Reich, "The New Face of Germany: Gramsci, Hegemony, and Europe," Harvard Working Paper Series, 1991.

55. See David Abraham, *The Collapse of the Weimar Republic* (Princeton: Princeton University Press, 1981).

56. Carl Friedrich and Zbigniew Brzezinski, *Totalitarian Dictatorship and Autocracy* (Cambridge: Harvard University Press, 1956). See also Juan Linz, "Totalitarian and Authoritarian Regimes," in *The Handbook of Political Science,* ed. Fred Greenstein and Nelson Polsby, vol. 3 (Reading, Mass.: Addison-Wesley, 1975); Hannah Arendt, *The Origins of Totalitarianism* (San Diego: Harcourt Brace Jovanovitch, 1973); Gabriel Almond and Sydney Verba, *The Civic Culture: Political Attitudes and Democracy in Five Nations* (Princeton: Princeton University Press, 1963); Seymour Martin Lipset, *Political Man: The Social Bases of Politics* (Garden City, N.Y.: Doubleday, 1963).

57. Gerard Braunthal, *Political Loyalty and Public Service in West Germany: The 1972 Decree against Radicals and Its Consequences* (Amherst: University of Massachusetts Press, 1990). For corroboration see also Joachim Hirsch, *Der Sicherheitsstaat* (Frankfurt am Main: Europäische, 1982).

58. Samuel Barnes and Max Kaase, *Political Action: Mass Participation in Five Western Democracies* (Beverly Hills, Calif.: Sage, 1979); Russell Dalton, *Politics in West Germany* (Glenview, Ill.: Scott, Foresman, 1989); Elisabeth Noelle Neumann, *The Germans—Public Opinion Polls, 1967–1980* (Westport, Conn.: Greenwood, 1981); and Thomas Risse-Kappen, "Public Opinion, Domestic Structure, and Foreign Policy in Liberal Democracies," *World Politics* 43 (1991): 479–512.

59. We recognize that this may be an overgeneralization to the extent that there are numerous exceptions to our claim about the relationship between subject and the level or method of analysis. One example might be the already mentioned Dahrendorf study, in which he integrates structural with historical analysis in addressing his variant of the German Question: "Why is it that so few in Germany embraced the principle of liberal democracy?" But we are describing the general thrust of types of study, not a steadfast rule that they all adhere to. See Dahrendorf, *Society and Democracy,* 14.

60. For confirmation on the stress on continuity in structural analysis, see Waltz, *Theory,* 65–68. For a variety of interesting perspectives on the security structure of Europe in the aftermath of the cold war, see Lynn-Jones, *Cold War and After.*

61. Mearsheimer, "Back to the Future," 174. For a realist critique of Mearsheimer, see Stephen Van Evera, "Primed for Peace: Europe After the Cold War," *International Security* 15 (1990–91): 7–57.

62. As an example of a substantive security study that does deal with the evolving international environment well, see Jack Snyder, "Averting Anarchy in the New Europe," in Lynn-Jones, *Cold War and After,* 104–40.

A Chronology

The following chronology presents an overview of events in the two Germanys and in international affairs affecting the collapse of the German Democratic Republic (GDR) in 1989 and its unification with the Federal Republic of Germany (FRG) in October 1990. The purpose of this exercise is in short form to pass in review the turbulent events of those months.

Arthur M. Hanhardt, Jr.

January 1989

1

New GDR law regulating foreign travel goes into effect.

11

Twenty GDR citizens who had staged a sit-in leave the office of the Permanent Representative of the FRG in East Berlin after being guaranteed quick action on their emigration requests.

15

In commemoration of the seventieth anniversary of the murders of Rosa Luxemburg and Karl Liebknecht, several hundred East Germans demonstrate in Leipzig. Eighty demonstrators are arrested.

20

George Herbert Walker Bush sworn in as forty-first president of the United States of America.

22

Erich Honecker announces that the Berlin Wall will remain in place for the "next hundred years."

February

6

Chris Gueffroy, age twenty, is shot and killed by GDR border guards at the Berlin Wall.

15
The last Soviet troops withdraw from Afghanistan.

16
Four GDR citizens ram their car into the gates of the FRG representative's office in East Berlin in an attempt to emigrate.

24
The Hungarian Socialist Workers party strikes its "leading role" from the Hungarian constitution.

March

11–12
The Leipzig spring trade fair is the occasion for some 600 demonstrators to seek exit from the GDR. The FRG cabinet ministers cancel visit to trade fair as a protest against shots fired at GDR citizens seeking to leave their country "illegally."

May

2
Hungarian border troops begin dismantling the "Iron Curtain."

7
Communal elections in the GDR post a turnout of 98.77 percent with 98.85 percent voting for the candidates of the National Front. Results challenged by citizens' groups charging election fraud.

13
Demonstrators in Beijing's Tienanmen Square begin hunger strike.

24
Fortieth anniversary of the founding of the FRG.

30–31
President Bush, visiting FRG, speaks of "partners in leadership" with the FRG during speech in Koblenz.

June

4
Bloodbath in Tienanmen Square as student demonstrations are forcibly ended by Chinese National Peoples Army.

7
Demonstration in East Berlin to protest alleged election fraud in May communal elections. Stasi and police scatter the demonstration and take more than one hundred demonstrators into custody.

8
A unanimous resolution of the GDR Volkskammer (parliament) shows "understanding" for the measures taken by Chinese leaders to "restore order and public safety through the use of armed force."

12–15
President Mikhail Gorbachev visits West Germany, leading to a wave of "Gorbymania." Gorbachev declares that the Berlin Wall can "disappear" when the conditions that lead to its construction are no longer present.

July

7
At the first East bloc summit since 1968, in Bucharest, Gorbachev declares an end to the Brezhnev Doctrine and says that each socialist country should pursue its own development.

16
GDR citizens seek refuge in the FRG embassy in Budapest.

August

1
The Axel Springer Verlag, publishers of *Die Welt* and *Bild Zeitung,* drop the quotation marks—"GDR"—that indicated the provisional status of the East German state.

3
GDR citizens occupy the FRG embassy in Budapest in growing numbers and begin occupying the FRG embassy in Prague.

8
The offices of the FRG representative in East Berlin are closed when 130 people occupy the premises, seeking to leave the GDR.

13
FRG embassy in Budapest is closed because of overcrowding.

19
During a festival of the Pan-European Union in Hungary, 661 GDR citizens flee across the Austrian border.

22

FRG embassy in Prague is closed because of overcrowding.

31

Hungarian Foreign Minister Gyula Horn meets GDR Foreign Minister Oskar Fischer in East Berlin. Horn declares that Hungarian policy regarding GDR citizens on its territory will be governed by international law on human rights and humanitarian concerns.

September

2

GDR refugees in Hungary now number over 3,500.

4

Monday night demonstration at the Nikolaikirche in Leipzig is broken up by police.

10

The oppositional group New Forum (Neues Forum) founded in East Berlin by Bärbel Bohley and Jens Reich.

10–11

Hungary announces opening of its borders to exiting GDR refugees effective at 0001 hours on the eleventh. This action was taken without consulting East Berlin. By the end of the month, 25,000 East Germans will have fled via the Hungarian opening.

12

The oppositional group Democracy Now (Demokratie Jetzt) founded in East Berlin.

18

In Leipzig, some one hundred persons are arrested for participating in an illegal demonstration following the Monday evening "Prayers for Peace" at the Nikolaikirche.

25

Erich Honecker, General Secretary of the Socialist Unity party and Chairman of the GDR Council of State, returns to his duties following several weeks of illness. In Leipzig over 8,000 persons participate in a Monday night demonstration protesting for freedom of expression and assembly, and against the rejection, by the state, of New Forum and other reform groups.

30

At the West German embassy in Prague, Foreign Minister Hans-Dietrich Genscher and Chancery Minister Rudolf Seiters announce that refugees in Prague and Warsaw may leave for West Germany via the GDR. East Berlin calls the refugees "traitors."

October

1

Democratic Awakening (Demokratischer Aufbruch), a reform group, founded in the GDR.

2

More than 20,000 participate in the now-regularized Monday night demonstrations in Leipzig. The demonstration is forcibly broken up by the police.

4

A second wave of GDR refugees crosses the GDR by train on its way to West Germany. There is violence at the Dresden train station, where 3,000 protest for their own emigration rights.

6

Mikhail Gorbachev arrives in East Berlin to mark the fortieth anniversary of the founding of the GDR. A "Common Declaration" of reform groups in the GDR demands free elections with secret balloting supervised by the United Nations. An officially sanctioned torchlight parade led by the Free German Youth celebrates the eve of the GDR founding.

7

Official demonstrations are held to observe the fortieth anniversary of the founding of the GDR, including an illegal military parade in East Berlin. Western Allies protest. Gorbachev publicly signals his views on the status of the GDR by remarking that "history punishes the tardy." In public appearances, Gorbachev is greeted with cries of "Gorbi, Gorbi help us!" Unofficial demonstrations demanding political and human rights take place in various East German cities, such as Plauen, Jena, and Potsdam. The demonstrations are broken up by Stasi and police with considerable brutality. The Social Democratic party in the GDR (SDP) is founded under the leadership of Ibrahim Böhme.

9

Massive Monday night demonstration in Leipzig—the largest demonstration in the GDR since the workers uprising on 17 June 1953. Some 70,000 demonstrators flood the streets of Leipzig under the banner: "We are the People! No Violence."

16

Over 120,000 demonstrate in Leipzig.

18

Erich Honecker asks to be relieved as head of party and state "for reasons of poor health," ending eighteen years of rule. Egon Krenz is unanimously named general secretary of the SED to replace Honecker. Krenz announces that the SED and the

GDR state leadership had misjudged the events of recent months and are about to undertake fundamental changes in a "turnabout" or Wende.

23

More than 300,000 demonstrate in Leipzig, warning against a "new concentration of power." Demonstrations, universally peaceful, now feature SED party leaders in conversation with "the people." SED media are discussing issues raised by demonstrators.

November

1

Egon Krenz ends visit to Moscow without a joint declaration. In his press conference, Krenz reports that GDR problems must be solved in Berlin. Krenz finds stimulating ideas in "New Thinking" and perestroika. German unification is "not on the agenda."

4

In East Berlin one million demonstrate for a reformed GDR. Speakers include prominent artists, writers, and political figures. Other demonstrations take place throughout the GDR.

7

The GDR Council of Ministers under Minister President Willi Stoph resigns.

8

A new SED Politburo is elected and an SED Action Program is presented at Central Committee meeting.

9

At an evening press conference, Günter Schabowski reads a statement setting the policy of the GDR government on travel. Asked if this meant that GDR citizens could leave via border crossings, Schabowski says yes. Thousands of East Germans move toward the border crossings into the western sectors of Berlin. Border guards lose control of the situation and scenes of a massive celebration of the fall of the Berlin Wall go around the world.

22

The SED offers to participate in "round table" talks with reform groups to discuss preparations for new elections, an electoral law, and changes in the constitution of the GDR.

28

Chancellor Helmut Kohl presents a Ten-Point Program designed to "overcome the division of Germany." Krenz responds that German unification is not on the agenda.

December

1

The GDR Volkskammer strikes the leading role of the working class and its party, the SED, from the GDR constitution.

3

The entire politburo of the SED resigns. Thus Egon Krenz loses his position in the SED party leadership.

4

At Monday night demonstrations in the GDR, persistent demands for German unification are being heard for the first time.

6

After forty-four days in office, Egon Krenz is forced to resign from his positions as head of the Council of State and the National Defense Council.

7

First meeting of the Round Table consisting of new and old parties and political organizations. First free elections scheduled for 6 May 1990.

11

The ambassadors of the four Allied Powers meet in Berlin to discuss the future status of Berlin.

16

The SED—Socialist Unity party of Germany—is renamed SED-Party of Democratic Socialism (SED-PDS).

20

President Mitterrand of France makes a state visit to the GDR, the first of the Western Allies to do so since World War II.

31

During 1989, 343,854 GDR citizens leave for West Germany.

January 1990

8

At the Monday might demonstrations in Leipzig the major themes are German unification, dissatisfaction with the pace of change in the GDR, and suspicion of the SED-PDS, which is identified with the old regime.

28

The Round Table moves the national election from 6 May to 18 March, responding to demands for more rapid change in the GDR.

30

GDR Minister President Hans Modrow visits Moscow and hears from Gorbachev that the four Allied Powers did not "in principle" question the right of the two German states to seek closer relations possibly leading to eventual unification.

31

58,043 people move from the GDR to West Germany in January, thus heightening pressures for internal economic and political change, and for quicker moves toward unification.

February

13

Chancellor Kohl and Minister President Modrow meet in Bonn to discuss common problems.

14

At the Open Skies conference in Ottawa, the Allied Powers in World War II, France, Great Britain, the Soviet Union, and the United States agree to "2 + 4" talks with the two Germanys. These talks will deal with the external aspects of German unification and the security concerns of Germany's neighbors.

24

Chancellor Kohl begins two-day visit to Washington, D.C. Kohl and Bush agree that a united Germany must remain in NATO. Kohl's waffling on the Polish border issue raises concerns about German unification.

March

8

The West German parliament passes a declaration guaranteeing the western boundary of Poland.

18

The first free parliamentary election in the GDR results in a victory for the conservative Alliance for Germany. The foreign ministers of the Warsaw Treaty Organization recognize the right of the Germanys to unify if so desired by their people.

April

14
Lothar de Maizière (CDU) becomes Minister President of the GDR in a Grand Coalition of the conservatives, the liberal parties and the Social Democrats.

27
In East Berlin the official negotiations for an economic, financial, and social union of the two Germanys begin.

May

2
FRG President Richard von Weizsäcker begins a state visit to Poland by stressing the inviolability of the Polish borders.

5
The first meeting of the "2 + 4" foreign ministers in Bonn. Main topic: the alliances to which the united Germany will belong.

6
Local elections are held in the GDR with essentially the same results as the parliamentary election in March.

18
The state treaty on the economic, financial, and social union of the two Germanys is signed.

June

3
At their summit meeting, Presidents Bush and Gorbachev declare that the alliances to which the united Germany may belong are a matter for the Germans themselves to decide.

21
The state treaty on the economic, financial, and social union is ratified by the parliaments of East and West Germany, which also renew guarantees for the western border of Poland.

July

1
The state treaty on the economic, financial, and social union goes into effect. Bonn now controls these fields for both German states.

6

Negotiations begin in East Berlin on the unification treaty between the two Germanys.

14–16

Chancellor Kohl and President Gorbachev meet in the Soviet Union. Gorbachev approves the unification of the two Germanys with full sovereignty and leaves the question of alliance membership for the Germans to decide.

16

First official meeting of the Treuhandanstalt or trust agency, charged with privatizing some 8,000 East German state-run companies.

17

The "2 + 4" talks, in their third round and with the participation of the Polish foreign minister, guarantee the western boundary of Poland.

August

22

Following a lengthy debate, the Volkskammer requests that the GDR be admitted to the Federal Republic of Germany according to Article 23 of the West German Basic Law (constitution).

31

The unification treaty between FRG and GDR is signed in East Berlin. Unification will become effective on 3 October.

September

12

The "2 + 4" talks conclude in Moscow with a treaty granting full sovereignty to a unified Germany. Remaining Allied rights will terminate on 3 October.

20

Unification treaty is ratified by the parliaments of FRG and GDR.

October

3

Unification Day: The GDR becomes a part of the FRG.

December

2

First parliamentary election in a unified Germany is won by the conservative-liberal coalition of Chancellor Kohl (CDU) and Foreign Minister Hans-Dietrich Genscher (FDP).

Index